C

UK Airfields

1 9 9 6

Published by
Camber Publications Ltd

ISBN 1 874783 80 2

Distributed to the aviation trade by:
AFE, Southside, Manchester Airport, Wilmslow, Cheshire SK9 4LL
Tel: 0161 499 0023 Fax: 0161 499 0298
AFE@airdata.u-net.com

Distributed to the book trade by:
AirData Publications, Southside, Manchester Airport,
Wilmslow, Cheshire SK9 4LL
Tel: 0161 499 0024 Fax: 0161 499 0298
books@airdata.u-net.com

Camber's UK Airfields 1996

Contributors & Compilers:
Nik Berry
Steve Dickinson
Judith Manfield
Tina Mathews
Phil Mathews
Jeremy M Pratt
Mike Rudkin
Rob Taylor

IMPORTANT
Camber's UK Airfields 1996 is a guide only and is not intended to be taken as an authoritative document. Whilst every care has been taken in compiling this guide, relying where possible on official information sources, the publisher and editorial team will not be liable in any way for any errors or omissions whatsoever. The inclusion of an airfield in this guide in no way infers that there is a public right of access.

INTRODUCTION

The airfields listed here are all considered to be those where there is reasonable access to the general public - either by air or road. For this reason solely military airfields and small farm strips have not been included. Nevertheless, the inclusion of an airfield in this guide in no way infers that there is a public right of access. If in doubt, please check with the airfield owners / operators.

Landing fee information and fuel prices are considered to be correct at the time of going to press, but obviously are subject to change. The symbol '+' means that the price is *plus* VAT, the word 'inc.' means that the price *includes* VAT. Car Hire and Taxi firms have their name printed in **bold** if they are known to be based on the airfield.

The inclusion of any organisation does not imply endorsement by the publisher.

All prices listed in the flying club section should include VAT, except where stated otherwise.

We want your help to keep this guide up-to-date. Any changes, additions or recommendations are welcomed - preferably in writing with a contact address for any further information.

Thank you for buying Camber's UK Airfields 1996 and happy landings!

England

Andrewsfield

4 miles west of Braintree, signposted from the A120
Andrewsfield Aviation Ltd, Saling Airfield, Stebbing, Great Dunmow, Essex CM6 3TH

Tel: 01371 856744 Fax: 01371 856759

The Americans arrived at Great Saling in 1942 - on July 4th appropriately enough - and work began on Great Saling airfield soon after. Renamed Andrew's Field, in honour of Lieutenant-General F. M. Andrews, operations began in 1943 with B17 Flying Fortresses and B26 Marauders. Later Mustang fighters also flew here escorting the bombers over Europe. Later still, East Anglia's first operational jet fighters - Meteors of 616 Sqn - made their operational debut from here.

Visitors today might wonder where and how these aircraft were housed. However, modern-day Andrewsfield with its single grass runway occupies only a small corner of the original wartime site. The odd piece of peri-track or dispersal area can be seen in the adjoining fields, but the original plan of the first USAF base built in England is much clearer from the air. The Andrewsfield Flying Club's tidy clubhouse has pictures of Andrewsfield past, a small collection of wartime memorabilia, and holds a number of commemorative social events during the year. There is a friendly welcome to visitors and the bar/cafe has a good menu and a nice view across the airfield.

Landing Fee
Single £3.00 multi £5.00 Helicopter £10.00. Overnight parking £2.00
Major credit cards except Amex and Diners

Fuel
AVGAS 100LL 67p inc. Available 0900-2100
Major credit cards except Amex and Diners

Flying Organisations

Andrewsfield Aviation Ltd	01371 856744
Chevron Foxtrot Golf Syndicate	01371 856744

Other Organisations

MK Aerosupport (maintenance)	01371 856796

Car Hire

M+M Car Hire	01376 325078

Taxis

Cabman Cars	01371 876363
Eastern Taxis	01371 873323
Joes Taxis	01376 328822

Public Transport
Buses from Braintree run close to the airfield. Braintree railway station 4 miles

Nearby Places of Interest

Working silk museum, Braintree, 4 miles.	01736 553393
Essex County Showground, 5 miles.	01245 362416
Wethersfield, 6 miles.	
Tour of former USAF base by arrangement.	01371 850161 ext.124/128
TIC Braintree	01376 550066

See also Earls Colne and Stansted

Food & Accommodation
Bar snacks at the club house, food available during airfield opening hours
The Kings Head pub in the pretty village of Stebbing - 2 miles

Elm Croft B&B, Stebbing - 2 miles	01371 856450
Hyfield B&B, Felsted - 2 miles	
(will collect/deliver to airfield)	01371 820372
Saracen's Head, Great Dunmow - 6 miles from £50	01371 873901

See also Earls Colne and Stansted

Bagby

2 miles south-east of Thirsk. See text for directions
Mr J. P. Lassey, Westwood, Bagby, Thirsk, North Yorkshire YO7 2PH.

Tel: 01845 597385 (airfield)   01845 597242 (operator)

Bagby, situated just off the A19, south of the Yorkshire market town of Thirsk, has the sort of welcome beloved of farm strip visitors. There are usually at least one or two interesting aircraft to look at and the cafe, while simple and basic, is of a reliably high standard - it is renowned for some of the best bacon butties to be found anywhere. The short runway, terminating in a hedge alongside the A19, is not for the faint-hearted pilot. If the wind is unfavourable, the first time flying visitor is recommended to telephone for advice. The local market town of Thirsk is pleasant and full of tourists in the summer, looking to identify parts of James Herriot's 'Darrowby' for themselves.

If arriving by road, follow 'Bagby' signs from A19. Entering Bagby village look for a narrow track on the right between two houses (one called 'Grestan'), the airfield is about 200 metres down this track.

Landing Fee
Business flights £5.00 All landings free with fuel uplift.
Major credit cards except Amex / Diners.

Fuel
AVGAS 100LL , maximum 60p inc. But you are invited to haggle for a better price if you like (ask for Philip)! Major credit cards except Amex / Diners.

Flying Organisations

Other Organisations
Graham Fox Aircraft Engineering 01845 597707

Car Hire
Moss Motors, Thirsk 01845 522042

Taxis
Prices Taxis, Thirsk. 01845 522709

Public Transport
Bus stop in Bagby village. G Fishwick (operators) 01347 868237. Thirsk railway station 3 miles.

Nearby Places of Interest
Falconry UK Bird of Prey and Conservation Centre,
Thirsk 2 miles 01845 587522
James Herriot Country, Thirsk and surrounding area - various attractions
Merlin Parachute Centre, Topcliffe, 3 miles 01904 626023
Yorkshire Gliding Club, Sutton Bank, 3 miles east 01845 597237

TIC 01845 522755

Food & Accommodation
Bar meals and club facilities available when airfield is open. Food normally available 12.00-14.00 weekdays. Parties and families catered for.

Greyhound Inn (with B & B), Bagby - 1 mile from £15 01845 597315

Black Lion Hotel, Thirsk - 3 miles from £20 01845 522615

Kirkgate Hotel, Thirsk - 3 miles from £25 01845 525015

Barrow (Walney Island)

1.5 miles north-west of Barrow in Furness

Vickers Shipbuilding and Engineering Ltd, Barrow/Walney Island Aerodrome, FAO ATC, Barrow in Furness, Cumbria LA14 1AB.

Tel: 01229 471147 / 471407 Telex: 65350 WALAIR G

Now operated by Vickers shipbuilders, the airfield opened at the end of 1941 as a training base for Air Gunners, with Lysanders and Ansons as the main types used. Nowadays, the main activity is that of the aircraft operated on Vickers' business. The airfield is reported by visitors to be friendly, but there are few facilities and no catering, so a fuel-stop is the most likely reason to visit here. That said, Barrow remains one of the few airfields within striking distance of the Lake District, which might be reason enough to bring an aircraft in for a weekend visit.

Landing Fee

£4.50 + per half tonne. 50% discount for PPL training.
Diners, cheques & cash only.

Fuel

AVTUR JET A-1
Diners, cheques & cash only.

Flying Organisations

Furness Aviation Ltd	01229 472404
Lakes Gliding Club	01229 471458

Other Organisations

Car Hire

Avis	01229 829555
Hertz	01229 836666

Taxis

Acacia Cars	01229 830055
D & S Contracts	01229 822020

Public Transport

Barrow railway station 1.5 miles

Nearby Places of Interest

The Furness Peninsula has a range of visitor opportunities including an early 14th Century castle and 2 international standard nature reserves.

The Dock Museum, Barrow in Furness	01229 870871
TIC	01229 580742

Food & Accommodation

Chandlers Country Cafe, Lindal in Furness, (Egon Ronay)

Abbey House 5 crowns, Barrow in Furness	01229 838282
Infield Hotel and Guest House, Barrow in Furness	01229 831381
Victoria Park Hotel, Barrow in Furness	01229 821159

Bembridge (Isle of Wight)

3 miles north-east of Sandown, Isle of Wight, on the B3330
Pilatus Britten-Norman Ltd, Bembridge Airport,
Isle of Wight PO35 5PR
Tel: 01983 873331/872511 Fax: 01983 873331
Telex: 86277 PBNBEM

The Isle of Wight is generally thought of as a pleasant and peaceful holiday resort, which undoubtedly it is. Somewhat less well recognised is that it is also home to an aircraft manufacturer of international renown, producing one of the most successful commercial aircraft ever built in the UK. Bembridge is home to the Islander, formerly the Britten-Norman Islander, more recently owned by the Swiss aircraft manufacturer Pilatus. Indeed the Islander is named after its birthplace, rather than the fact that it can be seen operating into tiny strips on small islands the world over, where other aircraft simply cannot operate commercially.

The airfield itself dates from 1915, although it saw little action during the First World War, and finally closed five years later. However, you'll find little here today that recalls the airfield's origins. The Pilatus Britten-Norman factory occupies the north-eastern corner of the airfield, with the tower. Unsurprisingly the assembly and test flying of PBN aircraft is the main activity of the airfield, although there is also an active glider club based here. The best place for viewing the activity is the Propeller Inn, on the B3395 on the southern edge of the airfield.

Landing Fee
Singles £8.00. Twins £15.00 inc. Cash and cheque only

Fuel
AVGAS 100LL 0.75 + AVTUR JET A1 25p +. By prior arrangement during operational hours. Cash, cheque and Amex

Flying Organisations

Bembridge Flight Training	01983 872050
Vectis Gliding Club	01983 853611

Other Organisations

Pilatus Britten-Norman Ltd (Maintenance)	01983 872511
Pleasure Flights	01983 872050

Car Hire

Avis	01983 615522
G P Economy Car Rental, Bembridge	01983 872904

Taxis

Bembridge Cars	01983 873395
Flint Cars and Private Hire	01983 872133/874132

Public Transport
Brading railway station 2 miles

Nearby Places of Interest

Osborne House, 5 miles	01983 200022
Carisbrooke Castle, 6 miles	01983 522107
Flamingo Park Water Fowl and Water Gardens, 3 miles,	01983 612153
Isle of Wight Wax Museum, 2 miles,	01983 407286
Bembridge Windmill, 2 miles,	01983 873945
TIC	01983 562905

See also Isle of Wight - Sandown

Food & Accommodation
The Propeller Inn (bar snacks) 01983 873611
The Seaview Hotel & Restaurant, Seaview 3 miles. Small Hotel / Pub / Restaurant with a nautical theme. The food is amongst the best on the island and there's a good selection of beers too. Rooms from £40 01983 612711

See also Isle of Wight - Sandown

Beverley (Linley Hill)

4 miles north east Beverley (see text for precise road directions)
Hull Aero Club, Linley Hill Aerodrome, Leven,
North Humberside, HU17 5LT
Tel: 01964 544994 Fax: 01964 544994

A former farm strip, Beverley (Linley Hill) airfield is situated a short distance from Leven, about 5 miles from the town of Beverley - whose imposing Minster dominates the local landscape. The airfield has been licensed and upgraded by the Hull Aero Club following their move from the nearby British Aerospace airfield at Brough.

The airfield still retains much of the atmosphere of a farm strip. The (now licensed) runway is larger and of a more reliable standard than many strips, and there are simple facilities in the club house. Resident aircraft are mostly the Cessnas of the Aero Club. If you are in the area the Museum of Army Transport, in Beverley town centre, is well worth a visit as it has a complete Blackburn Beverley (built at Brough) on display. This aircraft was flown into Paull airfield (now disused) near Hull, amid some local excitement as there was doubt that such a large aircraft could successfully land on the 600 metre grass runway. In the event only around half the runway was used. It was hoped to use the aircraft as a clubhouse for the resident flying club, but this proved impossible so the aircraft was eventually dismantled, transported by road, and re-assembled in situ.

Finding the airfield by road takes a certain amount of faith. In Leven village (Leven is on the A165, 5 miles north-east of Beverley) there is a small plane sign saying 'Airfield'. It is opposite the village bakery and a pub called 'The Hare and Hounds'. The airfield is 3-4 miles down this road which turns into a rather bumpy track about half-way along.

Landing Fee
£5.00 single inc. £10.00 multi inc. Overnight parking as per landing fee.
Cash or cheque only.

Fuel
AVGAS 100LL 68p inc.
Cash or cheque only.

Flying Organisations

Hull Aero Club	01964 544994

Other Organisations

Car Hire

Andrews	01482 867360
Bradcabs	01482 868396
Dennis Taylor	01482 861772
Beverley Ford	01482 866900

Taxis

Alpha	01482 881461
Bradcabs	01482 868396/868313
Flag Taxis	01482 858581
Westholme	01482 887227
-also arranged by aerodrome	01482 860794

Public Transport
Beverley railway station 5 miles

Nearby Places of Interest

Museum of Army Transport, Flemingate	01482 860445
Beverley Minster	01482 868540
Beverley Guild Hall	01482 867430
Beverley Race Course	01482 867488
TIC	01482 867430/883898

Architectural heritage dating from 11th century can be seen in many areas of Beverley

Food & Accommodation
Tea etc. in the club house

Lairgate Hotel convenient for racecourse	01482 882141
New Inn, Leven B&B from £20	01964 542223

Biggin Hill

3 miles south-east of Bromley on the A233
Regional Airports UK Ltd, Biggin Hill Airport, Kent TN16 3BN

Tel: 01959 571111 (Admin.) Fax: 01959 576404
Telex: 957045 BIGGIN G

Synonymous with the Battle of Britain, Biggin Hill is undoubtedly the most famous wartime airfield of all. The detailed exploits of Biggin Hill are beyond the scope of this guide, suffice to say, here is an airfield steeped in history like no other in the UK. In peacetime the RAF role for 'Biggin-on-the-Bump' was until recently as home to the Officers and Aircrew Selection Centre - together with a small chapel of remembrance dedicated to The Few. Since the OASC decamped to RAF Cranwell only the Chapel and its memorial remain, together with their Spitfire and Hurricane guardians, and the rest of the station is slowly deteriorating through neglect.

All this is in marked contrast to the rest of the airfield, where Biggin's claim to be London's premier GA airfield can scarcely be disputed. The GA Terminal in the tower building houses good flight briefing facilities, customs, duty-free and local information. On the other side of the runway you will find plenty of flying schools and aviation related companies. A large number of General Aviation aircraft types can be seen here, expensive business jets alongside training aircraft in profusion and occasional rarities like the Beech Queen Air and Grumman Widgeon amphibian. Facing the main road near the runway threshold you will find the airport cafe 'Scrambles', which offers a 'transport cafe' style menu. Food is also available at Kingair's bar.

Biggin Hill is a busy, commercial airfield and frankly not geared up to the casual visitor who just wants to wander around the hangers a bit. Nevertheless it's pretty much a 'must visit' type of place and is as welcoming as any airfield in the area. Recently the management announced plans for new facilities and reduced charges to prove that "Biggin Hill loves private owners". Watch this space.

Landing Fee
0-0.8 tonnes £15.28; 0.8-1.7 tonnes inc. £18.21; 1.7-2.5 tonnes £28.20. Parking fees daily: 0-0.8 £5.58; 0.8-1.7 £7.05; 1.7-2.5 £8.23.
All major credit cards (and a few minor ones too)

Fuel
AVGAS 100LL 56.5p +, AVTUR JET A1 25p +. 01959 574737
All major credit cards

Flying Organisations

A1 Aircraft	01959 575088 / 0860 872838
Air Touring Flying Club	01959 573133 / 573652
Alouette Flying Club	01959 573243
Biggin Hill School of Flying	01959 573583
Civilair Flying Club	01959 573853
Classair	01959 540495
EFG Flying School	01959 540400
Falcon Flying Services	01959 575923 / 572339
Hall Aviation	01689 855359
Kingair Flight Centre	01959 575088
London Flights (Biggin Hill) Ltd	01959 540079
Martin Evans	0181 9466950, 0959 540079
Metropolitan Police Flying Club (Biggin Hill Section)	01959 572350
Surrey and Kent Flying Club Ltd	01959 540579 / 5722255
Tropair Air Services	01959 576767

Other Organisations

Adams Aviation (aircraft spares)	01959 576660
Air Touring Services Ltd (Maintenance)	01959 573652
Avtech Ltd (Maintenance)	01959 575767
Bigginair Ltd (Maintenance)	01959 575923
Biggin Hill Ground School	01656 57191
Cobaircraft Co Ltd	01959 571553
Quantel Ltd	01959 574545
Shipping & Airlines Ltd	01959 573404
Skycare Handling	01959 574679
Testori (UK) Ltd (Maintenance)	01959 540052
The Flying Shop 01959 576370	

Car Hire

Avis	0181 6507067
Budget	0181 4647736

Taxis

Luxury Cars	01959 574677, 01860 379109

Public Transport

Bus stop outside the airfield gates to Bromley. Bromley South railway station 3 miles

Nearby Places of Interest

Knowle House, Sevenoaks	
TIC	01732 450305

Food & Accommodation

Scrambles cafe	
Oak Mount, Biggin Hill	01959 575443
Holmsdale House, Brasted 3 miles	01959 564834
The Chimneys, Tunbridge,	01732 773111
Kings Arms Hotel, Westerham 3 miles from £60	01959 562990
Clacket Lane Lodge, Westerham 3 miles from £38	01959 565577
Bromley Court Hotel, 15 mins by car from £69	0181 464 5011

Birmingham

5.5 miles south of Birmingham on the A45. M45 junction 6.
Birmingham International Airport plc, Birmingham International Airport, Birmingham, B26 3QJ
Tel: 0121 7677145 / 7675511 (Information Centre) Fax: 0121 7828802 Telex: 335582 BHXINT

Proposals for a municipal airport for Birmingham were put forward as early as 1928, but the airport was not opened until 1939 after the sort of political wrangling and environmental protest more familiar today than it was sixty years ago. The unusual terminal building was completed soon after and still stands on the cargo side of the airport, where the flying schools are based.

Birmingham's wartime role was primarily confined to training in Tiger Moths and flight-testing newly-built Stirlings and Lancasters from by the Austin Motor Co. factory a few miles away. Civilian operations recommenced in 1946 and now Birmingham is one of the UK's busiest airports outside London, with over 100 destinations claimed. The modern terminal complex is sited on the opposite side of the main runway to the old terminal, with British Airway's 'Eurohub' terminal next door. Both terminals offer all the facilities you would expect in a major international airport, and on the roof of the main terminal there is a cafe / viewing area with an aviation shop. One of Birmingham's prime advantages is its very good transport links. It is just off the M42 (which itself links the M6 & M5) and next door is Birmingham International railway station. This and the adjacent National Exhibition Centre complex are reached via the 'Maglev' monorail service from the main terminal (journey time 90 seconds!).

Recently the airport management shelved plans to close the second, shorter runway in the face of opposition from the GA community, and the handling agent based in the original terminal building - Execair - were voted 'Best UK FBO' in 1995. It seems that Birmingham is one of the few large UK airports that actually welcomes GA visitors!

Landing Fee

Up to 2 tonnes, £6.30 per 1/2 tonne + . First to hours parking free, then £2.01 per 500 kg per 24 hours.
Handling: single £12.50, multi £25. All major credit cards.

Fuel

AVGAS 100LL 58p + ; AVTUR JET A-1 28p +
All major credit cards.

Flying Organisations

Birmingham Aero Centre	0121 782 7755
Central Helicopters	0121 7823898
Jones Aviation	0121 7061845
Shakespeare	0121 7111717
Warwickshire Aerocentre	0121 7821011

Other Organisations

Aviation Hobby Shop	0121 782 2112
Execair (Handling)	0121 782 1999 (Fax 0121 782 1899)
Co Freq 122.35	
Maersk Air Engineering Ltd	0121 7823232
Midland Airport Services (Handling)	0121 782 7715 (Fax 0121 782 0530)
Teleydene Allvac/Vasco (Maintenance)	0121 7829888

Car Hire

Avis	0121 7826183
Budget	0121 7677810
Hertz	0121 7825158
Europcar	0121 7826507

Taxis

At terminals

Public Transport
Birmingham International railway station, connected to main terminal by Maglev link. 0121 643 2711

Weekday bus service (route 900) to city centre 0121 200 2601. National Express nation-wide coach services 0121 622 4373. United Counties Coach Link - Midlands services 01604 36681.

Nearby Places of Interest

Birmingham 5 miles	
Birmingham Museum of Science and Industry 6 miles	0121 2351661
Birmingham Bus Museum	
Birmingham Railway Museum	
National Motorcycle museum 2 miles	0121 7042784
National Exhibition Centre, 1 mile	0121 7804141
Cadbury World (prior booking is required)	0121 4514180
TIC	0121 6656116/7804321

Food & Accommodation
Usual eating and drinking facilities in the Eurohub and main terminal

Forte Post House (100 metres from cargo side) from £45	0121 782 8141
Novotel, Birmingham Airport	
(outside the main terminal) from £70	0121 7827000
Tristar, 1 mile from £30	0121 782 1010

Blackbushe

9 miles south of Reading, on the A30
Blackbushe Airport (85) Ltd, Blackbushe Airport, Camberley, Surrey
Tel: 01252 879449 (Management and Admin.) Fax: 01252 874444

Blackbushe was a wartime airfield whose resident squadrons served in a wide range of roles. Late in the war the airfield became a major receiving station for casualties from overseas, due to both the excellent transport links (especially to London) and the numerous local hospitals.

The airfield closed in 1946, but reopened for commercial use the following year and, like Northolt, Blackbushe was popular for commercial traffic due to its proximity to London. The name of Air Vice Marshal D.C.T. Bennett (of the 'Pathfinders') is closely associated with post-war Blackbushe. He first came here in 1949, setting up his commercial operation 'Fairflight' and he later came to the airfield's rescue when it was threatened with closure in 1960. He purchased most of the land which the airfield stood on, and operations continued. Later the airfield was owned and operated by the late Doug Arnold - the eccentric warbird operator and restorer - before being purchased by the present owners, British Car Auctions, in the 1980s. It remains a popular and busy GA airfield and jumping-off point for light aircraft bound for the continent.

Facilities in the main building are somewhat limited, but there is a cafe in the European Flyers clubhouse just across the car park.

Landing Fee
£15.00 inc. (single), light twins £22.50 inc. Up to 50% discount if refuelling. Major credit cards

Fuel
AVGAS 100LL 61p + AVTUR JET A1 24p+. Major credit cards (caution, fuel often not available on Public Holidays - call ahead to check).

Flying Organisations

Blackbushe School of Flying	01252 870999
European Flyers	01252 873747

Other Organisations

Air Hanson Engineering Ltd (Maintenance)	01252 890089
Air Hanson Ltd (Beechcraft, Sikorsky & McDonnell Douglas sales)	01252 890089

Car Hire

Avis	01344 417417
Europcar	01276 451570
Thrifty	01252 342624

Taxis

A2B Taxis	01276 64488
Hart Taxis	01276 33633
Yately Taxis	01528 60662

Public Transport
No convenient buses. Fleet railway station 3 miles.

Nearby Places of Interest

Hartley Wintey village 2 miles	
Bracknell, 6 miles, home of the Central Forecasting Office	01344 856267
The Countryside and Heritage Centre, Bracknell	01344 868222
Airborne Forces Museum, Aldershot 9 miles	01252 349619
Aldershot Military Museum, 9 miles	
Royal Army Medical Corps Museum, Farnborough 5 miles	01252 340212
TIC	01344 868196

Food & Accommodation
Cafe in European Flyers

The Ely Beefeater pub 1/2 mile on A30	01252 890487
Cartref - 3 miles, B&B from £19	01276 66888
Youlden Lodge - 3 miles B&B from £18	01276 61793
Railway Corner - 3 miles, B&B £17	01276 65880
Dial House Hotel - 5 miles from £60 (£40 weekends)	01344 776941

Blackpool

3 miles south of Blackpool, signposted off the A584/B5261, J4 M55
Blackpool Airport Ltd, Blackpool Airport, Lancs, FY4 2QY
Tel: 01253 343434 (Information Desk) Fax: 01253 405009

Blackpool might not spring immediately to mind when Britain's aviation heritage is referred to. However, an aircraft first landed on the racetrack that once stood here in 1909, making Blackpool second only to Farnborough historically. The airfield proper was built in 1919 and modest services to the Isle of Man and Liverpool were established in the 1930s. Later a factory was installed, which was in use into the late 1950s.

The discovery of natural gas fields in Morecambe Bay has brought a boost to the airport, justifying a separate helicopter terminal serving the gas rigs, some of which can be seen from the nearby beach. The old passenger terminal was replaced in 1995 with a much larger structure with improved facilities, indeed the whole airport is taking pains to modernise and redevelop itself. GA has always played a significant part in the airport's fortunes and Blackpool is regarded as a 'GA friendly' destination. There are four active flying clubs, air taxi operators, plenty of privately owned aircraft and modest scheduled services, including services to the Isle of Man. If you are flying in, the landing fees look steep at first glance. However, there are substantial discounts for cash payment - ask for details.

Landing Fee
£7.35 inc. VAT per half tonne up to 1 tonne, 1001-1500 kg £20.55, 1501-2000kg £27.40. Substantial discounts for cash payment. All major credit cards except Diners

Fuel
AVGAS 100LL 59p + , AVTUR JET A1 24p + All major credit cards except Diners

Flying Organisations

ANT Flying Club	01253 345396
Blackpool Air Centre	01253 341871
Comed Aviation Ltd	01253 349072
Helicentre Ltd	01253 343082
Westair Flying School	01253 404925

Other Organisations

Air Navigation & Trading Company Ltd (Maintenance)	01253 405093
Blackpool Air Centre (Maintenance)	01253 41871
Bond Helicopters Ltd (Maintenance)	01253 405222
Brian Seedle Helicopters (Maintenance)	01253 342754
Goldstar Engineering Ltd (Maintenance)	01253 404615
Survival Suit Centre	01253 404735
Westair Engineering Services Ltd	01253 404925

Car Hire

Avis	01253 397771
Europcar	01253 343547
Hertz	01253 404021

Taxis

Black taxi freephone in terminal	
Whitesides	01253 711611

Public Transport
National coach stop at main gate, Shuttle bus to Blackpool North railway station. Blackpool North railway station (with Intercity services) 3 miles. Squire's Gate railway station 0.2 mile towards the town centre, local services only.

Nearby Places of Interest
Blackpool, often derided by those who haven't visited, attracts - apparently - more visitors annually than Greece and all the Greek islands combined. What's more, much of this is within walking distance of the airport. If you're looking for a fun day-out this could be the place! Attractions include:
The Blackpool Tower, The Golden Mile, Pleasure Beach (with a huge rollercoaster, rides, amusements etc.), The Illuminations, Winter Gardens, Sealife Centre, Louis Tussaud's Waxworks, Theatres and cinemas, The World of Coronation Street etc. etc.
TIC 01253 21623

Food & Accommodation

'Brophy's' Bar / Cafe in the terminal
Harry Ramesden's Fish & Chips Emporium in the town - a must!
Accommodation information board in the terminal building. Blackpool has more hotel beds than Portugal (it says here) so you should be able to find something!
A couple of recommendations:

Highgate B&B (2 mins walk from airfield entrance)	01253 43418
Warwick Hotel 1 mile, from £40	01253 342192
Savoy Hotel from £22.50	01253 352561
Clifton Hotel from £22.50	01253 21481
The Old Coach House, from £23	01253 344330
The New Esplanade Hotel, from £17	01253 341646

Bodmin

3.5 miles north-east of Bodmin, signposted from the A30
Cornwall Flying Club Ltd, Bodmin Airfield, Cardinham, Bodmin, Cornwall PL30 4BU

Tel: 01208 821419/821463 Fax: 01208 821419

Nestled in a corner of Bodmin Moor, close to the main A30 trunk route through Cornwall, Bodmin is scarcely visible from the approach road. The airfield has been carefully located with an eye to the environmentally sensitive nature of the area, and but for the occasional arriving or departing aircraft there is little to betray its presence to a casual passer-by. Most of the buildings are single-storey and where possible taller structures such as the hangar have been constructed in hollows with earth banks to disguise their presence. This also has the additional advantage of deflecting some of the sound of aircraft taxying and running-up prior to departure. Airfields with sensitive neighbours will appreciate the efforts of the Cornwall Flying Club, the airfield's operators.

The airfield itself is small and simple, with only those facilities required by the flying club and local aircraft operators, but refreshments are available and the local area is particularly good for walkers and tourists. A few miles East along the A30 lies Jamaica Inn, complete with a remarkable museum. This houses a slightly macabre collection of Victorian curiosities, stuffed two-headed sheep and other strange exhibits.

Landing Fee
£6.00 inc. Visa/Access.

Fuel
AVGAS 100LL 72p inc. Visa/Access.

Flying Organisations

Cornwall Flying Club	01208 821419
Heliwest	01326 312371

Other Organisations

Bodmin Light Aeroplane Services Ltd (Maintenance)	01208 821535

Car Hire

Thomas and Williams	01208 77966
Westend Motors	01208 751656

Taxis

Bodmin Taxi Service	01208 73000

Public Transport

Bodmin railway station, 2 miles.	01208 79898

Nearby Places of Interest

Bodmin Moor, the airfield is ideally situated for direct access to moor for walking etc.

Jamaica Inn - see text	
Bodmin and Wenford Railway	01208 73666
Bodmin 3 miles	
TIC	01208 76616

Food & Accommodation

Pilot's Shop/Bar open 1000-1430	
Vending machine & Bar Food	
Lanhydrock House Restaurant	01208 74331
Cromarty B&B - 2 miles from £15	01208 74691
George and Dragon - 2 miles from £14	01208 72514
Mount Pleasant B&B -2 miles from £16	01208 821342
Priory Cottage B&B - 2 miles from £10	01208 73064
Mrs Pitlock B&B 5 mins from airfield	01208 821303

Bourn

7 miles west of Cambridge, off the A45
Rural Flying Corps, Bourn Aerodrome, Bourn, Cambridgeshire, CB3 7TQ
Tel: 01954 719602 Fax: 01767 640632

Operational by 1941, Bourn was to become one of the major bomber airfields of the war. Initially home to Stirlings, later squadrons were equipped with Wellingtons and Lancasters. The latter part of the war saw Bourn operating Mosquitoes and, later still, Spitfires. Closed in 1948, the land was returned to agriculture, but flying resumed here in the 1960s.

The airfield is run by the Rural Flying Corps, and indeed that name well sums up the atmosphere of this quiet airfield. Close to the end of the 01/19 runway are the resident aircraft on a small concrete apron and a grass parking area, the clubhouse, and a single hanger. There's usually somebody about and refreshments of the "help yourself to a cuppa" variety are always available to visitors. Lindsay Brown is the club CFI, well known in aerobatic circles and for his active work on behalf of AOPA.

To find the Rural Flying Corps by road, turn south off the A45, following the signs to Bourn village. The airfield is on your left after about 0·5 mile, accessed through a gate adjacent to an almost derelict barn. A small, discreet sign on the open gate directs you round the old (and pot-holed) peri-track to the parking area adjacent to the club premises.

Landing Fee
Singles £5, multi £10, Microlights £1. Overnight parking £5 single, £10 multi.
Visa, cheques or cash

Fuel
AVGAS 70p inc.
Visa, cheques or cash

Flying Organisations

Rural Flying Corps	01954 719602

Other Organisations

Rotortech Ltd	01954 210765 / 210901
Rural Flying Corps (Maintenance)	01954 719602

Car Hire

Avis	01223 212551
Eurodollar	01223 65438
Hertz	01223 418834

Taxis
By arrangement through the airfield.

Martin Nelson	01589 558735

Public Transport
Bus stop in Bourn village. Cambridge railway station 8 miles

Nearby Places of Interest
Viewing airside (not hangers) on request.

Duxford	01223 835000
Wimpole Hall, Park and Farm 3 miles	01223 207257
TIC	01223 463385

See also Cambridge and Little Gransden

Food & Accommodation
Tea, coffee and limited selection of sandwiches available in clubhouse
Duke of Wellington, Bourn village. (about 25 mins walk)
Golden Lion, Bourn village. (about 25 mins walk)

Ashlea (B & B)	01954 211539

On Bedford/Cambridge road - A428.
If stuck due to weather, the club can arrange something.
See also Cambridge and Little Gransden

Bournemouth (Hurn)

4 miles north of Bournemouth , signposted from B3073.
Bournemouth International Airport plc ,Christchurch, Dorset BH23 6SE
Tel: 01202 593939 (Information) 579748 (outside hours)
Fax: 01202 570266

Still known locally as Hurn, this airfield was a busy wartime site. Its location made it well placed for bomber raids into France, and in the run up to D-Day Hurn was crammed full of every conceivable aircraft type.

Today the airport at Bournemouth, bought by the local councils in 1969, is split into three main areas. The first, signposted from the A31 and A338, is where the pleasant modern terminal building houses the usual collection of shops, a cafeteria with a good viewing area and facilities for visiting pilots. There is also an 'information desk' whose main job, in our experience, is NOT to tell visiting pilots anything if at all possible! Maybe we caught them on a bad day. There are various flying organisations in the outlying buildings including several flying schools, PPSC (the commercial pilot ground school specialists), and Jet Heritage - the restorers and operators of privately-owned jet warbirds. Next to the terminal is the National Air Traffic Services school of Air Traffic Control .

The second area, to the north east across the swampy ground alongside the river, is home to more flying schools, air taxi operators and FR Aviation, whose fleet of Falcon 20s are kept busy target towing for various European armed forces.

The third area, to the north west, is given over to an industrial estate, and is where most of the support services can be found, together with a couple of flying organisations.

Bournemouth has an expanding range of scheduled, charter and cargo traffic. Light aircraft visitors are often passing through to the Channel Islands and mainland Europe and on a sunny weekend it gets to be pretty busy here.

Landing Fee

Up to 1000 kg £11.75, 1001-1499 kg £17.62, 1500 kg £23.50. Parking fees apply after 2 hours, Single engine at £5.00 per day. All major credit cards

Fuel

AVGAS 100LL 50.7p +; AVTUR JET A1 27.5p +. Available daily 0700-2130 and by prior arrangement with Esso outside these times 01202 594000. All major credit cards

Flying Organisations

A & G Aviation Ltd	01202 578558
Airbourne School of Flying	01202 582181
Airtime	01202 580676
Chase Aviation	01202 485172
Professional Air Training	01202 593366
SFT Aviation Ltd	01202 599888
Southern Flight Training Ltd	01202 590940
Spitfire Aviation	01202 582282

Other Organisations.

AIM Aviation (Jecco) Ltd (Maintenance)	0102 397388
Airtime Aviation (Maintenance)	01202 580676
Airwork Ltd (Maintenance)	01202 572271
Anglo American Aircraft Sales (Piper aircraft & parts, maintenance)	01202 570023
European College of Aviation	01202 599509
FLS Aerospace (Light Aircraft) Ltd (Maintenance)	01202 500200
GED (BBK Designs) Ltd (Maintenance)	01202 570629
IDS Aircraft Ltd (Cessna Citation Service Centre)	01202 573243
Jet Heritage	
Marilake Instruments Ltd (Maintenance)	01202 570055
Midair Aviation Ltd (Maintenance)	01202 581925
PPSC	01202 579819
SFT Aviation Ltd (Maintenance)	01202 499888
Source Aviation Services Ltd (Maintenance)	01202 578999
Wessex Air Maintenance	01202 590251

Car Hire

Avis	01202 293218
Hertz	01202 291231
Carwise	01202 471910
Europcar	01202 293357

Taxis

Available at terminal	
County Cabs	01973 709617
John's Taxis	01589 723804

Public Transport

Christchurch railway station 4 miles, Bournemouth railway station 6 miles. Both with services to London Waterloo.

Nearby Places of Interest

Bournemouth - 4 miles:	
Expo Centre, includes a Dinosaur Safari, The Bournemouth Bears and Mummies of the Pharaohs exhibition	01202 293544
Bournemouth Super Bowl	01202 291717
Bournemouth Water Zoo	01202 295593
Christchurch Ski & Leisure Centre	01202 499155
Place Mill, Christchurch	01202 487626
Harvey's Pleasure Boats, Poole	01202 666226
Sega World, Bournemouth	01202 316396
Tower Park Leisure Complex, Poole	01202 723671
TIC	01202 291715

Food & Accommodation

Cafe, bar and buffet at airport terminal	
Corkers Restaurant and Cafe Bar, Poole.	
La Mer Restaurant, Sandbanks, Poole	
La Roche Restaurant, Sandbanks, Poole	
Noel au Petit St Tropez, Brasserie and restaurant, Christchurch	01202 482522
Woolpack, Sopley 5 mins drive	01425 672252
Hurn Court Farmhouse 10 mins walk	01202 471336
Fishermans Haunt, Winkton - 3 miles. Real ale, excellent food, rooms from £35	01202 477283/484071
Hurn Court Farmhouse - 1 mile	01202 471336
Hogarths, West Parley 4 mins drive	01202 574769
Grosvenor House, 15 mins drive from £25	01202 558858
Chalkwood, Christchurch 5 mins drive	01202 474527
Tyrrells Ford Country House, Avon - 3 miles from £55	01425 672646
Belvedere Hotel, Christchurch - 3 miles from £20	01202 485978
For accommodation enquiries and bookings call	01202 290883

Breighton

5 miles east of Selby, signposted from A163
Real Aeroplane Company Ltd, Breighton Aerodrome, Breighton
Tel: 01757 289065, out of hours 01302 890633 Brian Brown

Breighton was built for RAF bombers, opening in 1942 with a squadron of Wellingtons, later re-equipping with Lancasters and Halifaxes.

Nowadays, much of the station has been redeveloped as an industrial estate, but a busy and popular airfield remains on one side of the original site. It is an excellent place to visit, there is always something going on and the friendly welcome is well known, as is the lack of a landing fee! The emphasis is on 'real' (i.e. interesting) aircraft. Some rare types can be found here, including an L39 jet trainer, which operates without difficulty from the 575 metre runway!

Catering is available at weekends offering good quality food, including excellent bacon buns, and tea and coffee are available during the week, if you make it yourself.

Landing Fee
Nil

Fuel
AVGAS 100LL 65.3p inc. cash or cheque only

Flying Organisations

Real Aeroplane Club	01757 289065

Other Organisations

Car Hire

Avis	01904 610460
Eurodollar	01904 612141
Hertz	01904 612586

Taxis
On request through the airfield

Public Transport
No convenient buses but flying club members are often willing to help out. Wressle railway station 2 miles

Nearby Places of Interest

Yorkshire Air Museum, Elvington 12 miles	01904 608595
Carlton Towers, Nr Goole 8 miles	01405 861662
Drax Power Station 4 miles	01757 618381
Selby Abbey 5 miles	
TIC	01757 703263

Food and Accommodation
Hot/cold food at the airfield at the weekends, including full cooked breakfast.

The Breighton Ferry , Breigton village - 1 mile	
The Old Poachers, Breighton village - 1 mile	01757 288849
Kings Arms, North Duffield - 2 miles	01757 288492
Mrs Davies B&B, Breighton - 1 mile	01757 288273
Londesborough Arms Hotel, Selby - 8 miles from £38	01757 707355

Bristol

8 miles south of Bristol on the A38. M5 junction 22 from south; junction 18 from north and west; M4 junction 19 (M32) from east.
Bristol Airport plc ,Bristol Airport, Bristol BS19 3DY
Tel: 01275 474444 Fax: 01275 474767
Telex: 449295 AIRPORT BRISTOL

Lulsgate Bottom, later Bristol Lulsgate, now merely Bristol, opened in 1940 as a training airfield. Situated on the western side of the country, the airfield was never going to be used for offensive purposes, but it was busy in a support and training role throughout the war. Bristol was developed for commercial use in the late 1950s and early 1960s, including a much-needed extension to the main runway. The main runway has since been extended further, and the airport is today a busy charter and scheduled base for South West England with a modern terminal alongside the A38 that houses the usual facilities. The support services and flying clubs operate from the north side of the airport, down the lane signposted to the village of Lulsgate Bottom. Unfortunately, recent development of the terminal has reclaimed the once popular viewing area, so at present there is no really satisfactory point from which to watch the aircraft, apart from the terminal's limited viewing facilities.

Landing Fee
£6.75 + per 1/2 tonne
All major credit cards except Switch.

Fuel
AVGAS 100LL 62p + ; AVTUR JET A1 20.3p +
All major credit cards except Switch.

Flying Organisations

Bristol Flying Centre	01275 474601
Bristol & Wessex Aero Club	01275 472514

Other Organisations

Global Trading Aviation Maintenance	01275 472484
RC Flight Simulations	

Car Hire

Avis	01275 472613
Hertz	01275 472807 or 0117 9779777

Taxis

Airport Taxis Ltd	01275 474812

Public Transport

National Express shuttle to Bristol coach station	0117 9557013
Bristol Temple Meads railway station 8 miles	0117 9294255

Nearby Places of Interest

Bristol 8 miles	
Bristol Industrial Museum, Prince's Wharf, Bristol	0117 9251470
City Museum and Art Gallery, Bristol	0117 9223571
Bristol Historic Dockyard, including the SS Great Britain	
The Clifton Suspension Bridge, Bristol	
The Cheddar Gorge 8 miles	
International Helicopter Museum, Weston-Super Mare, 10 miles	01934 635227

Food & Accommodation
Bars and restaurants on the first floor of terminal. Also vending machines.

Goblin Coombe Farm within walking distance B&B from £16	01934 862295
Jubilee Inn, Flax Bourton 5 mins drive B&B from £28 (recommended)	01275 462741
The Old Vicarage, Dundry 2 miles B&B from £18	0117 9784090
Eastfield Cottage, Flax Bourton 2 miles B&B from £12	01275 463936
Seymour Arms, Blagdon 4 miles B&B from £20	01761 462279

Cambridge

2 miles east of Cambridge. On the A1303, clearly signposted off the A45.
Marshall Aerospace, The Airport, Cambridge CB5 8RX
Tel: 01223 61133 Fax: 01223 321032
Telex 81208

Cambridge is operated by Marshall Aerospace - a company with a long and illustrious history as one of the UK's premier aerospace companies. Cambridge is Marshall's heavy engineering facility for the RAF, and a significant amount of work takes place here converting civilian airliners such as the L1011 Tristar to military transport and tanker roles. This is done alongside routine maintenance on anything from a Cessna trainer to Gulfstream business jets.

There is also a significant amount of business traffic, both for the university town, with its high-tech organisations, and for nearby Newmarket Racecourse. Add to this the modest scheduled services of Suckling Airways operated by their Dornier 228s, some seasonal charter flights, the aircraft of the flying clubs and the Bulldogs of the AEF and UAS and you will appreciate that the airfield is often moderately busy.

Flying visitors can make use of the staff canteen for refreshments, and visiting aircraft are handled promptly and efficiently, although the major nature of the engineering works undertaken here can mean that unscheduled maintenance can be difficult to arrange at short notice. Military contractors seldom encourage casual visitors and, as you might expect, Cambridge is a very security conscious airfield. There are no official viewing facilities, and hanger viewing not allowed. Nor is there any public access to the terminal area, except of course for pilots and passengers.

Landing Fee
Single £11.45 inc. if paid on day, multi £25.80 + if paid on day. Parking: £7.20 + each 24hrs period, first 3hrs free All major credit cards accepted.

Fuel
AVGAS 100LL 50.61p + available daily 0800-1745 (winter) 0700-1645 (Summer) 24 hours notice required all other times. AVTUR JET A1 28p + Mon-Fri 0800-1630 (winter) 0700-1530 (summer) 24 hours notice all other times including Sat, Sun and PH.
All major credit cards accepted.

Flying Organisations

Burman Aviation Ltd	01223 293396
Cambridge Aero Club	01223 373214
Cambridge Flying Group	01223 293343

Other Organisations

Marshall of Cambridge Aerospace Ltd (maintenance)	01223 61133

Car Hire

Avis	01223 21551
Hertz	01223 212551
Autorent	01223 312212

Taxis
Courtesy phone in terminal

Cabco	01223 51195

Camtax 01223 313131

Public Transport
Bus stop outside airport to town. Cambridge railway station 3 miles

Nearby Places of Interest
Cambridge 2 miles

University Museum of Archaeology, Cambridge	01223 337733
University Botanic Garden, Cambridge	01223 336265
Scott Polar Research Institute, Cambridge	01223 336540
American Military Cemetery 5 miles	01954 210350
Imperial War Museum Duxford 8 miles	
TIC	01223 322640

See also Duxford

Food & Accommodation

Cafeteria open 0730-1800, 3-course meal menu available 1230-1400.
Ancient Shepherd Pub, Fen Ditton (about 25-30 mins walk)
The Eagle, Benett Street, Cambridge. Former coaching inn with good food and real ales. The ceiling has been preserved as it carries the signatures of RAF and USAF airmen, made duringthe last war. 01223 301286

Abbey Guest House close to airfield £20	01223 241427
Hamden Guest House close to airfield	01223 413263
Hamilton Hotel £35	01223 365664
Helen Hotel, Cambridge from £35	01223 246465
Royal Cambridge Hotel, Cambridge from £70	01223 351631

Carlisle

5 miles east of Carlisle. Off M6 junction 44, take A689 following airport signs.
City and County Borough of Carlisle, Carlisle Aerodrome, Cumbria CA6 4NW
Tel: 01228 573641 (Information)
Fax: 01228 573310 (Flight Ops) Telex: 64476

Carlisle is an ex RAF airfield (formerly known as RAF Crosby-on-Eden) which lay dormant after the war until 1961 when Carlisle council opened the airfield as Carlisle Airport. Various attempts have been made to develop scheduled services here (usually to London), but none have flourished. Fortunately for visitors, the legacy of these attempts is a well-kept airfield with good facilities. It is next to Hadrian's Wall and convenient for Cumbria, Northumbria, the northern Lake District and the Scottish borders, and the terminal building offers modest but reasonable fare (in Henry's). In the summer you can sit at the tables outside the terminal and enjoy a good view of the airfield activity.

The three resident flying schools keep the airfield busy in good weather and there are a number of interesting light aircraft in the hangers. There are occasional military aircraft passing through (usually communications aircraft bringing visitors to the nearby Spadeadam ranges) and the usual mix of commercial and private aircraft traffic. There is a small museum and collection of military jets, including a Canberra, Lightning and Vulcan, maintained by Solway Aviation Society. The Vulcan is often open for inspection on Sunday afternoons and occasionally the systems are run-up.

One of the disused runways seems to be given over to vehicle storage, on a recent visit hundreds of vans in bright red Royal Mail livery were parked nose to tail along its length!

Landing Fee
Up to 1 tonne £13.31 +, 40% discount if paid cash on arrival. First 2 hours parking free, then £6 + per 24 hours. Access/Visa

Fuel
AVGAS 100LL 66p + AVTUR Jet A1 24p + .
Access/Visa

Flying Organisations

Border Air Training	01228 573490
Carlisle Flight Centre	01228 573333
Cumbria Aero Club	01228 573633

Other Organisations
Solway Aviation Society. Sundays 2-4 p.m. and by arrangement.

Car Hire

Eurodollar	01228 42707/8
Hertz	01228 512529
Avis	01228 590580

Taxis

Radio Taxis	01228 27575

Public Transport
Carlisle Citadel railway station
(West Coast Main Line) - 7 miles. Information 01228 44711

Nearby Places of Interest
Other nearby airports - Great Orton Airfield, Dalston; Kirkbride Airfield, Nr Wigton
Carlisle 7 miles

Discovery Walks of Historic Carlisle	01228 512444
Discovery tour of Carlisle Castle	01228 591922

Hadrian's Wall 10 miles

Visitor Centre (also book-a-bed Ahead service)	01228 512444
TIC	01228 512444

Food & Accommodation
'Henry's' bar and food in the main building. Open for food 1030-1500 weekdays; 1100-1500 Saturdays; 1200-1500 Sundays
B&B via the Cumbria Aero Club. Transport to/from the airfield provided, B&B from £15

Batt House, Cosby-on-Eden B&B from £12	01228 573366
Wallfoot Hotel & Restaurant from £20 (on road to airport)	01228 573696/573240
Newby Grange Hotel**, Crosby-on-Eden from £26	01228 573645
Crosby Lodge Hotel***, Crosby-on-Eden from £42	01228 573618

Chichester (Goodwood)

1 mile east of Chichester, signposted off the A286
Goodwood Aerodrome, Chichester, West Sussex, PO18 0PH
Tel: 01243 789660 Fax: 01243 536497

Just outside the cathedral city of Chichester on the Sussex coast, Goodwood airfield (known originally as Westhampnett) pre-dates the Second World War when it was home to Spitfires and Typhoons. It is perhaps better known for its motor racing heritage, however – the motor circuit was formed from the original perimeter track in 1947 most of the great post-war racers have competed here at some time or another. The Festival of Speed, held in June, commemorates the great days of motor racing.

The airfield, part of the Goodwood House estate, houses a number of interesting aircraft – Harvard, Stearman, Jungmann, several Tiger Moths and a two seat Spitfire, alongside the usual training and touring types. There are hopes to increase hanger capacity to accommodate more in the future. There is a pleasant cafeteria in Goodwood Flying School (the new caterers offering good quality food) with an excellent view of the airfield and a veranda. Goodwood Flying School offer pleasure flights, Stephenson Aviation offer helicopter pleasure flights.

Landing Fee
Singles £11.75 inc. Above 2 tonnes £15.25 + £5 per additional 500kg. Sundays £5.00 per engine - cash. Overnight parking £5.00 single, £11.75 twin. Half price if paid in advance.
Major credit cards except Amex and Diners.

Fuel
AVGAS 62p + JET A-1 28p +
Major credit cards except Amex and Diners.

Flying Organisations

Bushpilots	01730 895034
Cloudbase Aviation (Microlights)	01293 522465/0850 852610
Goodwood Flying School	01243 774656
Stephensen Aviation (Helicopters)	01243 530165
Vectair	01243 781652

Other Organisations

Goodwood Aerodrome (Maintenance)	01243 781934
Goodwood Motor Circuit	01243 789660
Peter Gethin Driving Courses	01243 778118
Stephenson Aviation (Maintenance)	01243 530165

Car Hire

Avis	01273 673738/01293 519900
Eurodollar	01273 202426/01293 51031
Hertz	01273 738227

Taxis

Dunnaways	01243 782403
Central	01243 776666

Public Transport
No convenient buses. Chichester railway station 3 miles with direct links to London, Gatwick, Portsmouth and Brighton. 01273 206755. Recorded information 01273 721032

Nearby Places of Interest

Chichester cathedral town - 1 mile	TIC 01243 775888
Goodwood Racecourse - 1/2 mile	01243 774107 (01243 774838 racedays)
Goodwood House - 1/2 mile	01243 774107
Tangmere Military Aviation Museum - 3 miles	01243 775223
Weald & Downland Open Air Museum - 4 miles	01243 811348

Food & Accommodation
Licensed bar & light meals at Goodwood Flying School - BLT recommended!
Anglesey Arms, Hanaker 1_ miles - good food
Clinchs Salad House (Egon Ronay) vegetarian restaurant, Chichester. 01243 788822
Sleepers B & B, Westerton House Farm - under 1 mile. £15PP. 01243 779479
Mrs D Fabricius B & B £20-25. 01243 774308 (recommended)
Jarvis Chichester Hotel - 1 mile. £85 (special weekend rates). 01243 786351
Goodwood Park Hotel **** - walking distance. 01243 775537

Clacton

1 mile west of Clacton, on the B1027
Clacton Aerodrome, West Road, Clacton-on-Sea Essex CO15 1BG
Tel: 01255 424671

The tiny airfield of Clacton, situated just a few metres from the coast at nearby Jaywick, is home to the Clacton Aero Club whose Cessnas, Piper Cubs and Tiger Moth work hard giving training and pleasure flights during daylight hours. Here also you may occasionally see the beautiful Dragon Rapide, which gives pleasure flights at the Duxford Air Museum, as it flies in and out for periodic maintenance.

Clacton is essentially a base for the aero club, who specialise in residential courses, tailwheel conversions and farmstrip flying. There is a simple cafe-bar area in the clubhouse offering drinks and snacks, and viewing is best done from the adjacent car park. If you feel energetic, you can take a walk along the public footpath that actually crosses the runway - but give way to the aeroplanes! Alternatively, the resort town of Clacton is only 10-15 minutes walk from the airfield.

By road, Clacton airfield can be reached by following the road along the coast from Clacton town centre to Jaywick. Alternatively, follow the signs from the A133 to St. Osyth and Jaywick, the airfield is on your left as you approach the sea.

Landing Fee
Single £3.00. Overnight parking £3.00
Visa/Access

Fuel

Flying Organisations

Clacton Aero Club (1988) Ltd	01255 424671

Other Organisations

CAS Engineering Ltd (Maintenance)	01255 424671

Car Hire

Taxis

Westons	01255 270630
AJ's	01255 474444

Public Transport
Clacton railway station 2 miles

Nearby Places of Interest
Clacton, a true English sea-side resort, is 10-15 minutes walk from the airfield.

Clacton Pier (rides, shows etc.)	01255 421115
Magic City, Clacton	01255 421115
Princes Theatre Clacton (Stars, Bands, Wrestling)	01255 422958
East Essex Aviation and Forties Museum, St Osyth, 5 miles	01255 423604
St Osyth Priory Picture Gallery	
TIC	01255 423400

Food & Accommodation
Tea, coffee and snacks from clubhouse
The club can offer accommodation from £10
Hundreds of eating, drinking and accommodation possibilities in Clacton

Cordy's, Clacton - 2 miles	01255 422910
Grand Hotel, Clacton - 2 miles	01255 222020
Chelsea House, Clacton - 2 miles B&B from £17	01255 421797
Chudleigh Hotel, Clacton - 2 miles from £20 (recommended)	01255 425407

Compton Abbas

3 miles south of Shaftesbury, signposted from the B3081
Compton Abbas Airfield, Ashmore, Nr Shaftesbury, Salisbury, Wiltshire SP5 5AP
Tel: 01747 811767 Fax: 01747 811167

On top of a hill, not far from Shaftesbury in picturesque Dorset countryside, Compton Abbas has many pilot's vote for "Britain's prettiest airfield". On a clear day the view from the airfield is magnificent. The pleasant airfield cafe has a terrace built to take advantage of the aspect, and the approach by air over a steeply sloping wooded valley is spectacular. The welcome is friendly, there's usually some interesting aircraft about, and the standard of catering is some way above that found in some airfield cafes, with a pub food style menu including particularly good home-made cakes.

Compton is usually quite active on any half-descent flying day, and also has a number of popular fly-ins each year. The airfield gained nation-wide prominence a few years ago when Asil Nadir, the disgraced Cypriot businessman on bail for alleged fraud, slipped out of the UK from here. For several days Compton got more press coverage than all the rest of the UK's GA airfields get in a year. When the fuss died down temptation got the better of the airfield and, exactly one year after Asil Nadir's departure, Compton held the 'Asil Nadir flew-out fly-in'!

Landing Fee
£7.00 inc.
All major credit cards except Amex, minimum £10

Fuel
AVGAS 100LL 0.579 +
All major credit cards except Amex, minimum £10

Flying Organisations
Abbas Air 01747 811767
GM Promotions 01373 463697
Fly a Stearman 01747 811767

Other Organisations
Carrill Aviation Ltd (Maintenance) 01747 812128

Car Hire
Arranged by the airfield

Taxis
A + B Taxis 01722 744744 / 0850 466311

Public Transport
Bus route in village of Compton Abbas - rural timetable. Regular services from Shaftesbury to other parts of county. Gillingham railway station 6 miles

Nearby Places of Interest
Shaftesbury, an ancient Saxon hilltop town with many interesting features including the now famous Gold Hill - the steeply cobbled street located behind the Town Hall (remember the Hovis advert?). It is a popular location for artists, film makers and photographers.
Shaftesbury Abbey 01747 852910
Blandford Forum, 8 miles.
Lots of picturesque countryside and drives.
TIC 01747 853514

Food & Accommodation
The Compton Abbas Airfield restaurant, 1000-1600 Mon-Fri and 1000-1700 weekends
Jesters Restaurant, Shaftesbury - 3 miles (Egon Ronay). 01747 854444
Byzant Restaurant, Shaftesbury - 3 miles 01747 853355
Ye Olde Two Brewers, Shaftesbury - 3 miles 01747 854211
Mr & Mrs L. Henstridge B&B 01747 854258
Grosvenor Hotel, Shaftesbury - 3 miles 01747 852282
Crofters, Shaftesbury - 3 miles B&B from £14 01747 852886
Museum Hotel, Farnham - 5 miles. Good beer, extensive wine list, excellent food. Recommended. From £50 01725 516261
Royal Hotel, Gillingham - 6 miles from £18 01747 822305

Coventry

3 miles south of Coventry, signposted off A45 and A46
Coventry Airport, Baginton, Coventry CV8 3AZ
Tel: 01203 301717 Fax: 01203 639451
Telex: 31646

Coventry has long been associated with the motor industry, but the airfield at Baginton was once home to Armstrong Whitworth Aircraft. Thousands of aircraft were built and assembled here, from Whitley and Lancaster bombers in wartime to Meteor, Seahawk and Hunter fighters and Argosy transports in later years. The name lives on in the Sir W G Armstrong Whitworth Flying Group, a local flying club still based on the airfield.

Coventry's role as a municipal airport has been eclipsed by Birmingham International, and the small terminal is in need of refurbishment or replacement as its facilities are basic, although the cafeteria has well priced food. Coventry has developed a niche as a GA and cargo base and Air Atlantique, operators of DC3s, DC6s and DC7s in freighter and pollution control roles, are based here. Air Atlantique have recently acquired ex-RAF Shackletons and a Scottish Aviation Twin Pioneer, which it is hoped will fly again. Together with the occasional Boeing 707 freighters, business jets and the busy local flying clubs and training schools, there is plenty going on here. Additionally, on the Rowley Rd to the north side of the airfield, the Midland Air Museum has a large collection of interesting aircraft including a Vulcan and an Argosy.

Most flying training takes place from buildings in a newly developed area off the Rowley road, adjacent to the modern tower building, and at the Coventry Aero Club's new premises a bar and cafe are under construction with what promises to be the best viewing area on the airport.

Landing Fee
Up to 1.5 tonnes 13.92 +, above 1.5 tonnes 13.98 per tonne
All major credit cards

Fuel
AVGAS 100LL 59.5p + AVTUR Jet A-1 30p +
All major credit cards

Flying Organisations

Armstrong Whitworth Flying Group	01203 301498
Atlantic Flight Training	01203 303010
Coventry Flying School/Coventry Aeroplane Club	01203 301428
Coventry Helicopters	01203 639206
Midland Air Training School	01203 304914
Senair	01203 307003
Solihull Flying Club	01564 826235
West Midlands Police Flying Club	0121 5502644

Other Organisations

Aeronanortec Ltd (Maintenance)	01203 307566
Airwing Aircraft Sales and Charter	01203 639254
Atlantic Aeroengineering Ltd	01203 307566
Aviation Training Associates	01203 639929
Coventry Aircraft Maintenance Ltd (Maintenance)	01203 302553
Executive Aircraft Maintenance	01203 511414
Flight Safety International	01203 305418
Flight Simulation	01203 511094
Midland Air Museum and Aerospace Education Centre	01203 301033

Car Hire

Avis	01203 225500
Eurodollar	01203 677042
Hertz	01203 251741
Europcar	01203 502111

Taxis

Lewis Taxis	01203 666666
Alan's Taxis	01203 555555

Public Transport
Metro Bus Service T route (not Sundays), 01203 559559. Coventry railway station 3 miles 01203 555211.

Nearby Places of Interest

The Lunt Roman fort, 1/2 mile	01203 832381
The Coventry Canal Basin	
(arts, crafts and boat related businesses)	01203 258318
Coventry 3 miles	
Heritage Motor Museum, Gaydon 14 miles	01926 641181
Coombe Abbey Country Park, 5 miles	01203 453720
Museum of British Road Transport	01203 832425
Bosworth Battlefield and Visitor Centre	01455 292239
National Motorcycle Museum, Solihull	
Warwick Castle	01926 408000
Kennelworth Castle	01926 52078
TIC	01203 832303
The Herbert Art Gallery and Museum	01203 832381

Food & Accommodation

Cafe in terminal
The Oak Pub (on the west side of the airport, near the terminal)
The Old Mill (in Baginton)

Treetops, Baginton _ mile B&B from £15	01203 304221
Mrs B Loughridge, Coventry 1_ miles B&B from £13	01203 413686
Mr and Mrs Smith, Coventry 1 mile B&B from £12.50	01203 412346
Mr J Freeman, Coventry 1_ miles B&B from £15	01203 416209
Coventry Knight Hotel, Ryton on Dunsmore	
2 miles from £55	01203 301585

Cranfield

7 miles south-west of Bedford. Signposted off the A509, M1 J14
Cranfield University, Cranfield Aerodrome, Cranfield,
Bedfordshire MK43 0AL
Tel: 01234 754784 (Admin.); 01234 751417 (Handing);
01234 750111 ext. 5584 (Accounts)
Fax: 01234 751805 (Admin. and accounts);
01234 751246 (Handling) Telex: 825072 CITECHC

Opened in 1937, Cranfield operated as a training base for a large part of the War. The College of Aeronautics was set up in 1946, and at the same time the Empire Test Pilots' School commenced activities here, later moving to Farnborough. The College of Aeronautics became the Cranfield Institute of Technology which still dominates the airfield today.

Apart from the Institute, whose campus occupies the majority of the airfield buildings, many other flying training organisations, maintenance organisations, air taxi operators and aircraft and equipment sales organisations operate from here. There are plenty of interesting aircraft around, from the Cranfield Institute's fleet to a number of privately owned ex-military jets. There is a cafe (the Dakota Club) overlooking the runway, and college accommodation is often available for a casual stopover if required. Cranfield is probably best known for the annual Popular Flying Association Rally and fly-in when over 1000 light aircraft from the UK and overseas, of every conceivable description, arrive at Cranfield. Over this weekend Cranfield becomes the busiest airport in Europe, and this year's Golden Anniversary rally (5th-7th July) promises to be the biggest ever.

Landing Fee

Cash - £4.50 per 500kg or part up to 3 tonnes, £9.00 per tonne or part thereof over 3 tonnes. Invoiced - double above rates.
Weekend cash landing charges 0-1500 kg £5.00 per landing, 1501-3000kg £10 per landing.
First 6 hours parking free. £4.00 per day or part up to 1500 kg, £8.00 per day or part 1501-3000kg
Major cards except Amex and Diners

Fuel

AVGAS 100LL 60.5p + AVTUR JET A1 27p + (up to 500 litres), then 26p +.
All major cards except Amex

Flying Organisations

Aardvark Aviation Ltd	0181 8109344
Bedfordshire School of Flying	01234 751403
Billins Air Services Ltd	01234 751400 0895 232044 (eves)
Bonus Aviation	01234 751800
Burman Aviation Ltd	01234 752220
Cabair College of Air Training	01234 751243
City Air Charter (London) Ltd	01234 751417
Euroair	01234 752262
Osprey Flying Club	01234 750197

Other Organisations

Bob Crowe Aircraft sales Ltd	01234 750442
Bonus Aviation Ltd (Maintenance)	01234 751800
Burman Aviation Ltd (Maintenance)	01234 752220
Cranfield Aeronautical Research Ltd (Maintenance)	01234 751181
International Aerospace Engineering Ltd	01234 750198
Kennet Aviation (Maintenance)	01234 752153
Westley Aircraft (Maintenance)	01234 751807

Car Hire

Avis	01908 281334
Eurodollar	01908 271077/ 01234 269566
Hertz	01908 374492

Taxis

Wharley End (on campus)	01234 750233
Raffles	01908 222222
Image Cars	01234 855536

Public Transport

Buses on campus to Bedford centre. Bedford & Milton Keynes railway stations 5 miles.

Nearby Places of Interest

Woburn Abbey 3 miles 01525 290666	
Houghton House, Ampthill 3 miles	
Bedford Museum, Bedford 8 miles	01234 353323
Bedford 8 miles	
Old Warden (Shuttleworth Collection) 10 miles	
TIC	01234 215226

Food & Accommodation

Good facilities on the campus site including news agents, hairdressers, garage, post office, bookshop, convenience store and NatWest bank with cashpoints.

The Dakota Club	01234 752087
Mitchell Hall (on airfield) room from £30.	
Booking 0900-1730 weekdays	01234 750111 ext. 3462
The Cranfield Cranfield Conference Centre and Lanchester Hall on the airfield also offer accommodation, book via the airfield switchboard	01234 750111
Carrington Arms Pub (good food), Mouslow 2 miles	01908 218050
Mrs P Eireby B&B from £12	01234 730596
Marston Manor B&B from £17	01234 768346
The Cock, North Crawley, 5 mins. drive from £20	01234 391222
The Swan, Cranfield Village 2 miles, B&B possible	
The Laws Hotel, Turvey from £42	01234 881213
Forte Travelodge, Marston Moretaine 2 miles room from £35	01234 766755
The Barns Hotel, Bedford 6 miles	01234 270044

Crowfield

4 miles east of Stowmarket, off the A140
Coddenham Green, Ipswich Suffolk IP6 9UN
Tel: 01449 711017 Fax: 01449 711054

After a long and sometimes bitter fight against local opposition, Crowfield's owner Andrew Williamson is to be congratulated for his success in turning his former farm strip into a licensed airfield, thereby bucking a trend for airfield closures. The grass runways are particularly well kept and there is a small flying school, modern clubhouse and hangarage facilities, all alongside a working farm. It is not over yet, however, and the Crowfield Airfield Supporters Group welcomes visitors to the airfield for their support - be it moral, financial, or otherwise.

In fact, Crowfield has a reputation of welcoming visitors (especially those who fly with due consideration to the airfield's neighbours) and is frequently commented on as a particularly friendly place to visit. Tea and (real) coffee are always on the go, and although food is a bit limited, chances are that you will be able to get a lift to Beacon Hill a few miles away, or some other eatery. As one of the few licensed airfields remaining in Suffolk, Crowfield is an excellent point from which to launch an exploration of this gentle and restful county. By surface travel the airfield is a little remote from public transport, so if you are planning to fly-in and then go exploring, planning transport in advance is advisable. Crowfield is close to the A45 dual carriageway. Take the A140 turning northbound, and about 0.5 mile from the Beacon Hill services take the right-hand turn signposted 'Coddenham Green'. Stay on this road /track and you will be able to follow signs to the airfield.

Landing Fee
£3.00 singles, £6.00 multi. Landing fee waived if 35 litres or more of fuel is purchased.
Overnight parking £2.35; £39.95 per month.
Cash or cheque only

Fuel
AVGAS 100LL 57p +
Cash or cheque only

Flying Organisations
Crowfield Flying School 01449 711017

Other Organisations

Car Hire
By arrangement, although a club member is usually willing to run people about.

Taxis

Stowmarket Taxis	01449 677777
Needham Cars	01449 722408
Bakers	01449 612071

Public Transport
Bus stop on the A140 (1·5 miles away). Needham Market railway station 5 miles.

Nearby Places of Interest
Close to A140 road access to Ipswich/Colchester/Norwich .
Constable country and the Norfolk Broads
Stowmarket Museum of East Anglian Life 4 miles 01449 612229
Mid Suffolk Light Railway Museum, Brockford Station, Stowmarket - 4 miles

Food & Accommodation
Tea, coffee and snacks at airfield

Aspens Restaurant, Stowmarket	01449 612038
Pipps Ford Hotel - 2 miles, from £25	01449 760208
Tamarisk House	01472 831825
Beacon Hill Little Chef	0800 850950
The Trowel and Hammer, Nr Stowmarket	01449 781234
Tamarise House B & B	0850 217190
Hotels Limes	01449 720305
Travelodge, Beacon Hill - 2 miles	0800 850950
Cedars Hotel, Stowmarket - 4 miles	01449 612668

Denham

2 miles east of Gerrards Cross, signposted from A412 (M25 junction 17, M40 junction 1)
Bickerton's Aerodromes Ltd, Denham Aerodrome, Uxbridge, Middlesex UB9 5DE
Tel: 01895 832161 (Admin.)

Denham's aviation heritage dates back to the First World War, when pilots were trained in the rudiments of groundschool before they went on to flying training. The airfield fell into disrepair after the war, until Martin-Baker set up here in the late 1920s. Because of its small size, Denham was never really suitable as an active duty airfield, and remained in a secondary role as a Relief Landing Ground for Booker during the Second World War.

Still a pleasant and popular airfield, civilian training has continued here more or less uninterrupted since the 1940s. Close to the M25 and M40, with good links to London via the A40, Denham is popular as a training base for Londoners and currently two busy flying schools (together with several flying groups), and helicopter training keep the airfield bustling and ATC have a reputation for being friendly even when the airfield is busy. Essentially the airfield has two main sites. To the south of the main runway is the Denham School of Flying, ATC and the Biggles restaurant. On the northside are hangers and the other flying schools and groups, the helicopter operators and maintenance companies. On this side of the airfield catering is pretty much limited to tea, coffee and whatever chocolate bars, crisps or biscuits you can get at the flying clubs.

Landing Fee
Up to 1 tonne £8.50 inc., up to 1·5 tonnes £12.50 inc., up to 2 tonnes £16.50 inc.; then £8 per additional tonne. Parking for 24 hours, half landing fee. Major credit cards

Fuel
AVGAS 100LL 58.72p + AVTUR JET A1 by prior arrangement only. Major credit cards

Flying Organisations

Denham School of Flying	01895 833327
Heli Air Ltd	01895 835899
The Pilot Centre Ltd	01895 833838

Other Organisations

Denham Aircraft Maintenance Ltd	01895 834187
European Helicopters Ltd (Maintenance)	01895 834777
Martin-Baker Aircraft Company Ltd (Maintenance)	01895 832214

Car Hire.

Lordship Motors	01753 883120
Eurodollar	01753 534442
Hertz	01753 820642

Taxis

Harefield Cars	01895 824024
Denham Station Cars	01895 834741 / 822863
Cabline	01895 270001

Public Transport
Denham railway station 1 mile. Uxbridge Underground station 4 miles.

Nearby Places of Interest
Northmoor Hill Woods - nature reserve and picnic area (woodland) adjacent to airfield boundary, 2-3 mins walking distance from either side of the airfield
London Heathrow airport 10 miles
Central London just 15 miles

Food & Accommodation
Biggles Restaurant & country club on airfield. Sunday lunch £11.00 01895 833120
Santucci coffee shop & pasta restaurant, Gerrards Cross - 2 miles
Accommodation details via the airfield
The Bull, Gerrards Cross - 2 miles from £44
Lambert Arms, New Denham. B&B 01895 255613
Master Brewer Hotel, Hillingdon Circus

Derby

6 miles south-west of Derby, signposted from A5132
Derby Aerodrome, Hilton Road, Egginton, Derby DE65 6GV
Tel: 01283 733803 Fax: 01283 75407

The story of Derby airfield is closely linked with the former airfield 3 miles away at Burnaston. Burnaston was home to the Derby Aero Club, until one day they were summarily informed that a huge car factory was to be built on the site, and there was no room for a little airfield or its occupants. The aero club, and in particular the owners Martin and Maggie Jones, fought a vigorous and determined campaign against the closure, aided by local and national supporters and AOPA. That battle was eventually lost, but not before the aero club had been allocated a 'green field' site on which to create a new airfield. The new Derby airfield opened in 1993, three years after Burnaston had been closed down, at Hilton - a few miles down the A38 from Burnaston.

This small airfield exists as tribute to the determination of the members of Derby Aero Club, Martin and Maggie Jones and their supporters. It is still growing and developing from its farmland origins and visitors are assured of a warm welcome. This year (on the 20th July) Derby is holding its first fly-in.

Landing Fee
£5.00 (singles), £10.00 (multi) , £10.00 (heli). 50% discount if refuelling.
Cash and cheques only

Fuel
AVGAS 100LL 73.5p inc.
Cash and cheques only

Flying Organisations

Derby Aero Club and Flying School	01283 733803
Sandwell Valley Aero Club	01922 648556

Other Organisations

Airspeed Aviation - CAA and PFA inspection (Maintenance)	01283 733803

Car Hire

Birmeston Garage	01332 513320
Avis	01332 200470
Eurodollar	01332 382251
Hertz	01332 205215

Taxis

Stretton Taxis	01283 511876
Weston Car Co	01332 331331
A1 Taxis	01283 838383

Public Transport
No convenient buses. Willington railway station 2 miles.

Nearby Places of Interest

Repton village, with a history dating back to 653AD	
Derby Industrial Museum - 6 miles	01332 255308
Derby Cathedral - 6 miles	01332 341201
Royal Crown Derby Pottery	01332 712800
TIC	01332 255802

Food & Accommodation

Drinks and snacks at the airfield	
Brook Farm Tea Rooms, Repton 3 miles (recommended)	01283 702215
Willington House Hotel, Willington 2 miles	01283 702104
La Villa 4 miles	01332 510161
Hilton House Hotel, Hilton 3 miles	01283 732304
Blenheim House Hotel, Etwall	01283 732254
Travel Inn, Derby 5 miles room from £35	01332 203003

Dunkeswell

14 miles north-east of Exeter, off the A373
Dunkeswell, Nr Honiton, Devon EX14 0RA
Tel 01404 891643/891271

Driving to Dunkeswell can be a frustrating experience. Not far from the M5, junction 28, the airfield lies just outside the village of the same name, about 3 miles off the A373 Honiton road. It sits atop a plateau, surrounded by steep valleys, through which the (poorly signposted) lanes lead to your destination. Chances are that just as you despair of finding it, you will round a crest in the road and there it is!

Dunkeswell entered the war quite late when Liberators of the USAAF arrived here, to be replaced by anti-submarine Liberators of the US Navy soon after. Joseph Kennedy, elder brother of John F. Kennedy, was killed while flying a Liberator from Dunkeswell in 1944. The airfield closed at the end of 1948 and was used by a gliding club for a while, but in 1967 the Aero Club was formed, and they built a clubhouse close to the newly built road which runs across the eastern part of the original airfield.

Now run by the Devon School of Flying the airfield is a popular base for airsports, and the pleasant clubhouse offers a good view of the airfield, still largely undeveloped beyond the light aircraft use it has today.

Landing Fee
£6.38 + (single), £3.50 + per 500kg (multi)
Visa/Mastercard/Delta/Switch. No cards under £10

Fuel
AVGAS 100LL 61p +
Visa/Mastercard/Delta/Switch. No cards under £10

Flying Organisations
Devon School of Flying 01404 891643

Other Organisations
Devon School of Flying (Maintenance) 01404 891643
R M Sport Parachuting Club

Car Hire
Turks Head Garage 01404 43440

Taxis
Canns Cosy Cars 01404 43440

Public Transport
Honiton railway station 4 miles

Nearby Places of Interest
North Hill Gliding Site - 2 miles
Wellington Monument - 9 miles
Fleet Air Arm Museum, Yeovilton - 20 miles
TIC 01404 43716

Food & Accommodation.
Cafe facilities at airfield
The Drewe Arms - 3 miles (Good Pub Guide 1995) 01404 841267
The Belfry Country Hotel, Yarcombe - 7 miles from £32 01404 861579
Godford Farm, Awliscombe - 3 miles B&B from £17 01404 42825
Lelamarie, Awliscombe - 3 miles B&B from £28 01404 44646

Duxford

8 miles south of Cambridge off the A505, next to Junction 10 of M11
Imperial War Museum/Cambridgeshire County Council, Duxford Airfield, Cambridgeshire CB2 4QR
Tel: 01223 833376 Fax: 01223 837267

The Imperial War Museum's vast site at Duxford is inarguably the greatest aviation museum in the country, possibly the finest in Europe. If you haven't yet visited it, you need to allow at least a full day to take it all in properly. Adjacent to junction 10 of the M11, access (especially from London) is easy by road and with Old Warden - home of the Shuttleworth Collection - just a few miles away, you could easily make quite a weekend of it. The Duxford airshows are a fine excuse to visit, and flying visitors are welcome most times; although on flying display days special procedures apply for arrivals by air.

Duxford opened in 1919, becoming first a training station, then a base for fighters between the wars. The RAF's first Spitfire was delivered to Duxford in 1938, leading to the formation of the first RAF Spitfire Squadron. Douglas Bader came here to command 222 Squadron early in 1940, and will always be closely associated with the station. The Americans arrived later in the war and the airfield remained in active service until 1961, latterly flying Hunters and Javelins. Closed due to a general state of disrepair and considered uneconomic to renovate to modern standards, the airfield first started to take its present form in the early 1970s. The warbird collector Ormond Haydon-Baillie kept a few aircraft here and the idea of a museum gathered momentum, culminating in today's huge aircraft collection, which includes the Concorde 002 prototype.

In addition to the Imperial War Museum and Duxford Aviation Society collections, several privately owned warbird collections are based at Duxford. Any number of restoration projects are underway at any one time together with maintenance and flying of classic and vintage aircraft of all shapes and sizes - this is very much a 'live' airfield. There are two cafe / restaurants and two museum shops. Latest news is the ongoing work on the £11m American Air Museum building, funded in part by the National Lottery Heritage Fund, which will house amongst others the giant B-29 Superfortress and B-52 Stratofortress. It is hoped that the building will open about mid-1997. And if all the aeroplanes get too much for you, try the impressive Land Warfare Exhibition Hall (connected to the rest of the museum by a light railway). There's simulator rides, a restored operations room, pleasure flying in a Rapide and more besides- what more could you ask for?

Landing Fee
Single £13.50 inc. multi £17 inc. Museum entry £6.00 for adults
All major credit cards

Fuel
AVGAS 100LL 59.5p + available 1030-1530 (winter) 1030-1700 (summer)
All major credit cards

Flying Organisation
Classic Wings Pleasure Flights

Other Organisations

Imperial War Museum	01223 835000
(Events Hotline)	0891 516816
B-17 Preservation Ltd (Engineering)	01293 883213
The Fighter Collection Ltd	01223 834973
Mitchell Aircraft Co. Ltd (maintenance)	01223 833113
Duxford Aircraft Preservation Society	

Car Hire

Avis	01223 21551
Eurodollar	01223 65438
Hertz	01223 212551

Taxis

Sawston Taxis	01223 833838

Public Transport
Details from 01223 835000. Cambus 103 weekdays, check weekends availability as times limited. Cambus information hotline 01223 423554. Also The Shuttleworth Collection Countrybus #14. Whittlesford railway station 3 miles. Cambridge railway station 8 miles

Nearby Places of Interest
Audley End house and miniature railway, 6 miles
TIC 01223 322640
See also Cambridge, Fowlmere and Old Warden

Food & Accommodation
Two cafe / restaurants on the airfield
John Barleycorn, Duxford 1_ miles pub & restaurant (recommended) 01223 832699
Duxford Lodge Hotel, Duxford 1 mile from £38 01223 836444
See also Fowlmere & Cambridge

Earls Colne

10 miles west of Colchester on the A1024, signposted off the A120
Bulldog Aviation Ltd, The Barn, Over Hall Hill, Earls Engaine, Colchester, Essex CO6 2NS
Tel: 01787 223943

Opened in 1942, Earl's Colne, like nearby Andrewsfield, was built by the Americans, who occupied it until 1944 flying B17 Flying Fortresses and B26 Marauders. Later RAF squadrons of Halifaxes established themselves here until 1946, when the airfield closed.

Like so many wartime airfields, that could have been the end of Earl's Colne. However, although much of the original airfield has been redeveloped for industrial use, a part has been re-established as an active airfield, used by the Essex Flying Club. Also on site is the Rebel Air Museum, open weekends in summer, which chronicles the airfield's history and has become something of a shrine to the 8th & 9th US Air Force. Recently the airfield has been taken over by a consortium led by newspaper magnate Eddie Shah, who plans to revitalise the whole site with an ambitious country club and leisure facility, in which the airfield will be an integral part. Certainly the building works already undertaken are impressive and the new flying club premises are smart, efficient and welcoming to visitors. The historic aircraft restoration companies based here also guarantee plenty of interesting aircraft on the airfield.

The extensive facilities are intended to make Earl's Colne an attractive destination for visitors. The sports complex is open to the general public and offers restaurant and bars, 27 holes for golf, a driving range, indoor and outdoor tennis courts, gym and swimming pool and wedding and conference facilities.

Landing Fee
Single £5.00, multi £9.00. Parking: Overnight £1.50 outside on grass
Major credit cards except Amex and Diners

Fuel
AVGAS 100LL 65p +
Major credit cards except Amex and Diners

Flying Organisations

Essex Flying School Ltd	01787 223676

Other Organisations

CDS Aviation Services Ltd (Maintenance)	01787 223006
Essex Golf & Country Club	01787 224466
Hawker Restorations Ltd	01449 740544 (Head Office)
Rebel Air Museum/Earls Colne Aviation Museum	

Car Hire

Braintree - Yellowline	01376 322771

Taxis

Braintree- Yellowline	01376 322771

Public Transport
Bus routes in villages. Braintree railway station 8 miles, Colchester railway station 10 miles , services to London Liverpool Street and Cambridge.

Nearby Places of Interest

Essex Golf & Country Club, on the airfield	01787 224466
Coggeshall, 2 miles. A small historic village known for its wide range of antique shops	
Marks Hall Country Estate & Visitors Centre, Coggeshall 2 miles	01376 563796
Paycocke's, Coggeshall 4 miles. Wool merchants house circa. 1500	01376 561305
Stour Valley Railway Centre 4 miles	
Colne Valley Railway, Castle Hedingham 8 miles	01787 461174
Colchester 10 miles. The oldest recorded town in Britain and capital of Roman Britain	
Colchester Castle, 10 miles	01206 282920
TIC	01206 282920

See also Andrewsfield

Food & Accommodation

Apart from the facilities at the sports complex, the flying club have tea/coffee machines, cold drinks vending machines and chocolate vending machines

The Woolpack & White Hart Inns, Coggeshall - 2 miles	
The Compasses, Pattiswick - 3 miles.	
Real ales, good food. Recommended	01376 561322
Poppy's Tea Room, Colchester - 10 miles	01206 765805
Elm House, Earls Colne - 1 mile B&B from £19	01787 222197
The Drum Inn, Earls Colne - 1 mile from £22	01787 222368
The Riverside Inn Motel, Earls Colne - 1 mile from £27	01787 223487
Drapers Mill - in village. A la carte restaurant & carvery.	
Accommodation from £35	01787 223666

East Midlands

7 miles south-east of Derby, signposted from A453. M1 J24 & 23A
East Midlands Airport, Castle Donington, Derby, DE74 2SA
Tel: 01332 810621 (information desk, 24 hours)
Fax: 01332 850393 Telex: 37543 EMAIR G

Originally called Castle Donington, the airfield opened in 1942 and served as a training and transport base until it closed in 1946. In the early 1960s a consortium of county councils effectively built a new airport was over the old one, as little remained of RAF Castle Donington. However, for a long time the old airfield was commemorated in the airport's RT callsign 'Castledon'.

East Midlands is today a busy and successful regional airport. It is the home base of British Midland and has also developed something of a speciality in the parcel-handling field, being the major UK base for DHL and UPS. Unfortunately this success has had an undesirable effect on light aviation visitors with compulsory handling for aircraft using the main apron and high landing fees.

Things are better for the flying schools here (based on a site to the west of the main airfield buildings with the maintenance companies), and there is also an interesting collection of preserved aircraft at the Aeropark. At the time of writing expansion work on the terminal (due to be completed this Spring) and apron area is putting the future of the Aeropark in doubt so phone ahead if you intend visiting it. The terminal cafeteria is adequate, in the way of many airport terminal cafes, but overall the welcome seems to have lost its polish.

Landing Fee
£12.43 under 1 tonne, £21.15 under 2 tonnes. First two hours parking free
All major credit cards

Fuel
AVGAS 100LL 60p + AVTUR JET A-1 25p + All major credit cards

Flying Organisations

Donair Flying Club	01332 810444
East Midlands Flying School Ltd	01332 850383
Eastwest Flying Training	01332 811418

Other Organisations

Aeropark and Visitors Centre	01332 852852 ext. 3361
Corporate Handling	01332 811179 (fax 811139)
Donington Aviation Engineering Ltd (Maintenance)	01332 812694
East Midlands Flying School Ltd (Maintenance)	01332 850383
Hunting Aviation Ltd Aircraft Engineering Division (Maintenance)	01332 810910
Rotortech Ltd (Maintenance)	01954 210901
Trent Aero Engineering Ltd (Maintenance)	01332 812348

Car Hire

Avis	01332 811403
Eurodollar	01332 382251
Hertz	01332 811726

Taxis

Donington Taxi Services	01332 810146
Airport Cars	01332 814225

Public Transport
Bus services to Derby, Nottingham and Leicester. Long distance coach services. Long Eaton railway station 5 miles, Loughborough railway station 9 miles, Derby railway station 12 miles

Nearby Places of Interest

Donington Park Motor Racing Museum - 1 mile	
Donington Race Track - 1 mile	01332 810048
Calke Abbey - 4 miles	01332 863822
Derby - 8 miles	
Derby Industrial Museum - 8 miles	
TIC	01332 255802

Food & Accommodation

The Donington Thistle, at airport entrance from £41	01332 850700
Bull and Swan Diseworth - 1/2 mile	
Little Chimneys Guest House, Diseworth - 1/2 mile	01332 812458
Park Farm House Hotel, Donington Park Racetrack -1 mile	01332 862409
Donington Manor Hotel, Castle Donington 2 miles from £30 (recommended)	01332 810253
The Four Poster Guest Ho, Castle Donington -2 miles from £20	01332 810335

Elstree

3 miles east of Watford, signposted from A41. M1 junction 5
Montclaire Shipping Co Ltd, Elstree Aerodrome, Borehamwood, Herts WD6 3AR
Tel: 0181 9537480

Visitors to Elstree might be surprised to learn that Handley Page Halifax four-engined bombers, converted to freighters, regularly operated from here in 1946. Less surprisingly, they soon moved operations to Stansted, with its longer runways. Since then Elstree has always had training, air-taxi and private aircraft as its main residents. From the air the airfield can be reminiscent of an aircraft carrier at times - a single runway with the areas either side covered with parked aircraft. On fine days at weekends the airfield can become very busy, particularly since the closure of Leavesden leaves it as one of the few airfields to serve North London.

The local area is quite noise-sensitive and certain types (e.g. Cessna 337) are not encouraged, but a number of interesting aircraft can be found here much of the time. Just now two Dakotas are parked up on the far side of the runway, waiting for a buyer. There is a small cafeteria, which offers a good cooked breakfast, and a Pooley's pilots' shop next door. There are two busy flying clubs, several maintenance organisations and an aircraft sales company. All they need now is more space to spread themselves over!

Landing Fee
Singles £6.50 + multi £13.00 +
Cash and cheques only

Fuel
AVGAS 100LL 66p +
All major credit cards except Diners

Flying Organisations

Firecrest Aviation Ltd	0181 2076201
London School of Flying	0181 9534343
Skysport	0181 8660562

Other Organisations

Airline Instruments Ltd (Maintenance)	0181 953 4912
Cabair Maintenance Ltd (Maintenance)	0181 953 3586
G-Air Aviation Services Ltd (Maintenance)	0181 953 8363
Light Aircraft Engineering (Elstree) Ltd (Maintenance)	0181 953 9341
Airtour International	0181 953 4870
Pooley's	0181 207 3749
MLP Aviation (aircraft sales)	0181 207 5133

Car Hire

Eurodollar	01923 233340

Taxis

Allied Taxis	01923 232505

Public Transport
Buses from village approx. 1 mile. Thameslink Elstree railway station 5 minutes. Bushey railway station 2 miles. Stanmore Underground station 5 minutes. Watford Junction intercity railway station 8 miles (about £7 by taxi)

Nearby Places of Interest

Mosquito Aircraft Museum, Salisbury Hall - 4 miles	01727 822051
RAF Museum, Hendon - 5 miles	0181 2052266
Elstree Film Studios - 2 miles	
St Albans - 7 miles	
Verulamium Museum, St Albans - 7 miles	01727 819339
Roman Theatre, St Albans - 7 miles	01727 835035
Central London - 12 miles	
TIC	01727 864511

Food & Accommodation
Cafe and restaurant facilities at the Elstree Cafe

The Battleaxes - 1/2 mile. Particularly good food, a range of beers and wines in pleasant surroundings overlooking the airfield. Recommended.	0181 9531049
La Casetta Italian restaurant, Kings Langley - 6 miles	01923 263823
North Medburn Farm, Elstree B&B	0181 9531522
Edgeware Hotel Elstree - 1 mile from £92	0181 9538227
Hilton National, Watford - 3 miles from £80	01923 235881
The Eagle Inn, Kings Langley - 6 miles from £18	01923 262563
The Noke, Thistle Hotel St Albans - 6 miles, from £89	01727 854252

Enstone

5 miles north-east of Chipping Norton next to the B4022
Enstone Aerodrome, Church Enstone, Oxfordshire, OX7 4NP
Tel: 01608 677208

A former RAF bomber airfield, with the original runways still clearly visible, Enstone is known as a base for gliding, motorgliding and microlighting. However there are a number of conventional light aircraft here (and one hanger even has a Buccaneer – non-flying) and the good condition of the main runway belies the appearance of much of the airfield, which has been given back to nature to a large degree. One flying school, the microlight school and the gliding club are on the southside of the airfield, accessed via the B4022/B4030 signposted to Church Enstone and Bicester. Follow the signs to the Enstone Industrial Estate, and pass through the gates at the far end of the access lane, onto the airfield. There is also a flying club on the northern side of the runway (which is where visiting pilots should report to), accessed by road via the B4022 on the west side of the airfield. Much of the access is by roughish perimeter track, so care is recommended, and some parts of the track are still used by aircraft.

Enstone has noise-sensitive neighbours and so is strict about its operating hours. No movements are permitted before 0800 and no departures after 1930, although landing is allowed till dusk.

The local area is particularly attractive, Cotswold stone villages and quaint local pubs abound and Enstone is an excellent base from which to explore them. Enstone village itself is typical and well worth the walk, it is about 2 miles from the southern side of the airfield.

Landing Fee
£6.00 singles, £12.00 multi. Overnight parking £2.75 inc. Cash and cheques only

Fuel
AVGAS 55p + Cash and cheques only

Flying Organisations

Enstone Eagles Gliding Club	01608 677461
Enstone Flying Club	01608 678204 / 0860 643424
Oxfordshire Sportflying Ltd	01608 677208
Pegasus Flight Training	01608 678741 / 0860 864445

Other Organisations

Car Hire
Europcar 01295 51787

Taxis
Aston Cars 01869 340460

Public Transport
Nothing convenient locally. Charlebury railway station 4 miles

Nearby Places of Interest
Lots of pretty Cotswold villages around area
Chipping Norton very popular old Cotswold wool town, the highest town in Oxfordshire at 650 ft above sea level
Whitney, 6 miles
TIC 01608 644379 / 644045

Food & Accommodation
In the nicely refurbished club house of Enstone Flying Club (on the south side of the airfield, next to the 26 threshold) you can get food at weekends. There is a transport cafe near the gliding club on the industrial estate, also on southern side of airfield, open through the week.
Swan Lodge 01608 678736
Nutters, Chipping Norton 6 miles. (Egon Ronay)

The Falkland Arms, Great Tew - 3 miles. A thatched roof, good old-fashioned pub with great beer and an excellent lunchtime menu. It's not unlike the Bell at Smarden (see Lashenden) in character. They have nice, cottagey bedrooms from about £40. There's only one drawback - they don't do evening food. Apart from that, it's well worth a visit.
The Forge House, Chipping Norton 6 miles from £32 01608 658173
Crown Inn, Enstone (about 2 miles from the airfield)
A popular Cotswold-stone pub next to a small river. Real ales (including Flowers Original - recommended), good bar food with friendly service and comfortable bedrooms from £30. There is only one hitch - they don't take credit cards, so be prepared. Otherwise, it's a fine place for a drink, a bite to eat and an overnight stop. 01608 677262

Exeter

4 miles north-east of Exeter, signposted from M5 (J29 & 30) & A30
Exeter Airport, Exeter Devon, EX5 2BD
Tel: 01392 367433
Fax: 01392 364593 (Airport authority)

Exeter Airport opened in 1937 as a municipal airport, the terminal building being completed the following year. The RAF used the airfield for a variety of roles during the Second World War, and maintained a presence here for sometime after, target towing Hunters flew from here as late as 1971, although the airport was chiefly given back to commercial aviation in 1947. There was little activity until the 1950s when Jersey Airlines (now Air UK) commenced operations from Exeter. Today the main operator is Jersey European Airways who have their maintenance base here. Privately owned ex-military jets (including Lightnings and Hunters) also liven things up a bit. All the usual feeding, watering, flight planning and viewing facilities are available in the small terminal building and the airport retains a cosiness lost at some busier, bigger places - perhaps because the structure and layout has changed little - many of the wartime buildings remain in use today.

Landing Fee
0-2000Kg £21.30 +
Visa and Access

Fuel
AVGAS 100LL 55p +, AVTUR JET A1 24.76p +. Fuel required after 1600 Sat/Sun must be requested in advance and a surcharge of £12.00 per hour will apply after that time.
Visa and Access

Flying Organisations

Airways Flight Training (Exeter) Ltd	01392 364216
Exeter Air Training School	01392 445197
Exeter Flying Club Ltd	01392 367653

Other Organisations

Goodridge (UK) Ltd (Maintenance)	01392 369090
JEA Engineering (UK) Ltd (Maintenance)	01392 362415

Car Hire

Avis	01392 59713
Eurodollar	01392 50858
Hertz	01392 57791
Europcar	01392 75398

Taxis
Taxis at terminal

Public Transport
Infrequent buses from terminal to Exeter. Exeter railway station 6 miles

Nearby Places of Interest
Exeter 3 miles
Exmouth, Budleigh Salterton, Sidmouth and the English Riviera 25 miles

Maritime Museum, Exeter	01392 58075
Underground passages, off the High Street, Exeter	01392 26588
TIC	01392 265700

Food & Accommodation
Bar and cafe in terminal

Old Mill, Ide - 6 miles	01392 59480
Blue Ball Inn - 3 miles	01392 873401
The Double Locks, Alphington - 3 miles Canalside pub. Large range of beers and good food.	01392 56947
Royal Clarence Hotel, Exeter - 5 miles from £39	01392 85464
Great Western Hotel, Exeter - 4 miles from £25	01392 74039
Clock Tower Hotel, Exeter city centre B&B from £15	01392 424545
The White Hart, Exeter. 15th century pub & restaurant. Rooms from £50	01392 79897

Fairoaks

2 miles north of Woking, signposted off A319. 5 miles from J11 M25
Fairoaks Airport, Chobham, Woking, Surrey GU24 8HX
Tel: Admin. 01276 857700 Fax: 01276 856898
Telex: 859033 FKSATC

Established as a private aerodrome in 1931 and reconstructed as a training airfield for the RAF in 1937, Fairoaks has always been associated with light aircraft and flying training. Its wartime role was largely confined to elementary flying training, using Tiger Moths.

Fairoaks is still busy training pilots. The airport has a pleasant and relaxed atmosphere and the staff are particularly helpful to visiting pilots. Two flying clubs operate from here, and the Fairoaks Flying Club has a small cafe from where visitors can view proceedings. Owned and operated by Alan Mann Helicopters since 1972, Fairoaks has a substantial amount of rotary-wing activity and numerous other businesses operate from here. The paved runway was laid in 1978 to overcome the persistent waterlogging problems posed to grass airfields in winter, and the airport continues to encourage development of business and commercial traffic. The airport operations staff are particularly helpful to visiting pilots, although non-flying visitors are asked to confine themselves to the public areas - car park, cafe, etc. in the interests of safety and security.

Fairoaks is just 5 miles from the M25 junction 11. Take the A319 towards Chobham and at the first roundabout signs to the airport appear.

Landing Fee
Singles up to 1 tonne £12.00, 1001-1500 kg £14.00. Overnight parking: singles, up to 1 tonne £5.88, 1001-1500 kg £7.05
Major credit cards

Fuel
AVGAS 100LL 58p + AVTUR JET A1 24p +
Major credit cards

Flying Organisations

Alan Mann Helicopters	01276 857471
EAA Aviation Ltd	01276 856969
Fairoaks Flight Centre	01276 858075

Other Organisations

Fairoaks Airport Services (handling)	01276 857444
Mann Aviation Ltd (Maintenance)	01276 857441
Spectro Oil Analysis Co (Maintenance)	01276 857511
British Helicopter Advisory Board	01276 856100
Flight Safety Committee	01276 855193
European Regional Airlines Association	01276 856495
Flying Colours, aircraft painting	01276 858600
Gama Aviation Ltd	01276 858485
Mann Aviation Sales Ltd	01276 856241
Northwright Aviation Services	01276 856548
Norman Pealing Ltd, Photography	01276 856039
Transair Pilot Shop	01276 858533

Car Hire

Moores Car Rentals	01276 857557

Taxis

Bluebird Travel	01932 347304
C.J. Edwards	01252 620278
Wolfhound (minibuses and executive service)	01276 858308

Public Transport
Woking railway station 3 miles. Trains every 15 mins to London Waterloo

Nearby Places of Interest
Convenient for Twickenham, Ascot, Sandown Park, Kempton Park and Epsom race courses

Brooklands Aviation and Motor Museum, Weybridge - 8 miles (highly recommended)	01932 857381
Royal Horticultural Society Gardens at Wisley - 8 miles	
Thorpe theme park - 5 miles	01932 562633
TIC	01483 444007

Food & Accommodation

Five Oaks Restaurant at airport (now under new management). 0700-1700 Mon-Fri, 0800-1700 weekends. They also prepare in-flight food and drink

Harvester Restaurant, Chobham - 2 miles	
Quails Restaurant, Chobham - 1 mile (Egon Ronay)	01276 858491
Blubechers, The Sun & Four Horseshoes pubs in Chobham (recommended) - 2 miles	
The Cricketer's, Downside Common - 2 miles Real ale & good food	01932 862105
Oaklands Farm, Chobham - 1 mile B&B from £25	01276 857268
The Litter Tree, Woking - 3 miles from £40	01483 762400
Northfleet Hotel, Woking - 3 miles from £60	01483 722971
Pankhurst, West End - 4 miles B&B from £27	01276 858149

Farnborough

1 mile north of Aldershot signposted from the A325
DRA, Farnborough, Hampshire, GU14 6TD
Tel: 01252 392231 (Mil)
Tel:01252 524440 (Farnborough Business Centre)
Telex: 858981 FNBAPT

Here, surely, is the birthplace of British aviation. Farnborough Common became a testing site for balloons and dirigibles in 1905, just 2 years after the Wright brother's first powered flight. Samuel Cody, the aviation pioneer, began testing kites and gliders here a year later, culminating in the first flight of an aeroplane in Britain – a Cody-built, Wright-derived design – on October 16th 1908. The Royal Aircraft Factory was established by 1912, and No.1 Squadron, Royal Flying Corps commenced activity the same year.

After WW1, the RFC became the RAF, so the Royal Aircraft Factory became the Royal Aircraft Establishment, boasting the country's first wind tunnel. Suffice to say, the full history of Farnborough is beyond the scope of this book, but its place in aviation history is irrefutable. The first 'Farnborough Show' took place in 1947 when the RAE opened its doors to the public - actually relatives and friends of staff. The first proper Farnborough show, under the auspices of the SBAC (Society of British Aircraft Constructors), was held the following year.

Today the biennial show is the major event in the UK aviation calendar, alternating with Paris as the premier European aviation showcase. The airfield is also home to the School of Aviation Medicine and the Air Accident Investigation Branch.

Fifty acres of the site have been released to General Aviation as an alternative to closing and redeveloping the airfield, and the RAE has its own museum here (unfortunately not open to the public, but available to researchers on request).

Landing Fee
Single £30 + multi £60 + (includes all handling charges). First 4 hours parking free, then £2 per hour.

Fuel
AVGAS 100LL 60p + JET A-1 23.5p +

Flying Organisations

RAE Bedford Gliding Club	01234 261079

Other Organisations

Farnborough Aviation Services Ltd	01252 372400
Farnborough Business Aviation Ltd (handling agents)	01252 524440
Mann Aviation Ltd	01252 395179
Royal Aircraft Establishment Aero Club Ltd	01252 392047/393649

Car Hire

Avis	01252 733644
APEX	01252 376160

Taxis
Can be arranged on arrival at airport

First Choice Taxis	01252 377777
Choice Cars	01252 377799
Farnham Taxis	01252 733373
A1 Rushmoor Radio Taxis	01252 333555
ABM Taxis	01252 622858

Public Transport
No convenient buses
Farnborough railway station 2 miles

Nearby Places of Interest

St Michael's Abbey, 1 mile	
The Parachute Regiment and Airborne Forces Museum, Aldershot 2 miles	01252 349619
Aldershot Military Museum, Aldershot 2 miles	01252 314598
Army Physical Training Corps Museum, Aldershot 2 miles	01252 24431
Royal Army Dental Corps Museum, Aldershot 2 miles	01252 24431
Royal Army Medical Corps, Museum, Aldershot 2 miles	01252 24431
Hero's Shrine and World War II Memorial, Aldershot 2 miles	
Wellington Monument, Aldershot 2 miles	
TIC	01252 811151

Food & Accommodation

Crew lounge in the GA Terminal has tea/coffee/snack vending machines but no cafe.

Snow Goose, Farnborough - 1 mile	01252 545132
The Swan, Farnborough - 1 mile	
Tumbledown Dick Inn, Farnborough - 1 mile	
The Ship Inn, Farnborough - 2 miles	
Harlington Centre Bistro, Fleet - 2 miles	01252 811222
Lismoyne Hotel, Fleet - 2 miles	01252 628555
The Johnnie Gurkha's Restaurant, Aldershot - 2 miles	01252 336482
Oak Tree Guest House, Farnborough - 1 mile B&B from £20	01252 545491
Falcon Hotel - 1 mile from £67	01252 545378
Forte Posthouse (free minibus service) - 1 mile from £99	01252 545051
Acacia , Fleet 2 miles B&B from £20	01252 623545
Terendak, Fleet - 2 miles B&B from £16	01252 613804
Bush Hotel, Farnham from £80	01252 715237

Fenland

6 miles east of Spalding signposted from B1168
Fenland Aerodrome, Holbeach St. Johns, Spalding, Lincolnshire, PE12 8RQ
Tel: 01406 540461, 01945 582891 (Mr. Coulten)

A small airfield, situated in the heart of the Lincolnshire Fens and a few miles from the bulb town of Spalding, Fenland tends to attract unusual homebuilt and sports aircraft. It also has a resident flying school, helicopter school and microlight operator and yet never seems to be overly busy except on certain weekends. The clubhouse has a nice restaurant and bar (which is closed Mondays) with a good view over the airfield and visitors by road or by air are made welcome.

Despite being within 15 miles from Peterborough, and less than 20 miles from the A1, Fenland remains a laborious airfield to reach by road. The principal problem is that the roads seldom continue in a straight line for more than a few hundred yards, before turning at right angles to navigate yet another fen. The easiest route by road is south from Holbeach, along the B1168 to Holbeach St. Johns, where the airfield is alongside the road. Alternatively, coming in from the west, be careful not to miss the B1168 north, again signposted to Holbeach St. Johns, as the signs from the other B roads (and smaller lanes) are less than clear. On a good day, of course, just look out for the aircraft in the circuit and follow your nose, but watch for the 90-degree bends!

Landing Fee
£5.00 inc.
All major credit cards except Amex and Diners

Fuel
AVGAS 100LL 58.7p +
All major credit cards except Amex and Diners

Flying Organisations

Fenland Flying School	01406 540461
Fenland Helicopter Centre	01406 540115
The Microlight School	01406 540542

Other Organisations

Fenland Aeroservices Ltd (Maintenance)	01406 534255

Car Hire

Avis	01733 349489
Eurodollar	01733 310283
Hertz	01733 893083

Taxis

Phoenix Taxi Service	01406 22807

Public Transport
Spalding railway station 7 miles

Nearby Places of Interest

Fenland Aviation Museum, Wisbech 8 miles	01945 585808
Ayscoughfee Hall Museum and gardens, Spalding 7 miles	01775 725468
Pinchbeck Engine and Land Drainage Museum, Spalding 7 miles	01775 725468
Gordon Boswell Romany Museum, Spalding	01775 710599

The Fens and nature reserves of the Wash are only 10 miles away, you may also see the RAF Tornadoes bombing the ranges!

TIC	01775 725468

Food & Accommodation
Restaurant and bar, closed Mondays

Cley Hall Hotel, Spalding - 7 miles food and accommodation	01775 725157
Red Lion Hotel, Spalding - 7 miles from £20	01775 722869
Bedford Court Guest House, Spalding - 7 miles B&B from £25	01775 722377
High Bridge House, Spalding - 7 miles B&B from £16	01775 725810
Travel Stop Motel, Spalding - 7 miles B&B from £20	01775 767290

Filton

4 miles north of Bristol on the A38; M5 junction 16 / M4 J20
Filton House, Bristol, BS99 7AR
Tel: 0117 9699094 Fax: 0117 9362474

Opened in 1910 by the British & Colonial Aeroplane Company Limited, later Bristol Aeroplane Company, Filton was soon producing Bristol Boxkites for the War Office. A long and distinguished history follows, by way of Blenheim, Beaufort and Beaufighter, and engines such as the Hercules and Centaurus which powered not only its own designs, but also types as diverse as the Sea Fury and Lancaster.

After the war, the runway was extended to accommodate the greatest design from the Bristol stable, the extraordinary Brabazon airliner, which never got past the prototype stage. Engine development was also continuing though, culminating in the Bristol Olympus which powered the Vulcan Bomber, and still propels Concorde (which was also built here).

Nowadays, Bristol's engine building facility has been absorbed into Rolls Royce, who still have a large factory on the airfield site, and the airframe section is a division of British Aerospace, as part of the Airbus consortium. The airfield remains active, partly due to BAe's activities, but also because the airfield management are sufficiently enlightened to encourage General Aviation. A small flying school and various business operators regularly fly from the pleasant GA terminal (with a good met/pre-flight briefing facility) alongside the A38, and the operations staff have a particularly good reputation as being friendly and helpful in their wish to encourage traffic.

Landing Fee
£13.00 per tonne up to 3 tonnes. Over 3 tonnes £12.80 per tonne. Training rebate of up to 75% available. Parking free first 4 hours. Thereafter up to 3 tonnes 95p per 500 kg per hour.
Visa, Mastercard, Switch, Delta, Diners. Not Amex

Fuel
AVGAS 100LL 58.6p + AVTUR JET A1 25p +
Visa, Mastercard, Switch, Delta, Diners. Not Amex

Flying Organisations
Bristol Aero Club 0117 936 8935 or 962 2678

Other Organisations

British Aerospace Aerostructures Ltd	0117 9693831
British Aerospace Airbus Ltd	0117 9693831
Flight Operations	0117 9365656/9362400

Car Hire
Available through Operations, who may be able to obtain special rates

Taxis
Available through Operations
AMB 0117 9314431

Public Transport
Bus stop by main gate on A38. Bristol Parkway railway station 1 mile, 15 minutes walk

Nearby Places of Interest
Bristol 4 miles
See Bristol (Lulsgate) entry

Food & Accommodation
Coffee/tea available at Operations. BAe canteen may be available. Transport cafe close to entrance
Food available at Horseshoe pub by main gate
Travellers Rest (excellent food)
Accommodation can be booked through Operations who may be able to negotiate special rates

Aztec Hotel 1 mile from £65	01454 201090
Crest Hotel 1 mile from £91	0117 9564242
Rockleaze House B&B from £18	0117 9692536
Rowan Lodge B&B from £22	0117 9312170

Fishburn

3 miles north of Sedgefield, County Durham, signposted off A177
John Morgan, Fishburn Airfield, Fishburn, County Durham
Tel: 01913 770137 (Airfield), 01913 720213/770448 (Admin.)
Fax: 01642 605383 (Skyshow Aeros)

Something of a rarity - a new airfield! Fishburn was officially opened on the 30th June 1995 by Tony Blair the Labour leader (who lives just a few miles away).

Fishburn is a very friendly strip, with a pleasant club house in a caravan where tea and coffee are available. The hangar houses some rare Chinese Nanchang CJ6 trainers, which may be seen if the owner (and keyholder) is available. The local area is noise sensitive, so flying visitors are requested to avoid the local villages and approach and depart with the usual discretion. As a recent addition to the chart, Fishburn may well be on your list of airfields to visit. If the warmth of the welcome received is any yardstick you will return, despite the rather daunting aspect on the approach due to crops being grown right up to the edge of the strip.

Landing Fee
£2.00 (singles), £5.00 (multi)

Fuel

Flying Organisations

Skyshow Aerobatics	01642 676115
Howe Aviation Ltd	01585 227026

Other Organisations

Car Hire

Avis	01325 368800
Eurodollar	01325 353659

Taxis
Phone numbers at clubhouse

Public Transport
Billingham railway station 10 miles

Nearby Places of Interest
Sedgefield Horse Racing 3 miles
Car Boot Sale every Sunday at Sedgefield, over 150 stalls
Durham, 10 miles
Darlington, 10 mile

TIC	01325 382698

Food & Accommodation
Light refreshments on the aerodrome
Regatta - Old English Tea Rooms, Durham.

(Egon Ronay)	0191 384 2378
Station House Hotel, Durham	0191 3846906

Accommodation 2 miles from the aerodrome, booking via the airfield operators

Hardwick Hall Hotel 1 mile	01740 620253

Fowlmere

8 miles south of Cambridge sign posted from the B1368
Modern Air Ltd, Fowlmere Aerodrome, Royston, Herts SG8 7SJ
Tel: 01763 208281 Fax: 01763 208861

Close to Duxford, Fowlmere has actually been two airfields. The first opened in 1918, the present site, some way removed from the first, dates from 1940 and hosted various fighter squadrons with Spitfires, Hurricanes and later P51 Mustangs, flown by American USAAF pilots. To find out more a visit to the 16th century Chequers pub in Fowlmere village is strongly recommended. The pub sign commemorates the RAF and USAAF pilots from Fowlmere who once frequented the pub, and inside there are photographs of Fowlmere airfield past. The Chequers has the added attraction of specialising in very good food with an impressive wine list too.

Back at the airfield, most has returned to agriculture. What is left is a hanger, some outbuildings and a single grass strip. Several light aircraft are based here and visitors are made welcome. There is no catering on the airfield, although you can get tea or coffee in the Modern Air building.

Landing Fee
Singles £8.00, multi £12.00
Cash or cheque only

Fuel
AVGAS 100LL 64p +
Cash or cheque only

Flying Organisations

Modern Air	01763 208281

Other Organisations

Modern Air (Maintenance)	01763 208281

Car Hire

Kirkham Cars	01763 261116
Ford	01763 242084

Taxis

Meltax	01763 244444
Sawston Taxis	01223 833838

Public Transport
Shepreth railway station 2 miles, Royston railway station 4 miles
Bus service 78 and 79 (Gatwick - Cambridge) call at Royston, 4 miles, every 2 hours
Bus service 346 and 347 (Gatwick - Cambridge) call at Royston, 4 miles, every 2hr 30 mins

Nearby Places of Interest

Imperial War Museum, Duxford - 2 miles	01223 835000
The National Trust Wimpole Hall and Home Farm, Arrington, 5 miles	01223 207257
RSPB reserve - 1 mile	
TIC	01279 655261
See also Duxford and Cambridge	

Food & Accommodation

Chequers Hotel, Fowlmere - 1 mile (recommended-see text)	01763 208369
Maguires, Fowlmere -, 1 mile	01763 208444
Sheen Mill Hotel and Restaurant, Melbourn - 2 miles from £45	01763 261393
Goldington Guest House, Melbourn - 2 miles	01763 260555
Fairhaven, Kneesworth - 4 miles B&B from £16	01763 249471

Full Sutton

7 miles east of York sign posted off the A166
Full Sutton Airfield, Stamford Bridge, York, YO4 1HS
Tel: 01759 372717/306492 Fax: 01759 372991

Full Sutton opened in 1944 with a squadron of Halifax bombers, and later became home to Dakotas, Lancasters and Lancastrians. Between 1946 and 1963, when the airfield was finally closed by the RAF, it saw sporadic activity, but for the most part was put on Care and Maintenance.

The land became an industrial estate and later a maximum security prison was built on part of the site, but a section of the airfield remains and was reopened as a licensed airfield in 1995. A pleasant club house has been built for the resident flying club, housing a bar area and the usual briefing facilities, and the small hangar houses the club training and touring aircraft. There is also a microlight operator on the airfield. The owners and operators are keen to develop the airfield, so a welcome is assured for visitors.

By road, the airfield is best reached from the A166 York-Bridlington road. Follow the signs for the industrial estate, turning left at the T-junction at the end of the estate access road and follow the disused main runway to the hangars and clubhouse.

Landing Fee
Singles £3.00, multi £10.00, Microlights £2.00

Fuel
AVGAS 100LL by arrangement

Flying Organisations

Full Sutton Flying Centre	01759 372717
Aerosport UK	01759 373063

Other Organisations

Car Hire

Avis	01904 610460
Eurodollar	01904 612141

Taxis

Hessel's Cab	01759 303176

Public Transport
York railway station 10 miles

Nearby Places of Interest

Stamford Bridge 2 miles, ancient battleground	
Yorkshire Air Museum, Elvington 8 miles	01904 608595
York 10 miles	
TIC	01904 620557
See also York Rufforth	

Food & Accommodation

Bar and light refreshments in the clubhouse	
Three Cups, Stamford Bridge - 2 miles	01759 371396
Cuckoo Nest Farm, Wilberfoss - 2 miles B&B from £18	01759 380365
Kexby Bridge Hotel, Kexby - 3 miles from £45	01759 388223
Ivy House Farm, Kexby - 3 miles B&B from £16	01904 489368
Meltonby Hall Farm, Meltonby - 3 miles B&B from £15	01759 303214
See also York (Rufforth)	

Gloucestershire

4 miles west of Cheltenham signposted from A40, M5 junction 11, A417, A419 (often signposted by its old name of Staverton)
Gloucestershire Airport, Cheltenham, Glos, GL51 6SP
Tel: 01452 857700 Fax: 01452 715174

Still known to many as Staverton, the airfield opened in 1936 as the new site for the Cotswold Aero Club, which had started operations four years earlier from a site on the other side of the A40. The site was extended and improved by the RAF in 1938 who established Staverton as a training base. Several famous names in aircraft engineering subsequently moved here, including Rotol (the propeller manufacturer - now part of the Dowty Group, still a major employer on the site), Folland and Gloster Aviation.

Given back to civilian operations in 1950, the airfield now serves as a popular destination for General Aviation and is home to several busy flying clubs and operators. Several attempts over the years to establish the airfield as a base for commercial operations have met with little success, and the airfield now seems to be developing itself as a base for light aircraft and flying training. The hangars house a variety of interesting aircraft including ex-Navy Herons and a rarely seen Spitfire. Some redevelopment has taken place in recent years, with a modern Tower building and there are plans for a new terminal to replace the ramshackle wooden building used until recently. With the closure of the Red Baron pub adjacent to the car park, catering is limited to a small cafe opposite the tower.

Landing Fee

£10.00 if less than 2 tonnes. 23 tonnes £20.00. Parking fees apply 2 hours, £5.00 per 24 hour or part thereof. All major credit cards

Fuel

AVGAS 100LL 61p + AVTUR JET A1 31p +
All major credit cards

Flying Organisations

Aeroshow Flying Club	01452 857419
Archer Flight Training	01452 713830
Burman Aviation	01452 712388
Cotswold Aero Club	01452 713924
Gloucester and Cheltenham School of Flying	01452 857153
Pilot Flight Academy	01452 713555
Staverton Flying School	01452 712388

Other Organisations

Air Fabrication Services	01452 859878
Aircraft Mart (aircraft sales)	01452 855525
American Aviation Services (FAA Ground School, Aircraft Sales)	01452 714747
Bodycote (UK) Ltd	01452 714440
Cotswold Aero Engineering Ltd	01452 714525
Diamond Aircraft Sales (UK)	01452 856888
Dowty Aerospace Aviation Services Gloucester	01452 713111
Eurojet Aviation Engineering Department	01452 713456
Gloucester Pilot Shop	01452 854371
Gloucestershire Aviation Museum Collection, (currently moving into temporary premises at the airport)	01242 515533 / 577240
Holder Aviation Insurance	01452 713355
J Jones Aircraft Interiors	01452857177
Mid-West Engines Ltd	01452 857456
Midwest Aviation Sales	01452 857800
Police Aviation Services Ltd	01452 857999
RGV Aviation Ltd (maintenance & avionics)	01452 855501

Car Hire

Avis	01452 380356
Eurodollar	01452 421133
Hertz	01452 421461

Taxis

Cheltax 01242 525191
Associated Taxis 01242 523523

Public Transport

Bus stop outside airport entrance, served 4 times daily by Gloucester - Cheltenham service. Bus stop 1/2 mile, served every 15 mins by Gloucester - Cheltenham service. Cheltenham railway station 5 miles (about £6.00 by taxi), Gloucester railway station 5 miles

Nearby Places of Interest

Brickhampton Golf course next to airport	01452 859444
Cheltenham regency town 3 miles	
Cheltenham Racecourse, 6 miles	01242 513014
Gloucester, 4 miles ancient Roman city and port	
Gloucester Docks & National Waterways Museum (recommended)	01452 318054
Bugatti Trust 10 miles	01242 677201
Tewkesbury historic town 10 miles	
The Cotswolds 15 miles	
Forest of Dean 20 miles	
TIC	01242 522878 & 01452 421188

Food & Accommodation

Sky Catering cafe, centre of airfield so access from 'ground side' can be difficult. Super view of runways, "when it's sold we shut" so late in the day arrivals MAY be disappointed 01452 857929

Hope Orchard B&B - 1 mile from £16	01452 855556
The White House Hotel ***, - 1 mile from £48	01452 713226
The Golden Valley Hotel - 2 miles from £37	01242 232691
Longford Travel Lodge room from £32	01452 523519
The Hatherley Manor - 2 miles B&B from £35	01452 730217
Travel Inn, Uckington - 3 miles room from £35	01242 233847

Halfpenny Green

5 miles east of Bridgnorth signposted off B4176, A449 and A454
Halfpenny Green Aerodrome, Bobbington, Nr. Stourbridge, West Midlands, DY7 5DY
Tel: 01384 221350 (admin), 01384 221378 (ATC)
Fax: 01384 221514

The present day Halfpenny Green opened during the 1960s as a home for private flying and training. The original wartime airfield (RAF Bobbington) was a home to training squadrons and even today the style of the airfield typifies that of many wartime Service airfields. Halfpenny Green houses several busy flying training organisations and a Police helicopter operations unit. A small cafe on the first floor of the tower building offers snacks and fry-ups to the hungry visitor and a Sunday Market operates every week. A curiously shaped hangar in the South West corner of the airfield is often the road visitors first sight of the airfield. It is home to one of Richard Branson's advertising airships which can be seen around the country in its role as a mobile hoarding.

Halfpenny Green is a busy light aviation airfield. In addition to the aircraft of the locally based flying schools, it is a popular venue for cross-country training and being close to the Midlands puts it within easy reach of a great many other GA airfields. Curiously, it always seems somewhat difficult to spot from the air, and more than one aircraft approaching from the north has approached the quite different RAF Cosford instead!

Landing Fee
£8.00 per tonne up to 4 tonnes. Private, Club and training if paying cash £13.00 (singles) £20.00 (twins). 50% discount if fuel is uplifted. Cash or cheque only

Fuel
AVGAS 100LL 62p + AVTUR JET A1 27p + available 0900-1715 All major credit cards

Flying Organisations

Aceair	01384 221470
Bobbington Air Training School	01384 221292
Halfpenny Green Flying Centre	01384 221456
Midland Flight Centre	01384 221011

Other Organisations

Bobbington Estates Limited	01384 221328
Central Counties Air Support Unit	01384 221377
Midland Aircraft Maintenance	01384 221302
Premier Aircraft Maintenance Ltd	01384 221009
Pyramid Aviation	01384 221459

Car Hire

Martin Thomas	01746 765315
Europcar	01902 453544
British Car Rental	01384 442287

Taxis

Albro	01902 22525
3Cs	01384 77772

Public Transport
Wolverhampton railway station 7 miles, Stourbridge railway station 10 miles

Nearby Places of Interest

Halfpenny Green Vineyard, Halfpenny Green 1 mile	01384 221387
Severn Valley Railway, 8 miles	
Aerospace Museum, Cosford 12 miles	01902 374112
Wolverhampton Race Course, Wolverhampton 10 miles	
Ironbridge Gorge Museum (highly recommended) 15 miles	01952 433522
Midland Motor Museum, Stanmore Hall, Bridgnorth 6 miles	
TIC	01384 457494

Food & Accommodation

High Flyer Cafe (in Tower) open 0900-1700 7 days a week	01384 221403
The Crown, Claverley - 3 miles good food and real ale	
Camp site directly opposite airfield entrance	
Blakelands, Bobbington - 1 mile B&B from £21	01384 221464
Travel Lodge, Dudley - 7 miles room from £31	01384 481579
Stourton Castle (built 1184, luxury weekend breaks a speciality). Limo pick up from airfield is arranged by hotel on request/booking	01384 872208
The Copthorne Hotel, Merry Hill - 10 miles from £60	01384 482882
Goldthorne Hotel, Wolverhampton - 10 miles from £51	01902 714801

Hawarden

4 miles west of Chester, signposted from A55/A459
Hawarden Airport, Broughton, Clywd North Wales CH4 0BA
Tel: 01244 522013 Fax: 01244 523035 / 520521

Four miles from Chester, on the main A55 trunk road, Hawarden was built in 1937 as a factory, producing large numbers of Wellington bombers. It was also used as an Operational Training Unit equipped with Spitfires, some of the RAF's best known aces flew a Spitfire for the first time here.

After the war aircraft production continued for de Havilland producing Doves, Vampires and Mosquitoes. In recent times the airfield has built the BAe (nee HS) 125 business jets, and wing sets for Airbus. These are transported by road the 35 miles to Manchester International, where they are loaded onto Airbus Industrie's Guppy (and recently Beluga) freighters for shipment to Toulouse for final assembly.

At one time Hawarden gave a distinctly frosty welcome to GA aircraft, and flying training took place sporadically over the years. This was a shame, not least because Hawarden has an enviable weather record and many attractions to the flying visitor including long runways, navaids and radar. Recently the airfield's policy on light aircraft operations has warmed-up considerably. There is now some flying training taking place, and it would appear that General Aviation visitors are much more welcome.

Landing Fee
Up to 2000Kg £15 inc.

Fuel
AVGAS 100LL 55p + AVTUR JET A1

Flying Organisations

Chester Flying School	01244 534353

Other Organisations

Raytheon Corporate Jets Incorporated (Maintenance)	01244 520444

Car Hire

Avis	01244 311463
Eurodollar	01244 390008
Hertz	01244 374705
Europcar	01244 312893

Taxis

Airport Service	01244 346550
Abbey Taxis	01244 311804
Dee Cars	01244 671671

Public Transport
Chester railway station 4 miles

Nearby Places of Interest
Factory tours possible by appointment
Chester, Roman town 4 miles. Lots of historic interest here, allow a day to see it properly
Hawarden Castle 2 miles
TIC 01244 317962

Food & Accommodation

Tea and coffee at airfield	
Chester Grosvenor Hotel Library, Chester (Egon Ronay)	01244 324024
Plenty of accomodation in Chester, details via the TIC	
Curzon Hotel, Chester 3 miles from £25	01244 678581
Grosvenor Arms Hotel, Pulford 3 miles from £35	01244 570560

Hinton in the Hedges

2 miles west of Brackley, signposted from the A422
Hinton-in-the-Hedges Airfield, Steane, Nr Brackley, Northants
NN13 5NS
Tel: 01295 811235 Fax: 01295 811147

This charmingly named airfield opened in 1940 with as a training and operational conversion base. Later in the war, research into beam approach landing systems was conducted from here, part of the advantage being Hinton's remote location. It is bizarre to think that the predecessor to the modern day Instrument Landing System, used at all the world's major airports, was developed in such a quiet, rural spot.

Nowadays, the airfield has mostly returned to agriculture. Most of the flying here is conducted in gliders and motorgliders, although the runways are quite adequate for conventional light aircraft. The welcoming clubhouse can offer light refreshments, and there is no shortage of traditional village pubs in the locality for good food.

Hinton can be tricky to find by road. Take the A422 from Brackley towards Banbury and follow the signs to Hinton-in-the-Hedges down a sharp left turn about 3 miles out of Brackley. Follow the narrow lane to the airfield at the end of the lane. Even here, the presence of the airfield is not obvious, farm buildings block the view of the clubhouse.

Landing Fee
None charged and no parking fees for a short stay.
After 24 hours parking £1.25 (single) £2.00 (multi)

Fuel
AVGAS 100LL 71p inc. Cash and cheque only

Flying Organisations

Aquila Gliding Club	01295 811056
Pilot Flight Training	01295 812775
The Motor Glider Centre	01295 812775 / 0836 787421

Other Organisations

Holdcroft Aviation Services Ltd (Maintenance)	01295 810287
Mike Tate Aero Engineering (Maintenance)	01295 812131

Car Hire
None convenient

Taxis

P & J Cars	01280 704330

Public Transport
Banbury railway station 10 miles

Nearby Places of Interest

Sulgrave Manor 5 miles	01295 760205
Aynho Park 5 miles Grand country house and gardens	
Aynho - pretty village, shame about traffic!	
TIC	01280 700111
See also Turweston	

Food & Accommodation

Tea and coffee at Pilot Flight Training	
Bed and Breakfast on the airfield (recommended)	01295 811235
Fox Inn, Farthinghoe village 2 miles	01295 710393
See also Turweston	

Humberside

10 miles west of Grimsby signposted from the end of the M180
Humberside Airport, Kirmington, Ulceby, South Humberside, DN39 6YH
Tel: 01652 688456 (info desk), 01374 721746 (out of hours)
Fax: 01652 680524

Humberside Airport is a busy regional airport with increasing amounts of schedule and charter jet traffic up to the size of MD83/87 and B757, but still the predominant activity is General Aviation. Five organisations offer flying training and Bond Helicopters operate a busy station servicing the more southerly North Sea gas and oil rigs. Despite all this activity, Humberside still has plenty of quiet periods, and light aircraft are always welcome. The terminal is small (sometimes a little too small, when a 757 is on the ground!) but possesses all the expected facilities, including a pleasant cafeteria with an excellent, reasonably-priced, breakfast - all too rare these days.

By road the airport is about 3 miles from the M180 and well signposted, by the village of Kirmington (by which name the RAF knew the airfield when it opened in 1942, equipped with Wellingtons). It is also quite close to the Humber Bridge, the longest suspension bridge in the UK, and one of the longest in the world. Many visiting pilots make a small diversion to view the structure from the air.

Landing Fee

£6.75 per 0·5 tonne up to 3 tonnes. Discount for payment on arrival. First 2 hours parking free, then £3.30 per 24 hours or part of up to 3.5 tonnes
Amex, Diners, Visa and Mastercard

Fuel

AVGAS 100LL 56p +, AVTUR JET A1 21p +
Amex, Diners, Visa and Mastercard

Flying Organisations

Frank Morgan School of Flying	01652 688859
Humber Flying Club	01652 680746
Humberside Flight Training Ltd	01652 688056
Soloflight Captains Club	01652 688833
Triple 'A' Flying Ltd	01652 680564

Other Organisations

Bond Helicopters Ltd (Maintenance)	01652 688417
Bostonair Ltd (Maintenance)	01652 680446

Car Hire

Avis	01652 680325
Europcar	01652 680338

Taxis

At terminal	
Blythe taxis	01652 688684

Public Transport

Infrequent bus service (twice daily) Brigg to Thornton Curtis, stops at airport entrance
Barnetby railway station 3 miles

Nearby Places of Interest

Brigate Lodge and Golf Course	
Wrawby Post Mill - 6 miles	01652 653699
Elsham Hall Country Park - 6 miles	01652 688698
Humber Bridge, the worlds longest single span suspension bridge - 12 miles	
Cleethorpes - 12 miles usual seaside attractions	
Grimsby - 10 miles, major fishing port	
National Fishing Heritage Centre, Grimsby	01472 344868
TIC	01652 657053 or 688586

Food & Accommodation

Licensed buffet in terminal	
New Inn, Limber - 2 miles. Good food, and B&B from £25	01469 560257
Station Hotel, Barnetby - 2 miles B&B from £25 (Pilots are welcome as the owner is a PPL)	01652 688238
Holcombe House, Barnetby - 2 miles B&B from £12.50	01652 680655
Hawthorne Farm - 2 miles B&B from £15	01652 688272
The Exchange Coach House Inn - 8 miles from £35.00	01652 657633
Arties Mill Lodge - 8 miles from £25	01652 652094
Briggate Lodge Inn, Broughton - 10 miles (recommended)	01652 650770

Ipswich

2 miles south-east of Ipswich, signposted from the A45
Ipswich Airport, Nacton Road, Ipswich Suffolk IP3 9QF
Tel: 01473 720111 Fax: 01473 710055

A cloud hangs over Ipswich Airport. It has been under threat of closure and redevelopment for the last five years and has already had one last-minute stay of execution. Closure is still a real possibility, and is much in the mind of the resident flying schools and parachute school.

Easy to reach, just 2 minutes off the main A45 and close to the A12 trunk road, the airport is a small site without large hangars, and with predominantly single and two-storey buildings.

For a time in the 1980s Suckling Airways flew scheduled services from here. These days facilities are limited, which is a shame because with a little development the 1930s terminal building could be quite pleasant. The unfortunately named Pitts Bar is in the terminal building and you can also get tea and coffee at one or other of the flying clubs. An old Dakota languishes in a corner of the airfield. It flew in for the making of a film several years ago, and was left behind by the departing crew on completion of filming. One hopes the airfield will not suffer the same undignified end.

Landing Fee
£10.00 single, £13.35 multi. Overnight parking £3.50
Major credit cards except Amex and Diners

Fuel
AVGAS 100LL 59.5p + AVTUR Jet A1 on request
Major credit cards except Amex and Diners

Flying Organisations

Horizon Flying Club Ltd	01473 714840
Ipswich School of Flying	01473 729510
Suffolk Aero Club	01473 713312
Parachute Club	01473 710044

Other Organisations

Car Hire

Avis	01473 273366
Eurodollar	01473 219851/216962
Hertz	01473 218506
Europcar	01473 211067

Taxis

Avenue Taxis	01473 257777
Flash Cabs	01473 259777
Jet Cabs	01473 729656/720584

Public Transport
Town bus from airfield entrance. Ipswich railway station 2 miles

Nearby Places of Interest

Ipswich, with over 600 listed buildings, 2 miles	
Ipswich Museum, Ipswich	01473 213761
Ipswich Transport Museum	01473 832260
Tolly Cobbold Brewery, tours available, Ipswich	01473 231723
Sutton Hoo, Woodbridge, (Viking burial ground),10 miles	
Felixstowe major port, 10 miles	
TIC	01473 258070

Food & Accommodation
Pitts Bar in terminal, 'transport cafe' type menu. Open 0900-2300 everyday
The Brewery Tap, Cliff Rd, Ipswich (below the brewery). The full range of Tolly Cobbold beers - as you'd expect - and good food. 01473 281508
Mrs Debenham B&B 01473 723172
Aaron House B&B 01473 715001
Suffolk Grange Hotel - 3 mins walk, from £65 (weekdays), £45 (weekends) 01473 272244

Isle of Man (Ronaldsway)

10 miles south-west of Douglas, signposted off A5
Isle of Man Airport, Ballasalla, Isle of Man, IM9 2AS
Tel: 01624 821600 Fax: 01624 821611

Ronaldsway can trace its origins back to 1926, when the site was first used as a landing ground - Sir Alan Cobham's Flying Circus visited in 1929. Scheduled operations started in the 1930s, and the airfield was considerably extended in 1943 when the airfield became RNAS Ronaldsway. The airfield reverted to civilian use in 1948, and the runways were extended and widened in 1957 to accommodate larger, more modern aircraft.

These days the airport is a busy commercial concern, having invested £7m over the last five years. Around 550 000 passengers passed through in 1995 using the many scheduled services to the UK and Ireland, the busiest ones being to Heathrow and Liverpool with Manx.

Facilities are better since the new terminal extension was opened in 1994. Visiting pilots can now clear customs, special branch, security and flight briefing in one location. The restaurant is OK, albeit a little pricey, and there is a shop where Manx Kippers can be bought.

Traffic, indeed the whole island, gets a bit hectic during TT week (usually end May/early June) when you can't move for motorbikes. In keeping with the racing theme, the island is also hosting this year's Schneider Trophy Air Race (12-14th July).

Ronaldsway has also become the first UK airport with its own Internet site, including a plan of the airport and live ATC radar pictures, it's at http://www.enterprise.net/airport/airport.htm .

Landing Fee
£6.50 + per 0·5 tonne to 3 tonnes
Access or Visa

Fuel
AVGAS 100LL 71.16p + AVTUR JET A1 31.42p + Available 0700-2030 local and by arrangement 01624 823311 ext. 233
Cash, cheque or Visa

Flying Organisations
Manx Flyers Aero Club 01624 822926
Ashley Gardner School of Flying 01624 823454

Other Organisations
Manx Airlines Ltd (maintenance) 01624 82411

Car Hire
Athol Car Hire 01624 822481
Mylchreests 01624 823533

Taxis
At terminal

Public Transport
Regular coach service to Douglas, Ballasalla railway station 1 mile

Nearby Places of Interest
Lots of holiday activities, beaches, boats, scenery, walks, sports etc.
Castletown historic town - 1 mile
Douglas - 10 miles, island capital
Port St Mary - 5 miles, fishing village
Spanish Head, for general views and scenery - 7 miles
Steam Railway, Ballasalla - 1 mile 01624 663637
Manx Electric Railway - 13 miles 01624 663637
TIC 01624 686766

Food & Accommodation
Enough Restaurants, Cafes, Hotels, Guest houses and B&Bs to fill a whole book. Locally to the airport:
Castletown Golf Links Hotel - 1 mile from £35 01624 822201
The Rowans - 1 mile B&B from £16.50 01624 823210
Fern Lea, Nr Ballasalla - 2 miles B&B from £17 01624 824192
The Golf Links Hotel 01624 822201
The Cherry Orchard 01624 833811

Isle of Wight (Sandown)

1 mile west of Sandown, signposted off A3056
Isle of Wight Airport, Sandown, Isle of Wight PO36 9PJ
Tel: 01983 405125 Telex: 86686

Lea Farm Airport opened for business in the 1930s, with scheduled services to London and Portsmouth, but closed during the war, when activity moved to Bembridge, Somerton and Foreland (presumably four airfields was thought excessive for such a small island!).

Officially reopened in 1948 with extended runways as 'Isle of Wight (Sandown) Airport' a number of airlines operated services here until as late as 1967. The airport closed again in 1974, but escaped redevelopment into a housing estate, and reopened soon after. NDN Aircraft opened a factory to build the Firecracker, the Freelance and the Fieldmaster in 1980 and later the ARV Super2 was built here, but this also failed to find a suitable market.

Despite this chequered history, the airfield remains an inviting and friendly destination. A number of the NDN project aircraft can be seen in the hangars, and at the beginning of this year German aircraft collector Josef Koch announced that he was moving in his collection of 18 historic aircraft (including a Dragon Rapide). There are plans to open a museum and vintage aircraft centre - watch this space!

Landing Fee
£7.70 (singles) up to 2 tonnes, over 2 tonnes £14.00. Cash and cheque only

Fuel
AVGAS 100LL 64p +. Cash and cheque only

Flying Organisations

Airbourne School of Flying	01202 582181

Other Organisations

Aeronortec Ltd , Sandown (Maintenance)	01983 403468
Vectis Aviation Services (Maintenance)	01983 405520

Car Hire

Manor House	01983 402321
South West Rentals	01983 864263
Wilton Car Hire	01983 864414/866889

Taxis

Lake Taxis	01983 402641
Cheap Taxis	01983 404747
Danny Cabs	01983 402403

Public Transport
Sandown railway station 2 miles

Nearby Places of Interest

The usual seaside attractions at Shanklin and Sandown	
Arreton Manor, 1200 years of history -3 miles	01983 528134
Boat trips from Sandown Pier,	
Solent and Wight Line Cruises	01983 564602
Brading Roman Villa - 2 miles	01983 406223
Robin Hill Country Park - 4 miles	01983527352
Isle of Wight Rare Breeds Park - 6 miles	01983 852582
Museum of Smuggling History, Ventnor	01983 853677
Shanklin Chine, historic gorge	01983 866432
TIC	01983 403886
See also Bembridge	

Food & Accommodation

Cafe at airfield	
Francine's - about 3 miles. Recommended for its Sunday lunches in particular	
White Lion Pub (with food), Arreton - 3 miles	
Fisherman's Cottage Pub (with food), at the base of Shanklin Chine	
Jolly Sailor, Sandown - 2 miles, pub and steakhouse	01983 406115
Belmont Hotel, Shanklin - 2 miles	01983 862864
Osbourne House Hotel, Shanklin - 2 miles from £22.50	01983 862501
Cliff Tops Hotel, Shanklin - 2 miles	01983 863262
See also Bembridge	

Lands End (St Just)

5 miles west of Penzance signposted off B3306
Lands End Aerodrome, St Just, Cornwall TR19 7RL
Tel: 01736 788771(operator) Fax: 01736 788366

Conceived originally as a base for regular services to the Scillies, scheduled services to St. Mary's began in 1937 and the 20 minute journey compared favourably with the 4 hour ferry crossing. Scheduled services to St. Mary's are still operated, these days by Islanders, from the modest terminal which offers good value food and drink from the small cafe. The airfield is operated by Westward Airways, which itself is owned by the operators of the ferry, so neatly hedging their bets!

The airfield remains largely unchanged and the grass runways have steep gradients in places. The Lands End Flying Club, part of Westward Airways, have a pleasant clubhouse and the views out to sea can be quite striking.

One word of warning for flying visitors. This end of the country is surrounded on three sides by the sea and, especially in south-west winds, low cloud and advection fog can arrive rapidly. The weather at the airfield has been known to close-in completely in moments, so don't plan to arrive with minimum fuel on board!

Landing Fee
£6.50 (single), £12.50 (multi) inc.
All major credit cards - but not debit cards

Fuel
AVGAS 100LL 70p, AVTUR Jet A-1 31p
All major credit cards - but not debit cards

Flying Organisations

Lands End Flying Club	01736 788771 / 788719

Other Organisations
Westwards Airways (Lands End) Ltd (Maintenance) 01736 788601

Car Hire

Budget	0800 181181
Tucker Garage	01736 62980/60078

Taxis

Tom's Taxis	01736 871442
Stone's Taxis	01736 63400

Public Transport
Land's End to St. Ives bus service 3 times daily. Penzance Railway station 6 miles

Nearby Places of Interest
Cape Cornwall, scenic coastal views - 2 miles
Sennen Cove - 3 miles. Take the coastal path from here to Land's End

Chysauster Ancient village - 5 miles	01736 61889
Geevor Tin Mine - 2 miles	01736 788662
Land's End - 5 miles	01736 871501
Trinity House National Lighthouse Centre - 8 miles	01736 60077
St. Michael's Mount - 10 miles	01736 710507
Flambards Village Theme Park (with Cornwall Aero Park) - 15 miles	01326 564093
TIC	01736 62207 / 62341

Food & Accommodation

Restaurant and club facilities
Hundreds of eating and accommodation possibilities, here's a few:

The Lobster Pot - 6 miles	01736 731251
Trewellard Meadery	01736 788345
Bosavern House, St Just - 1 mile, B&B from £13.75	01736 788301
Cape Cornwall Golf and Country Club - 2 miles, B&B from £18	01736 788611
The Old Success Inn - 2 miles	01736 871232
Sunny Bank Hotel - 2 miles B&B from £13	01736 871278
Land's End Hotel - 3 miles	01736 871844

Lasham

5 miles south-east of Basingstoke signposted off A339
Lasham Aerodrome, Lasham, Alton, Hampshire, GU34 5SS
Tel: 01256381 322

Mosquitoes of the Pathfinders once flew from Lasham. Later, it was home to another famous name in British aviation, as Lasham was Dan Air's maintenance base.

Today, the most numerous traffic here is of the unpowered kind - there are 3 glider clubs at Lasham. However, if the airfield seems a bit larger than your average glider site, that is because Lasham is also home to a clutch of engineering companies that specialise in airliner conversion and maintenance work - a legacy of Dan Air's tenure here. Thus Lasham is one of the few places were you can find B727s in the circuit with single-seat sailplanes. For powered flying visitors the airfield is strictly Prior Permission Required. Given that, powered aircraft are welcomed and there are refreshments and briefing facilities in the gliding school clubhouse.

On the north side of the airfield, east of the main gliding site, is the Second World War Aircraft Preservation Society. The name is slightly curious as all of the society's aircraft are post-war types! Nevertheless there are displays more closely aligned with WW2, and the museum site does command a good view of the airfield. Admission is free, and the collection is open Sundays and Bank Holidays 10:00-18:00.

Landing Fee
On application

Fuel

Flying Organisations

Imperial College Gliding Club	0181 7885489
Lasham Gliding Society	01256 381322
Surrey & Hants Gliding Club	01256 381270

Other Organisations

ATC-Lasham Ltd (Maintenance)	01256 56123
Chase Aerospace (UK) Ltd (Maintenance)	01256 381507
FLS Aerospace Ltd (Maintenance)	01256 56123
Three Counties Aero Engineering (Maintenance)	01256 381330
Second World War Aircraft Preservation Society	

Car Hire

Avis	01256 63600
Hertz	01256 55000
Eurodollar	01256 477777

Taxis

Alton Taxis	01420 84455/83657
Ames Cars	01420 83309
1 Atax	01420 88888 / 88886

Public Transport
Bus service 208 linking Petersfield and Basingstoke stops at Lasham village (1 mile) 5 times daily, Alton railway station 8 miles

Nearby Places of Interest

Curtis Museum and Allen Gallery, Alton - 8 miles	01420 82802
Abbey of Our Lady and St John, Alton - 8 miles	01420 562145
Jane Austen's House, Chorton - 9 miles	01420 83262
The Watercress Line, Alton - 8 miles	01962 733810
Bass Brewery, Alton - 8 miles (tours available)	01420 541177
TIC	01420 84399

Food & Accommodation

Tea and coffee etc. at airfield	
Alton House Hotel, Alton - 8 miles from £32	01420 80033
The French Horn, Alton B&B from £30	01420 83269
The Grange Hotel and Restaurant, Alton from £49	01420 86565
Swan Hotel, Alton from £39	01420 83777
B&B can be arranged by the Lasham Gliding Club	

Lashenden (Headcorn)

The Aerodrome, Headcorn, Ashford, Kent TN27 9HX. Off the A274 south of Headcorn
Tel: 01622 890226. Outside hours 01622 890236
Fax: 01622 890876 Telex 966127

Just outside the pretty Kent village of Headcorn lies the aerodrome mostly known as Lashenden. Confusingly, the former wartime airfield of Headcorn - a totally different airfield - lay a few miles to the north. However the present day Lashenden is also widely known as Headcorn. Confused? The policy of not naming an airfield after the nearest village was adopted in wartime to confound invaders. In truth, it continues to baffle the natives today! During the War, Lashenden hosted squadrons of Spitfires and Mustangs, 'Johnnie' Johnson flew from here in 1943, and the Lashenden Air Warfare Museum on the airfield houses a good collection of aircraft and memorabilia.

The Lashenden was returned to Shenley Farm, the landowners, in 1946 and has remained an active aerodrome ever since. Something of a local centre for airsports, the airfield boasts a thriving parachute centre, together with several locally based flying instructors, working together under one roof. Aerobatics and even hot air balloons are a not uncommon sight overhead and Headcorn became the new home of The Tiger Club several years ago when they were obliged to move out from Redhill. All this activity gives Lashenden / Headcorn a great variety of aircraft, from Polish Wilgas and Lots, through the ubiquitous Cessnas and Pipers to Tiger Moths, Turbulents and some fairly exotic competition aerobatic hardware. The busy cafe does reasonable 'pub grub' type food seven days a week.

Landing Fee
£5 single, £10 multi. Overnight parking free
Cash or cheque only

Fuel
AVGAS 100LL 74p inc. AVTUR JET A-1 34p inc.
Cash or cheque only

Flying Organisations

Bateleur Aviation	01233 613549
Martin Evans	0181 946 6950
The Tiger Club	01622 891017
Thurston Helicopters	01622 891158
Weald Air Services	01622 891539

Other Organisations

Headcorn Parachute Club	01622 890862
Shenley Farms (Engineering) Ltd (maintenance)	01622 890226
Lashenden Air Warfare Museum	01622 890226

Car Hire

Avis	01622 683002
Eurodollar	01622 684844
Hertz	01622 34677

Taxis
01622843384

Public Transport
No convenient buses, Headcorn railway station 2 miles

Nearby Places of Interest

Headcorn Flower Centre and Vineyard, Headcorn 2 miles	01622 890250
Leeds Castle, Maidstone 6 miles	01622 765400
Kent and East Sussex Railway 8 miles	
TIC	01622 673581

Food & Accommodation

Cafe open 7 Days a week 0800-1800

Little Silver Country Hotel, 6 miles, from £100 (recommended) 01233 850321

Geoff & Shereen Cook, 18 Kings Rd, Headcorn 2 miles from £16 01622 891293

Mrs G. Skippon, 2 Station Rd., Headcorn 2 miles from £16 01622 890627

The Chequers Inn, Smarden 3 miles from £20 01233 770217

The Bell, Smarden
A beautiful Kent pub with a pretty garden and some really good beers about 2 miles from the airfield. Inside the pub you'll a games area, and also cosy rooms (candle lit by night), real fires and low beams. Food is good, the atmosphere friendly and there is a vintage car gathering on the second Sunday of each month. The simply furnished rooms are comfortable and in the morning you make your own 'continental' style breakfast in a small kitchen area outside the rooms. We first stayed here years ago and have been coming back ever since. If you visit once, we think you will return too. Rooms from £20.

01233 770283

Leeds Bradford

6 miles north-west of Leeds signposted off A658 & M62
Leeds Bradford International Airport, Yeadon, Leeds, Yorkshire, LS19 7TZ
Tel: 0113 2509696 (information desk)
Fax: 0113 2505426 (admin.) Telex 557868

Built on top of a hill, Leeds Bradford Airport is sometimes a victim of low cloud and crosswinds, nevertheless it remains a friendly and helpful place to light aircraft visitors. The Yorkshire Aeroplane Club - which opened the airfield in 1931 - is still here, with a pleasant clubhouse and bar on the western side of the airport, the other side of the runway from the modern terminal. The airfield's major wartime role was as home to a shadow factory for Avro, building Ansons, Lancasters, Lincolns and Yorks in large numbers.

These days, large charter aircraft operate services all year round and an increasing amount of scheduled traffic is seen here. A major development of terminal finished in Spring 95, and it is generally modern, efficient and pleasant, with catering to a good standard (full breakfast recommended) and the usual flight briefing and viewing facilities. By road, the airport is reached after a lengthy trek around the ring roads of Leeds and Bradford, but is well signposted from either city centre, and from the M62 motorway. Allow at least 30 minutes for the drive from the M62.

Landing Fee
£12.80 + per tonne or part of. Parking 1-1·5 tonnes £5.16 + , 1·5 -2 tonnes £6.88 +
All major cards, but Amex has a £100 limit.

Fuel
AVGAS 100LL 56p +. Avail 0800-1800 with Yorkshire Light Aircraft, AVGAS refuelling not avail for helicopters. All major credit cards
AVTUR JET A1 by prior arrangement only 0113 2503133.

Flying Organisations

Knight Air Flying School	0113 2391339
Yorkshire Aeroplane Club	0113 2503840

Other Organisations

Knight Air (Maintenance)	0113 2391339
Yorkshire Light Aircraft Ltd (Maintenance)	0113 2503133

Car Hire

Avis	0113 2503880
Eurodollar	0113 2777957
Hertz	0113 2504811
Europcar	0113 2509066

Taxis
At terminal

Telecabs	0113 2792222

Public Transport
Horsforth railway station 3 miles, Leeds railway station 7 miles

Nearby Places of Interest

Leeds 7 miles:	
City Museum	0113 2478275
Granary Wharf	0113 2446570
Tetley's Brewery Wharf	0113 2420666
Bradford 9 miles:	
Transpierience - Transport Discovery Park	01274 690909
Industrial Museum	01274 631756
National Museum of Photography, Film and TV (recommended)	01274 727488
Harewood House 7 miles	0113 2886225
Shipley 8 miles canal cruises	01274 595914
TIC	0113 2468120

Food & Accommodation

Brasserie 44, Leeds	0113 2343232
Sous Les Nez Des Villes, Leeds (Egon Ronay)	0113 2440108
Harry Ramsden's (the famous fish & chips emporium), Leeds	
Bradford is a must for curry lovers, try the Kashmir,	01274 726513
Park House Guest Home 1 mile B&B from £18	0113 2505503
Aaron Lodge 1 mile B&B from £20	0113 2506777
Travel Inn (2 mins drive) room from £35	01582 414341
Forte Post House 3 miles from £59	0113 2842911
Hilton National 8 miles from £55	0113 2442000

Leicester

4 miles east of Leicester. See text for road directions
Leicester Aerodrome, Gartree Road, Leicester, LE2 2FG
Tel: 0116 2592360 Fax : 0116 259 2712

A former wartime airfield, Leicester's ancestry is apparent in the triangular runway layout and standard wartime control tower. However, Leicester is definitely not an airfield rooted in the past. Leicester Airport (as it was officially renamed in 1977, having been Leicester East before) is operated by Leicestershire Aero Club from the restored Tower building. The well-organised club house has all the usual briefing and flight planning facilities, and a nice bar/cafe upstairs, which does good value food, but is closed on Mondays. A number of interesting aircraft are resident here and there is an excellent annual airshow each August, well attended and deservedly popular. An outdoor karting track by the entrance can provide an entertaining afternoon.

Leicester has also distinguished itself recently by opening two new asphalt runways to compliment the existing main 10/28 runway. Together with the two grass runways that gives 10 possible landing directions - no crosswind problems here! Leicester's investment in the future of their airfield deserves the congratulations and support of the GA world.

Finding Leicester by road is not always straight-forward as it is some way from the city centre, so here are some pointers:

From the M6 junction 21 initially follow signs for 'Outer Ring Road' heading East.

From the A47, turn off at Houghton on the Hill next to the Total garage, signposted to Stretton. Go through the village and keep going for 2-3 miles until you get to a T-Junction. Turn right towards 'Great Stretton' and the airfield is about of a mile on the right.

From the A6 turn off at Oadby on the B667 (signs to Staughton, Great Glen and the Strettons), turn right at the T-junction at the end of the road. The airfield will appear on your left after about 2 miles.

Landing Fee
Single £7.50, multi £20.50 inc. £5.00 inc. at weekends. Free if fuel uplifted
All major credit cards except Diners

Fuel
AVGAS 100LL 59p +
All major credit cards except Diners

Flying Organisations

Leicestershire Flying Club	0116 259 2360
Capital Helicopters	01889 505 611

Other Organisations

RN Aviation (Leicester Airport) (Maintenance)	0116 2593629
Stretton Circuit (karting)	0116 2593144

Car Hire

Avis	0116 2626523
Eurodollar	0116 2510455
Hertz	0116 8521803

Taxis

Astons	0116 2555111

Public Transport
Bus service 196 into City centre. Bus stop approx 1/2 mile from airfield. Leicester railway station 3 miles.

Nearby Places of Interest
Castle Park an area of gardens, churches, riverside walks, ancient walls and gateways, interesting shops and museums, Leicester - 2 miles 01162 650555
Bruntingthorpe Airfield, British Aviation Heritage and the Lightning Preservation Group, Bruntingthorpe - 10 miles
The Snibston Discovery Park, Coalville -10 miles 01530 510851
Great Central Railway - Leicester 3 miles 01509 230726
Percy Pilcher Museum, Stanford Hall,
Lutterworth -15 miles 01788 860250
TIC 01162 650555

Food & Accommodation

Restaurant upstairs in tower. Open 1200-2000 Tue-Fri and 1030-1600 weekends

The Yews	01162 2593369
Bel Air restaurant, Leicester	01162 532397
The Cherry Restaurant, Leicester	01162 544773
Belmont Hotel, Leicester - 2 miles	01162 544773
Grand Hotel, Leicester - 2 miles	01162 555599
Hermitage Hotel, Oadby - 2 miles from £30	0116 271 9441

Little Gransden

5 miles south-east of St Neots
Yak UK, Little Gransden Airfield, Fullers Hill, Little Gransden, Sandy, Beds SG19 3BP
Tel: 01767 51950 Fax: 01767 51665

Home of Yak UK, importers of every PPL's favourite (and most attainable) warbird, the Yak 52, Little Gransden can usually be relied upon for unusual and interesting aircraft.

Not to be confused with the former wartime bomber base of Gransden Lodge, which is a couple of miles to the north-east, Little Gransden offers the cosy atmosphere more associated with a private strip, although the field is licensed and training takes place here. Tea and coffee are available to visitors, although there are no other refreshments. A picnic table by the intersection to the runways offers a pleasant spot on a sunny day if you take your own food.

Access to Little Gransden (also known as Yak city) by road is through a farmyard, just off the B1046, not far from the A14. Southbound on the A1198 towards Royston, it is signposted 'Gransden airfield'. Take the B1046 right hand turn towards 'Gamlingay' and 'Gransdens'. Three miles further on, take the left turn on the corner signposted 'Gamlingay 2', the airfield is 1/2 mile on the right.

Landing Fee
Single £5.00. Long term parking not normally available
Cash or cheque only

Fuel
AVGAS 100LL 57p +
Cash or cheque only

Flying Organisations
Skyline School of Flying 01767 651950

Other Organisations
Yak UK 01767 651156
Vintech Aero Engines 01767 561794

Car Hire
Avis 01908 281334/ 01908 230110
Eurodollar 01908 271077/ 01234 269566
Hertz 01908 374492

Taxis
Dereks taxis 01767 260443

Public Transport
Buses from Gamlingay. Sandy railway station 7 miles

Nearby Places of Interest
Gransden Lodge gliding site 2 miles,
Cambridge University Gliding Club 01767 677077
See also Bourne, Duxford and Old Warden

Food & Accommodation
Only chocolate bars and soft drinks at the airfield itself
Mrs Bygraves B&B 01767 677459
Gransden Lodge Farm, Little Gransden B&B from £15 01767 677365
Mrs Gorton B&B 01767 650581
Model Farm, Little Gransden B&B from £16 01767 677361

Liverpool

7 miles south-east of Liverpool signposted off A561
Liverpool Airport Plc, Liverpool, L24 1YD
Tel: 0151 4868877 Fax: 0151 4863339
Telex 629323

The original airfield site, known as Liverpool Airport North, was built on the land of the Speke Hall Estate in 1928, and the art-deco terminal added a few years later in 1939. Speke Hall, one of the best preserved half-timbered houses in Britain, still stands between the two airport sites next to the link taxiway.

A new main runway was later built alongside the river Mersey, over a mile south of the old site and connected to the north airfield by the link taxiway. An apron, and modern terminal followed, and the old terminal finally closed in the early 1980s. The north airfield still houses the flying clubs and their maintenance facilities, but its old runways are no longer available for take-off and landing. The new terminal houses the usual facilities, customs, cafeteria, flight briefing in an efficient modern setting. At the time of writing the terminal is being extensivley refurbished, and so further improved facilities are expected. The 'Blenhiem' restaurant has been relocated to the old British Midland lounge. Liverpool hosts modest scheduled services, mostly to Ireland and the Isle of Man, and a fair amount of charter and freight traffic with annual passenger numbers of around 450 000.

The airport is signposted on all the major routes into Liverpool. These lead you to the main terminal, however to reach the north airfield and the flying schools, you should take a turning off the A562 next to 'TOTAL' petrol station (a mile after the main airport turning from the east, a mile before it from the city). At this entrance there are numerous billboards and signs for the clubs, turn here and bear right past the old terminal building to the security gate, where you will be directed to the club of your choice.

Landing Fee
£15.00 + (single) £25.00 + (multi) includes 24 hours free parking. Parking fees £6.00 (singles) £9.00 (multis) per 24 hours
All major credit cards

Fuel

AVGAS 100LL 63.01p + AVTUR JET A1 32.78p + via Esso	0151 486 7084
Available H24 All major credit cards	

Flying Organisations

Airnova Flight Centre	0151 4277909/4277908
Cheshire Air Training School	0151 4868383
Deltair Aviation Services Ltd	0151 4922040
Liverpool Flying School	0151 4277449
Merseyside Aviation	0151 4943924/0831 662738
Keenair	0151 4277449
Southport and Merseyside Aero Club	0151 7097494

Other Organisations

Air Nova (Maintenance)	0151 4278093
Keenair (North West) Ltd (Maintenance)	0151 4273275 / 4274048
Bond Helicopters	0151 4480030

Car Hire

Avis	0151 4866686
Eurodollar	0151 4480020
Hertz	0151 4867111
Europcar	0151 708 9150

Taxis
At terminal

Public Transport
Buses from terminal to Liverpool, also to Garston railway station. Garston railway station 2 miles. Train times 0151 709 9696

Nearby Places of Interest

Speke Hall - 1 mile	
Liverpool FC Stadium tour	0151 2601433
Tate Gallery, Liverpool	0151 7090507
Walker Art Gallery	0151 2070001
Liverpool Museum	0151 2070001
Aintree Race Course	0151 523 2600
Haydock Park	01942 725963
Liverpool Docks including Customs and Excise Exhibitions and Beatles Story	0151 7088574
Merseyside Maritime Museum	0151 2070001
Warship Preservation Trust, Birkenhead Docks	0151 6501573
Numerous maritime attractions in the Liverpool/Birkenhead area.	
Birkenhead 5 miles	0151 6501573
TIC	0151 7092444

Food & Accommodation

Airport bars/cafeteria in the main terminal	
Albert Dock, Liverpool (all sorts of eating & shopping here)	0151 7088574
Cavern Club (made famous by the Beatles)	0151 2361957
La Grande Bouffe, Liverpool	0151 2363375
Far East Chinese restaurant, Liverpool	0151 7093141
Casa Italia, Liverpool	0151 2275774
Somersby Guest House - 4 miles	0151 7227549
Aacher - 4 miles B&B from £22	0151 7093477
Dolby	0151 70872
Atlantic Tower, Liverpool from £34	0151 227 4444
Liverpool Moat House - 4 miles from £95	0151 7090181

London (City)

6 miles east of the City of London signposted off the A1011
Royal Dock, Silvertown, London E16 2 PX
Tel: 0171 4745555 (Information) Fax: 0171 5111040
Telex: 264731

For a few years City airport, and the Docklands development it is closely associated with, looked to be destined to become an empty monument to the 'yuppie' years of the late 1980s.

A Dash 7 first landed at Heron's Quay in 1982, although work did not begin on the airport until 4 years later. City opened in 1987, but for sometime the short runway - and steep approach path required - placed severe restrictions on the aircraft that could operate here. Despite the airport's proximity to London city centre, the lack of public transport links and restricted range of services kept passenger numbers low. The public transport situation improved slowly and a runway extension was opened in 1992, allowing in for the first time jet aircraft such as the BAe146. More than 500 000 passengers used the airport in 1995 (compared with just 170 000 in 1991) and it now has 14 'business' destinations through Europe - although Paris remains the prime route. Many types of executive jets and turboprops are allowed in, and even a Cherokee landed here recently - although it was an emergency landing due to engine trouble!

If you are visiting by road, use the long term car park if at all possible. You can get an hour's free parking here and it's only three minutes from the terminal. By comparison the short term car park is very expensive.

Landing Fee
On application

Fuel
AVTUR JET A-1

Flying Organisations

Other Organisations
FLS Aerospace Engineering
Business and Conference Centre 0171 4763999
Business Air (Handling agent) 0171 4745555
Servisair 0171 4745555

Car Hire
Europcar 0171 4760309
Hertz 0171 4767151

Taxis
At terminal, Desk in terminal operated by Computer Cab 0171 4746545

Public Transport
Silvertown/London City Airport railway station (north London line) 300 metres. Red Shuttle Bus every 20 mins to Liverpool Street railway station (£4.00 one-way, journey time about 30 mins). Yellow Shuttlebus operates a high frequency service to Canary Wharf allowing direct connection to Docklands Light Railway, info. 0171 4745555. Bus route 473 from Stratford railway station. Docklands Light Railway 0171 9184000, London Transport 0171 2221234.

Nearby Places of Interest
Comprehensive airport shop 0171 7474555
Canary Wharf, London, and all that. Only 15 mins to the City and 30 mins to the West End (driving times)
TIC 0839 123456 / 0171 8248844

Food & Accommodation
Brasserie Restaurant, buffet and bar in terminal 0171 4731944
Numerous restaurants, cafes, bars, etc. within 10 miles
General travel services (hotel reservations, mobile phones, coach hire, sightseeing tours, flowers and theatre tickets, tickets for shuttle buses, travel cards etc.) at the General Services Desk 0171 4766428

London (Gatwick)

3 miles north of Crawley signposted off M23 Junction 9 & 9a
London (Gatwick) Airport, West Sussex, RH6 0NP
Tel: 01293 535353 Fax: 01293 505093
Telex: 877725 GAL

Gatwick has in the past suffered from the problem of being viewed as very much secondary to Heathrow. Scheduled airlines wanted to be at Heathrow if at all possible, and much of the traffic here was IT charter, giving Gatwick a 'bucket and spade' image, rather than being a serious international airport. Like most stereotypes, this view of Gatwick is some way off-target, especially given the airport's growth in recent years. Scheduled services are dominant now, and some major airlines have actually begun to move services here from Heathrow.

The more recent development of the airport seems to have been driven largely by the desire to create a major shopping complex, and it has been said - presumably in jest - that the accountants would rather lose the aeroplanes than the shops! Certainly the shopping, eating and drinking facilities are impressive, even on the 'public' side, and it is rumoured that the airport has become a popular day out for those who have no intention of flying anywhere!

There is a good viewing terrace on roof of the south Terminal, where the BuchAir enthusiast's shop is also located. Unfortunately there are no such facilities at the north Terminal.

If you are flying out of Gatwick, be sure to restrict your hand luggage (as indeed we're all meant to). Reaching most of the gates involves an impressive amount of footwork, and moving walkways are few and far between.

Landing Fee
BAA rates. As low (!) as £50 off-peak

Fuel
AVTUR JET A-1

Flying Organisations

Other Organisations

British Airways plc (Maintenance)	01293 567000
Bristow Helicopters Ltd (Maintenance)	01293 502131
Caledonian Airways Ltd (Maintenance)	01293 668350
Cityflyer Express Ltd (Maintenance)	01293 507482
GB Airways Ltd (Maintenance)	01293 664226
IAP Aircraft Maintenance Ltd	01293 502288
Nordic Aero Ltd (Maintenance)	01293 502512
Nordisk Aviation Products UK Ltd (Maintenance)	01293 502139
Ogden Aviation Engineering Ltd (Maintenance)	01293 507331
Over 70 shops and restaurants	
Buchair enthusiast's shop	
Interflight (handling)	01293 540409

Car Hire

Avis	01293 539721
Eurodollar	01293 619368
Europcar	01293 531062
Hertz	01293 530555

Taxis
At terminals

Public Transport

Gatwick railway station connects to south terminal. Express service to London Victoria every 15 mins (30 mins off-peak). About 30 mins to Victoria. One-way fare about £9.00

Network South Central - sales, enquiries and ticket telesales	01273 206755
London British Rail (to East Anglia, the South and South East)	0171 9285100
London British Rail (to the West of England and South Wales)	0171 2626767
London British Rail (to the West Midlands, North West and Scotland)	01713877070
London British Rail (to the North East and Scotland)	0171 2782477

Regular shuttle buses to central London, Heathrow, Luton, Stansted. Fare to central London about £9.00, about 1hr 10 mins journey

Crawley Buses	01293 525173/524287

Various national coach companies serve Gatwick, information on 01293 502116 (south terminal); 01293 502320 (north terminal)

Nearby Places of Interest

Central London 30 minutes by train, as is Brighton

Vallance By-Ways - 6 miles Historic aircraft collection with a 550m grass strip	01293 862915/0836 666817
Gatwick Zoo - Russ Hill, Charlwood. Open March-October	01293 862312
Tilgate Lake - Crawley, watersports	01293 851854
MGM Cinema	01293 527497
Tilgate Park and Nature Centre - Crawley	01293 521168
TIC	01293 560108

Food & Accommodation

Plenty of restaurants at airport, most are of reasonable quality and value

Fortune Villa Chinese Restaurant - Crawley	01293 520432
Bengal Spices - Crawley	01293 571007
The Copthorne London Gatwick, from £98	01342 714971
Forte Crest Gatwick, North Terminal, from £99	01293 567070
London Gatwick Airport Hilton - Crawley from £140	01293 518080
London Gatwick Airport Travel Inn (North Terminal), from £34.50	01293 568158
Forte Travelodge - Crawley from	01293 533441
Brooklyn Manor Hotel - Crawley. from £30. Courtesy bus	01293 546024
The George - Crawley from £58	01293 524215
Berrens Guest House - Horley from £20. Courtesy bus	01293 786125
Chalet Guest House - Horley from £24. Courtesy bus	01293 821666
Laurel Cottage Guest House from £30. Courtesy bus	01342 718984

London (Heathrow)

12 miles west of central London, Junction 4 M4 (J14 M25). Also access via A4 & A30
London Heathrow Airport, Hounslow, Middlesex, TW6 1JH
Tel: 0181 759 4321 (Enquiries) Fax: 0181 7454290
Telex: 934892

As soon as you start talking about London Heathrow, the statistics start flowing. It is the world's busiest international airport. Something like 51m passengers pass through each year - almost equivalent to the population of the UK! There are 380 000 flights each year and 90 airlines flying to 220 destinations from here. Few people brave the traffic and crowded terminals just because they happened to be passing - and it's nobodies idea of a quiet Sunday afternoon's outing!

The public transport links are almost a book in themselves. By road Heathrow is (of course) easy to get to, but the traffic jams through the tunnel to terminals 1,2 & 3 have been known to back onto the motorway link road. Driving to & from central London is anything from 45 mins (if you're Damon Hill and it's 3 am) to nearer 2 1/2 hours in the rush hour.

Once you get to Heathrow it's well worth seeking out the handy 'Heathrow Airport Pocket Guide', available at the information desks. It lists services, what's where, useful telephone numbers etc. and could save you a lot of hassle. The viewing terrace and shop are accessed via Terminal 2, the security personnel do not encourage viewing elsewhere and there are no proper viewing facilities in Terminal 4.

A recent Egon Ronay report cited Heathrow's food as very good. Mind you, it was only compared to 3 other airports, one of which was Paris Charles de Gaulle - so it wasn't what you'd call stiff competition. Nevertheless, coming best out of the report were The Upper Crust and The Granary (best coffee of all) in Terminal 3, and the Seafood Bar.

Landing Fee
BAA rates. Minimum at peak hours (if you're daft enough to try it) is £400 +

Fuel
AVTUR JET A1

Flying Organisations

Other Organisations

British Airways plc (Maintenance)	0181 5625531
British Midland plc (Maintenance)	0181 9905033
Dunlop Ltd (Maintenance)	0181 7591086
Hunting Business Aviation Ltd (Maintenance and handling)	0181 7592141
Heathrow Business Centre	0181 759 2434

Car Hire

Avis	0181 899 1000
Eurodollar	0181 897 3232
	0181 751 6466
Europcar	0181 897 0811
Hertz	0181 897 3343

Taxis
At all terminals

Public Transport

Underground stations all terminals (Piccadilly Line) 1 hour 5 mins / £3.50 to central London
Airbus 1hr 20 mins to central London, Euston and Victoria - about £6.00
Average taxi fare to central London £33
Shuttle buses to Gatwick, Stansted and Luton
Express coach links with Reading and Woking railway stations
Numerous London Transport bus routes and national coach company services

24 hour London Transport Travel Information	0171 2221234
Surrey Traveline Travel Information	01737 223000
Bucks Traveline Travel Information	0345 382000
London United Busways Limited	0181 9776665
National Express nationwide coach routes	0171 730 0202

Nearby Places of Interest

London 12 miles, reputed to have some tourist attractions
Heathrow Airport Visitor Centre. An interactive exhibition of the airport's past, present and future; a community information centre; good runway views and a job centre. Located in Newall Road, off the A4 Bath Road, close to the Ramada Hotel. Nearby bus stops for routes 81, 105, 111, 140, 190/192, 222, 285. Open Friday 10-7 pm Saturday 10-5 pm. Final entry 1 hour prior closing. 0181 7456655
TIC 0171 824 8844

Food & Accommodation

Restaurants, buffets and bars in all terminals. Burger King Terminal 3 recommended!
Terminal 2 Roof Garden cafe (with viewing) 0181 7455259
Oakley Court, Boaters Brasserie,
Windsor, 6 miles (Egon Ronay) 01628 74141
Eton Wine Bar, Eton, 5 miles (Egon Ronay) 01753 854921
All terminals have hotel reservation desks, and these are generally a much better bet than arranging your own accommodation, unless you specifically want to stay at a certain hotel
Hotels (all around airfield) central booking number 01904 679999
British Hotel Reservation Centre - covers Hotels, B&B and Hostels.
In the T1,2,3 Underground station 0181 564 8808
in the T4 underground station 0181 564 8211
Heathrow Guest House from £30 0181 384 3333

London (Stansted)

3 miles east of Bishops Stortford, M11 junction 8
Stansted Airport Ltd, Stansted, Essex, CM24 1QW
Tel: 01279 680500 (Switchboard) 662520 (Information)
Fax: 01279 815249 Telex 818708 STN LTD G
For many years, even after it had been officially designated London's third airport, Stansted had the feel of a 'white elephant'.

Stansted was built as a USAF bomber base in 1943. Civilian operations commenced after the war, but fortuitously the US Air Force returned in the mid-1950s to lengthen the runway. After this they lost interest in the airfield, but their legacy was a 3000m runway which has been Stansted's saviour, guaranteeing that, at least, freight companies and overhaul companies would be attracted here.

Even into the 1980s the airport was grossly under-developed. Those who knew the airport at this time will recall the rather tatty terminal building and the staff 'greasy spoon' canteen, housed in a wartime Nissen hut (motto "whatever you want, it's off"). Aside from the sparse scheduled services, traffic was mostly freight, charter and executive aircraft.

Much of this has changed since the new terminal opened in 1991. This impressive steel and glass structure is generally liked by users, and indeed the whole airport now has far more the air of a significant international airport. With its own railway station and good motorway links Stansted is at last in a position to fulfil its promise.

Landing Fee
BAA rates. Around £30 for singles off-peak

Fuel
AVGAS 100LL AVTUR JET A1. Available north side, 0700-2300 daily. At other times a callout charge of £100 will be levied unless fuel is required for medical flights or prior arrangements have been made. Esso 01279 663178/9. Southside, AVTUR JET A1 available H24

Flying Organisations

Other Organisations

AEM Ltd (Maintenance)	01843 591381
FLS Aerospace Ltd (Maintenance)	01279 680068
Heavylift Aircraft Engineering Ltd (Maintenance)	01279 680611
Hunting Aviation Business Aviation Division (Maintenance and handling)	01279 680167
Inflite Engineering Services Ltd (Maintenance)	01279 680736
Kearsley Airways Ltd (Maintenance)	01279 871000
World Aviation Support Ltd (Maintenance)	01279 663186
Universal Aviation (UK) Ltd (Handling)	01279 680349
Executive Airways (Handling)	01279 680290
Hascombe Aviation Services (Handling)	01279 680291

Car Hire

Avis	01279 663030
Budget	01279 681194
Europcar	01279 680240
Hertz	01279 680154

Taxis
At terminal

Stansted Airport Cars	01279 662444

Public Transport
Stansted Airport railway station 0171 928 5100. Stansted Express runs to London Liverpool Street every 30 mins, average 50 mins travel time. About £11.00 one-way Extensive local and national coach services, direct services to Heathrow. Cambridge Coach Services 01223 236333, Eastern National 01245 353104, Greenline 01279 426349/421971, Speedlink 0181 6687261, Town Link 01279 426349/421971, National Express 0171 730 0202, Essex Busline 0345 000333

Nearby Places of Interest

Tours of old world war two buildings at the airport	01279 662709
Essex Leisure Link, phone service with details of activities in Essex (premium number)	0898 345386
Adventuress River Cruises, Sawbridgeworth	01279 600848
Mountfitchet Castle and House on the Hill Toy Museum, Stansted. Award winning Norman motte and bailey castle and fully animated toy museum	0891 424103
Mole Hall Wildlife Park	01799 540400
TIC	01279 652274
See also Andrewsfield	

Food & Accommodation

Reasonable eating and drinking facilities in the terminal	
The Cake Table Tea Room, Thaxted - 7 miles	01371 831206
Hotel Reservation Service, in the International Arrivals Concourse	01279 662929
Hilton National Hotel, (at airport) from £50	01279 6800800
The Thatch, between Saffron Walden and Bishops Stortford on the B1383 from £15	01799 543440
The Laurels, Stansted. Courtesy car to airport, from £29	01279 813023
Norman House, Stansted from £18	01279 812343
The Old Post Office, Broxted - 3 miles from £16	01279 850050
See also Andrewsfield	

Luton

2 miles east of Luton off the A505. M1 junction 10, or A505 off the A1(M) at Hitchin
London Luton Airport Ltd, Percival House, Percival Way, Luton, Bedfordshire LU2 9LY
Tel: 01582 405100 (switchboard) Fax: 01582 395313 (Admin.)

Luton Airport (or 'London Luton Airport' as it now likes to call itself) has recently gained a reputation for not wanting light aircraft visitors. A steep rise in landing fees for light aircraft - a £100 surcharge at certain times of the day - led to the home-based Luton Flight Training closing down. A light aircraft that flew one practice ILS at Luton received an invoice for nearly £60! Even visitors by road might be put off by the sign in the car park warning that a lost car parking ticket will be charged at a minimum £140!

Not surprisingly, light aircraft visitors are now few and far between. This is ironic as Luton was once home to Percival, makers of some of the finest light aircraft ever built in Britain. Modern-day Luton is the base for charter operators Monarch and Britannia, who both have major engineering and training facilities here. It is also developing something of a speciality as a destination for budget priced scheduled routes - indeed Luton has just announced passenger numbers up 40% year-on-year.

The terminal has good facilities and catering outlets, open 24 hours a day. There is also a dedicated Spectators area - with viewing facilities and cheap car parking.

Landing Fee

Up to 2 tonnes £14.40, but big penalties at certain times of the day. Handling to 5 tonnes £40

Fuel

AVGAS 100LL 68p + Shell Oil 01582 417659 (out of hours). AVGAS supplies limited, available 0600-2359, other times by arrangement with a surcharge. AVTUR Jet A-1 30p +

Flying Organisations

Delta Helicopters	01582 405250
Eagle Flight Training	01582 420007
Britannia Flying Club	01582 428065

Other Organisations

Helitech (Luton) Ltd (Maintenance)	01582 27828
Magec Aviation Ltd (Handling & maintenance)	01582 24182
Hunting Business Aviation (Handling)	01582 38322
HPB Aviation (Group) Ltd (refurbishment)	01582 26266
Metro Business Aviation (Handling)	01582 38322

Car Hire

Eurodollar	01582 411435
Avis	01582 36537
Europcar	01582 413438
Alamo	01582 486414

Taxis

Airport Cars	01582 373737

Public Transport

A useful 'passenger information guide' is available from the Airport. Buses to Luton railway station 2 miles. Thameslink 01582 27612, Intercity 0171 387 7070. Local bus services 0345 788788, Jetlink (to Heathrow & Gatwick etc.) 0181 668 7261. National Express 0990 808080. Stagecoach United Counties 01604 20077. Cambridge Coach Services 01223 236333

Nearby Places of Interest

Luton Museum and Art Gallery, Luton	01582 36941
Luton Hoo 2 miles	01582 22955
Luton TIC	01582 401579

Food & Accommodation

Reasonable quality cafe, restaurant, KFC & bar in terminal

Hotel Ibis from £32	01582 424488
Chiltern Hotel	01582 575911
Stathmore Thistle	01582 34199
Red Lion & Lodge Hotel	01462 76281

Lydd

1 mile east of Lydd, signposted from B2075
Lydd Airport, Lydd. Romney Marsh Kent TN29 9QL
Tel: 01797 320401 Fax: 01797 321615
Telex 966310

Lydd was built in 1953 in this remote corner of Kent specifically as a civil airport for channel crossings. The style of architecture and the general demeanour of the place reminds the visitor that this airfield's heyday was the 1950s and 60s when Bristol Freighters and Carvairs of Silver City Airlines flew a regular car-ferry service to France. Black and white pictures in the terminal, depicting famous patrons such as Diana Dors, hark back to this stylish past. The last car ferry flew from here in 1978 for Silver City, but after this the airport continued to see a regular traffic - either one of the ill-fated attempts to resurrect a cross-channel service, or light aircraft clearing customs and stocking up on the duty frees for continental trips.

With the arrival of 'one Europe' and the relaxation of customs requirements for continental travel, this role has also diminished. However, the airport management are proud of the airfield's history and are keen to revitalise Lydd by attracting GA aircraft flying to and from the continent. The regular flow of UK and foreign registered aircraft, from microlights to corporate Boeings, is testament to their efforts. While Lydd rarely bustles with activity, there are often unusual and foreign-registered aircraft passing through. The reasonable cafeteria boasts a large viewing area, and customs facilities and duty-free are available. Even better, the airfield offers free landing fees to pilots who buy fuel en-route to the continent.

Landing Fee
Singles to 1500kg £7.00 +, 3000 kg £14.50 + Free if going foreign and buying fuel. Other offers apply at different times. Overnight parking £5.00
All major credit cards except Diners

Fuel
AVGAS 59p + AVTUR JET A1 29p +
All major credit cards except Diners

Flying Organisations

Romney Marsh Aviation	01797 320734

Other Organisations

Car Hire

Romney Car and Van Hire	01797 363189
Cycle Hire, Dymchurch Cycle Shop, Dymchurch	01303 875296

Taxis

Shepways Taxi Service	01679 66842 0836 775014 / 0860 759534

Public Transport
Appledore railway station 5 miles. Info 01732 770111

Nearby Places of Interest

Clay Pigeon shooting, Lydd	01679 20179/20185 or 01860 249379
Go-karting, Lydd	01679 20179/20185 or 01860 249379
Jet Ski, Lydd	01679 21895
Sand Yachting, New Romney	01679 66770
Dungeness Power station trips, Romney Marsh - 4 miles	01797 321815
Dungeness RSPB nature reserve, Lydd - 3 miles	01679 20588
Romney Hythe & Dymchurch Railway, New Romney Station - 3 miles	01797 362353
Brenzett Aeronautical Museum Trust, Brenzett - 8 miles	01233 627911
TIC	01303 258594

Food & Accommodation
Refurbished cafe / flight reception area open 7 days a week 0800-1800

The Dolphin, Lydd 2 miles from £15	01679 320259
The Bridge Inn, Lydd from £10	01679 362187
Chatswood Lodge, Lydd B&B from £16	01679 320410
Waterside Guest House, Dymchurch 4 miles B&B from £15	01303 872253
Chantry Hotel, Dymchurch 4 miles from £20	01303 873137

Manchester (Barton)

5 miles west of Manchester on the A57, Junction 2 M63
Lancashire Aero Club, Barton Aerodrome, Liverpool Road, Eccles, Manchester M22 5PA
Tel: 0161 7894785 (Flying Club), 0161 7877326 (Clubhouse)

Opened in 1930, Barton was intended to become Manchester's main airport, but the poor local drainage (the airfield sits atop 80 feet of peat) coupled with the short runways led most activity being transferred to Ringway by 1938. During the war, Percival Proctors were assembled here, and there were occasional visits by aircraft as large as Lancasters.

The original tower, a distinctive 1930s design and now a listed building, still stands on this busy GA airfield. At weekends Barton resembles a beehive, with extensive activity by fixed-wing, rotary-wing and microlights alike, and the Greater Manchester Police Helicopter is based on the airfield, operating day and night. There are number of rare and interesting types in the hangers, and the active local PFA Strut is based here. Lancashire Aero Club, Britain's oldest established flying club, have operated the airfield for many years and are based in the tower building. Their clubhouse (next to the carpark) offers a bar, good catering, and views over the airfield from inside, or outside on a warm day. Also next to the car park is the Barton Visitor Centre (due to re-open late Spring) which includes a coffee shop, museum and souvenir shop. Outside is a Vampire T11, ME108, and Canberra nose section.

Barton's future is not absolutely clear at the moment. There are ambitious plans – including a tarmac runway 24/06, new hangers and an aviation museum based around the tower and Pemberton hangar – to coincide with the 2002 Manchester Commonwealth games. As always, much will depend on the attitude of the local authority who own the airfield and what support the airfield can gather.

Landing Fee
£5.00 inc. All major credit cards

Fuel
AVGAS 100LL 60p + AVTUR Jet A1 30p + All major credit cards

Flying Organisations

Lancashire Aero Club	0161 7877326
Manchester Helicopter Centre	0161 7877125
Mainair Microlight School	01706 55134

Other Organisations

Light Planes Lancashire (Maintenance) Ltd	0161 7877326
Taurus Air Services	0161 707 7064
Historic Aviation Society	
Flightline (Pilot's Shop)	0161 707 9695

Car Hire

Avis	0161 2366716
Eurodollar	0161 8343000
Hertz	0161 2362747

Taxis

Lyles	0161 707 4444
Roadrunner	0161 776 2426
H & L	0800 122422

Public Transport
Bus stop at gate, services to Manchester city centre

Nearby Places of Interest
See Manchester International
TIC 0161 489 6412

Food & Accommodation
Lancashire Aero Club clubroom (the door says members only, but visiting pilots are always welcomed)
Coffee shop in the Barton Visitor Centre
Airport Hotel (at the gate). Bar snacks and restaurant facilities.
Rooms from £32.50 (weekdays) and £25 (Fri, Sat, Sun) 0161 789 6543
Wendover Hotel - 1 mile from £39.50
(£29.50 at weekends) 0161 789 7811
See also Manchester International

Manchester

8 miles south-west of Manchester, Junction 5 M56
Manchester Airport plc, Manchester Airport, Manchester M90 1QX
Tel: 0161 4893000 (switchboard) Fax: 0161 489 2889
Telex: 665457

Ringway, as it was then known, became Manchester's official airport in 1938 - taking over from nearby Barton. The runways were paved in 1942 when the three large hangars on the southside of the airfield built. These still bear the faded camouflage markings applied over fifty years ago and were used as assembly sheds for Avro prototypes, separate from the main factory at Woodford, 5 miles away. The prototype Avro Manchester, Lancaster, Lincoln, York and Tudor were all built and made their maiden flights from here. On the West side of the airport, where the fire station now stands, was Fairey Engineering, from where Fairey Battles and Barracudas were built, and also Halifaxes for Handley Page. After the war, Gannets and the prototype Fairey Delta, the supersonic test bed and Vulcan development aircraft, were built and flown from this site.

The first of the new terminals was built in 1962, along with an extension to the main 06/24 runway. This terminal was modernised and extended in 1985, and a second terminal opened in the early 1990s. Manchester is the UK's third largest gateway after Gatwick and Heathrow, with something like 15m passengers passing through annually. Despite this, Manchester still accommodates a healthy GA community in the old Avro hangers on the southside. Light aircraft visitors have to comply with some fairly complicated PPR procedures, and shun the peak hours if you want to avoid an 'excess' charge, but ATC are well disposed towards GA - perhaps because many of the controllers here are active pilots too. However, the tenure of the flying schools and light aircraft on the southside may be limited. To allow further expansion, the airport wants to build a second, parallel runway. The result of the protracted public enquiry is still awaited, but if it does get the go-ahead, this second runway will run right through the present southside area.

Back at the main airfield site you'll find all the facilities you would expect at a major international airport. In fact, in many people's opinion the facilities are somewhat better than many airports, with above average eating, drinking and shopping. The coffee shop in Terminal 1 (international) departures has a good view across the runway, though arguably the best value food on the airport is at the Burger King in Terminal 1 (international) arrivals. There is a shop on the viewing terraces, accessed via Terminal 1 (international) departures, and also a viewing area on the southside of the airport. Unfortunately there are no viewing facilities at all in the newer Terminal 2.

Reaching the main airport by road is merely a question of following the signs from about 30 miles around. The M56 passes by (exit Junction 5), and this itself connects to the nearby M6, M62 and M63. To reach the southside, leave the M56 at junction 6 and negotiate the rather complicated roundabout affair following signs for 'A538 Wilmslow'. This will take you past the cargo section (near the old Fairey /Dan Air hangers) and through a tunnel under the runway. After exiting the tunnel, the southside turning is signposted on the left after 200 metres. If you pass the Moat House hotel on the left - you just missed the turning!

Landing Fee
£4.65 per 500kg + All major credit cards. Minimum £70 during peak hours

Fuel
AVGAS 100LL 71p + AVTUR JET A1 30p + All major credit cards

Flying Organisations

MSF Aviation (UK) Ltd	0161 499 1444
Ravenair	0161 4368848 / 4991632

Other Organisations

Air Kilroe Ltd (maintenance & handling)	0161 4362055
Airline Services Ltd	0161 4893173
Airplan Flight Equipment (pilot supplies)	0161 499 0023
Aviation Shop, Spectators Terraces, airport guided tours etc	0161 4990303
Information line, Manchester Airport	0891 227318
Northern Executive Aviation Ltd (handling & maintenance)	0161 436 6666
Ravenair (maintenance & handling)	0161 4368848
FLS Aerospace Ltd	0161 4993999
Sky Wheels Ltd	0161 4989780

Car Hire

Avis	0161 4362020
Eurodollar	0161 4993320
Hertz	0161 4378208
Europcar	0161 436 2200
Manchester Airport Self Drive	0161 498 8188

Taxis

Outside all terminals, 24 hours

Public Transport

Bus and coach station outside terminal 1 international arrivals, extensive local buses and national coaches. Local Bus & rail info. 0161 228 7811.
National Express 0161 228 3881.
Airport railway station with services every 15 minutes to Manchester Piccadilly and beyond 0161 832 8353

Nearby Places of Interest

Manchester 8 miles
Museum of Science and Industry Air and Space Gallery (recommended) 0161 832 2244 - 8 miles
Granada Studios (recommended) - 8 miles
Quarry Bank Mill and Styal park (recommended) - 2 miles
Terminal 1 TIC (in the international arrivals hall) 0161 436 3344
Terminal 2 TIC 0161 489 6412

Food & Accommodation

Ship Inn, Styal - 1 mile from southside. Food recommended
Etrop Grange, at airport. Food recommended, rooms from £65 0161 499 0500
Manchester Airport Hilton, at airport from £113 0161 436 4404
Forte Crest, at airport from £70 0161 437 5811
Travel Inn Heald Green -1 mile £35.00 0161 436 8921
The Wilmslow Moat House - 1 mile from southside. From £92 (£52 weekends) 01625 889988
Stanneylands Hotel, Wilmslow - 3 miles from £47 01625 525225
Rylands Farm Guest House - 1 mile from southside from £30, courtesy transport to airport 01625 535646, 548041
The Grove Guest House, Wilmslow - 3 miles from £28 01625 548484

Manston

3 miles west of Ramsgate, signposted from A253 Ramsgate Road on B2190
Kent International Airport, PO Box 500, Manston, Kent CT12 5BP
Tel: 01843 823333 Ops 0860 649578 Commercial
Fax: 01843 821386 (Ops), 01733 328004 (Commercial)

Military and civil operations coexist at Manston in a sort of uneasy cohabitation. Access to the terminal by road from the Canterbury side is across the military airfield on a main road, controlled by traffic lights. These days there is not as much military activity since the (controversial) closure of the SAR helicopter facility, but on a recent visit large numbers of newly-retired Buccaneers could be seen, lined up with geometric precision at the Eastern end of the airfield. Manston has a proud military background, flying from here dates to 1915 and it was a front-line station during the Battle of Britain. The initial trials of the 'dam busters' bouncing bomb were made here and 'Roly' Beaumont, later to become the famous Lightning test pilot, flew Typhoons here.

The 'Kent International Airport' terminal is pleasant enough, but empty for much of the time. If you really need to find somebody, try the corridor on the left as you enter the building, which leads to the main office. Flight briefing facilities and the restaurant are accessible and parking is no problem. The airfield is perhaps most remarkable these days for the unusual visitors it attracts, particularly large Ilyushin jet transports operated by Air Foyle and dilapidated 707s and DC8s, which come here to the Jet Support Centre for servicing and occasionally to be broken up for spares and scrap. Most interesting resident right now is a privately owned executive 707 that flew in a few months ago and has stayed ever since. Judging by the writs attached to it lots of people would like to speak to the owner. Chances are that it will be sold-off just to pay for the landing and parking fees!

Landing Fee

Much depends on what distance you have flown, so pay attention as they may ask questions.

Up to 1 metric tonne £14.36. 1-11/2 tonnes £21.54, 11/2-2 tonnes £28.72. 50% discount if your flight originated within 100 miles of Manston, plus a compulsory £4.50 'terminal handling fee' - even if you don't handle the terminal presumably. They do say 75% discount for training flights though. First 2 hours parking free. Thereafter, per 24 hours of part thereof: 1 tonne £4.50, 2 tonnes £6.50.

All major credit cards

Fuel

AVGAS 100LL 62p + AVTUR JET A1 28p +

All major credit cards

Flying Organisations

Seacoat's Flying Club	01843 822022
TG Aviation / Thanet Flying Club	01843 823520

Other Organisations

Modern Jet Support Centre Ltd (Maintenance)	01843 823661
TG Aviation Ltd (Maintenance)	01843 823656
Hurricane & Spitfire Memorial Building	01843 823351 Ext. 2219

Car Hire

Budget Car Hire	01843 860310
Spains	01843 592149

Taxis

Minicabs Ltd	01843 581581

Public Transport

Ramsgate railway station 3 miles. South Eastern Trains Info and Booking 01732 770111

Nearby Places of Interest

Hurricane & Spitfire Memorial Building (recommended)	01843 823351 ext. 2219
Ramsgate 3 miles	
Maritime Museum, Ramsgate 3 miles	01843 587765
Motor Museum, Ramsgate	01843 581948
Go Karting	01843 588005
Margate, 4 miles	
Shell Grotto, the only underground shell temple in the world	01843 220008
Margate Lifeboat Station	01843 221613
Margate cave, 1000 years of history	01843 220139
Laser Games in Margate	01843 295354
24 lane Ten Pin Bowling Alley	01843291010
Broadstairs, 4 miles	
Dickens House Museum	01843 862853
Dickens festival in June	

TICs - Ramsgate 01843 591086, Margate 01843 220241, Broadstairs 01843 862242

Food & Accommodation

Airport cafe (does a good set lunch, but the sandwiches are expensive)
Merlin Cafe (near Hurricane and Spitfire Memorial Building). Good value

Accommodation Booking Services	01843 865650
Innsbrook Hotel Margate from £14	01843 298946
Nayland Rock, Margate, from £19	01843 299992
Jarvis Marina, Ramsgate from £32	01843 588276
The Regency Hotel Ramsgate from £18	01843 591212

Netherthorpe

2 miles west of Worksop. See text for road directions
Netherthorpe Aerodrome, Thorpe Salvin, Worksop, Nottinghamshire
Tel: 01909 475233, 01909 473428

First opened in 1935 by the Sheffield Aero Club (who are still here) the airfield has, to all intents, always been a small, grass, light aviation aerodrome.

A surprising variety of aircraft live here, including a handful of multi-engine types (Aztec, Comanche) and several PFA types. The clubhouse has a friendly, licensed bar which serves good quality bar meals, and landings are free to PFA members. It's a good place to drop in just for a looksee, the atmosphere is friendly and informal and there is usually something going on. Remember though, Netherthorpe IS a small airfield, the longest runway (06/24) is just 450m and if you are flying in for the first time you may be asked about your short field experience.

Arriving by road is also different, although the airfield is only 3 miles from the M1 (J30). From the A619, 2-3 miles outside Worksop, take the turn signposted "Thorpe 2½". Opposite there is a billboard "Steetley Chapel". 400yds from the main road take the first left which looks like the entrance to a farm yard. Go past the Chapel along a narrow lane for about a mile until you reach a small cross-roads. Take the right hand turn and the airfield should be visible ahead, about 0·5 of a mile away. From the A57, take the signs to Shireoaks. Turn right 200 yards after the level crossing (the road goes left, you carry on straight ahead) then left for Thorpe Salvin again and the airfield is just around the next bend.

Landing Fee
Singles £3.00, multi £6.00 (although the airfield is not too keen on visiting twins).
Helicopters £5.00. For PFA members landings are free. Overnight parking as landing fee.
Cash or cheques only

Fuel
AVGAS 100LL 68p (65p to SAC members)
Cash or cheques only

Flying Organisations

Sheffield Aero Club	01909 475233
Phoenix Flying Club	01909 481802

Other Organisations

Dukeries Aviation Ltd	01909 481802
Sky Ads Banner Towing	01909 482981

Car Hire

DC Cook	0114 2484484
Eurodollar	0114 2754111
Hertz	0114 2760121
Budget	01909 476821

Taxis

Nunns	01909 500005

Public Transport
No local buses. Shireoaks railway station 1 mile, Worksop railway station 3 miles

Nearby Places of Interest

South Yorkshire Aviation Museum, Firbeck - 5 miles	01709 372821
Clumber Country Park -5 miles	
Sheffield - 12 miles	
Roche Abbey - 6 miles	01709 812739
TIC	0114 273 4671/2

Food & Accommodation

Licensed Restaurant facilities available at the airfield	
Parish Oven, Thorpe Salvin - 1 mile	01909 770685
Tom Cobbleigh/Half Moon - 2 miles	01909 720225
Forte Travel Lodge, Worksop - 3 miles room from £35	01909 501528
Hardwick Guest House, Worksop - 3 miles prices B&B from £17	01909 473162
Regency Hotel, Worksop - 3 miles from £27	01909 474108
Sherwood Guest House, Worksop - 3 miles B&B from £17.50	01909 474209

Newcastle

5 miles north-west of Newcastle-upon-Tyne on the A696
Newcastle International Airport Limited, Woolsington, Newcastle-Upon-Tyne NE13 8BZ
Tel: 0191 2860966 information desk ext. 3305/3350/3334

Newcastle's modern, busy airport was first established at Woolsington in 1935 after a protracted search for a suitable site.

Nowadays the airfield has seen extensive development and the terminal benefits from a dedicated rail link to the city. Newcastle Airport is also easy to reach by road, being well signposted from the A1. Newcastle has a good range of scheduled services and charter flights (particularly in the summer season) and the occasional military visitor. There are viewing facilities on the roof of the terminal which has all the usual airport facilities, at usual airport prices. Encouragingly, the airfield management have a progressive attitude towards GA which thrives on the southern side of the airfield. A new GA Terminal, with briefing facilities, light refreshments and a small pilot shop opened in the early 1990s, and the nearby Newcastle Aero Club bar does a roaring trade at lunchtimes. The GA apron is often full of a wide variety of types, from trainers to bizjets. To find the GA side by road, follow the 'maintenance' signs from the terminal, then signs for 'Aeroclub' and 'General Aviation'.

Landing Fee
£6.35 per 500kg +. All major credit cards

Fuel
AVGAS 100LL 59.5p + Littlewings Engineering Ltd 0191 2860966 ext 4232; daily 0800-1900 (winter), 0700-1800 (summer) except 1 May-30 Sept when 0700-1900. And by arrangement with 24 hours notice. Out of hours surcharge applies. All major credit cards
AVTUR Jet A1 25p + AirBP or Conoco 0191 286 0966 ext 4290 or 0191 2862252; 0600-2000 (winter) 0500-2100 (summer) and by arrangement. All major credit cards

Flying Organisations

Newcastle Upon Tyne Club	0191 2861321

Other Organisations

Gill Aviation Ltd	0191 2869665
Littlewings Engineering Ltd	0191 2716485
Samson Aviation Services Ltd (Handling & Pilot's Shop)	0191 2144111

Car Hire

Avis	0191 2860815
Budget	0191 2140077
Hertz	0191 2866748
Europcar	0191 286 5070

Taxis
At terminal

Public Transport
Metro link to central Newcastle (journey time 22 minutes). Regular shuttle to Newcastle Central railway station, 7 miles. Extensive local buses, including service to city centre every 30 mins 0191 232 6262. Coach services to Northern England and Scotland

Nearby Places of Interest
North East Aircraft Museum - 10 miles (follow signs for Nissan works) 0191 5190662
Bede's World (museum of early medieval Northumbria, access by Metro from airport) 0191 4892106
The North of England Open Air Museum - 8 miles. 01207 231811
Newcastle - 5 miles (Quayside, restaurants, shops, outdoor market, boat trips etc.)
TIC 0191 2610610

Food & Accommodation
Standard airport fare in terminal - on the pricey side
Good bar meals at the Newcastle Aero Club

Airport Moat House Hotel	01661 824911
The Rise Guest House - 1/2 mile, from £25	0191 2864963
The Wheatsheaf Hotel - 1/2 mile, from £35	0191 2869254
East Farm - 3/4 mile, from £20	01661 872480

North Weald

4 miles south-east of Harlow, signposted off the A414, junction 7 M11
North Weald Airfield, Epping, Essex, CM16 6AA
Tel: 01992 524510

North Weald has perhaps as rich a history as any ex-RAF airfield in the country. It was active as early as 1916, and played a key role during the Battle of Britain. Although is never received the same recognition as Biggin Hill, much of the film "The Battle of Britain" was filmed at and around North Weald. In post war years the famous Black Arrows were based here, whose 22-Hunter formations astonished Farnborough crowds in the 1950s.

Military activity ceased in 1960, and the airfield reverted to civilian use. For many years the main residents were gliders. However, since the mid-1980s that has changed with the arrival of Aces High, whose historic aircraft are based here, and the bi-annual Flight Business and General Aviation Exhibition.

The airfield's history is commemorated by 'The Squadron' operating from a collection of original huts on the airfield with a fascinating collection of memorabilia and fully working replica WWII RAF fighter base. This should a 'must visit', if only for the food from the NAAFI-style cafe, which offers a good view of proceedings from the terrace. There are number of air displays and fly-ins throughout the summer, details from 01992 522210. Even on non-display days the large collection of vintage and historic warbirds and interesting visitors make a visit well worthwhile. The airfield is right alongside the M11, (junction 7 offers easy access) and only 20 miles north-east of London. Some pilots use North Weald rather than the better known, and more expensive, London airfields (the nearest underground station is less than 10 minutes by taxi). However, it is worth remembering that North Weald is definitely a VFR airfield, with no navaids on site.

Landing Fee
Singles £5 inc. multi £10 inc. Nil for members of 'The Squadron'
Cash or cheque only

Fuel
AVGAS 100LL 55p + AVTUR JET A1 23p +
Cash or cheque only

Flying Organisations

The Squadron	01992 524510 Fax: 01992 522238
Essex Gliding Club	0181 8026663

Other Organisations

North Weald Flying Services Ltd (Maintenance)	01992 524510
Aces High Flying Museum	
39 Restoration Group	

Car Hire

Arranged via The Squadron	
Hertz	01279 433316
Avis	01279 414040

Taxis
Arranged via The Squadron

Public Transport
Buses from Epping - 3 miles, and Chipping Ongar - 3 miles. Harlow railway station, 6 miles (8 minutes by taxi). Epping London Underground station - 3 miles (£5.00 by taxi)

Nearby Places of Interest

North Weald Airfield Memorial Museum, North Weald	01992 522044
Blake Hall. Garden, Ops Room and Air Scene Museum, Chipping Ongar 3 miles	01277 362502
TIC	01245 283400

Food & Accommodation

Restaurant and bar facilities at The Squadron	
The Clock Tower Cafe Restaurant, Chipping Ongar	01277 362431
Local hotel and B&B can be arranged by The Squadron	
Bumbles, Ongar 3 miles B&B from £16	01277 362695
Uplands, Epping 4 miles B&B from £16	01992 573733

Northampton (Sywell)

5 miles north-east of Northampton signposted off A43
Sywell Aerodrome, Northampton NN6 0BT
Tel: 01604 644917

A large, and busy grass airfield, Sywell dates from 1928 when the Northamptonshire Aero Club held a 'Great Aerial Pageant' to raise funds for their first aircraft. Flying training on Tiger Moths and Ansons took place here throughout the war and a major overhaul unit, servicing Wellingtons, opened on a site on one side of the airfield. These large hangers now house a number of storage warehouses, making this part of the airfield a bit of a maze.

Civilian operations resumed in 1947. In its early years, the PFA held their annual Rally here, until its size forced a move to a bigger location. There is a fixed wing flying club and several helicopter operators (including Robinson distributors Sloane), who keep the airfield busy whenever the weather is suitable. A hotel on the airfield, adjacent to the parking area, offers food and refreshments - Sunday lunches recommended - and the rare opportunity to open your curtains in the morning and see aircraft right outside the window. Visitors can also get light refreshments at the Aero Club's clubhouse, near the Tower.

Northampton is easy to find by air (look for the large reservoir 2 miles to the north-east of the airfield) and by road - follow the 'Black Truck' signs for 'Sywell' from the A43.

Landing Fee
£7.50 (single) inc. multi £15, Helicopters £15, microlights £5 . Overnight parking £5.00
All major cards except Amex/Diners or Direct debit cards

Fuel
AVGAS 100LL 61p + AVTUR JET A1 29p +
All major cards except Amex/Diners or Direct debit cards

Flying Organisations

C J Helicopters	01604 760760
Flylight Air Sports	01604 494459
Northampton Microlight Club	01604 812290
Northamptonshire School of Flying Ltd	01604 644678
Sloane Helicopters	01604 790595

Other Organisations

March Helicopters Ltd (Maintenance)	01604 493137
Northamptonshire School of Flying (Maintenance)	01604 644678
Sloane Helicopters Ltd (Maintenance)	01604 790595
Taylor Aircraft Services Sales and Brokerage (Maintenance)	01604 492160

Car Hire

Avis	01604 602323
Eurodollar	01604 259101
Hertz	01604 768488
Europcar	01604 785178

Taxis

A1 taxis	01604 22227

Public Transport
Northampton railway station 8 miles

Nearby Places of Interest

Sywell Country Park	
Pitsford Water, fishing, boats for hire, picnicking etc. - 2 miles	01604 781350
Castle Ashby, Gardens, Craft and Rural shopping yard - 10 miles	01604 129250
Holdenby House - 12 miles (where Charles I was imprisoned)	01604 770074
Althrop House 12 miles (home of the Spencer family)	01604 770209
TIC	01604 671200

Food & Accommodation
Tea, coffee and snacks at Northamptonshire School of Flying

The Aviator Motel (on airfield) from £27.50 (weekdays) and £22.50 (w/e)	01604 642111
Horseshoe Tavern Chef & Brewer pub, about 500 meters along the road to Northampton	
Ashley House, Pitsford 2 miles B&B from £16	01604 880691
Falcon Hotel, Castle Ashby 10 miles from £45	01604 696200

Norwich

3 miles north of Norwich City centre signposted from A140
Norwich Airport Ltd, Norwich, NR6 6JA
Tel: 01603 411923 Fax: 01603 487523
Telex: 97209

RAF Horsham St. Faith was a busy wartime airfield, with bomber, fighter and reconnaissance aircraft based here. Later Hornets, Meteors, Hunters and Javelins operated from the huge concrete dispersals that are still visible around the airfield perimeter. The RAF left in 1960, and commercial aviation got off to a slow start, but by 1970 the merger of several small operators formed Air Anglia, which itself later became part of Air UK.

Nowadays, Norwich Airport is busy with Air UK's operations (their major engineering base is here), helicopter fleets servicing the North Sea oil and gas fields, and numerous GA movements. Viewing is encouraged, and the terminal is well equipped. Recent developments have produced a dedicated GA section with hangarage, maintenance and a small cafe/bar area just off the main A140, heading north. The maintenance area - also accessed from the A140 but to the south of the main airport terminal area - occupies the older part of the airfield. Here can be found the remainder of the GA operators, together with another cafe (no shortage of catering facilities here!), by the entrance to the airfield site. Norwich never appears to be very busy, but appearances in this case can be deceptive, and the occasional military visitor can enliven proceedings quite nicely.

Landing Fee

Up to 1 tonne ,£10.52 inc. standard, £6.18 training (pre-booked). 1-2 tonnes £18.40 inc. standard, £7.57 training (pre-booked). 50% discount with fuel uplift (minimum 30 lt singles, 100 lts multi). First 2 hours parking free, then £1.91 per 500kg per 24 hours or part.
All major credit cards accepted

Fuel

AVGAS 100LL 64p +, AVTUR Jet A1 24p +
All major credit cards accepted

Flying Organisations

East Coast Flight Training	01603 787187
Norfolk County Flying Club	01603 404600
Sterling Helicopters Ltd	01603 417156
The Norwich School of Flying	01603 403107

Other Organisations

City of Norwich Aviation Museum (on the airfield boundary)	01603 625309
Air UK Engineering Ltd (Maintenance)	01603 424244
Alan Mann Helicopters Ltd (Maintenance)	01603 417156
Sterling Helicopters Ltd (Maintenance)	01603 417156
Roper Aircraft Maintenance	0836 695794
Norwich Handling	01603 420645

Car Hire

Avis	01603 416719
Europcar	01603 400280
Hertz	01603 404010

Taxis

At terminal	01603 424044

Public Transport

Airport Park and Ride (£1.50 for 5 people). Full bus service, details 01603 761212.
National coach services. Norwich railway station 4 miles 01603 765676

Nearby Places of Interest

Norwich 3 miles with Cathedral and Castle	
Royal Norfolk regiment Museum 3 miles	01603 223649
Steam Museum, Buckenham 9 miles	
Norfolk Broads, boating contact	01603 31133 ext. 5005
TIC	01603 666071

Food & Accommodation

Bar and restaurant in Norfolk County Flying Club. Similar to a good pub with a selection of bar snacks and meals, all at a reasonable price, with a good view of the airfield overlooking the threshold of Rwy 09. It's open to all during the day, but restricted to members only in the evenings. From the main terminal entrance follow the road towards the Park and Ride, keep going along this road and you can't miss it.

Cafe/restaurant in terminal

Britons Arms Coffee House, Norwich	01603 623367
Stakis Airport Hotel from £60	01603 410544
Berrie Rise - 1 mile B&B from £13	01603 890713
Elm Farm Hotel - 1 mile B&B from £29	01603 898366
Arlington Hotel Norwich - 3 miles from £44	01603 617841
Friendly Lodge, Norwich from £77	01603 741161

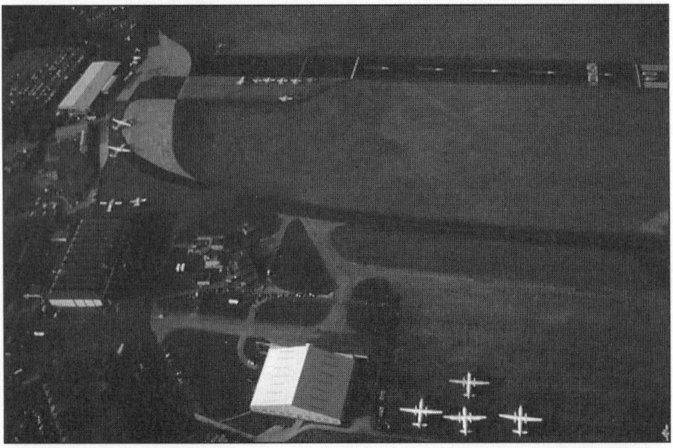

Nottingham

3 miles south-east of Nottingham signposted from A52
Nottingham Airport, Tollerton, Nottinghamshire, NG12 4GA
Tel: 01602 815050 Fax: 01602 811444

Still known locally as Tollerton, Nottingham airport is a pleasant, quiet airfield typical of many Midlands GA airfields with a wartime heritage. Leicester and Halfpenny Green are very similar, both in layout and atmosphere to Nottingham, which makes them attractive places on a sunny summer afternoon when the circuit is busy with training, and arrivals.

Opened in 1930, Nottingham Flying Club moved in a year later, but military training did not start until 1937, with Magisters and Ansons. When the war started, the trainers moved out and bombers moved in: a major maintenance base for heavy aircraft, Hampdens, Halifaxes, Liberators and Lancasters among them, was established here by Fields Aviation Services. After the war, the same company used the Tollerton facilities to dismantle and scrap large numbers of Lancasters.

Nowadays, the airfield is operated by Trumanair, whose premises include the clubhouse with bar and cafe and briefing facilities. There is also a restaurant on the airfield's southern side, which does lunches to a good standard.

Landing Fee
£10.00 (singles, half price Sat/Sun), multi from £14.00

Fuel
AVGAS 100LL 62p + AVTUR Jet A1

Flying Organisations

The Sherwood Flying Club Ltd	01159 332334
Truman Aviation Ltd	0115 9815050

Other Organisations

Truman Aviation Ltd (Aircraft sales & maintenance)	01159 815050

Car Hire

Avis	0115 9501872
Eurodollar	0115 9503385
Hertz	0115 9580575

Taxis
By arrangement

Public Transport
Nottingham railway station 3 miles

Nearby Places of Interest

The Caves of Nottingham	0115 9241424
The Lace Hall	0115 9484221
The Galleries of Justice	0115 9520558
Nottingham Goose Fair, held in October	0115 9470661
The Tales of Robin Hood	0115 9483284
Nottingham Castle	0115 9482626
Brewhouse Yard Museum, Nottingham	0115 9483504
Museum of Costume and textiles, Nottingham	0115 9483504
Canal Museum, Nottingham	0115 9598835
Greens Mill and Science Centre, Nottingham	0115 9503635
Nottingham Forest Football Club	
Holme Pierrepont Country Park, Nottingham	0115 9821212
TIC	0115 947 0661

Food & Accommodation
Club facilities and pub food at the aerodrome

Loopers Restaurant, Nottingham -3 miles (Egon Ronay)	0115 9632175
Sonny's, Nottingham - 3 miles	0115 9473041
Forte Crest, Nottingham - 3 miles	0115 9470131
Stakis Hotel, Nottingham - 3 miles	0115 9419561
Royal Moat House Hotel, Nottingham - 3 miles	0115 9414444
The Rutland Square Hotel, Nottingham - 3 miles	0115 9411114

Old Sarum

2 miles north of Salisbury, signposted from the A338
Hangar Three, Old Sarum Aerodrome, Salisbury, Wiltshire SP4 6BJ
Tel: 01722 322525 Fax: 01722 323702

The second oldest operational aerodrome in the country, Old Sarum dates back to 1915 when farm land was requisitioned to build a site for training and fighter aircraft. The wooden hangars which lend the airfield much of its distinctive character were constructed in 1917 and are now listed buildings. Today they house a variety of interesting aircraft, from the converted Shadow microlights of the Aviation for Paraplegics and Tetraplegics Trust, through various training and touring types to less common aircraft such as Siai Marchetti SF260 and DeHavilland Dove.

Re-licensed for training by the Old Sarum Flying Club in 1992, the airfield continues to grow, having recently acquired the former tower structure from Southampton Airport. The club runs a popular cafe overlooking the airfield, which offers a wide variety of home-cooked meals presented to a high standard. The menu changes frequently and, to quote the chef, 'there is not a freezer bag in sight'. On a summer's day, with the spire of Salisbury Cathedral clearly visible just 3 miles away, this is a destination that takes some beating.

Arriving by road follow signs for 'Old Sarum', then 'Old Sarum Castle'. As you near this you will see signs for the airfield itself.

Landing Fee
£7.00 (single) £4.00 (microlight). £14.00 (multi) Parking £3.50 per night. Access or Visa only

Fuel
AVGAS 100LL 64p inc. Access or Visa only

Flying Organisations

Bushpilots	01730 895034
Old Sarum Flying Club	01722 322525
Old Sarum Microlight Club	01722 414770 / 0850 516404
Shadow Flight Centre Ltd	01722 410567

Other Organisations

FLS Aerospace (Lovaux) Ltd (Maintenance)	01722 321812
Old Sarum Engineering (Maintenance)	01722 322525/410711

Car Hire

AVH Car Rental	01722 338644
Budget	01722 336444
Church Field Vehicle Rentals	01722 324306
Europcar	01722 335625

Taxis

A + B Taxis	01722 744744
Salisbury Taxis	01722 334343

Public Transport
No convenient buses. Salisbury railway station 2 miles

Nearby Places of Interest

Salisbury 2 miles	
Salisbury Cathedral	01722 328726
Salisbury Museum	01722 332151
Old Sarum Iron Age Fort, 3 miles off A36	0171 9733434
Stonehenge, 8 miles 01980 62556	
TIC	01722 334956

Food & Accommodation

The Old Sarum Restaurant in the flying club, open 0900-1700	
Don Giovanni's Italian Restaurant, (close to Salisbury Cathedral)	01722 330053
The Kings Arms, Salisbury's oldest hostelry	01722 327629
Victoria Lodge, Salisbury - 3 miles, from £25	01722 320586
Edwardian Lodge, Salisbury - 3 miles B&B from £20	01722 413329
Hayburn Wyke Guest House, Salisbury - 3 miles B&B from £21	01722 412627
Ratfyn Barrow House, Amesbury - 6 miles B&B from £24 (recommended)	01980 623422

Old Warden (Biggleswade)

6 miles east of Bedford. 2 miles due west of A1 where it bypasses Biggleswade
The Shuttleworth Collection, Old Warden/Biggleswade Aerodrome, Northill, Biggleswade, Bedfordshire SG18 9EP
Tel: 01767 627288 Fax: 01767 627745

A small airfield in open countryside, a collection of hangers backing onto woodland. Grass runways, uneven in places, and a few sheep wandering around. It could be any one of a number of English airfields - but for the residents of the hangers. Old Warden is guardian to the Shuttleworth Collection, one of the world's premier collections of vintage aircraft.

The collection was founded in the 1930s by Richard Shuttleworth, and he established the airfield on a corner of his estate. Richard Shuttleworth was killed in a flying accident after joining the RAF in the Second World war, but thankfully the collection he founded has flourished and grown.

The difference between Shuttleworth and an ordinary museum is simple - the majority of the aircraft still fly. Even on an 'ordinary' day there will be plenty to see. The five hangers house the main collection, and there are many supporting displays. There is a collection of vintage cars in the garage, and there is a shop, playground and restaurant. There are flying days during the season when the home-based aircraft are joined by warbirds of every flavour and the other machinery of the airshow circuit.

But if you really want to indulge in the heady atmosphere of Old Warden, try to attend one of the summer 'sunset displays'. On these evenings, if conditions are just right, the oldest and most frail of the collection's aircraft take to the air. To see them airborne, evening light reflected on their fabric and wood structures, is to sense the flying spirit of the pioneer years. In case you haven't guessed, it's a must!

Landing Fee
Admission to museum charged for arrivals by air. £5 per adult, £2.50 children. Under 5s free.

Fuel
AVGAS 100LL By arrangement only

Flying Organisations

Other Organisations

Shuttleworth Collection	01767 727288

Car Hire

Avis	01908 281334/ 01908 230110
Eurodollar	01908 271077/ 01234 269566
Hertz	01908 374492
Biggleswade Motor Company	01767 313788

Taxis

Maurice Taxis	01767 316438 01234 262222

Public Transport
Biggleswade railway station 3 miles - Great Northern and Network South East route to London Kings Cross. Midland mainline route to London St Pancras stops at Bedford 8 miles. Infrequent local bus services from aerodrome on United Counties route 180. Tel: 01234 262151 or Bedford County Council Leisurelink Services 01234 228337

Nearby Places of Interest

Swiss Garden (one of the UK's top gardens. Adjacent to the airfield)	01767 627666
Duxford	
Bedford 8 miles	

Food & Accommodation

Old Warden Guest House, Old Warden - 1 mile B&B from £20	01767 627201
Stratton House Hotel, Biggleswade	01767 312442
Bedfordshire Farmhouse Accommodation: Bedford 01234 870234 or Sandy	01767 682332
Kings Arms, Sandy	01767 680276
Rose & Crown Hotel, Potton	01767 2660221
Sandy Hotel	01767 692220

Oxford

Off the A44 just north of Oxford
Oxford Airport, Kidlington Oxford OX5 1RA
Tel: 01865 841234 (Ops) Fax: 01865 841165

Oxford airport is known, like the city itself, as a seat of learning. Kidlington opened in 1938 as a training ground for reserve aircrew, but became a satellite station and relief landing ground for Abingdon, Little Rissington and Brize Norton. At one time over 100 Harvards were in use from this airfield. The Oxford Air Training School (now part of CSE) has been training commercial pilots and engineers here since its origins in 1961, and the activities of CSE dominate the site. The training school teaches students for airlines around the world who fill the circuit most flying days. This and the maintenance hangars and aircraft sales help to produce a steady flow of visitors and the airfield is usually very active. The main building (under the tower) houses an excellent operations and flight planning department, a pilot shop and a good restaurant. By road the airfield is easy to reach, sandwiched between the A44 and A4260 and the airfield is visible from the A44, about two miles north of the interchange with the A40. However, public access by road is restricted by a manned security barrier and generally only those on airfield business get through.

Landing Fee
£12.00 Singles. 50% rebate with fuel uplift. Overnight parking £10.00 up to 3 tonnes.
All major credit cards

Fuel
AVGAS 100LL 60p + AVTUR JET A1 26p + All major credit cards

Flying Organisations

Oxford Air Training School	01865 841234
Air Med Pilot flight training at Air Med - scenic flights	01865 842887
McAlpine Helis (Inc Eurocopter and Turbomecca)	01865 841188
Pilot Flight Training	01865 370814
Oxair Services/Ox Helicopters	01865 370739

Other Organisations

CSE Aviation Ltd (Maintenance)	01865 841234
McAlpine Helicopters Ltd (Maintenance)	01865 841188
Oxford Aircraft Refurbishers	01865 841234
Pilots shop in operations department	
Kartex indoor karting	
RD Aviation Ltd (pilots shop near airfield)	01865 841441

Car Hire

Target (adjacent to airfield)	01865 379691
Avis	01865 249000
Eurodollar	01865 240471
Hertz	01865 57291

Taxis

James Cars	01865 375742
Woodstock Travel	01993 813434

Public Transport
Shuttle bus service into city centre. Bus stop by main gate. Oxford railway station 6 miles

Nearby Places of Interest

Oxford and all that 5 miles	
Guided walking tours of Oxford	01865 726871
Oxford Bus Museum, Long Hamborough - 2 miles (only open Sundays)	01993 883617
Morrells Brewery Tour, Oxford, every Sat and Sun	01865 792013
Woodstock - 2 miles	
Blenheim Palace - 2 miles	01993 811091
TIC	01865 726871

Food & Accommodation

Restaurant in main block, open airfield hours	
Wise Alderman canalside pub, 10 mins walk from airfield (turn right out of the airfield entrance) real ale, food and accommodation	01865 372281
Linden Tea Rooms, Woodstock - 2 miles	
Brothertons Brasserie Woodstock - 2 miles (recommended)	01993 811114
Bowood House Hotel, Kidlington - 1 mile from £38	01865 842288
Feathers Hotel Woodstock - 2 miles. THE place to eat and stay if your wallet will stretch to it. Rooms from £80	01993 812291
Regent House, Woodstock - 2 miles B&B from £40	01993 811004
Marlborough Arms, Woodstock - 2 miles from £40	01993 811227
The Vicars, Woodstock - 2 miles	01993 811212

100's of eating and accommodation possibilities in Oxford itself. Try the TIC for details

Panshanger

3 miles west of Hertford sign posted off the B1000
Panshanger Airfield, Cole Green, Hertford, Herts, SG14 2NH
Tel: 01707 391791 Fax: 01707 392792

Until a few years ago Panshanger looked destined to fade away, but a change of ownership has brought about a remarkable turnaround and now the airfield seems to have, quite literally, a new lease of life. Used partly as a decoy airfield for nearby Hatfield, Panshanger was originally known as Holywell Hyde, but was renamed in 1943 when elementary flying training took place here in Tiger Moths and, later, Chipmunks. The original wartime site has now been redeveloped as housing for Welwyn Garden City, indeed arriving aircraft taxy past rows of back gardens on their way to the parking areas.

The recently renovated clubhouse is equipped with a large wood-burning stove, and has (literally) a warm welcome for visitors. Refreshments and light snacks are available and now that the hangar is being rebuilt it is hoped that the number of resident aircraft will increase.

If arriving by road, take the B1000 from Hertford (turn left, just behind the railway station) towards Welwyn and Digswell. About 1-2 miles outside Hertford take the left turn signposted 'Cole Green', the airfield is about 1/4 of a mile up the hill. Alternatively take junction 6 off the A1(M). Although the B1000 is badly signposted from here try following signs for Tewin. The airfield sits just off a lane heading south from this road, about halfway between Hertford and Welwyn.

Landing Fee
Singles £5.00, multi £10.00
Cash and Cheques only

Fuel
AVGAS 100LL 55p +
Cash and Cheques only

Flying Organisations

East Herts Flying School & Pitts Special Experience	01707 391791

Other Organisations

Car Hire

Hertz	01707 331433
Europcar	01438 715888

Taxis

Castle Cabs	01992 501002
B. A. Taxis	01992 503222
County Cabs	01992 504111

Public Transport
Hertford railway station 3 miles, frequent services to London. Bus 339 Panshanger village to Welwyn and Watford once a hour, Mon-Sat. Bus 724 (Stansted - Heathrow via Welwyn and Watford) stops at Panshanger village every hour Mon-Sat and 4 times on Sun.

Nearby Places of Interest

Hertford Castle - 3 miles	01992 584322
Hertford Museum - 3 miles	01992 582686
Hatfield House - 5 miles	01707 262823
Ware Museum - 5 miles	01920 487848
Roman Baths, Welwyn by pass - 4 miles	01707 271362
Knebworth House and Gardens - 8 miles	01438 812661
TIC	01707 339664

Food & Accommodation

Snacks at aerodrome	
Homestead Court Hotel, 2 miles	01707 324336
Hatfield Lodge Hotel & Conference Centre, 4 miles from £25	01707 272661
The Hall House, 3 miles from £48	01992 582807
Mrs Cook, Welwyn Garden City, B&B from £20	01707 322724
Mrs Densham, Welwyn Garden City, B&B from £15	01707 323868

Perranporth

2 miles south-west of Perranporth signposted from B3285
The Airfield, Higher Trevellas, St. Agnes, Cornwall, TR5 0XS
Tel: 01872 552266, 553310

Today, other than the hard runways, little remains of the former wartime airfield of Perranporth, although it should be said that the airfield was never more than sparsely equipped in the first place. Envisaged as a satellite for Portreath, Spitfires were operated from here and, later in the war, Avengers and Swordfish came here to mount coastal patrols in the run up to Operation Overlord - the D Day landings. After the war, the airfield's small size and windswept cliff-top location led to its closure for military service in 1946, but it reopened as a civil aerodrome in 1951, unfortunately with little commercial success. Nowadays the airfield is used for gliding and private flying training, based in the old control tower building, and the operators encourage visitors. In 1995 Perranporth won the removal of restrictive conditions that the local council had sought to place on movements - an important victory in GA's fight for wider recognition.

The nearby town of Perranporth is a charming, typical North Cornish town, and the rugged coastline offers some spectacular walks. The airfield is alongside the B3285, at Trevellas, which is the locals' name for the airfield.

Landing Fee
Two seat aircraft £8 inc. four seat aircraft £10.50 inc.
Cash or cheque only

Fuel
AVGAS 100LL 63p +
Cash or cheque only

Flying Organisations

Perranporth Flying Club (Truro Aviation Ltd)	01872 553310
Cornish Gliding & Flying Club	01872 572124

Other Organisations

Car Hire

Avis	01326 211511
Eurodollar	01637 850750

Taxis

Atlantic Taxis	01872 572126

Public Transport
Newquay railway station 8 miles, Truro railway station 8 miles

Nearby Places of Interest

The World in Miniature 2 miles	01872 572828
Cider Farm, Penhallow 3 miles	01872 573356
Tehidy Country Park 5 miles	01209 714494
Truro 8 miles	
Flambards Theme Park 10 miles	01326 564093
Goonhilly Down Earth Station 12 miles	01326 221333
TIC	01872 573368

Food & Accommodation

Beach Dunes Hotel - 1 mile from £47	01872 572263
Mount Pleasant Farmhouse - 2 miles B&B from £13.50	01872 572418
Villa Margarita - 2 miles B&B from £21	01872 572063
Aviary Court - 5 miles B&B from £54	01209 842256
Cliffside Hotel - 2 miles from £13.50	01872 573297
Oak Tree Restaurant, food and accommodation	01872 561111

Peterborough (Conington)

7 miles south of Peterborough, signposted off the A1
Klingair Limited, Peterborough Business Airfield, Holme, Peterborough PE7 3PX
Tel: 01487 832022 Fax: 01487 832614

Known variously as Conington or Peterborough Business Airfield today, the airfield on this site was called Glatton in 1943 when it was built. It was home to USAAF squadrons of B17 Flying Fortresses, and later large numbers of Liberators and Lancasters used the airfield.

Only a portion of the original site remains in use today, although it is still well-kept. A new clubhouse/reception building has just been built, which should offer better facilities than the old portable buildings it replaces, but at the moment only parts of it are in use. The operators hope

to develop the airfield for business and recreational use, with the intention of attracting more and varied aircraft types to base themselves here. The airfield is clearly signposted from the A1 south of Peterborough, and from the A1 is just through the small village of Conington.

Landing Fee
£9.00 inc.(singles), £18.00 + (light twins).
Visa, Mastercard, Diners. No Amex/Switch

Fuel
AVGAS 100LL 63p + AVTUR Jet A1 28p +
Visa, Mastercard, Diners. No Amex/Switch

Flying Organisations
Klingair Flying Club 01487 832022

Other Organisations
Klingair Ltd (maintenance & sales) 01487 832022

Car Hire
Avis 01733 349489
Eurodollar 01733 310283
Hertz 0173 3893083

Taxis
Anglis Taxis 01733 66661
1st Ace Hereward cabs 01733 67060
3 Star Ambassador Taxis 01733 6777/244440

Public Transport
Viscount Bus and Coach Company, info. 01733 54571. Peterborough railway station 6 miles

Nearby Places of Interest
Nene Valley Railway 6 miles 01780 782854
Fotheringhay, birthplace of Richard III, prison and execution place of Mary Queen of Scots, 8 miles 01833 274333
Guided walks around Peterborough, contact TIC
Peterborough Cathedral 7 miles 01733 343342
Museum and Art gallery 7 miles 01733 343329
TIC 01733 317336
See also Peterborough Sibson

Food & Accommodation
Snack bar and club facilities in the new GA building
Admiral Wells Pub, 1/2 mile. Bar food & restaurant
Mrs B. McCoy B&B, Conington village 1/2 mile 01487 832642
Bell Inn, Stilton - 3 miles from £55 01733 241066
See also Peterborough Sibson

Peterborough (Sibson)

6 miles west of Peterborough on the B671
Walkbury Flying Club, Sibson Aerodrome, Wansford,
Peterborough PE8 6NE
Tel: 01832 280289, 01733 235187

Opened in 1940, pilots began training here in 1941, on Oxfords and Tutors, later arrivals being Masters and the occasional Hurricane. Today Sibson houses a wide variety of unusual aircraft, including a number of PFA types, and a large transporter for the resident parachute club. In recent years this has been a Skyvan, a Pilatus Porter and a Polish Turbo LET, but currently the ubiquitous Cessna 206 fills the role. The parachute club has a bar and cafe, but this is not open all the time, so check before setting off if you are relying on catering. You can, however, get a coffee and a chat in the 'tower' (on the side of the main hanger), and there are a number of excellent pubs and restaurants in the adjacent villages - especially at Wansford.

RAF Wittering's circuit is clearly visible from Sibson, and the area can get quite busy when they are recovering their Harriers. The A1 is visible from the tower and access to Sibson by road is straightforward - take the A605 to Elton from the A1 south of Peterborough, then north up the B671. Alternatively, from the north or west, head south onto the B671 from the A47, just off the A1. From either direction Sibson Airfield is well signposted.

Landing Fee
£5.88 single. £11.75 multi. Overnight parking free. Longer period by arrangement.
Access and Visa only with a 5% surcharge

Fuel
AVGAS 100LL 59.5p +
Access and Visa only with a 5% surcharge

Flying Organisations

Walkbury Flying Club	01832 280289

Other Organisations

Busy Bee Aero Engineering	01832 280579
Parachute Centre	01830 280490

Car Hire

Avis	01733 349489
Eurodollar	01733 310283
Hertz	0173 3893083

Taxis

Anglis Taxis	01733 66661
1st Ace Hereward cabs	01733 67060
3 Star Ambassador Taxis	01733 6777/244440

Public Transport
Viscount Bus and Coach Company, info. 01733 54571. Peterborough railway station 8 miles

Nearby Places of Interest
No spotters airside. Hangers viewed by request.

Nene Valley Railway - 3 miles	01780 782854
Rutland Water & attractions - 10 miles	01780 460321
East of England Showground - 5 miles west of Peterborough	01733 234451
RAF Wittering - 3 miles, the RAF's oldest operational station and home to Harrier. Guided tours available though opening is limited.	01780 64501 ext. 7470
TIC	01733 317336

Food & Accommodation
The Birdland bar (01832 280404) is open Wed-Sun, 0800-2200 in the summer and 0800-1800 at weekends only during the winter. It is open to all and does snack type food and breakfasts.
Possible accommodation at Para Centre on the airfield

Cross Keys, Wansford - 3 miles (recommended)	01780 782266
Haycock Hotel (****),Wansford - 3 miles	01780 782223
Paper Mills Pub and B&B, Wansford - 3 miles	01780 782328

Plymouth (City)

5 miles north of Plymouth, signposted off A386
Plymouth City Airport, Crownhill, Plymouth Devon PL6 8BW
Tel: 01752 772752 (information) Fax: 01752 793067
Telex: 45465

A small but quite busy airfield, conveniently close to Plymouth town, the airfield was established in 1931 with commercial services to Cardiff commencing the following year. During the Second World War, the airfield was pressed into service as Exeter became overcrowded.

Commercial activity recommenced in 1946, and the most significant development came with the arrival of Brymon Airways in 1975. Now part of British Airways, Brymon operate the distinctive 4-engined STOL commuter turboprop, the deHavilland Canada Dash 7 whose characteristic steep approaches into Plymouth's short runways are a remarkable sight. Also in evidence here are the Grob 115s of the Royal Navy's flying grading flight. The terminal building can get a bit busy when a scheduled flight arrives or departs, but the restaurant offers a well-prepared, if limited, menu and a good cup of tea. The airport is well signposted from the A30 which runs through Plymouth, and lies just to the north of the town centre off the A386.

Landing Fee
200-500Kg £8.70 + ; 500-1499Kg: £15.52 + ; 1500-1990Kg £22.97 +
All major credit cards

Fuel
AVGAS 100LL 62.36p + AVTUR JET A1 27.25p +
All major credit cards

Flying Organisations

Plymouth School of Flying Ltd	01752 773335

Other Organisations

Maersk Air Engineering Ltd (Maintenance)	01752 705151
Plymouth Executive Aviation Ltd (Maintenance)	01752 786611

Car Hire

Avis	01752 221550
Eurodollar	01752 220877
Hertz	01752 705819
Europcar	01752 669859

Taxis
Available at terminal

Public Transport
Plymouth railway station 3 miles

Nearby Places of Interest

Dartmoor National Park - 8 miles	01822 890567
Plymouth - 3 miles, is full of things nautical including Plymouth Hoe and the Naval Dockyards at Devonport	
Plymouth Boat Cruises	01752 822797
Tamar Cruising	01752 822105
RAF Mountbatten, tours arranged via Blue Badge Tour Services	01752 775841
TIC	01752 264849

Food & Accommodation

Restaurant in terminal	
The Lopes Arms, Roborough - 1 mile	01752 769633
Midway, Roborough - 1 mile	01752 733221
The China House pub & restaurant, overlooking Sutton Harbour, Plymouth	01752 260930
Loma Loma, Plymouth Hoe B&B from £15	01752 661859
Plymouth Moat House, Plymouth centre from £30	01752 662866
Georgian House Hotel, Plymouth Hoe from £25	01752 663237
Travel Inn, Crabtree - 3 miles from £35 per room	01752 600660

Popham

9 miles north of Winchester. Alongside the A303
Popham Airfield, Winchester, Hampshire, SO21 3HB
Tel: 01256 397733 Fax: 01256 397114

Owned and operated by Charles Church (Spitfires) Ltd, alas the Spitfires are not here, being kept and restored a few miles away. What you will see is a fine and varied collection of light aircraft, including several Luscombes, Beagle Pups, Jodels, Austers and Yak 52s. In fine weather anytime, and particularly at the weekends, the airfield comes alive with activity from microlights to twin-engined tourers. There are a number of fly-ins throughout the season and it is also rumoured that occasionally impromptu cricket matches are held on the runway (on non-flying days presumably!).There is an excellent cafe, with a terrace alongside the runway, and tea and coffee are always available. The lunches are popular and are served "until we run out", so get in early if eating is your intention, or even better call ahead and book a table. The local PFA Andover Strut meets here the second Monday each month, and the Spitfire Club has social evenings the last Friday each month.

The airfield is alongside the A303, just before it joins the M3. From the east, take the second exit for Micheldever Station (and Overton), and a quick right-left across the road at the bottom of the slip-road (signposted to Popham) puts you on the lane to the airfield. From the west, leave the A303 on the sliproad to Micheldever Station and Overton before the services (the airfield water tower may be visible to your right), turn right under the A303 at the bottom of the slip road, and right again as if to rejoin the A303 in the opposite direction.

Landing Fee
£4.00 non members inc. Members free
Cash or cheque only

Fuel
AVGAS 100LL 67p inc.
Cash or cheque only

Flying Organisations
Airbourne Aviation 01256 398254

Other Organisations
Wiltshire Aircraft Maintenance 01256 398372

Car Hire

Martins Auto Rent	01256 244448
Avis	01256 63600
Eurodollar	01256 477777
Hertz	01256 55000

Taxis
Via the airfield, or
Grassby's Taxis 01256 21904

Public Transport
Micheldever railway station 2 miles

Nearby Places of Interest

Winchester 6 miles	
Winchester Cathedral	01962 866854
City Mill, Winchester	01962 870057
Peninsula Barracks Military Museum, Winchester	01962 864176
Basingstoke Canal Centre 10 miles	01252 370073
TIC	01256 817618

Food & Accommodation

Airport Cafe, Sunday lunches recommended	
The Cathedral Refectory, Winchester (Egon Ronay)	01962 853224
Elizabethan Restaurant, Winchester	01962 853566
The Copper Beeches Hotel 5 miles from £20	01256 28528
Audleys Wood Thistle Hotel 5 miles from £46	01256 817555
Hilton National, Basingstoke 5 miles from £74	01256 460460

Redhill

2 miles south-east of Redhill, 2 miles off the A25
Terminal Building, Redhill Aerodrome, Surrey RH1 5YP
Tel: 01737 823377 (Admin) Fax: 01737 822110
Telex: 929100REDAIR G

Redhill Aerodrome traces its origins back to 1933 when the first planning permission was granted for use of the land as an aerodrome. During the Second World War Spitfires flew here, although the station's activities were somewhat eclipsed by those at nearby Biggin Hill.

In the 1970s, the airfield became the base of operations for Bristow Helicopters whose buildings dominate the airfield and whose helicopter activity on the airfield is considerable. In addition to Bristow, two other helicopter operators are based here, alongside the fixed-wing flying clubs, and a microlight operator. Redhill has a thriving GA community, and the airfield has plans to expand and encompass the whole range of GA. Ironically, these plans have probably been aided by the recent refusal to grant planning permission to develop the airfield into a commuter feederliner airport with links to nearby Gatwick.

If you're looking for the airfield by road, take the 'South Nutfield' turning off the A25. Stay with this road and you will see airport signs as you near it.

Landing Fee
0- 1·5 T £10.50 +, 1·5 - 2 T £14.50 +. Heli - single £12.00 +, multi £30.00 +. 50% rebate if uplifting fuel. Overnight parking: single £5.00, multi £6.50. Visa/Access/Diners

Fuel
AVGAS 100LL 57p+ AVTUR JET A-1 27p + (01737 823518). Available 0900-1630 (winter) 0800-1830 (summer). Visa/Access/Diners

Flying Organisations

Bristows Helicopters Ltd	01737 822353
Cabair Flight Training (Redhill)	01737 822166
Cloudbase Aviation	01737 822423/0850 852610
Cubair	01737 822124
Redhill Aviation	01737 822959
Redhill Helicopter Centre	01737 823287
Rotorvation Helicopter Training School	01322 865992/862289

Other Organisations

Acebell Aviation (Acebell) Ltd (Maintenance)	01737 822212
Aviation Furnishings International Ltd (Maintenance)	01737 822751/2
Bristow Helicopters Ltd (Maintenance)	01737 822353
Redhill Engineering (Maintenance)	01737 822959

Car Hire

Avis	01293 529721
Hertz	01293 530555

Taxis

Belfry	01737 766111
Roadrunners	01737 645555

Public Transport
Redhill railway station 2 miles

Nearby Places of Interest

Central London 15 miles	
Croydon site of London's original airport 10 miles - the old terminal is still there	
Croydon Clock Tower includes museum and art gallery	0181 2531030
Reigate Priory Museum 5 miles	01737 245065
London Gatwick Airport 5 miles	
TIC	0181 2531009

Food & Accommodation

Vending machines in the tower building	
Cafe in Redhill Aviation open 1000-1600, bar lunchtimes and evenings	
Arun Lodge Guest House, Redhill - 2 miles B&B from £25	01737 761933
Lynwood Guest House, Redhill - 2 miles B&B from £20	01737 766894
Nutfield Priory, Redhill - 2 miles from £95	01737 822066
Reigate Manor Hotel, Reigate - 5 miles from £58	01737 240125
Travel Inn, Salfords - 2 miles room from £35	01737 767277

Retford (Gamston)

2 miles south of Retford on the B6387. Signposted from the southbound A1
Retford/Gamston Airport, Retford, Nottinghamshire, DN22 0QL
Tel: 01777 838593/838594, 01777 838521 (out of hours)
Fax: 01777 838035

These days, little evidence of a wartime station (RAF Gamston) remains, although the RAF operated here well into the 1950s. The buildings are modern and the airfield has a neat, tidy appearance, as befits an operation which is keen to develop private and business operations. The main building, which houses the tower, flight briefing and operations, also has a small rest area with coffee and snack machines, but as yet there are no more substantial catering facilities. The airfield staff are keen to develop the airfield however, and visitors can expect a warm, and helpful reception. The resident operators mainly fly Beech/Cessna/Piper types, but with a number of King Airs and Sikorsky S76s. Flying training is at present restricted by the airfield's planning licence, but advanced instruction, microlighting and gliding take place here. If you have time hanger viewing is possible if you ask first at operations, if you are in a hurry they say they specialise in quick turnarounds.

The airfield is close to the A1 and A57 near Worksop and Retford, and is well signposted. It is 35 mins from Sheffield, 25 mins from Doncaster

Landing Fee
Single £5.11 +, Heli £6.00 +, Multi £4.00 per 500kg or part thereof + Parking: Singles £5.00, helis £7.50, multis £7.50 (up to 2500kg) All major cards except Amex

Fuel
AVGAS 100LL 59p + AVTUR Jet A1 25p +
All major cards except Amex

Flying Organisations

ALH Skytrain	01777 838202
Dukeries Gliding Club	01909 501032
Eastern Air Centre Ltd / The Flight Centre	01777 838222
Roylair Services Ltd	01777 839049

Other Organisations

Lambson Aviation Ltd T/A Knight Air (Maintenance)	01777 838595

Car Hire

Via operations	
Budget	01909 476821

Taxis

Via operations	
BJ's (discount for visiting pilots)	01777 228999/0860 876766

Public Transport
Gamston village 1/2 mile served by Nottingham - Doncaster bus 3 times daily. Retford railway station 3 miles

Nearby Places of Interest

Doncaster races (25 mins by road)	
Sundown Adventureland - 2 miles	01777 248274
The World of Robin Hood - 3 miles	01623 836003
Bassetlaw Museum - 3 miles	01777 706741
Ollerton Country Park and Abbey - 6 miles	01623 824153
Sherwood Forest Visitor Centre - 10 miles	
TIC	01777 860780

Food & Accommodation

Local pubs 1 mile - details from operations	
Travel Lodge - 3 miles room from £33	01909 591775
West Retford Hotel from £29	01777 706333
Barneys Country Club - 3 miles	01623 860210
The Barns Guest House - 3 miles B&B from £19	01777 706336
Clumber Park Hotel - 5 miles, from £45	01623 835333

Rochester

2 miles south of Rochester, signposted from A229 M2 junction 3
Rochester Aerodrome, Rochester, Kent ME1 2XX
Tel: 01634 816133 / 816127

Rochester Airport is owned and operated by GEC Marconi Avionics, who occupy the buildings first used by Short Bros. in 1934 to build Scylla flying boats. During the War four-engine Stirling bombers were built here in some numbers although flying activity was limited - not surprising given the size of the airfield!

Nowadays Rochester Aviation operate a flying school here using Robin DR400s and visiting pilots can get a coffee and snacks from a vending machine in their rooms below the tower. Unfortunately this is the extent of the catering available on site, although a hotel at the airfield entrance offers restaurant and coffee-shop facilities, at a price. A number of privately owned aircraft occupy the hangar and parking area in front, and the Beech Expeditor owned by a local aircraft restoration group has become something of a fixture.

Rochester scores high on the 'friendliness' scale. The ATC and flying school staff go out of their way to make visitors welcome and hanger visits are OK if you ask first.

Arriving by road, the airport is more properly in Chatham, alongside the A229 and close to the M2 (junction 3). Access via either the M2 or M20 (junction 6) is simple from the M25. The airfield entrance is on a dual-carriageway section of the A229, just after a blind bend which must be negotiated with caution - look for the signs to the Forte (now Granada) Hotel. Traffic lights control access to the airfield across the end of the runway - ignore them at your peril!

Landing Fee
£6.00 single, £10 multi. Overnight parking £3.50/£5.00
Cash and cheque only

Fuel
AVGAS 55p + AVTUR Jet A1 25p +
Cash and cheque only

Flying Organisations

Cherokee Flying Group	01322 666345
London Aerial Tours	0181 946 6950
Rochester Aviation Ltd	01634 816340
Rotorvation Helicopter Training School	01322 865992
Three Point Flying	01634 861265

Other Organisations

GEC Avionics Ltd (Maintenance)	01634 844400
Kent Aerospace Castings plc (Maintenance)	01634 660831
Medway Aircraft Preservation Society	
Spitfire/Hurricane workshop open weekends	01634 816492

Car Hire

Kennings	01634 845145

Taxis

Medway Cab Co	01634 848848
New Cabs	01634 818777
Strood Cabs	01634 710001
Volkes	01634 843601/222222

Public Transport
Chatham - Maidstone 101 bus stop outside gate, Public Transport information 0800 696996
Chatham railway station 3 miles, 35 mins to Victoria, Rail Enquiries 01732 770111

Nearby Places of Interest

Rochester 2 miles	
Guided walks, Rochester - 2 miles	01634 843666
Rochester Tours, Rochester - 2 miles	01634 405228
Paddle Steamer cruises,	
Chatham Historic Dockyard & Rochester Pier	01634 827648
Medway Heritage Centre, Chatham	01634 407116/408437
Historic Dockyard, Chatham	01634 812551
TIC	01634 843666

Food & Accommodation

Vending machines in the Flying Club

Forte Crest Hotel / Forte Posthouse on boundary of field. Food reasonable but not cheap.

Accommodation from £69 (weekdays) and £49 (weekends)	01634 687111
Dukes House Chatham 5 mins walk B&B from £12	01634 843977
Regent Guest House, Chatham 5 mins walk from B&B from £12	01634 841810
Kings Head Hotel, High Street, Rochester - 2 miles from £20	01634 842709
Phoenix Hotel 5 mins walk	01634 409980

Sandtoft

7 miles south-west of Scunthorpe signposted off A18, M180 J2
Sandtoft Aerodrome, Belton, Doncaster, South Yorkshire, DN4 1PN
Tel: 01427 873676 Fax: 01427 874680

Once a huge bomber airfield, opened in 1944 as a training unit with Halifaxes, nowadays only a small part of Sandtoft airfield remains active for flying purposes, the majority of it has returned to farmland or become and a vague, sprawling collection of warehouses called the Sandtoft Industrial Estate. Clearly visible from the M180 - if you know where to look between junctions 1 and 2 - the airfield lies on a lane which parallels the motorway, about 1/4 mile to the south.

There are two entrances to the airfield, either side of the runway, but the tower, flying club and restaurant/bar occupy the two-storey building on the eastern side of the runway. There are a good number of aircraft based here, including a Jet Provost and Rockwell Turbo-Commander 690 used for aerial survey work, but the aircraft are scattered around the airfield in two or three locations and difficult to see all in one go. The restaurant, and adjacent bar are well appointed and of a good standard.

By road, leave the M180 at junction 2 following directions for 'Gainsborough' initially. In the village of Belton (less than a mile from the motorway) turn right at the mini-roundabout opposite a post office. The airfield is a couple of miles along this road, on your left.

Landing Fee
£5.00 (singles) £10 (multi)
Visa, subject to 3% surcharge

Fuel
AVGAS 100LL 59p +
Visa, subject to 3% surcharge

Flying Organisations

Sandtoft Aero Club	01427 873676
Yorkshire Microlight Centre	01132 563049 0860 496060

Other Organisations

Cooper Aerial Surveys Engineering Ltd	01427 874423

Car Hire

Avis	01302 310154
Eurodollar	01302 310061

Taxis

A1 24hr Taxis	01724 871827
Epworth taxis	01427 874569

Public Transport
Thorne railway station 4 miles

Nearby Places of Interest

Sandtoft Transport Centre - 1 mile	01302 842948
Doncaster Race Course	01302 320066
The Doncaster Bowl, Doncaster - 8 miles	01302 531122
Cusworth Hall, (includes museum of South Yorkshire Life)	01302 782342
The Dome, Doncaster.	
Europe's largest indoor leisure complex	01302 370888
Epworth Old Rectory, Epworth - 5 miles	01427 872268
TIC	01302 734309

Food & Accommodation

Restaurant and bar at airfield	
The Gateway Inn and restaurant - 6 miles	01302 882849
The Red Lion, Epworth - 5 miles B&B	01427 872208
Brickmakers Arms, B&B	01427 890375
Campanile Hotel, Doncaster Leisure Park.	
Accommodation and food, competitive rates.	01302 370770

Scilly Isles

1 mile east of Hugh Town, St. Mary's
St. Mary's Airport, St. Mary's, Isles of Scilly, TR21 0NG
Tel: 01720 422677 Fax: 01720 422226

Scheduled services between here and Land's End (St. Just) began in 1937, and even today aircraft maintaining the air links to the mainland are the main users of St Mary's.

Nowadays the modernised airport - the present terminal and tower buildings opened in 1975 - caters for commercial traffic from Penzance Heliport and Plymouth, as well as the modest service maintained from Land's End and other mainland airports in the summer. The runway was lengthened in 1990 but even so commercial visitors are restricted to Twin Otters, Islanders & Skyvans. Apart from the lifeline for the islanders, the Scilly Isles' own individual attractions provide ample tourist traffic and arrival by air avoids a two hour ferry trip. There are few resident aircraft to view, but that is not the attraction here. There is catering on the airfield, in the terminal building, but a short and pleasant walk from the airfield brings one to the beach, complete with a small cafe. St Mary's is a popular light aircraft destination in the Summer. One recent visitor to the airport reports an unusual piece of aerodrome information passed by Air Traffic: "Golf - Tango Sierra, the cow in your ten o'clock IS tethered!"

Landing Fee
Singles £10.85 inc. multi £16.05 inc. Parking £4.65 (single), £5.65 (multi) per 24hr period.
Cash and cheque only

Fuel

Flying Organisations

Other Organisations

Car Hire
Most prefer not to!

Taxis

Scilly Cabs	01720 422901 (mobile 0836 253063)
Paul's London Taxis (bit far from home isn't he?)	0374 299885
Allan's Taxis	01720 422635 (mobile 0836 737824)

Public Transport
"Not really" we were told!

Nearby Places of Interest

Longstone Heritage and Leisure Centre, Hugh Town - 2 miles	01720 22924
Isles of Scilly Museum - 2 miles	
Scuba Diving	01720 22595
Sailing	01720 22037/23041
Tresco Gardens	01720 422849
Cromwell's Castle, Tresco	
King Charles Castle, Tresco	
Glorious QUIET beaches	
The other islands (escape before the Scillonian docks to more peace and quiet)	
TIC	01720 422536

Food & Accommodation

Buffet & bar in terminal	
Tregarthen's Hotel, Little Western Bar, St Mary's (highly recommended)	01720 22540
Island Hotel Restaurant, Tresco. Good food, rooms from £60	01720 22883
Mermaid Inn, Hugh Town - 2 miles, at the harbour	
Atlantic Hotel, St Mary's from £44	01720 422417
The Harbourside Hotel, St Mary's from £36	01720 422352
Blue Carn Cottage, Hugh Town B&B from £16.50	01720 422309
New Inn, Tresco, from £40	01720 422844

Seething

9 miles south of Norwich signposted from B1332
Seething Aerodrome, Brooke, Norwich, NR15 1EL
Tel: 01508 550453 (airfield), 01508 558013 (Seething Aviation Ltd), 01502 711852 (out of hours)

Most days Seething is quiet and peaceful (although it can get busy at weekends) and it might be difficult to imagine Seething as it is was when the 448th had their Liberators here. There is a memorial here to the 448th Bomber Group which is worth reading as it gives a sense of the wartime life and death existence that was once the daily routine here.

Halfway between the A146 and the B1332, about 10 miles south east of Norwich, the airfield has a smart clubhouse, and a number of resident aircraft but catering facilities are limited. In recent years, time and money have been spent improving the airfield, including resurfacing the runway. Hopefully, given enough visitors, the facilities will be further developed in time. Seething is a nice place for a cup of tea and a chat, well worth a Sunday afternoon's outing - particularly as the airfield has been getting good recommendations from recent visitors.

Landing Fee
Business flights -£6.00 (singles), £12.00 (multi). Cash and cheque only. No landing fee for private flights, but a donation to assist in runway maintenance would be appreciated

Fuel
AVGAS 100LL 62p +
Cash and cheque only

Flying Organisations
Waveney Flying Group 01508 550453

Other Organisations
Seething Aviation (maintenance) 01508 558013
Station 146 Tower, memorial to 448th Bomb Group, Seething

Car Hire
Budget 01603 484004

Taxis
Bestway 01603 624444

Public Transport
No convenient buses
Beccles railway station 9 miles

Nearby Places of Interest
The Norfolk Broads 01502 713196
Hales Hall - 4 miles a 16th century manor
Norfolk and Suffolk Aviation Museum - 5 miles 01502 562944
TIC 01502 713196

Food & Accommodation
Snacks, hot and cold food at aerodrome
Numerous pubs in the vicinity, the airfield staff will point you in the right direction
Park Farm, Bungay - 5 miles B&B from £22 01986 892180
Shrubland Farm, Beccles - 9 miles B&B from £18 01502 677241
Green farm, Geldeston - 7 miles B&B from £18 01508 518028

Sherburn-in-Elmet

6 miles west of Selby
Sherburn-in-Elmet Aerodrome, Lennerton Lane, Sherburn-in-Elmet, West Yorks, LB25 6JE
Tel: 01977 683699 Fax: 01977 683699

Even the most casual visitor to Sherburn-in-Elmet will probably notice the references to Ginger Lacey, the wartime ace stationed here, who subsequently had a long association with the Sherburn Aero Club. His exploits are recounted in a panel and display case in the smart clubhouse bar, which incidentally serves excellent food and drink - the all-day breakfast deserving special mention - with a varied menu of freshly prepared meals.

The airfield dates from 1918, when Blackburn Aircraft established a factory to build seaplanes and carrier-borne aircraft here. Hurricanes were based here during WW2 and the airfield was a base for repair, maintenance and aircraft manufacture - Swordfish aircraft were built here in large numbers. In the 1960s and 70s Grumman aircraft were assembled here and each year Sherburn hosts a fly-in when Grumman aircraft from all over Europe arrive back at their 'birth place'.

The former main tarmac runway is now a vehicle test track so Sherburn uses three excellent grass runways for the busy flying club and various resident aircraft. The airfield is easy to reach by road, and id about three miles east of the A1, just off the B1222. From Cawood take the B1222 signposted for 'Sherburn' and look for the signs to the Aero Club on your right a few hundred yards after crossing the railway line from Sherburn.

Landing Fee
£3.00 (singles), £6.00 (multi) Helicopters £6.00 inc. Overnight parking singles £6.00 inc. multi £8.00 inc.
Major credit cards except Amex and Diners

Fuel
AVGAS 100LL 65p inc.
Major credit cards except Amex and Diners

Flying Organisations	
Sherburn Aero Club Ltd	01977 682674
Other Organisations	
Sherburn Engineering Ltd (Maintenance)	01977 685296
Car Hire	
Avis	0113 2439771
Eurodollar	0113 2777957
Hertz	0113 2504811
Taxis	
Windmill Private Hire	01937 832979
Speedway (yes, really)	01977 681381
Public Transport	
South Milford railway station 2 miles	
Nearby Places of Interest	
Selby Abbey - 5 miles	01757 703123
Roman remains in Castleford - 6 miles	
Castleford Museum	01977 559552
TIC	01757 703263
Food & Accommodation	
Restaurant facilities at airfield	
Wheelgate Guest House,	
Sherburn-in-Elmet B&B from £20	01977 682231
Granada Lodge, junction 33 of M62 - 6 miles from £39	0800 555300
Londesborough Arms Hotel, Selby - 8 miles from £38	01757 707355
Brook Street Guest House, Selby - 8 miles B&B from £12	01757 708208

Shipdham

4 miles south of East Dereham signposted from A1075
Arrow Air Services (Engineering) Ltd, Shipdham Aerodrome, Thetford, Norfolk IP25 7SB
Tel: 01362 820337/820162

Home, in 1942, to the B24 Liberators of the 44th Bomb Group 8th Air Force, whose "Flying 8-ball" motif still abounds on the airfield, Shipdham played a significant part in the bomber offensive over Europe in the second half of the war. As with many of the bases constructed solely for the Americans, Shipdham closed soon after hostilities ceased.

Reopened in 1970 by Arrow Air Services, who still operate the airfield and its associated flying club, the wartime atmosphere still lingers. There is an interesting collection of memorabilia housed in the clubhouse, recalling life as it was when the 44th were here. Around the airfield much of the land has returned to farmland, many of the buildings have succumbed to disrepair and the paved surface has deteriorated in places. However, there are serious plans afoot to improve the airfield, although nothing confirmed at the time of writing.

The bar offers good hospitality and excellent cooked food, and apart from the training fleet there are a few interesting aircraft around. The airfield is visible from the A1075, to the east of Shipdham village, halfway between East Dereham and Watton. In any case the airfield is clearly signposted from Shipdham itself, on the left as you enter the village from the north.

Landing Fee
Free during daytime - 'donation to runway fund' please.
Night landing - £3.50 +. Block Booking £12.50 +

Fuel
AVGAS 100LL 63p.
Major credit cards except Amex / Diners

Flying Organisations
Arrow Air Centre Ltd 01362 820162

Other Organisations
Arrow Air Services (Engineering) Ltd 01362 820337

Car Hire
Hertz 01842 761362

Taxis
Anglia taxis 01362 690050

Public Transport
No convenient buses. Wymondham Railway station 10 miles

Nearby Places of Interest
The Norfolk Broads 01502 713196
Horse Riding
Thetford, Fakenham, Wymondham, East Dereham and Swaffham all with 30 mins drive
TIC 01603 666071

Food & Accommodation
Licensed bar and restaurant in clubhouse, open evenings also. 'Pub Grub' food available from Sunrise to Sunset (it says here) everyday of the year except 25, 26 and 27 December
The George Hotel, East Dereham- 3 miles, a la carte restaurant, bar meals and accommodation 01362 696801
The Old Game Bird Cottages, Cranworth - 1 mile from £75 for a 2 night break 01362 821011
Charterhouse B&B, Honingham - 8 miles. Owned by Nigel (who operates the airfield). Favourable rates for visitors to Shipdham including transport to/from airfield 01603 880772

Shobdon

6 miles west of Leominster. Follow 'Shobdon' village signs from the A4110 and B4632, airfield is signposted in Shobdon village
Herefordshire Aero Club, Shobdon Aerodrome, Leominster, Hereford, HR6 9NR
Tel: 01568 708369 Fax: 01568 708935

Built as a glider training station, Shobdon first saw life in 1940 as Pembridge Landing Ground, but was renamed in 1942 after development into a larger airfield.

Gliding is still a significant part of the aerial traffic here, and indeed you'll find most types of aerial activity at Shobdon, from paragliding and microlighting through to fixed wing and helicopter training. Perhaps because the flying school and cafe are in the original nissen huts, perhaps because of the unspoilt nature of the airfield and the surrounding countryside, Shobdon still has a strong nostalgic ambience - in the nicest possible way.

In fair weather Shobdon fairly bustles with activity. The clubhouse, cafe and bar face the runway and parking area, with a pleasant patio area where meals can be taken if weather permits. The cafe is run by Mary, and the Sunday lunches in particular have gained something of a reputation locally for quality and value.

In the hangar behind the nissen huts there are a variety of aircraft and the maintenance facilities. Resident aircraft occupy tie-downs on the grass and are mainly popular trainer/tourer types, although there are one or two rarer examples around. Helicopters operate from their own clubhouse just east of the main hanger.

Landing Fee
£7.00 inc. (single) £2.00 (microlight) £14.00 (multi)
Visa/Mastercard/Switch/Delta. Amex and Diners NOT accepted

Fuel
AVGAS 100LL 68p inc. AVTUR JET A1 29p inc. Not available after 1700 (summer) or 1630 (winter).
Visa/Mastercard/Switch/Delta. Amex and Diners NOT accepted

Flying Organisations

Herefordshire Aero Club	01568 708369
Tiger Helicopters	01568 708028
Herefordshire Gliding Club	01568 708908
Paraglide International Flying School	01568 708075, 0831 348665
Sabre Air Sports	01568 708168

Other Organisations

Shobdon Aircraft Maintenance Ltd	01568 708855
Plane Wrappers	01568 708620
Active Omega Adventure Centre	

Car Hire

Watson's Leominster	01568 612060
Mortimer's Garage	01568 81271

Taxis

Markham's	01568 768208

Public Transport
Lifts to accommodation by arrangement, usually available. Bus in Shobdon village - Primrose Motors #496, but the service is irregular.

Nearby Places of Interest
Shobdon lies at the heart of the Marches, the beautiful and historic borderlands of England and Wales. Rolling countryside, half-timbered villages and rural pubs are the order of the day. Sightseeing (by air or surface) is a delight. The historic towns of Leominster, Presteigne and Knighton are all within 10 miles of Shobdon.

Shobdon Sports and Leisure Club 1/2 mile	
Croft Castle - 4 miles, open May-Sept	01568 780246
Offa's Dyke can be seen at Knighton - 10 miles	
Leominster - 7 miles. Town trail guide available from the TIC	
TIC	01568 616460

Food & Accommodation

Mary runs the cafe - Sunday roasts recommended (as are the bacon butties). Open 0830-1730 (summer); 0830-Sunset ish (winter) 7 days a week
The bar is called Woodies
Bateman Arms, Shobdon village (30 mins walk) real ale and food
Post office and stores in Shobdon village
Bell Inn, Yarpole - 5 miles (good pub food) 01568 780359
On-site camping with showers and caravanning. Tents £2, caravan £3.50 per night 01568 708369
Victoria House B&B - 1 mile 01568 708881
Mortimers Cross Pub - 2 miles B&B 01568 708741
The Elms B&B - 3 miles from £18 01544 388405
Eardisland Tea Room B&B - 3 miles from £14 01544 388226

Brick House Farm B&B, Presteigne
- 5 miles (recommended) 01544 267306
New Inn, Pembridge 2 miles.
Pembridge is a pretty black-and-white village typical of the area, and the New Inn is very much in keeping with it. The rooms are snug and traditionally furnished with a real fire for winter. Ruddles is the main beer, with other 'visiting' real ales. Food is well above normal 'pub grub' in both variety and quality - but is also good value. You'll want to stay - and you can. Rooms from £20. Recommended 01544 388427

Shoreham

1 mile west of Shoreham By Sea, signposted from A27 / A259
Shoreham by Sea, West Sussex BN43 5FF
Tel: 01273 452304 Fax: 01273 440146
Telex 877246 SOUTHN G

Shoreham claims to be the oldest licensed aerodrome in the country, and there's no reason to disbelieve it. Flying started from the site in 1910 on land owned by the Miles family of aircraft manufacturing fame, and has taken place continuously ever since. Other famous names associated with Shoreham in the early days include Avro, Farman and Cecil Pashley. Work commenced on the wonderful Art-Deco terminal in 1934. Soon airlines such a Lufthansa, KLM, Sabena, Air France and Imperial Airways were operating from Shoreham, which found itself as the focus for commercial aviation with the outbreak of the Second World War, as activity shifted away from Croydon.

After the war civilian flying resumed in earnest, but with mixed success. To make ends meet the airport was leased to Miles Aircraft, and later Beagle Aircraft, whose excellent Pup and ill-fated Basset were built here, before the company folded in the early 1970s.

Nowadays Shoreham is best known as a GA airfield, with several busy flying schools and associated support services. The Grade II listing terminal building, often seen in films and TV programs that need a 1930's airport location, has been sympathetically preserved. A pleasant licensed cafeteria occupies much of the ground floor with an excellent view of proceedings from inside, or from outside on the terrace in fine weather. The whispering gallery above the first floor landing of the entrance hall was recently restored and it is here that you will find the headquarters of the Popular Flying Association, appropriately enough for an airfield so closely linked to British light aviation.

There's plenty of interesting aircraft around including a few Tiger Moths and a Harvard, and a small museum behind the hangers.

Landing Fee
£13.00 up to 1500Kg, £13.00 per tonne above, less £2.00 for ultralights (max. weight 500 kg). £6.00 for overnight parking for aircraft up to 1500Kg.
Visa/Diners/Mastercard

Fuel
AVGAS 100LL 61p + AVTUR JET A-1 27p + Available up to 30 mins before airfield closes. Visa/Diners/Mastercard

Flying Organisations

Airbase	
Air South Ltd	01273 462874
Barry Aviation Flying Club	01444 451177
Fast Helicopters Limited	01273 465389
Premier / Jade Flying Club	01273 462277
Sky Leisure Aviation Ltd	01273 464422
Southern Air Ltd	01273 461661
Sussex Flying Club Ltd	01273 440852
Transport Command Limited	01273 462784

Other Organisations

Popular Flying Association	01273 461616
Air South Engineering Ltd (Maintenance)	01273 462874
Jade Air Engineering Ltd (Maintenance)	01273 464013
KB Aviation (Maintenance)	01273 453333
Northbrook Aviation (Maintenance)	01273 461198
Rollason Aircraft & Engines Ltd (Maintenance)	01273 462680
Southern Air Ltd (Maintenance)	01273 461664
Museum of D Day Aviation (Mobile)	0374 971971
Shoreham Aviation Heritage Centre in terminal building	
Shoreham Aircraft Preservation Society, Shoreham	
Bonner Engineering	01273 440250
Marston Corporate Finishes	01273 461310
Record Racing Rally Association	01273 461182

Car Hire

Avis	01273 673738
Eurodollar	01273 329332
Hertz	01273 738227

Taxis

Streamline	01273 747474
Airport Taxi Bookings	01273 461655

Public Transport

Various buses running between Worthing and Brighton stop in Shoreham village.
Shoreham railway station 1 mile

Nearby Places of Interest

Brighton - 6 miles:	
Brighton Pier, Pavilion etc.	
Sussex Toy and Model Museum, Brighton	01273 749494
Volks Electric Railway on the seafront	01273 681061
Foredown Tower, Hove - 3 miles	01273 422540
The Body Shop Tour, Worthing - 5 miles	01903 731500
TIC	01273 455566

Food & Accommodation

The Shoreham Airport Restaurant in the terminal.	
Open every day 0800-2200	01273 452300
Food For Friends, Brighton	01273 202310
The Mock Turtle tea shop , Brighton	01273 327380
The Sussex Pad Hotel (overlooking the airfield) from £45	01273 454647
The Crabtree - 1 mile B&B from £15	01273 463508
Upton Farm House - 2 miles B&B from £20	01903 233706
Chatsworth Hotel - 3 miles from £25	01903 336103
Berkley Hotel - 3 miles from £25	01903 820000
The Grand Hotel - 4 miles from £59	01273 202694

Sleap

10 miles north of Shrewsbury, signposted off the B5476
Sleap Aerodrome, Myddle, Shropshire SY4 3HE
Tel: 01939 232882 / 232045 Fax: 01939 235058

Opened early in 1943, Sleap (pronounced "Slape") housed Whitley bombers and Horsa gliders and was primarily used by the RAF as a training airfield. Operated by the Shropshire Aero Club since 1964, the airfield is normally a quiet spot during the week, and is closed on certain weekdays. At weekends, however, things are busier – particularly at weekends when other local flying schools come in to use the circuit and the gliding club is active. The clubhouse is in the old tower building, one of the few wartime structures remaining. That itself is something of a marvel, as the tower was demolished by runaway Whitley bombers not just once, but twice during the RAF's tenure. On the first floor of the tower you will find a comfortable bar and cafe where you can usually get hot and cold snacks. There is also a fine view of across the airfield but, mindful of this building's chequered history, you might not want to relax too much as you watch the training aircraft thrashing around the circuit!

The airfield is at the end of a long track, well signposted off the B5476 Shrewsbury / Wem road, about 4 miles south of Wem. There is nothing significant within walking distance of the airfield, and it's a long trek to the B5476 road, so pre-arranged transport is a must if you want to explore this pretty corner of Shropshire.

Landing Fee
£5.00 (single) £10.00 (multi) Overnight parking £7.50 (single) £10.00 (multi)

Fuel
AVGAS 100LL 75p inc.

Flying Organisations

Shropshire Aero Club Ltd	01939 232882
Shropshire Soaring Group	01939 232045

Other Organisations

Kilroe (maintenance)	01939 290861

Car Hire

Europcar	01743 236623

Taxis

Derek	01939 234562

Public Transport
Infrequent buses to Wem from the B5476. Wem railway station 4 miles, Shrewsbury railway station 7 miles

Nearby Places of Interest

Sweet Pea Festival, annually in July, Wem	01948 840779
Shrewsbury - 7 miles	
Shrewsbury Castle	01743 361196
Clive House Museum, Shrewsbury	01743 354811
Haughmond Abbey - 8 miles	01743 709661
The Meres, Ellesmere - 8 miles	01691 622981
Hawlestone Hall and Gardens - 10 miles	01939 200300
Shrewsbury Quest Abbey, Foregate - 10 miles	01743 354811
TIC	01691 622981

Food & Accommodation
Bar meals available weekends

Old Post Office, Wem - 4 miles, pub and bistro	01939 235046
Horse and Jockey, Wem - 4 miles	01948 710427
Maypole Tea Rooms, Wem - 4 miles	01939 234791
Cellar Restaurant, Ellesmere - 8 miles	01691 622433
The Old Vicarage - 3 miles B&B from £19	01939 234835
Foxleigh House, Wem - 4 miles B&B from £17	01939 233528
Soulton Hall, Wem - 4 miles B&B from £21	01939 232786
Ellesmere Hotel - 8 miles from £21	01691 622055

Southampton (Eastleigh)

4 miles north of Southampton, signposted off A335 and M27 J5
Southampton Airport, Southampton, SO18 2NL
Tel: 01703 629600 Fax: 01703 629300 Telex 477981 SOUAPT G

If you haven't visited Southampton Airport for a year or two, you could be forgiven for thinking you have arrived at the wrong place, such is the extent of the redevelopment which has taken place. The new terminal building with shops, car hire and taxi desks, bar & restaurant (airport average in quality and price) has been developed sympathetically. The distinctive arch-roofed style of architecture of the old airport buildings has been retained, in keeping with the similarly-styled Ford factory just across the M27.

A busy airport, the Channel Islands are a popular destination and scheduled services run daily from here to various destinations, usually in commuter turboprop types although the occasional jet can be seen. The two resident flying schools operate a variety of light single and twin-engined types also. There is a good flight-briefing unit in the terminal and a railway station adjacent to the main car park, about 200 metres from the terminal. Also within the terminal is a plaque commemorating a landmark in Britain's aviation history when, on the 5th March 1936, the first prototype Spitfire took to the air from here.

Landing Fee
£13.64 per tonne. All major credit cards

Fuel
AVGAS 100LL 56.96p + AVTUR JET A1 27.04p + All major credit cards

Flying Organisations

BM Aviation	01962 842555
Carill Aviation Flying School	01703 627225
Solent Flight Ltd	01703 650300 / 650005

Other Organisations

Osprey Aviation Ltd (Maintenance)	01703 620727
Skycare (Handling)	

Car Hire

Avis	01703 616061
Eurodollar	01703 227373
Hertz	01703 638437
Europcar	01703 740100

Taxis
At terminal

Bee Line	0703 617517

Public Transport
Buses at terminal to Southampton. Southampton Parkway railway station outside terminal. Services to Southampton, Bournemouth etc. and London Waterloo 01703 229393

Nearby Places of Interest

Winchester Cathedral	01962 866854
Southampton 3 miles:	
Guild Hall	01703 632601
Art Gallery	01703 632601
Hall of Aviation, Southampton	01703 635830
The Docks - ships all shapes and sizes	
Ocean Village and Marinas	01703 228353
International Boat Show, usually September	01784 473377
TIC	01703 221106
Portsmouth 12 miles:	
The Historic Dockyard including Mary Rose, HMS Victory, HMS Warrior, various nautical museums	0839 407080
Royal Naval Museum	01705 733060
Royal Navy Submarine Museum	01705 529217
Beaulieu Motor Museum 10 miles	01590 612123

Food & Accommodation

Bar and restaurant in terminal	
Hedgehog and Hogshead Pub, Southampton	01703 581124
Travel Lodge, Eastleigh (5 mins drive, opening Summer 96) room from £35	01582 414341
Novotel - 3 miles from £52	01703 222158
De Vere Grand Harbour - 3 miles from £57	
Anchor Cottage - 5 miles B&B from £15	01489 894935
Acton Lodge Hotel - 7 miles from £35	01329 231200
Pendennis - 7 miles B&B from £13	01329 281379

Southend

2 miles north of Southend on Sea, signposted from A127, A1159 and B1013
London Southend Airport, Southend on Sea, Essex SS2 6YF
Tel: 01702 340201 Fax: 01702 331715

Like Blackpool, Southend is a municipal airport which has recently benefited from the development of a new passenger terminal. Although still uncompleted in Spring 1996, and with something of a 'Marie Celeste' feel, it is hoped that facilities in the terminal will open in time for the summer. The intention is to return Southend to the traffic levels of its heyday when nearly 750 000 passengers a year passed through.

Flying on this site dates back to 1915 when Bleriot monoplanes were deployed here in an effort to protect London from Zeppelins. The airfield opened as a civilian airport in the 1930s and was little used by the military in the second world war. Civilian flying resumed in 1946 and in 1948 Freddie Laker began his aviation career here with his company Aviation Traders. Cross-channel Carvair car ferries flew here in the 60s and 70s, and the Viscounts of British Air Ferries were a long standing feature at Southend. Now British World Airlines have taken their place with BAC-111 and BAe146 aircraft. The freighters of Heavylift, the cargo airline, are often in evidence here and the various maintenance companies attract a wide range of airliners for engineering work.

Apart from the terminal's (hoped for) facilities, most of the flying clubs can provide refreshments and snacks, although Aviators (by the Vulcan) have a larger selection of bar meals. Most of the flying schools are based along the eastern perimeter road (running towards the 24 threshold), take the road to the right of the terminal as you turn towards it from the main road. To reach Southend Flying Club (which is near the 06 threshold) take the second airport entrance, rather than the first which leads to the terminal.

Landing Fee
Up to 1 tonne £12.10 inc., 1-2 tonnes £24.10, 2-3 tonnes £35.25, night surcharges apply 2300-0600. First 2 hours parking free, then £7.05 inc. per 24 hours, (up to 4 tonnes).
All major credit cards

Fuel
AVGAS 100LL 55.67p + AVTUR JET A1 26.3p +

Flying Organisations

Aviators Flight Center	01702 542497
Direct Helicopters	01702 546420
Seawing Flying Club Ltd	01702 545420
Southend Flying Club	01702 545198
Willowair Flying Club Ltd	01702 531555

Other Organisations

Air Livery (aircraft refurbishers & resprays)	01702 540710
Central Flying Services (Maintenance)	01702 540380
Flightspares Ltd	01702 548989
Heavylift Aircraft Engineering Ltd (Maintenance)	01702 541616
Ipeco Aerospace Ltd	01702 549371
Isenburg Engineering Ltd (Maintenance)	01702 547490
JRB Aviation Ltd (Maintenance)	01702 54543
RFS Aircraft Engineering Ltd (Maintenance)	01702 543000
Routair (handling)	01702 544594
Routair Aviation Services Ltd (Maintenance)	01702 540380
Vulcan Restoration Trust	
World Aviation Support Ltd (Maintenance)	01702 348604/348601

Car Hire

Avis	01702 480481
Hertz	01702 546666

Taxis

Rank outside terminal	01702 334455
Andrew's Taxis	01702 548005

Public Transport
Bus stop outside main gate. Thameway 01268 287541. Southend transport 01702 355711. Rochford railway station 1 mile,
Southend railway station 2 miles 01702 544139 or 01268 775854. 9A bus to Southend railway station every 30 mins

Nearby Places of Interest
Southend 2 miles, a seaside resort town with all the usual attractions including modern shopping mall, Southend Sealife Centre, Southend Planetarium and Peter Pan's Adventure Island.
Roller City (in the old Air Museum building adjacent to the airport)
01702 541111
Southend Pier (the world's longest pleasure pier,
trains to the end if you don't fancy the walk!)
01702 215622
Southend Sea Life Centre
01702 462400
Southend Planetarium
01702 330214
The Lynn Tait Gallery
01702 471737
Palace Theatre, Westcliff on Sea 4 miles
01702 342564
TIC
01702 215120

Food & Accommodation
Bar, restaurant and coffee shop in terminal. Hopefully
Bar and food at Aviators, sandwiches at Seawing
Olham's fish restaurant. Westcliff on Sea - 3 miles
Hundreds of accommodation possibilities, recommended are:

Airport Moat House less than 1 mile from £26	01702 546344
Camelia Hotel, Thorpe Bay - 3 miles from £35	01702 587917
Westcliff Hotel, Southend - 3 miles from £26	01702 345247
Roslin Hotel, Thorpe Bay, from £26	01702 586375
Hotel Renouf	01702 541334

St Mawgan

4 miles east of Newquay, signposted off the A3059 and B3276
RAF St Mawgan, Newquay, Cornwall TR8 4HP
Tel: 01637 872201 ext. 2045/2046. 01637 860551 (civilian handling by Brymon Airways / British Airways Express)
Fax: 01637 874032

This airfield is perhaps better known in the airline world as Newquay, however it continues to be called St Mawgan by pilots and probably will be for many years. St Mawgan was best known in the past as RAF St Mawgan - home of the RAF's Maritime Patrol units. From here Nimrod aircraft flew out deep into the south-west approaches and into the Atlantic, submarine hunting and providing search and rescue cover - saving countless lives. Today the Nimrods have gone, although they sometimes pass through on military exercise. In their place have come Sea King helicopters. There is an active Sea King squadron, training unit and maintenance base here.

The development of the airport is now concentrated on attracting scheduled and charter traffic. The new terminal opened in March 1994 with a bar and snacks, a car rental desk and freephones to hotels. So far the main operators are BA Express (formerly Brymon) to Dublin, Cork, Jersey and Plymouth; and Skybus to the Isles of Scilly and Bristol.

Landing Fee
Are you ready for this? Weekdays for a single £13.50, + £10 handling, + £8.50 MOD insurance, plus £4.00 per passenger on departure (even for a private flight apparently). First two hours parking free, then £2.20 per 24hrs. Some of this is plus VAT, some isn't - they couldn't tell us which.
All major credit cards (just as well)

Fuel
AVTUR Jet A1 32p + available from Brymon Airways.
All major credit cards

Flying Organisations

Other Organisations

Car Hire

Avis	01326 211511
Eurodollar	01637 850750
Europcar	01637 860337

Taxis

Taxi rank at bus station 4 miles	01637 872487

Public Transport
Newquay railway station 4 miles

Nearby Places of Interest

The Land of Illusion - 4 miles	01637 877531
Spirit of the West Theme Park - 4 miles	01637 881160
Trenance Leisure Park - 4 miles	01637 875982
Lappa Valley Steam Railway - 4 miles	01872 510317
Sealife Centre- 4 miles	01637 872822
Newquay - 4 miles	
Surfing at Newquay - 5 miles	01637 877083
TIC	01637 871345

Food & Accommodation

The Falcon, St Mawgan - 1 mile. Real ale, good food, rooms from £18	01637 860225
Hotel Victoria - 4 miles from £15	01637 872255
Hotel Mordros - 4 miles from £15	01637 876700
Headland Hotel - 4 miles from £35	01637 872211
The Chonaill Lodge Hotel - 4 miles from £85	01637 876492

Stapleford

5 miles north of Romford, signposted from the A113
Stapleford Aerodrome, Stapleford, Nr Romford, Essex RM4 1SJ
Tel: 01708 688272, 0181 5598253 Fax : 014028 421

Stapleford airfield dates back to the 1930s, when it was a base for Hillman Airways. Hurricanes flew from here during the Battle of Britain, and after the war the airfield reverted to civilian use in the hands of the Herts & Essex Aero Club.

Stapleford is still largely a training airfield. The Cessnas of Stapleford Flight Centre make up much of the activity, although there are a several unusual types tucked away in the hangers on the western side of the airfield. For many years Stapleford was somewhat overlooked compared to the other GA airfields close to London, despite Stapleford's claim to be the closest of all - being just 16 miles from Tower Bridge. Perhaps this was because Stapleford was a grass airfield (and a very pleasant one at that). This may change now that Stapleford have invested in a tarmac strip on part of the main 04/22 runway, and of course there is still the Lambourne VOR/DME just off the airfield near the 04 threhold. Other attractions remain the same. There is a small pilot's shop and the club house serves appetising, reasonably priced food; the cooked breakfasts are particularly popular. It says 'members only' on the door, and has done for 20 years, but everybody ignores this and visitors are welcomed.

Situated in open countryside, Stapleford still has a rural feel, despite the M25 passing within a mile. Frustratingly there is no nearby access from either the M25 or the M11. Best bet is to leave the M25 at junction 28 (Brentwood) and then follow signs for Chipping Ongar, Navestock and then Abridge. However you get to Stapleford, chances are that you will be well rewarded.

Landing Fee
Single £5 + ; multi £10 +
Visa/Access

Fuel
AVGAS 100LL 60p +
Visa/Access

Flying Organisations

Stapleford Flight Centre	01708 688380

Other Organisations

Aeromega Helicopters (Engineering) Ltd	01708 688361
Stapleford Flying Club Maintenance	01708 688449
Thurston Avionics Ltd (Maintenance)	01708 688341/4

Car Hire

Hertz	01708 721882

Taxis
On request

Public Transport
Theydon Bois underground station, 3 miles (Central Line)

Nearby Places of Interest

Epping Forest - 10 miles	0181 508 0028
Queen Elizabeth's Hunting Lodge, Chingford - 7 miles	0181 529 6681
Lee Valley Regional Park - 3 miles	01992 713838
Hainault Forest Country Park - 3 miles	0181 500 7353
The Brentwood Centre - 5 miles (touring venue, particularly comedy)	01277 262616
TIC Brentwood	01277 200300

Food & Accommodation

Newhouse Farm (Tudor Farmhouse), Stanford Rivers - 1 mile B&B from £16	01277 362132
Parsonage Farm, Theydon Bois - 2 miles B&B from £40	01442 814242
Longacre, Stanford Rivers - 2 miles B&B from £16	01277 372954
Red House Farm, Doddingshurst - 8 miles B&B from £20	01277 372336
Forte Posthouse, Epping - 8 miles from £60	01992 573137

Sturgate

4 miles south-east of Gainsborough, signposted from B1241
Sturgate Aerodrome, Nr Gainsborough Lincolnshire DN21 5PA
Tel: 014278 3280/703 Fax: 014278 3416
Telex 56387 EASTEX G

Sturgate is a wartime airfield that very nearly didn't happen at all. Built too late in the Second World War to house any operational aircraft, Sturgate was closed almost before it had opened. However, the Americans moved in with jet fighters during the Korean War, and stayed until 1964, thus establishing the airfield.

These days most activity at Sturgate is provided by the Lincoln Aero Club, who operate mainly at weekends. Eastern Air Executive will probably meet you during the week, but whenever you visit catering is rather limited - the sandwich van due around mid-day being the best bet! For cooked meals, the nearby town of Gainsborough is probably the place to go and the airfield staff will give you their current recommendations. Visit weekday or weekend you receive a friendly welcome, but don't expect to find a hive of airborne activity.

The airfield lies between Heapham and Upton, south of the A631 eastbound from Gainsborough. It is not far from the B1241, 2 miles after it leaves the A156 south from Gainsborough for Lincoln.

Landing Fee
£5.00 (singles) £15.00 (multi)

Fuel
AVGAS 100LL 60p +

Flying Organisations

Lincoln Aero Club (weekends)	01427 838305
(weekdays)	01777 702417/01522 721411

Other Organisations

Eastern Air Executive Ltd (Maintenance & Resprays)	01427 838280

Car Hire

Avis	01522 511200
Eurodollar	01522 512233

Taxis
Arrangement can be made through Eastern Executive ops on request

Public Transport
Gainsborough railway station 4 miles

Nearby Places of Interest

Bomber Country Aviation Museum 4 miles	01427 668809
Gainsborough (Britain's most inland port) 4 miles:	
Gainsborough Old Hall	01427 612669
Gainsborough Hertitage Centre	01427 838629
TIC	01427 615411

Food & Accommodation

Local pub meals available, ask for a recommendation	
Hickman Hill Hotel and Restaurant - 4 miles from £24	01427 613639
Ivy Lodge Hotel and Tea Rooms - 4 miles from £18	01427 763723
Church Farm - 5 miles B&B from £13	01427 668279
Black Swan Coaching Inn - 5 miles from £22	01427 718878

Teesside

5 miles south-east of Darlington on the A67
Teesside International Airport Ltd, Darlington, County Durham DL2 1LU
Tel: 01325 332811 Fax: 01325 332810
Telex: 587635

Opposite the main terminal at Teesside Airport stands the St.George's Hotel, commemorating the original name of the airfield, Middleton St. George. RAF bombers flew here during the war, and the airfield was active as a military station until 1964, flying Hunters and Javelins. Development as a civil airport began almost immediately the RAF had left, and the passenger terminal was completed two years later.

The airfield retains much of the atmosphere of a large RAF station and many of the ex-military buildings remain in use today, indeed the hotel is the former Officers' Mess. Teesside is not too busy, however, to extend a welcome to light aviation, including the three resident flying schools. The terminal houses the usual facilities, including a pleasant restaurant which serves good food, at the expected prices. There are a growing number of scheduled and charter destinations, but GA looks to be the main activity at Teesside for some time to come.

Well signposted from the A1/A167 junction, and the A19 trunk roads, the airport lies on the A67 between Yarm and Darlington.

Landing Fee
£13.10 + per tonne.
Access / Visa

Fuel
AVGAS 100LL 62p + AVTUR Jet A1 25p + via Conoco.
Access / Visa

Flying Organisations

Cleveland Flying School Ltd	01325 332855
St George Flying Club	01325 333431
Teesside Aero Club/Teesside Flight Centre	01325 332752 / 333142

Other Organisations

Flight Calibration Service	01325 333317
Guided tours of airport available	01325 332811 ext 173

Car Hire

Avis	01325 332091
Europcar	01325 333329
Hertz	01325 332600

Taxis

Teesside Airport Taxis	01325 332177
Chalies Taxis	01325 382819
Arena Cars	01325 482979
C & D Taxis	01325 307221

Public Transport
Buses available at terminal to Darlington. Railway station at airport. Helplines 01482 326033 (8am-8pm) and 0191 2326262 (7am-10.45pm) daily.

Nearby Places of Interest

Croft Circuit, Dalton on Tees, rallycross etc	01325 484829
Darlington Cricket and Football Ground	01325 466415 (cricket), 01325 465097 (football)
Darlington Railway Centre and Museum	01325 460532
Quaker Veteran Commercial Vehicle Rally held in May	
TIC	01325 382698

Food & Accommodation

St George Hotel, at airfield (A la carte menu, bar meals, buffets, banquets and private functions). From £70	01325 332631
Copper Kettle Tea Rooms, Middleton-St-George - 1 mile	01325 333192
Old Farmhouse Inn, Middleton-St-George - 1 mile	01325 333372
Devonport Hotel - 1 mile from £35 (Collection service from airport)	01325 332255
Newbus Arms Hotel and Restaurant 5 mins from airport. From £45	01325 721071

Thruxton

4.5 miles west of Andover, signposted from A303
Thruxton Aerodrome, Nr Andover, Hampshire, SP11 8PW
Tel: 01264 772352/772171 Fax: 01264 773913

The cafe under the control tower at Thruxton is called the Jackaroo, named after the curious Thruxton Jackaroo 4-seater aircraft converted from Tiger Moths here in the late 1950s. Today, though, aviation plays a secondary role to the motor racing circuit which has flourished here in recent years.

Originally built in 1940, Thruxton was an RAF airfield during the second world war. Civilian flying by the Wiltshire Aeroplane Club continued in peacetime on a modest scale, and the airfield perimeter track soon became the racing circuit.

Today the airfield is a busy and interesting destination, although access to the airfield on race days can be difficult due to the crowds. However at other times Thruxton offers plenty of diversion to the visitor - helicopters, gliders and parachutists operate alongside the fixed-wing training, and the motor circuit is often host to an entertaining variety of testing traffic. By road Thruxton is easy to find, lying just off the main A303 to the west of Andover. Follow the signs to 'Thruxton Circuit', NOT Thruxton village, and you will have no difficulty.

Landing Fee
£5.88 inc. (single) 11.75 (multi) inc. Overnight parking (tie down) £2.00
Access and Visa

Fuel
AVGAS 100LL 55p + AVTUR JET A-1 29p +
Access and Visa

Flying Organisations

Fast Helicopters Ltd	01264 772508
Western Air Training	01264 773900
Thruxton Gliding Club	01264 773274

Other Organisations

Earthline Ltd (Maintenance)	01264 771327
Fast Helicopters Ltd (Maintenance)	01264 772508
Heliwork Services Ltd (Helicopter sales & maintenance)	01264 773422
Thruxton Motor Racing Circuit	01264 772607/772696
Skid Pan	01628 527387
Ian Taylor's motor racing school	01624 773511

Car Hire

Avis	01264 356187
Eurodollar	01264 338181
Kennings	01264 773944

Taxis
01264 353536/0860 747403

Public Transport
Bus route to Thruxton village 1 mile approx. to Andover. Andover railway station 5 miles

Nearby Places of Interest

Hawk Conservancy, Andover 4 miles	01264 772252
Andover Museum, Andover 6 miles	01264 366283
Museum of the Iron Age Andover 6 miles	01264 366283
Middle Wallop, with the Museum of Army Flying 6 miles	01264 384421
TIC	01264 324320

Food & Accommodation
The Jackeroo in the control tower building (on the 'public' side of the motor racing circuit). Open airfield hours for drinks and snacks. Lunches 1200-1400, bar open until 2300.

The Old Barn, Amport - 1 mile from £21	01264 710410
Broadwater, Amport - 1 mile from £20	01264 772240
Lains Cottage, Quarley 1 mile B&B from £20	01264 889697
Fair Deal Motel	01980 629542
Ashley Court, Andover - 4 miles from £50	01264 357344

Turweston

2 miles east of Brackley, signposted from the A43
Turweston Aerodrome, Brackley Northamptonshire NN13 5DD
Tel: 01280 701167 Fax: 01280 701167

Another airfield developed initially for bomber training, Turweston became a satellite station to several larger bases in the area, operating from time to time Wellington, Mitchell and Boston aircraft until its closure in 1946.

Most of the airfield returned to agriculture, but in recent years an attempt has been made to encourage light aviation from the site, and modest development has taken place. Unfortunately there was vociferous local opposition to the planning consent, which was only granted after a lengthy and bruising Public Enquiry. There is a small flying club here, and also a cafe that has a good reputation locally.

Turweston lies off the A43, to the north of Brackley. Turn right off the bypass, through the village of Whitfield, and the airfield is on your right hand side a couple of miles further on.

Landing Fee
£5.78 (single) £9.90 (multi)
Cash or cheque only

Fuel
AVGAS 100LL on request

Flying Organisations
India Mike Charlie 01280 705749

Other Organisations

Car Hire
By arrangement

Taxis
P & J Cars 01280 704330

Public Transport
Banbury railway station 12 miles

Nearby Places of Interest

Stowe Landscaped Gardens - 2 miles	01280 822850
Silverstone Circuit - 4 miles	01327 857273
John Watson Performance Driving School, Silverstone	01327 857177
Sulgrave Manor - 5 miles	01295 760205
Towcester Race Course - 7 miles	01327 353414
Banbury historic town - 10 miles	
TIC	01280 700111
See also Hinton-in-the-Hedges	

Food & Accommodation
Proper Charlies, on airfield - choci cake highly recommended
Accommodation can be arranged by flying club
Mrs Field, The Thatches, Brackley
- 2 miles B&B from £14 01280 850358

Wellesbourne Mountford

4 miles east of Stratford upon Avon, next to the B4086
Wellesbourne Mountford Aerodrome, Stratford upon Avon,
Warwickshire CV35 9EU
Tel: 01789 842000

One of the busiest and most popular airfields in the Midlands, Wellesbourne Mountford was

built as a training station for bombers and remained an active military airfield until 1964. These days, much of the airfield has become an industrial estate, and one of the former runways is used for vehicle storage. On the active airfield the five flying clubs, helicopter training school and numerous private aircraft - including a number of interesting types - keep the airfield busy. Even the Vulcan (now joined by a Buccaneer) is occasionally fired up and taxied across the airfield! Recently a number of buildings have been improved a new licensed bar and cafe (the Fly Inn) is building on the old cafe's reputation for good value food.

By road, the airfield is less than 5 miles east of Stratford-upon-Avon, visible from the A429 as you bypass the village of Wellesbourne (look for the Vulcan). From the M40, take the exit for the A46 but continue round the roundabout to the A429. After the village of Barford, take the second turning on the right (signposted to Charlecote). Continue through Charlecote village, over the bridge to the crossroads at the end. The airfield is then visible straight ahead, the main entrance is the third on your left, by the old propeller.

Landing Fee
Single £7.00 inc. multi 12.00 inc. Parking free on grass.
Visa/Diners/Mastercard. No Switch

Fuel
AVGAS 100LL 59p + AVTUR JET A-1 24p +
Visa/Diners/Mastercard. No Switch

Flying Organisations

Avon Flying School	01789 470727
Heli Air Ltd	01789 470476
R S Pilot Training	01789 470434
South Warwickshire Flying School	01789 840094
Take Flight	01789 470424
Wellesbourne Aviation Ltd	01789 841066/841067

Other Organisations

Wellesbourne Wartime Museum	01789 293127
Wellesbourne Aircraft Maintenance	

Car Hire

Ford	01789 267446
Listers	01789 294477
LCS (Warwick)	01926 495188

Taxis

007 taxis	01789 414007
Shakespeare Taxis	01789 414100
Main Taxis	01789 414514

Public Transport
No convenient buses. Stratford upon Avon railway station 4 miles

Nearby Places of Interest
Charlecote House (& gardens) - 1 mile
Stratford Upon Avon - 4 miles, with all its attractions including:

The Royal Shakespeare Theatre	01789 295623
Anne Hathaways's Cottage	01789 293127
Heritage Motor Museum - Gaydon 10 miles	01926 641181
Warwick Castle - 10 miles	01926 408000
TIC	01789 293127

Food & Accommodation

The Fly Inn at the airport	
Charlecote Pheasant Hotel - 1 mile. Food recommended	
Fox Inn, Loxley - 1 mile. Food recommended	01789 840991
Kings Head, Wellesbourne - 2 miles (popular with local pilots)	01789 840206
Chadley House, Wellesbourne - 1 mile from £40	01789 840994
The Croft, Stratford - 4 miles B&B from £17	01789 293419
Braeside, Stratford - 4 miles B&B from £16	01789 261648
The Moat House, Stratford - 4 miles from £70	01789 414411

White Waltham

2 miles south-west of Maidenhead
White Waltham Aerodrome Ltd, White Waltham Aerodrome,
Nr Maidenhead, Berks SL6 3NJ
Tel: 01628 823272/3/4 Fax: 01628 826070

White Waltham opened in 1935 for the de Havilland School of Flying, and indeed its history has always been closely associated with training. Its most famous pupil was probably the Duke of Edinburgh, who flew Chipmunks and Harvards here in 1953.

The original wooden buildings still stand, and today house the flying school and a very agreeable bar and restaurant. The bar food comes from a varied menu, is reasonably priced and produced to a high standard. By all accounts the restaurant is equally good. Sitting in the wicker chairs with a good view across the grass runways, there are reminders of White Waltham's wartime stint as headquarters of the Air Transport Auxiliary. The ferry pilots of the ATA became legendary for making over 300 000 flights during the war, delivering a huge variety of aircraft.

The aircraft resident here today are no less varied and interesting, and at weekends this is a busy and popular destination. Visitors are welcomed and the airfield management are working hard to promote White Waltham as one of London's premier GA airfields.

Access to White Waltham is easy via the motorway network. Leave the M4 at J8/9 on to the A404(M), and at junction 9B take the A4 towards Maidenhead. Then follow signs for White Waltham and continue through the village of Cox Green. At the roundabout by the Esso petrol station turn left and White Waltham is about 1/4 mile on the right.

Landing Fee

£6.75 singles. £13.50 multi or £6.75 if picking up fuel. Parking £5.88 singles. £9.40 multi. per night

Fuel

AVGAS 70p, AVTUR JET A-1 30p inc. Available 0800-SS-30 Winter, 0700-SS-30 Summer

Flying Organisations

Aeros/AN2	0707 262774
Avia Special Ltd	01707 262774
Freestyle Aviation (aerobatic training)	01628 37732
Sloane Helicopters Ltd	01628 829369
West London Aero Club	01628 823272

Other Organisations

Richard Goode Aerobatics (Sukhoi Distributor)	0171 3123166
White Waltham Airfield Ltd (Maintenance)	01628 823276

Car Hire

Eurodollar	01628 838914
Hammants (1/4 mile)	01628 823211

Taxis

Park Cars (limos)	01628 836726
U-want	01628 822110
Taxi	0860 514978
Airport Cars	01628 836726

Public Transport

Bus stop opposite airfield entrance. National Coach information and bookings 01865 791579. Maidenhead railway station 2 miles

Nearby Places of Interest

Courage Shire Horse Centre, Maidenhead - 2 miles	01628 824848
Ascot racecourse	01344 22211
Windsor Castle	01753 868286
Crown Jewels of the World Museum, Windsor	01753 833773
The Museum of Berkshire Aviation, Reading - 10 miles	01734 340712 / 448089
TIC	01628 830267

Food & Accommodation

West London Aero Club - bar snacks and restaurant
Several local pubs within walking distance

Shirley's B&B - 200 yds. B&B from £20	01628 824318
Beehive Manor, Cox Green - 1 mile. B&B from £36	01628 20980
Thames Riviera Hotel, Maidenhead - 2 miles. From £80	01628 74057
Holiday Inn, Maidenhead - 2 miles. From £99	01628 823444
Ye Olde Bell Hotel, Hurley - 3 miles. From £50	01628 825881

Wickenby (Lincoln)

8 miles north-east of Lincoln, signposted off A46
Wickenby Aerodrome, Langworth Lincolnshire LN3 5AA
Tel: 01673 885345/6 01522 754520 (out of hours)
Fax: 01673 885391

Like so many airfields in this part of the country, Wickenby was built for Bomber Command during the Second World War. Also, like many other local airfields, flying activity is now limited to a corner of the former site. And yet, Wickenby seems to particularly retain the atmosphere of its past. Maybe it's the number of original buildings, now empty and overgrown, dotted around the airfield. Maybe it's the memorial at the gate to the 2000 plus Wickenby aircrew lost in just a couple of years. Whatever, on a misty autumn morning it is not hard to imagine that you might chance upon a Lancaster parked on a remote dispersal, appearing out of the gloom. In a sense, the whole airfield is a memorial to those who flew from here and did not return.

The Wickenby of today is a relatively quiet airfield. There are a few interesting resident aircraft, and a locally based flying club, but catering in the clubhouse does not extend beyond tea, coffee and a snack vending machine.

On a clear day Lincoln Cathedral can be seen from the tower across the flat Lincolnshire fens. The airfield is situated about halfway between Lincoln and Market Rasen, being signposted from the B1202, about 5 miles south of Market Rasen.

Landing Fee
Cessna 152 £6.00 +

Fuel
AVGAS 100LL on request

Flying Organisations

Wickenby Aviation Ltd	01673 885345

Other Organisations

Wickenby Aviation (Maintenance)	01673 885345

Car Hire

Avis	01522 511200
Eurodollar	01522 512233

Taxis
Arranged on request

Public Transport
A8 bus Caistor to Lincoln stops in Wickenby village. Lincoln railway station 10 miles

Nearby Places of Interest
North Kesteven Airfield Trail - a tour of active and former airfield sites in mid-Lincolnshire 01529 414294

Market Rasen Horseracing, 5 miles	01673 843434
Burghley House 5 miles	01780 52451
Lincoln 8 miles:	
Cathedral	01522 544544
Castle	01522 511068
National Cycle Museum	01522 545091
Museum of Lincolnshire Life	01522 528448
Roman Remains inc. mint wall, aqueduct, Newport Arch	01522 529828
TIC	01522 529828

Food & Accommodation

Tea, coffee and snacks at the clubhouse	
The Limes Country House Hotel,	
Market Rasen - 5 miles from £35	01673 842357
Beechwood Guest House,	
Market Rasen - 5 miles B&B from £15	01673 844043
Lea Holme - 4 miles B&B from £18	01522 868749
Wig and Mitre pub restaurant, Lincoln - 8 miles	01522 523705
The Castle Hotel, Lincoln - 8 miles from £48	01522 538801
Hollies Hotel, Lincoln - 8 miles from £25	01522 522419
Abbaye Guest House, Lincoln - 8 miles B&B from £20	01522 531385

Woodvale

5 miles south of Southport, next to the A565
RAF Woodvale, Formby, Liverpool L37 7AD
Tel: 01704 872287 Fax: 01707 824805

Woodvale was hurriedly opened in 1941 with Spitfires, Beaufighters and Mosquitoes defending Liverpool's docks and factories, and covering Irish Sea shipping convoys.

After the war, the runway was extended to accommodate Meteor jets, but by the early 1970s the military activity was mainly confined to the aircraft of the Air Experience Flight and University Air Squadrons, which remain here today.

Because Woodvale is still an active military station, facilities for civilian visitors are confined to those provided by the two resident flying schools, both of which have a members' bar, and can provide basic snacks, but there is no cafeteria or restaurant and casual visitors by road will be met by security barriers at the airfield entrance. The airfield nevertheless maintains a pleasant and relaxed atmosphere and can be recommended, especially during the summer, when the seaside towns of Formby and Southport are busy. When the Open Golf Championship is taking place at nearby Royal Birkdale (approximately 2 miles from the airfield) some of the professional golfers' private aircraft stay at Woodvale for the duration, but otherwise the resident aircraft are almost entirely Bulldogs, Cessna and Piper trainers.

The airfield is alongside the A565, about 5 miles south of Southport.

Landing Fee
£20.00 (single) £30.00 (multi) MOD rates + £8.00 Crown Indemnity. Parking fees apply after 2 hours £5.00 (single) £10.00 (multi) MOD rates
Cash or cheque only

Fuel
AVGAS 100LL 59p+ AVTUR JET A1 30p +

Flying Organisations

Woodvale Aviation Co Ltd	01704 874456
West Lancs Aero Club	01704 872610

Other Organisations

Woodvale Hangers Ltd (maintenance)	01704 874497

Car Hire

Dewerdens (Vauxhall Dealer)	01704 533066

Taxis

White taxis	01704 527777
Yellow Taxis	01704 531000
Formby Taxis	01704 831212

Public Transport
Bus stop 100 yards outside main gate for both directions every 20 mins to/from Southport and Formby. Freshfield or Ainsdale railway station both 1 mile from Woodvale.

Nearby Places of Interest
Southport - seaside town with the usual seaside town entertainments - 7 miles
British Lawnmower Museum (yes, really),

Southport - 7 miles	01704 535369
Southport Zoo	01704 538102
Southport Railway Centre	01704 530693
Southport Pleasureland	01704 532717
TIC	01704 53333

Food & Accommodation
Bar and snacks at both flying clubs
Southport 7 miles, wide selection of eateries and accommodation - all price ranges

Stutlea Hotel and Leisure Club, Southsea from £37.50	01704 544220
Sycamore from £31	01704 530308
Royal Clifton Hotel	01707 533771
Scarisbrick Hotel from £25	01704 543000
Leicester Private Hotel from £22	01704 530049

Wycombe Air Park (Booker)

3 miles south-west of High Wycombe on the B482, Junction 4 M40
Airways Aero Association Ltd, Wycombe Air Park, Booker, Marlow, Bucks SL7 3OR
Tel: 01494 529261

Wycombe Air Park, also well-known as Booker, was opened in the 1930s as Marlow Airport. The airfield was used for training in the Second World War, and the proximity of the Bomber Command (later Strike Command) HQ at nearby High Wycombe kept the airfield busy as a base for military communications aircraft.

The military have long since gone, but Wycombe is now arguably one of the busiest GA airfields in the country. There are three fixed-wing flying schools, two helicopter schools, a glider club and numerous privately owned aircraft - needless to say the airfield is often busy. However, inarguably the most interesting aircraft on the airfield can be seen courtesy of the Blue Max Museum of Film Flying, run by Bianchi Aviation Film Services. Here you can see a vista of rare and historic aircraft - Spitfires, Yaks, Stampes etc. There is the chance to see the ongoing maintenance and restoration work, and most of the aircraft are airworthy so maybe you'll see one airborne. You can also expect to see some fairly exotic aerobatic machinery, including the latest CAP aircraft, courtesy of Tony Bianchi's Personal Plane Services, housed in the same hanger.

Across from the hangers The Red Baron serves an upmarket 'pub grub' menu during the day, and offers a good view across the airfield.

Landing Fee
Up to 1·5 tonnes £12.00 (£10 if fuel uplifted). 1·5 to 2 tonnes £21.00 (£18 if fuel uplifted)
Overnight parking Singles £6.50, multis £12.00.
All major cards except Amex

Fuel
AVGAS 100LL 58p + AVTUR JET A-1 26p +
All major cards except Amex

Flying Organisations

Air Training Services	01494 445412
Booker Gliding Club	01494 442501
British Airways Flying Club	01494 529262
Mc Carthy Helicopter Services	01494 451111
Skyline Helicopters Ltd	01494 451111
Tiger Fly (pleasure flights in Tiger Moths)	01697 371472
Wycombe Air Centre Ltd	01494 451703

Other Organisations.

'Blue Max' Museum of Film Flying (open 10-5 daily)	01494 529432/449810
Airways Aero Associations Ltd	01494 532997
Booker Air Services	01494 529263
McCarthy Helicopter Services Ltd (Maintenance)	01494 451111
Personal Plane Services Ltd (Maintenance & sales)	01494 529432
Pooley's Pilots Shop (Open 9-5)	01494 526107
Skyline Helicopters Ltd (Maintenance)	01494 451111
Wycombe Air Centre Ltd (Maintenance)	01494 443737

Car Hire

Avis	01494 450750
Eurodollar (will deliver to airfield)	01494 527853
Thrifty Car Rental	01494 441456

Taxis

Neales	01494 463399/444984

Public Transport
Bus stop outside main gate. Wycombe Bus Company 01494 520941, Chiltern Bus 01494 464647, National Express 0121 6266226. For all bus and rail info. call 01345 382000. High Wycombe railway station 3 miles Chiltern lines info 01494 441561 (office hours) or 0171 3333179 (24 hours).

Nearby Places of Interest

Viewing of hangers under supervision by request	
Marlow - 2 miles (pretty town next to the Thames)	
Ercol Furniture Ltd, tours available	01494 521261
Wycombe Local History Museum	01494 421895
West Wycombe Caves, West Wycombe Village - 3 miles	01494 533739
West Wycombe Park - 3 miles	01494 523720
Hughenden Manor - 3 miles, former home of Disraeli	01494 532580
TIC	01494 421892

Food & Accommodation

The Red Baron, open 0900-2300	
Live and let live, Booker Common, walking distance lunches only	
Malvern House - 1 mile	016194 445688
Hare and Hounds, Marlow - 2 miles (food and Rebellion IPA recommended)	01628 483343
Post House, by M40	01494 442100
Alexandra Hotel, Wycombe - 2 miles from £50	01494 463494
Red Barn Farm - on the corner of the airfield. B&B from £20	01494 882820

The George & Dragon, West Wycombe - 2 miles
A rambling 15th Century coaching house in the centre of pretty West Wycombe. There's a nice garden at the back for sunny afternoons, and a real log fire for cool evenings. It's a friendly place where you're certain to be made welcome. There is usually a good range of beers on tap, and the bar food is excellent and good value too. The bedrooms are comfortable and the full English breakfast is a delight - provided you haven't overdone the real ale the night before! We haven't stayed since the building was renovated and the bedrooms refurbished, but we are assured that there have been no significant changes - which sounds good to us! West

Wycombe Park is within easy walking distance, and there is a fine view of the village from atop the hill. Beer, food, accommodation and walk all well recommended! Rooms from £40

01494 464414

York (Rufforth)

3 miles west of York, signposted from B1224
Rufforth Aerodrome, York, YO2 3QA
Tel: 01904 738694

Alongside the B1224, 3 miles west of York, the airfield of Rufforth was built in 1942 as a bomber airfield. After the war, little activity continued other than training and glider flying.

Today it is the gliders which are still associated with Rufforth. Extensive training takes place here under the auspices of the York Gliding Centre, on conventional gliders and SLMGs (Self-Launching Motor Gliders). There is also a microlight training school on the eastern side of the airfield, and a couple of privately owned aircraft are also based here. Unless the aircraft owners are around, it is unlikely that casual visitors will be allowed access to the hangars for viewing purposes, but the Gliding Centre has a clubhouse which offers basic snacks and refreshments courtesy of vending machines.

The airfield is about 3 miles from the main A64 trunk road past York. From the west, turn at the Buckles Inn (signs to the York Gliding Centre), or from the east leave the A64 at the Copmanthorpe flyover, following the signs to Askham Richard. The airfield and the Yorkshire Gliding Centre are signposted from here.

Landing Fee
£5 for singles.
Cash or cheque only

Fuel
AVGAS 100LL 60p
Cash or cheque only

Flying Organisations	
York Gliding Centre	01904 738694
York Flying Club	01482 865518
The Microlight Flying School	01904 628105, 0831 417499
Other Organisations	
McLean Aviation (maintenance)	01904 738653
Car Hire	
Avis	01904 610460
Eurodollar	01904 612141
Taxis	
	01904 623332
Public Transport	
York railway station 5 miles	
Nearby Places of Interest	
York with all its attractions 5 miles:	
National Railway Museum (recommended)	01904 621261
White Rose Line-Cruises	01904 628324
Yorkshire Museum	01904 629745
Micklegate Bar Museum	01904 612490/634436
Jorvic Viking Centre (recommended)	01904 643211
York Minster Visitor Centre (recommended)	01904 637134
York Castle Museum	01904 653611
TIC	01904 620557
Food & Accommodation	
Snacks on airfield at weekends	
Pub lunches at The Tankard, Rufforth - 1 mile	
Kilby's Restaurant, Skelton - 4 miles	01904 670222
All manner of eating, drinking and accommodation possibilities in York	
National Trust Tea Rooms, next to York Minster. Recommended.	01904 659282
The Royal York Hotel, York - 5 miles from £50	01904 653681
Mount Royale Hotel, York - 5 miles from £36	01904 628856
Hotel Fairmount, York - 5 miles from £26	01904 638298

Alderney

1 mile south-west of St Anne's, Alderney
States of Guernsey, States of Guernsey Airport, Guernsey, Channel Islands
Tel: 01481 822851

Alderney is the oldest of the Channel Island airfields, but also the smallest. This is in keeping with the islands itself, islanders will tell you that Alderney is the most unspoilt of the islands, with the best beaches and the best value hotels.

It is a small island (only 3 square miles), the 'capital' St Anne's is just 10 minutes walk from the airfield gates. The sense is very much of relaxed informality, an ideal place to get away from it all. Traffic is generally light and, a big plus in our view, caravans are not permitted. You can hire bicycles from a number of places and in the summer there is a regular bus service from St Anne's to the five main beaches.

Aurigny are the main users of the airfield, with scheduled services to the Jersey and Guernsey, the UK mainland and France, in their distinctive yellow Trislanders which also carry the night mail. The airfield has a rural feel, you can hand in your customs forms and pay landing fees with the firemen (next to the curious 'tower on stilts' that houses ATC) and everybody is pretty easygoing. Unlike the other two Channel Island airfields Alderney has three runways, so crosswinds are not often a problem. It also has a very pro-GA attitude. The facilities have been improved recently and AVGAS, engineering and a duty free shop now available.

Alderney's 12th annual fly-in takes place from the 14th-16th of June this year. In recent years the fly-in has attracted up to 125 aircraft - which must be quite a sight on this small airfield!

Landing Fee
£5.20 (cash), £10.40 (non cash) per metric tonne or part thereof. Parking fees apply after the first 72 hours. Visa/Access/Mastercard

Fuel
AVGAS 100LL 39p no VAT. Visa/Access/Mastercard/Amex

Flying Organisations
Stratair 01481 822549

Other Organisations
Evans Aviation Ltd (maintenance) 01481 824081
Alderney Flying Club (fly-in organisers) 01481 822297

Car Hire
J.B. Cycle Hire 01481 822294/822762

Taxis
Alderney Taxis 01481 822611/822992

Public Transport
See main text.

Nearby Places of Interest
All of the island, basically.

Food & Accommodation
Buffet and shop in terminal
Inchalla restaurant and bar, St Anne's 01481 823220

Rose and Crown Hotel, Le Huret. The place to stay for aviators. They offer a special package deal for pilots and passengers that includes £10 B&B for 'safety pilots', free landing, 72 hours free parking at Alderney and free use of car. There's an extensive home-cooked menu (excellent food by all accounts) and the Rose & Crown is Les Routiers recommended. Its also recommended by aviators who have stayed here. Book early would seem to be the only sensible advice!
01481 823414 Fax: 823615

Guernsey

3 miles west of St Peter Port
States of Guernsey Airports, Guernsey, Channel Islands
Tel: 01481 37766 Fax: 01481 38728

Guernsey opened in 1939 as a civil aerodrome with services to the UK mainland and the other Channel Islands. A hurried evacuation of over 300 islanders preceded the German occupation of the island in 1940 and the airfield was used by the Luftwaffe until 1945.

Civilian commercial services soon resumed and the airport remains a busy and popular facility, with scheduled services by Aurigny in their distinctive yellow Trislanders, and Air UK and British Airways in more conventional airliners. Guernsey can now boast over 20 scheduled destinations, in addition to the regular freight flights by Channel Express.

To many Guernsey is a quieter and less hectic place than Jersey. There is an island-wide speed limit of just 35mph and many holidaymakers choose to hire bicycles instead of cars.

The recently expanded terminal houses all the usual facilities, and the airport is becoming increasingly popular with GA aircraft visiting the Channel Islands, not least for the annual Guernsey International Air Rally. The 1995 event was the best attended for many years, and this year's rally, celebrating 25 years of the rally and competition, is being held from the 13th-15th September. More details from 01481 65267

Landing Fee
£5.90 per tonne (cash) no VAT
Mastercard, Visa and Switch

Fuel
AVGAS 100LL 36.8p no VAT. AVTUR JET A-1 31.4p no VAT. 0815-2030 daily (winter), 0515-1930 daily (summer).
Visa and Mastercard

Flying Organisations

Channel Aviation Ltd	01481 37217
Guernsey Flying Training/Guernsey Aeroclub	01481 65254

Other Organisations

Aircraft Servicing (Guernsey) Ltd	01481 65750
Anglo Normandy Aeroengineering	01481 66333
Eagle Airways (Handling)	01481 35455

Car Hire

Avis	01481 35266
Hertz	01481 35376

Taxis
Outside terminal

Public Transport
Regular buses to St Peter Port

Nearby Places of Interest

German Occupation Museum, Forest	01481 38205
Fort Grey Shipwreck Museum, Rocquaine Bay	01481 726518
German Military Underground Hospital, St Andrew	01481 39100
Castle Cornet, St Peter Port (watch out for the daily cannon firing at noon!)	01481 721657
TIC	01481 723552

Food & Accommodation
Buffet at airport. Viewing area on roof of terminal
The Absolute End (French restaurant), St Peter Port 01481 723822
The TIC accommodation bureau (01481 723555) and the airport information desk are your best bet for booking accommodation. Here are some recommendations:

Old Government House, St Peter Port from £46	01481 724921
Hotel De Havelet, St Peter Port from £40	01481 722199
L'Atlantique Hotel, Perelle Bay from £30	01481 64056
Midhurst House, St Peter Port from £30	01481 724391

Jersey

4 miles west of St Helier, States of Jersey
States of Jersey Airport, Jersey, Channel Islands
Tel: 01534 43925 Fax: 01534 46831
Telex: 4192332 AIRJER G

The largest of the Channel Islands, and a tax haven to boot, Jersey is the busiest of the Channel Islands and naturally enough its airport is the biggest and busiest of three airfields in the island group.

Jersey is a popular holiday and business destination. Commercial traffic is busy during the summer season, the runways can accommodate aircraft in the B737/757 class and the freight aircraft of Channel Express are also much in evidence. Most weekends May to October will see an influx of visitors arriving not just from the UK but from France and the rest of continental Europe too. 1.8 million passengers passed through the airport in 1994, and when you know that the island's population is only 85 000 or so you get the idea. A long awaited £20m improvement program started in late 1995, designed to ease the peak-hour congestion.

If you are flying to Jersey it is worth knowing that the Jersey Met office now offer a comprehensive met forecast and information service on the Internet (there's even up-to-date satellite pictures). Find the Jersey Met Office Index at http://user.itl.net/~jmet/ .

If you do arrive by private aircraft you are likely to be parked some way from the terminal. Don't make the mistake of walking across the apron - they don't like it! An Aviation Beauport mini-bus will come out and take you to the terminal (for free). Each of the Channel Island airports has it's own annual rally, the Jersey International Air rally is normally held at the beginning of May.

Landing Fee
Up to 1 tonne £10, then £5.00 per _ tonne to 3 tonnes. No VAT. Visa/Mastercard/Amex

Fuel
AVGAS 100LL 36.4p No VAT, AVTUR JET A1 27p No VAT. Refuelling not available after 1930 local time for AVGAS, or after 2100 local time for JET A1, except by arrangement. Visa and Access

Flying Organisations
Jersey Aero Club 01534 43990

Other Organisations
Aviation Beauport Ltd (Handling) 01534 42128
Channel Island Aero Services Ltd (Engineering) 01534 42373
Jersey Aircraft Maintenance Ltd 01534 45124

Car Hire
Avis 01534 499499
Hertz 01534 45621

Taxis
Outside terminal

Public Transport
Bus to St Helier, every 15 mins

Nearby Places of Interest
Lots and lots of places to visit. Here's a selection:
Jersey Motor Museum, St Peter's Village
(includes aero-engine collection and railway section) 01534 482966
German Underground Hospital, St Lawrence 01534 863442
Kempt Tower Visitor Centre, St Ouens Bay 01534 483651
St Peter's Bunker Museum, St Peter's Village 01534 481048
The Living Legend, (Jersey's past and present), St Peter 01534 485496
Mont Orgueil Castle, Gorey 01534 853292
TIC 01534 500700

Food & Accommodation
Restaurant and buffet at terminal. Viewing from terminal roof
The Admiral, St James Street, St Helier (cosy surroundings, excellent food, good choice of beers) 01534 30095
Tipsy Toad Town House, St Helier (fine range of beers - even has its own mini-brewery! Food's pretty good too)
Every sort of accommodation is available. Advance Booking via the TIC is strongly advised, especially in the peak summer months. A couple of recommended hotels:
Royal Yacht Hotel, St Helier from £40 01534 20511
Millbrook House, St Helier from £25 01534 33036
Cliff Court Hotel, St Helier from £25 01534 34919

Northern Ireland

Belfast (International)

12 miles north-west of Belfast, signposted off M1 and M2
Belfast International Airport Ltd, Belfast International Airport, Belfast, BT29 4AB
Tel: 018494 22888 Fax: 018494 423883
Telex: 747980 Airport Duty Ops Officer

Aldergrove is the oldest airfield in Northern Ireland, it opened in 1918 as a factory site for Harland & Wolff (better known for shipbuilding) to build bombers for Handley Page. During WW2 a number of units were established here and Aldergrove developed a major role as a base for Anti-Submarine, and Coastal Command convoy escort squadrons patrolling the North West approaches. The RAF and Army Air Corps still have presence here, operating mostly helicopters on the south side of the airport.

The airfield's role became primarily civilian when a 'modern' purpose-built terminal was opened in 1963 and Aldergrove became formally 'Belfast Airport'. 'Belfast International', it is now known, is the major airport for Belfast and Northern Ireland - and a major success story. Privatised in July 1994, scheduled destinations doubled in 1995, with passenger numbers expected to be about 2.5 million in that year. There are numerous charter and freight services and, as if to mark the growing status of this airport, Air Lingus re-introduced services to New York and Boston in July 1995 after a break of over 20 years.

The terminal has all the usual services and facilities, and viewing is possible from the 1st floor departures. What's next? The answer to that question depends more on politics than aviation, although recently the management at Belfast International have been rumoured to be interested in buying Belfast City.

Landing Fee
£7.65 up to 15 tonnes. Minimum £12.50 +

Fuel
AVGAS 100LL, 63p + 01849 422789, available 0900-1700 local. Out of hours Woodgate Air Service or Aldergrove Flight Training Centre AVTUR JET A1 via BP.
Visa/Access/Diners

Flying Organisations

Aldergrove Flight Training Centre	01849 423747
Helicopter Training & Hire Ltd	01849 453663
Woodgate Air Services	01849 422789

Other Organisations
Aldergrove Flight Training Centre handle all GA aircraft under 2 tonnes.
Tel: 01849 423747 Fax: 01849 412777
Eurojet handle all GA aircraft over 2 tonnes. Tel: 01849 422888 ext. 4040/4041
Fax: 01849 422640. Woodgate Air Maintenance Ltd 018492 422789

Car Hire

Avis	018494 22333
Eurodollar	018494 52565
Europcar	018494 23444
Hertz	018494 22533

Taxis
At terminal

Public Transport
Buses every 30 minutes to central Belfast. Antrim railway station 5 miles

Nearby Places of Interest

Belfast 12 miles	
Belfast Botanic Gardens Park 8 miles	01232 324902
TIC	01232 246609

See also Belfast City and Newtownards

Food & Accommodation
Buffet and bar in terminal

Aldergrove Airport Hotel ***, (on airport) from £65	01849 422033
Lansdowne Court Hotel ***, Belfast - 12 miles from £40	01232 773317
Malone Guest House, Belfast - 12 miles from £25	01232 669565
Camera Guest House, Belfast - 12 miles from £18	01232 660026
Dukes Hotel, Belfast - 12 miles from £45	01232 236666
Plaza Hotel, Belfast - 12 miles from £50	01232 333555

See also Belfast City

Belfast (City)

East side of Belfast Docks, 1.5 miles from Belfast city centre, via A2
Belfast City Airport Ltd, Belfast City Airport, Sydenham By-Pass, Belfast, BT3 9JH
Tel: 01232 457745 Fax: 01232 459198

Flying operations at this site date back to the 1930s on land alongside the harbour, and the airport proper was opened in 1938. With such a large deep-water harbour alongside, it is perhaps unsurprising that Short Brothers made their name here building large and sophisticated flying boats.

Belfast Harbour (now Belfast City) is still home to Short Brothers, whose successful Shorts 330 & 360 commuter aircraft, and Tucano military trainer, are built here. Opened to commercial traffic in 1983 - some years before the similar venture at London City airport - the main advantage the airfield has is its proximity to Belfast city centre, being only a few minutes' drive away. Hence City has become the main airport for commercial traffic and together with the Short Brothers factory the airport has become a major local employer. The growth in regional airline routes has benefited Belfast City, and it recorded a spectacular five-fold increase growth in passenger numbers in 1995. The busiest route is London Stansted, but there are also flights to Prestwick, East Midlands, Newcastle, Exeter, Birmingham, Edinburgh, Glasgow and Manchester.

Landing Fee
2 tonnes, landing £14 + £14 Nav charge = £28. £25 min. charge for invoicing if not paid at airport.
Training rates by arrangement up to 50% discount.'Off-peak' flights not subject to navigation fee. £3.70 per tonne to 2 tonnes, £7.40 per tonne above.

Fuel
AVGAS 100LL 70.76p + AVTUR JET A-1 28.7p + . Cash, cheque or Diners only

Flying Organisations

Other Organisations
Short Brothers plc 01232 458444

Car Hire
Avis 01232 452017
Europcar 01232 450904
Hertz 01232 732451

Taxis
Airport taxi rank

Public Transport
Regular buses to city centre. Sydenham Halt railway station 100 metres from airport entrance

Nearby Places of Interest
Belfast 1 mile
Belfast Castle and Cave Hill Woods, 2 miles 01232 776925
Lagan Lookout Centre, Belfast City Centre 01232 315444
Ulster Folk and Transport Museum 7 miles 01232 421444
TIC 01232 246609
See also Belfast International & Newtownards

Food & Accommodation
Buffet and bar in terminal (unfortunately it is reported to be distinctly average)
Manor House Cantonese restaurant,
43 Donegal Pass, Belfast (Egon Ronay) 01232 238755
Strand Restaurant Wine bar & bistro,
12 Stranmillis Road, Belfast 01232 682266
The Warehouse, 35 Hill Street, Belfast 01232 439690
Roscoff (famous French restaurant),
Shaftesbury Square Belfast 01232 331532
See also Belfast International

Enniskillen (St Angelo)

5 miles north of Enniskillen
Fermanagh District Council, Enniskillen, Co. Fermanagh Northern Ireland
Tel: 01365 322771

A pretty airfield in glorious countryside, a friendly welcome to visitors and local services and amenities at reasonable prices. If you're wondering how you've missed this gem, you need to look a bit further west on your map, to the south-west corner of Northern Ireland.

Visiting pilots are assured of a warm welcome in the tower, where you can take in the modern facilities - paid for from European Union funds apparently. The resident aircraft have a hangar near the tower building and the runway distances available have recently increased. The airfield site is bisected by a road, on the far side of which army helicopters operate. When the tower is closed the army base will usually answer radio calls. The beautiful Upper Lough Erne borders the airfield on its western boundary, and the rolling hills of County Fermanagh beckon beyond.

Landing Fee
Singles £5.00 inc. Multi £10.00 inc.

Fuel
AVGAS 100LL 69p + by prior arrangement only

Flying Organisations

Other Organisations

Car Hire

Lochside Garages	01365 324366
Country Cars	01365 322727

Taxis

Call-A-Cab	01365 324848
Diamond Taxis	0800 123444
Star Taxis	01365 323232
Westend Taxis	01365 325999

Public Transport
No convenient buses or railway stations. Enniskillen coach station 01365 322633

Nearby Places of Interest

Beautiful countryside, hills, loughs	
Enniskillen Castle - 5 miles	01365 325000
Marble Arch Caves - 8 miles	01365 348855
Devenish Island (in Upper Lough Erne) - 5 miles	
Castlebowlervision (leisure complex), Enniskillen - 5 miles	01365 324172
Numerous boat and cruiser hire companies - details from TIC	01365 323110

Food & Accommodation

Tea and coffee at the airfield	
Mulligan's Bar & Restaurant, Enniskillen - 5 miles	01365 322059
Franco's restaurant, Enniskillen - 5 miles	01365 324424
Saddlers Restaurant, Enniskillen - 5 miles	01365 326223
Fort Lodge Hotel, Enniskillen - 5 miles £25	01365 323275
Railway Hotel, Enniskillen - 5 miles £25	01365 322084

Londonderry (Eglinton)

7 miles east of Londonderry, signposted from the A2
City of Derry Airport, Airport Road, Eglinton, Londonderry
Northern Ireland BT47 3PY
Tel: 01504 810784 Fax: 01504 811426

In 1941 the airfield at Eglinton opened without finished runways, and it was only able to accept the resident Hudsons and Hurricanes four months after the HQ staff had moved in. Later the airfield became home to various American squadrons, flying Spitfires and Corsairs. Training continued after the war until the end of the 1950s and Eglinton was used for military aviation until 1966, when it became Londonderry Airport. The airfield now boasts a smart new terminal, courtesy of European Union funds, which houses the usual facilities, including a pleasant cafeteria serving light refreshments of a good standard. Welcoming and friendly, the airfield receives good reports from fly-in visitors for its helpful ATC staff. Access to the hangars housing resident aircraft is limited by virtue of their distance from the terminal, tucked away in a corner of the airfield.

As we go to press Jersey European Airways have announced that their daily London Stansted to Belfast route is being extended to Londonderry, and a direct service Londonderry to Birmingham is also being introduced - good news indeed and hopefully a sign of things to come.

Landing Fee
Single-engine, club and private £6.05 + . multi, club and private £12.10 +
All major credit cards

Fuel
AVGAS 100LL 69p + AVTUR JET A1 26p +
All major credit cards

Flying Organisations
The Eglinton Flying Club 01504 810962

Other Organisations

Car Hire
Avis 01265 43654
Ford Rentacar 01504 360420

Taxis
Available at terminal. On average £6 into town.

Public Transport
Bus stop on the main road, about 3-4 mins walk from the terminal, with regular services into town.

Nearby Places of Interest
Foyle Valley Railway, Londonderry - 7 miles 01504 265234
Tower Museum, Londonderry - 7 miles 01504 372411
City Walls, Londonderry - 7 miles
(the most complete city wall in Ireland. You can walk along it, about 1 mile in all)
The Giant's Causeway - 20 miles

Food & Accommodation
Cafe in terminal
Longfield Farm B&B from £20 01504 810210
Banks of Faughan Motel from £21 01504 860242
Eglinton Guest House - 1 mile B&B from £15 01504 810377
Everglades Hotel, Londonderry 01504 46722

Newtownards

9 miles east of Belfast on the northern shore of Strangford Lough
Newtownards Aerodrome, Portaferry Road, Newtownards, County Down, Northern Ireland B23 3SG
Tel: 01247 813327/811409 Fax: 01247 814575

In 1934 The Marquis of Londonderry donated 50 acres of his estates to the construction of Newtownards and the airfield quickly became the busiest airfield in the country, with services to several cities on the British mainland. Extended for wartime operations, it reverted to civilian use after the War and services to England resumed including car-ferry schedules, operated by Silver City.

With the rise of Aldergrove and Belfast City, the airfield has settled back into the more tranquil role as the unofficial Northern Ireland centre for light aircraft. The Ulster Flying Club are based here and the area's good weather record makes it a popular destination. As elsewhere in Northern Ireland visitors are assured of a warm welcome whether they arrive by surface or by air. There is usually something interesting to watch, and Newtownards is probably the only UK airfield with its own Chinese restaurant. It's called the New Dragon Palace and you'll find it in the flying club. By all accounts it's very good, and eating there will certainly make a change from the usual cup of tea and a cheese sandwich!

Landing Fee
Singles £8.00, multi £18.00 inc. Parking £2.35 (singles), £5.88 (multi) inc.
Visa and Access

Fuel
AVGAS 100LL 79p inc. available as airfield hours.
Visa and Access

Flying Organisations

Helicopter Training and Hire Ltd	01247 820028
Ulster Flying Club	01247 813327

Other Organisations

Claddagh Air Maintenance (N.I.) Ltd	012665 58609
Kenboag Aviation Ltd (Maintenance)	01247 811241
Trenchard Ltd (Maintenance)	01846 651749

Car Hire

A1 Car and Van Hire	01247 464447

Taxis

Crabo Taxis	01247 810360

Public Transport
Bangor railway station 8 miles

Nearby Places of Interest
Castle Espie Wildfowl & Wetlands Centre,
Comber - 5 miles 01247 874146
Located just a few miles from Newtownards along the shore of Strangford Lough, this is the largest collection of wildfowl in Ireland including many rare species. You will also find hides, landscaped gardens, woodland walks and fine wildlife paintings. Pilots might also wish to bear in mind that thousands of birds migrate to the center annually!
Bangor - 5 miles
North Down Heritage Centre, Bangor - 5 miles
TIC 01232 246609
See also Belfast (Aldergrove) and Belfast City

Food & Accommodation

New Dragon Palace, in the flying club	01247 816800
Bay Tree Cafe, (Egon Ronay), Holywood - 6 miles	01232 426414
Culloden Hotel & Cultra Inn, Holywood - 6 miles	01232 425223

See also Belfast (Aldergrove) and Belfast City

Scotland

Aberdeen

7 miles north-west of Aberdeen, on the A96
Aberdeen Airport Ltd, Aberdeen Airport, Dyce, Grampian Scotland AB2 0DU
Tel: 01224 722331 (Information desk ext. 5312)
Fax: 01224 723714 Telex: 73120 CAA

Dyce opened to scheduled services in 1934 serving routes throughout Scotland and, eventually, to Norway. The Second World War saw Dyce in a number of roles, including Coastal Patrol, Convoy Escort and training, and a military presence was retained here until the late 1950s.

But for the discovery of North Sea Oil, the aerodrome would probably have faded into obscurity. Now, however, Aberdeen is the largest and busiest heliport in Europe, serving the hundreds of gas and oil rigs throughout the North Sea. As a result scheduled services have flourished, feeding the airport with traffic from the rest of the UK and Northern Europe.

Many of the original wartime structures remain, alongside much more modern development, including the unusual, pyramidal tower building, likened to a Ziggurat. The terminal facilities have recently been improved, including much better shopping and catering outlets. If you're looking for the flying school by road, follow the "Airport East" signs from the main terminal.

Landing Fee
Under 2 tonnes £15 +. First hour's parking free, then 64p per tonne to 23 hours, thereafter 6p per tonne per quarter hour. All major credit cards accepted

Fuel

AVGAS 100LL 69.5 + Aberdeen Refuellers Ltd	01224 772127 / 0860 310313
JET A1 28.35 + Shell & BP	01224 772127 / 0860 310313

All major credit cards accepted

Flying Organisations

Aberdeen Flying Club/Tayside Aviation Ltd	01224 725333
Bond Helicopters Ltd	01224 725505
British International Helicopters	01224 771353
Bristow Helicopters Ltd / Caledonian Helicopters Ltd	01224 723151/2

Other Organisations

Caledonian Airborne Engineering Ltd	01224 770222
Maersk Air Engineering Ltd	01224 724825

Car Hire

Avis	01224 722282
Eurodollar	01224 626955
Hertz	01224 722373
Budget	01224 771777
Europcar	01224 770770

Taxis
Available at the terminal. About £8.00 to city centre.

Public Transport
Dyce railway station 2 miles, Aberdeen railway station 7 miles. Buses to city centre and railway station every 40 mins, fare £2.10 Info. 01224 664586 & 633333

Nearby Places of Interest
Aberdeen - the granite city 7 miles
The Grampian Highlands to the west
More castles with ghosts than you can shake a stick at. The nearest is Castle Fraser, south of Kemnay (10 miles) 013303463
Aberdeen TIC 01224 632727

Food & Accommodation
Reasonable eating and drinking facilities in the main terminal
Information board with direct freephone connection in terminal - next to the information desk
Prince of Wales Pub, 7 St Nicholas Lane, Aberdeen (recommended)

Skean Dhu Hotel (at Airport) from £95	01224 725252
Speedbird Inn 400 metres from airport, from £40	01224 772884
Travel Inn £35 per room, Dyce - 2 miles	01224 821217
The Beeches, Dyce - 2 miles B&B from £20	01224 722249

Barra

Foreshore of Traigh Mhor, Isle of Barra
HIAL, Barra Aerodrome, North Bay, Castle Bay, Isle of Barra, Western Isles PA80 5XY
Tel: 01871 890283, 890212 Fax: 01871 890220

The famous 'airfield on the beach' - where operating hours are dictated by the tide, and the runways are under water at least a third of the time! When the tide is out the Twin Otters of Loganair / British Airways Express share the ridged sand of the beach with cockle harvesters - Traigh Mhor (pronounced Tray Vor) means Cockle Strand.

If the arrival to Barra is the most romantic of any UK airport, the island itself does not disappoint. The film 'Whisky Galore' was shot on Barra, although the SS Politician and its cargo of 250 00 bottles of whisky was in fact wrecked on the nearby island of Eriskay in 1941. It's easy to see why Barra would appeal to film makers - it is everybody's idea of what a Hebridean island should look like. One road circles the part of the island south of Traigh Mhor, the main town of Castlebay is about 7 miles south of the airfield on this road. From Castlebay you can take boat trips past Kisimul Castle to the small islands south of Barra, and ferries operate to the other islands and the mainland. A causeway allows you to cross to Vatersay. Alternatively you can take the road north from the airport to Eoligarry with its two mile beach, where ferries leave for South Uist.

Recently larger aircraft have sometimes been used on the daily flights to Barra, and there has also been talk of laying a tarmac runway on the island. Inter-island gossip is that Barra's inhabitants are opposed to both moves. They like their island (and the airport) the way it is, and most visitors will probably agree.

Landing Fee

Private light aircraft up to 3 tonnes £10.50 inc. if paid cash/cheque on arrival. No parking fees (because if you stay too long, the tide comes in!).
To operate outside notified hours you must sign (and have accepted) an indemnity form obtained from Highland and Islands Airports Ltd, tel: 01667 462445, fax: 01667 462579. Even if you do not *intend* to fly outside the published hours you are strongly recommended to consider signing this form in advance. However, remember that at Barra 'outside hours' may well mean 'under water'!

Fuel

Flying Organisations

Other Organisations

Car Hire

Taxis

Hatcher's Taxis	01871 810486
Campbell's	01871 810216

Public Transport

Post bus, details from TIC

Nearby Places of Interest

Eoligarry village, 2 miles	
Castlebay (main town) 5 miles	
Golf Course, Grean Head	
Halaman Bay, Tangasdale, 7 miles. Fine beach	
Castlebay TIC (open April - October)	01871 810336
Stornoway TIC (open all year)	01851 703088

Food & Accommodation

Tea room at airport	
Kisimul Gallery Cafe, Castlebay - 5 miles	01871 810645
Isle of Barra Hotel, Tangasdale - 7 miles from £35	01871 810383
Castlebay Hotel, Castlebay - 5 miles from £30	01871 810223
Craigard Hotel, Castlebay - 5 miles from £30	01871 810200
Northbay House, Northbay, 10 minutes from airport B&B from £17	01871 890355

Benbecula

Western side of Benbecula, on the B892 at Balivanich
HIAL, Benbecula Aerodrome, Balivanich, Isle of Benbecula, Outer Hebrides, HS7 5LW
Tel: 01870 602051 / 603147 Fax: 01870 602278
Telex 777736

The airfield on Benbecula pre-dates the Second World War. The RAF station opened here in 1942 and its predominant role was as a base for anti-submarine operations. Benbecula was relinquished by the RAF in 1946 and services by BEA (later British Airways' Highlands & Islands division) commenced. These were taken over by Loganair, and now the wheel has come full circle as Loganair are today flying in British Airways colours under the franchise of British Airways Express.

The airfield still has close military connections. The army missile testing range on Benbecula is responsible for a huge danger area that stretches far out into the Atlantic, past St Kilda. In fact, the MOD is the major employer on the island, and vital to the local economy on an island that was previously regarded as merely a stepping stone between North Uist and South Uist - it is connected to both by causeways.

Benbecula can be fairly described as windswept with a barren, treeless landscape. The islanders take a certain pride in this, as well as the lack of litter and graffiti on the island, and the fact that cars and houses can be left unlocked at night with no risk of burglary. However, Benbecula seems a busier island that many of those in the Outer Hebrides and facilities are good at Balivanich which is adjacent to the airport. The airport itself has good length runways, navaids and fuel - something of a rarity in the Hebrides!

Landing Fee
Private light aircraft up to 3 tonnes £10.50 inc. if paid cash/cheque on arrival. Parking £1.56 per tonne per 24 hours. All major credit cards.
To operate outside notified hours you must sign an indemnity form obtained from Highland and Islands Airports Ltd, tel: 01667 462445, fax: 01667 462579. Even if you do not *intend* to fly outside the published hours you are strongly recommended to consider completing this form in advance, as the weather is more than capable of wrecking the best laid plans!

Fuel
AVGAS 100LL 0.81p +, AVTUR JET A1 0.465p + 01870 603147 .By prior arrangement. Quantities limited. Outside published hours 48 hours notice is required, fuel is subject to surcharge. Cash or cheque only

Flying Organisations

Other Organisations

Car Hire

MacLennan's	01870 602191
Ask	01870 602818

Taxis

Buchanan's	01870 602277
MacVicar's	01870 602307
MacLennon's	01870 602191

Public Transport
Details from TICs

Nearby Places of Interest

Several good beaches and castle ruins	
Kallin harbour, Grimsay 4 miles	
Liniclate (town with sports centre) 4 miles	
North Uist and South Uist	
North Uist TIC (April - Oct)	01876 500321
South Uist TIC (April - Oct)	01878 700286
Stornoway TIC (open all year)	01851 703088

Food & Accommodation

Light refreshments at aerodrome cafe/bar	
Creagorry Hotel, 15 mins from airport from £27	01870 602024
Dark Island Hotel, Liniclate - 4 miles from £30	01870 603030
Culla Bay View, Balivanich - 1 mile B&B from £15	01870 602201

Cumbernauld

16 miles north-east of Glasgow, signposted off the A80
Cumbernauld Aerodrome, Duncan McIntosh Road, Ward Park North, Cumbernauld G68 0HH
Tel: 01236 781711 Fax: 01236 781676 Telex: 778156 CUAIR G

Duncan McIntosh Road is the main access road to Cumbernauld's modern airport. Named in honour of the founder of Loganair it recognises his contribution to aviation in Scotland at virtually every level. Cumbernauld itself, in common with many modern airfield developments, feels as much an industrial estate as an airfield. This is probably because it is one of the few new airfield developments of recent times - in other words it did not start life as a wartime military base.

The airfield houses the West of Scotland Flying Club, recently moved from their former base at Glasgow Airport, and Dollar Helicopters. Additionally Cormack Aircraft Services Ltd, the airfield owners, operate Caledonian Seaplanes in a Loch some way to the north, hence the occasional appearance of a Cessna 206 on amphibious floats.

Upstairs in the main building is the pleasant 'Ozone' bar, serving good bar food and snacks with a good view over the apron. At a time when nearby Glasgow does not seem to be encouraging light aircraft visitors, Cumbernauld is more and more becoming the obvious GA airfield destinations for mid - Scotland.

Landing Fee
Singles up to 2000kg £8.50, then £5.60 for any subsequent landings within 48 hrs, over 2000kg £25.00, then £15.00. Multi up to 2000kg £25.00, then £15.00 for any subsequent landings within 48 hrs, 2001-5700kg £35.00, then £25.00.
All major credit cards

Fuel
AVGAS 100LL 65p +, AVTUR JET A1 30p + . All major credit cards

Flying Organisations

Caledonian Seaplanes	01236 457777
West of Scotland Flying Club	01236 451000

Other Organisations

Cormack Aircraft Services Ltd (Maintenance)	01236 457777
European Helicopters Ltd (Maintenance)	01236 457567

Car Hire

Avis	0141 8872261
Eurodollar	0141 2041051
Hertz	0141 2043373

Taxis

East Field Cars	01236 730009
Black Cab Taxis	01236 738383

Public Transport
No convenient buses. Glasgow Central railway station 16 miles

Nearby Places of Interest
Glasgow about 25 minutes by road
Edinburgh about 35 minutes by road
Just along the northern edge of the airfield are the remains of the Antonine Wall, an ill-fated attempt by the Romans to build a new frontier north of Hadrian's wall. It didn't work, and today the ditch and turf wall is all that remains of what was once the Roman Empire's northern boundary. In a valley below the wall is a disused canal, where you can walk along the towpath.
TIC 0141 2044400

Food & Accommodation
'The Ozone' bar, open 1100-0100, 7 days a week

Wayside Lodge	01324 840310
Wester Dullatur	01236 723218
Travel Inn, Cumbernauld £35	01236 725339

Dundee

1 mile south of Dundee, alongside the A85
Dundee Airport, Riverside Drive, Dundee, DD2 1UH
Tel: 01382 643242/641709 Fax: 01382 641263
Telex: 76431

On the north bank of the River Tay, 1 mile upstream from William McGonegal's famous Tay Bridge, Dundee Airport sits neatly and economically alongside the town, conveniently located for the centre and the industrial areas to the South and West of the town centre. The airfield uses remarkably little land, as the runway parallels the riverbank and only the small collection of airport buildings intrude from the shoreline.

Dundee, like Cumbernauld and Glenrothes (Fife), is quite typical of recent 'new-town' airfield development, where the emphasis is on the airport as a tool for business rather than a travel centre. At present Dundee has one scheduled service, to Edinburgh and Manchester. The runway was extended last year in an attempt to bring more scheduled traffic to Dundee, and there are plans for new terminal but no date yet. The existing terminal is getting on for 15 years old and has minimal facilities.

Don't let this put you off. The location is ideal for travellers to the area, and flying visitors will be well looked after. Tayside Aviation have a small coffee bar area with views over the runway and the river, and the pleasant town centre of Dundee is a short walk or taxi ride.

Landing Fee
£6.50 inc. Parking £3.83 + on grass; £4.60 on apron.
All major credit cards

Fuel
AVGAS 100LL 66p +, AVTUR JET A1 24p +
All major credit cards

Flying Organisations
Tayside Flying Club/Tayside Aviation Ltd 01382 644372

Other Organisations
Tayside Aviation (Engineering) Ltd 01382 68838

Car Hire
Avis 01382 832264
Eurodollar 01382 24037
Mitchells 01382 23484

Taxis
01382 515573

Public Transport
Dundee railway station 1 mile

Nearby Places of Interest
Dundee 1 mile
Discovery Point, 1 mile 01382 201245
Sea Life Centre, St Andrews, 10 miles 01334 74786
St Andrews Castle, 10 miles 01334 77196
The Secret Bunker, 20 miles. Scotland Nuclear Bunker now open to public, also used in WWII, full of all sorts of bits and pieces. Well recommended by those who have visited. 01333 310301
TIC 01382 434664

Food & Accommodation
Snack and canned drinks vending machines in terminal
Tea and Coffee in the Tayside Flying Club
Raffles Restaurant, Dundee. (Egon Ronay) 01382 26344
Bruce Hotel 01382 223021
Discover Quay Travel Inn - 2 miles, room from £35 01382 203240
Westend Hotel 01382 25712
The Angus Thistle, Dundee - 2 miles from £32 01382 26874

Edinburgh

5 miles west of Edinburgh on the A8; signposted from the M9, M8 and A90
Edinburgh Airport, Edinburgh Lothian, Scotland EH12 9DN
Tel: 0131 333 1000 Fax: 0131 3177126
Telex: 72615 EDI LTD

The story of Edinburgh airport is the story of two airfields. The Turnhouse site dates from 1916. The runways were paved during the second World War and RAF Hurricanes and Spitfires moved in. RAF Turnhouse also played host to many USAF bombers, staging through on their way to bases further south. The RAF station is still open and active hosting, among other things, a University Air Squadron, an Air Experience Flight, and many interesting military aircraft on stopovers. Two of the three flying schools based at Edinburgh are sited on this side of the airfield.

The main airport, in the guise of the passenger terminal (built in 1971) and the newer long runway, occupies virtually a separate site on the western side of the airfield off the A8. Here you will find the pleasant terminal, with all the usual facilities and viewing on the 2nd floor. There is also a GA terminal located about halfway between the Edinburgh and Turnhouse sites, where business jets sit alongside the Cessnas of Edinburgh Air Centre.

This winter a £4m expansion plan has started, designed to reduce congestion and add more shops to the terminal. At present Edinburgh has around 30 scheduled destinations with 11 carriers, 3.2 million passengers passed through in 1995. Edinburgh is a reasonably 'GA friendly' airfield and it is worth noting that last year Edinburgh's movements rose, compared to the fall at nearby Glasgow. Handling is not compulsory, however visiting pilots are probably best advised to use Execair's facilities at the GA terminal - not least to avoid ending-up several miles from where they want to be on this larger than average airport site!

Landing Fee
£15.00 single. Parking; 0-2 tonnes £11.50 per 24 hours or part.
All major credit cards

Fuel
AVGAS 100LL 71.36 + AVTUR JET A1 30p +
All major credit cards

Flying Organisations

Edinburgh Air Centre	0131 3398888
(Adjacent to the GA terminal, reached from the main terminal site)	
Edinburgh Flying Club	0131 3394990
Turnhouse Flying Club	0131 3394706

(For Turnhouse and Edinburgh Flying Clubs follow A8 towards the city centre, and 2 miles beyond the terminal take signs to the left for 'RAF Turnhouse')

Other Organisations

Aircraft Engineers (Maintenance)	0131 3334150
Execair (Handling)	0131 317 7447

Car Hire

Avis	0131 3331866
Europcar	0131 3332588
Hertz	0131 3331019
Alamo	0131 3335100

Taxis
Available at terminal

Public Transport
Regular buses to city centre and Waverley Bridge station. Waverley Bridge railway station 5 miles

Nearby Places of Interest

Edinburgh 5 miles	
Princes Street and its shops, voted the most beautiful street in Britain	
Edinburgh Castle	0131 2259846
Scotch Whiskey Heritage Centre, Royal Mile, Edinburgh	0131 2200441
Camera Obscura (recommended)	0131 2263709
Forth Road and Rail Bridges (huge toll this one - 20p per car) 5 miles	
National Museums of Scotland	
- Museum of Flight, East Fortune 20 miles	01620 88308
TIC	0131 5571700

Food & Accommodation

Restaurant, buffet and bar in terminal - rated as 'average airport food' by visitors. Many aircrew eat at the adjacent Stakis hotel instead

Stakis (on airport, opened June 1995) from £89 mid-week, £35 weekends	0131 519 4400
Commodore Hotel (recommended) 5 mins, courtesy bus to/from GA terminal £35	0131 336 1700
Royal Highland Lodge, adjacent to airport, from £50	0131 333 4331
Glenlivet (recommended) Edinburgh, B&B from £18	0131 334 1188
Kenvie Guest House, Edinburgh B & B from £16	0131 6681964

(Accommodation prices tend to rise during the Edinburgh Festival)

Fife

2 miles west of Glenrothes. Leave M90 at junction 5, follow signs for "Glenrothes / Glenrothes South", airfield is then signposted from the B921

Fife Aerodrome, Glenrothes, Fife, KY6 2SL

Tel: 01592 753792 Fax: 01592 612812

Just outside the new town of Glenrothes lies the new airport of Fife (Glenrothes). Recently reopened after a closure of three years, the airfield is now run by Tayside Aviation, operators of nearby Dundee Airport - another 'new' airfield development. Like Dundee, the airfield is remarkably compact , although this is perhaps in part because little development has taken place here in recent years.

The new operators are keen to build up activity and already a busy flying school operates from here. The airfield restaurant, bar and lounge (the Tipsy Nipper) has been refurbished and is already receiving rave reviews from those who have eaten there. All visitors are made welcome and the feeling is of an airfield being re-vitalised - an attractive idea in itself. The beautiful local scenery and the fact that Glenrothes is only 30 minutes by road from Edinburgh make Fife an attractive destination.

Landing Fee

Single £6.00, multi £12.00. 50% discount if fuel uplifted or more than £6.00 spent in restaurant.

Major credit cards except Amex & Diners

Fuel

AVGAS 100LL 64p +

Major credit cards except Amex & Diners

Flying Organisations

Fife Flying Club / Tayside Aviation Ltd 01592 753792

Other Organisations

Pooley's Pilot's Shop in club house

Car Hire

By arrangement with the airfield

Taxis

01592 611111

Public Transport

Thornton Junction and Marchinch railway stations 4 miles. Kirkcaldy mainline railway station 7 miles

Nearby Places of Interest

Portmoak Gliding Centre 6 miles 01592 840355

Golf wherever you look

Falkland Palace, 8 miles 01337 857397

TIC 01333 429464

Food & Accommodation

Licensed restaurant and club facilities at the 'Tipsy Nipper'.

Open Tues-Sun 10.00-23.00, high teas on Sunday 16.00-19.00

Kind Kyttock's Kitchen, Falkland - 8 miles (Egon Ronay) 01337 57477

Rescobie Hotel, Glenrothes - 2 miles from £40 01592 840220

Grange House Hotel (ask for Leslie it says here) 01592 742143

Glasgow

6 miles west of Glasgow. M8 Junction 29, signposted from A726
Glasgow Airport Limited, Paisley, Strathclyde PA3 2ST
Tel: 0141 8871111 Fax: 0141 8484586 Telex 776613

Abbotsinch airport opened in 1932 as a municipal airport, and during the Second World War was home to both the RAF and Royal Navy (whose part of the airfield was known as HMS Sanderling). The RAF moved out to nearby Renfrew during the war, leaving the airfield entirely for Naval use, and some operations by Scottish Airways. The Navy finally left in 1963 and in the large, modern terminal the Sanderling Bar commemorates the long standing Royal Navy presence.

Since the airfield returned to purely civilian operation growth in traffic has been steady, particularly since the breaking of Prestwick's monopoly on transatlantic traffic in the late 1980s. These days Glasgow is indisputably the busiest airport in Scotland, with 13 carriers serving 40 destinations - including USA; in 1995 5.4 million passengers passed through.

Easy to reach by road, the airport is adjacent to the M8, although General Aviation is less well served. Handling is mandatory for all visiting aircraft. Furthermore, several of the resident flying schools and light aircraft have been persuaded to leave, presumably to accommodate an expected increase in traffic numbers. The result - a 2% FALL in movements! The one remaining flying club (maybe more favoured by the airport now) has moved to tidy new premises on the Abbotsinch road, while a new home is found, hopefully still on the airfield.

Landing Fee
Under 2 tonnes £15 +, over 2 tonnes £4.55 + per tonne. Plus minimum £25.00 compulsory handling fee. For GA aircraft handling is compulsory through Execair. All major credit cards.

Fuel
AVGAS 100LL 72p + AVTUR Jet A1 30p +. Through Execair, all major credit cards.

Flying Organisations
Glasgow Flying Club 0141 8894565
(Leave M8 at junction 28 and follow the 'RVP' and 'Renfrew' signs. At the Travel Inn roundabout turn left to 'Renfrew', Glasgow Flying Club is 3/4 mile on Abbotinch Rd)

Other Organisations
Loganair Ltd (Maintenance) 0141 8891311
Scottish Aerotech Services Ltd (Maintenance) 0141 8480040
Execair (Handling) 0141 848 4712

Car Hire
Avis 0141 8872261
Hertz 0141 8872541
Europcar 0141 887 0414

Taxis
Outside terminal

Public Transport
Paisley (Gilmore St) railway station 2 miles 0141 204 2844
Coaches to city centre very 20 minutes, Edinburgh hourly 0141 332 9191
Local buses to Paisley and Renfrew

Nearby Places of Interest
Glasgow 6 miles
Museum of Transport, Glasgow 0141 3311854
Prince's Square Shopping Centre
Hutchesons Hall, City Centre 0141 5528391
The Tenement House, Nr Sauchiehall Street 0141 3330183
Paddlesteamer excursions from central Glasgow along the river Clyde 0141 2218152
TIC 0141 2044400

Food & Accommodation
Tea and coffee available at Glasgow Flying Club. They have plans to extend their facilities in the spring Restaurant, buffet and bars in terminal
Babbity Bowster Glasgow (Egon Ronay) 0141 552 5055
The Jenny Traditional Tea Rooms, Glasgow 0141 2044988
Glynhill Leisure Hotel - 1 mile from £36 0141 8865555
Regent Guest House, City Centre B&B from £20 0141 4221199
Ewington Hotel, City Centre from £37.50 0141 4222030
Travel Inn at airport - from £35 per room (courtesy bus to terminal) 0141 842 1563
Forte Crest (on airport) from £40 0141 887 1212

Glenforsa (Isle of Mull)

1 mile east of Salen on the Isle of Mull
D S Howitt, Airfield Bungalow, Salen, Isle of Mull PA72 6JN
Tel: 01680 300402/812475

Glenforsa, on the island of Mull, is said by many to be one of the most beautiful airfield locations in the UK. On the northern coast close to the A849 and roughly halfway between the main towns of Tobermory (10 miles north) and Craignure (9 miles south), the airfield is bounded by the Sound of Mull to the north, and green forest to the other sides. The adjacent Glenforsa Hotel run by Jean and Paul Price (seafood highly recommended) and the spectacular local scenery are reward enough, and a visit by air or sea to see the stunning basalt pillars and resident puffins of Fingal's cave on the Isle of Staffa is highly recommended.

The island seems to have more than its fair share of attractions and facilities, and the visitor can choose from sailing, fishing trips, sight seeing tours, whale watching and even a miniature railway; in addition to the abundant local history, walks through the dramatic scenery and wildlife. The island has two Tourist Information Centres (see below) and a monthly business and leisure guide 'Round & About', available from Mull Laser Print on 01688 302451. Tobermory is regarded by those who know as being the prettiest town of all the islands, with brightly coloured houses around the bay, watching the 'Cal Mac' ferries leaving for the outer islands. The bay is reputed to be the final resting place of a 16th century Spanish galleon, and in such a enchanting place it is not difficult to believe in such legends.

Back at the airfield, there is a popular annual fly-in each May. Whenever your planned visit, flying visitors should phone well in advance for details of the airfield, a weather briefing, and to give the operators time to clear the sheep off the runway!

Landing Fee
£4.15 per half tonne +
Cash or cheque only

Fuel
AVGAS 100LL available on prior notice, usually only in the summer
Cash or cheque only

Flying Organisations

Other Organisations

Car Hire

Bayview Garage	01680 812444
Mull Travel & Craft (car & bike hire)	01680 812487

Taxis

Tommy's Private Hire	01688 302204

Public Transport
Details from the Glenforsa Hotel

Nearby Places of Interest

Duart Castle (home of MacLean Clan)	01680 812309
Old Byre Heritage Centre, Dervaig - 14 miles	01688 400229
Tobermory Distillery (the only distillery on the island) - 10 miles	01688 302645
Sea-Life Surveys, Dervaig - 14 miles (whale/dolphin watching)	01688 400223
Turus Mara, Dervaig - 14 miles (cruises to Staffa, Iona etc.)	01688 400242
Mull and West Highland Narrow Gauge Railway	01680 812494
Tobermory TIC	01688 302182
Craignure TIC	01680 812377

Food & Accommodation

Glenforsa Hotel, Norwegian Lodge hotel next to the airfield, from £30	01680 300377
Puffer Aground Restaurant, Aros - 2 miles	01680 300389
Back Brae Restaurant, Tobermory - 10 miles	01688 302422
The Western Isles Hotel, Tobermory - 10 miles from £40	01688 302012
Mrs Adam B&B, Salen - 2 miles from £15	01680 300386

Inverness

7 miles north-east of Inverness, signposted from A96, B9039 and B9006
Inverness Aerodrome, Invernesshire IV1 2JB
Tel: 01667 462445 Fax: 01667 462586

Opened in 1940 as an RAF airfield, Inverness became the main civil airport for the Highlands following a major extension to the runway in 1974. British Airways are the dominate operator, with 3 daily flights to London Heathrow using B737s. Currently about 300 000 passengers pass through each year. £4 million has recently been spent on general improvements on the airfield and there are plans to upgrade and expand the terminal. Of particular interest to visiting pilots there is now a 'one stop' flight planning office in the terminal where fuel, landing fees, met information etc. can all be dealt with without having to shuttle to different parts of the airfield.

Happily, Inverness retains the atmosphere of a small, regional airfield. Flying training and air taxi work is undertaken by Air Alba, who are part of Air Atlantique. Additionally DC3s of Air Atlantic's Marine Pollution Control Unit are based here to be used for the dispersal of oil slicks at sea. To reach Air Alba by road take first left turning after the main gate.

Interestingly Inverness enjoys a much better weather record than many would expect, with excellent visibility over the spectacular Highlands and coastline of north east Scotland for much of the time.

Landing Fee
Private light aircraft up to 3 tonnes £10.50 inc. if paid cash/cheque on arrival. Parking £1.56 per tonne per 24 hours. To operate outside notified hours you must complete and have had accepted an indemnity form obtained from Highland and Islands Airports Ltd (tel: 01667 462445, fax: 01667 462579), and send them a copy of your insurance certificate. Even if you do not *intend* to fly outside the published hours you are strongly recommended to consider doing this in advance. All major credit cards

Fuel
AVGAS 100LL 69.49p + from Air Alba, Mon-Fri 0900-1630 local. Sat-Sun 1000-1600 01667 462664. AVTUR JET A-1 28.45p + from Air BP, Mon-Fri 0600-1830 local. Sat-Sun 0600-1700 (W) 0600-1830 (S) local. Only Diners accepted. Both fuels attract an out of hours surcharge. All major credit cards.

Flying Organisations
Air Alba 01667 462664

Other Organisations
Merlin Maintenance 01667 462642

Car Hire
Avis 01667 462787
Eurodollar 01463 238084
Hertz 01463 224475

Taxis
Available at the terminal

Public Transport
Regular buses to Inverness railway station. Inverness railway station 7 miles. Nairn railway station 6 miles

Nearby Places of Interest
Culloden, site of the battle - 3 miles 01463 790607
Fort George - 3 miles 01667 462777
Cawdor Castle and Gardens - 4 miles, 01667 404615
Loch Ness and the monster etc. etc. - 20 miles
Inverness Museum and Art Gallery, Inverness 01463 237114
Edwardian Bridges span the river Ness at Inverness - the eastern extremity of the Caledonian Canal which bisects Scotland along the fault line of the Great Glen.
TIC 01463 234353

Food & Accommodation
Refreshments and bar at the terminal
For local information the BA staff at check-in desk 1 in the terminal are usually helpful
Culloden Pottery Vegetarian Restaurant,
Gollanfield - 1 mile. (Egon Ronay) 01667 462749
The Claymore House Hotel, Nairn - 6 miles from £42 01667 453731
Clach Mhuilinm, Inverness - 6 miles B&B from £18 01463 220062
Moyness House, Inverness centre - 6 miles B&B from £25 01463 233836
Palace Hotel, Inverness centre - 6 miles from £29 01463 223243

Islay

5 miles north of Port Ellen, next to the A846
Islay Aerodrome, Isle of Islay, Argyll Scotland PA42 7AS
Tel: 01496 302361 Fax: 01496 2096

Situated not far from the Scottish mainland, and with reasonably long tarmac runways and good navaids, Islay is an obvious first stopping point for an aviator exploring the Western Isles.

When you do arrive at Islay, wait until the engines have stopped and then listen. Chances are that you will hear very little man-made noise. Now mentally adjust to a slower pace of life and a different perspective, and you have a much better chance of enjoying these magical islands.

Not all airfields in the Highlands and Islands are as well equipped as Islay, but in many ways it is a typical destination. The airfield opening hours are closely linked to the regular Loganair (now franchised as British Airways Express) services so a copy of British Airways' Scottish timetable can be very useful. Islay has no fuel, no hangerage and no resident aircraft. Despite (or perhaps because of) this visitors are greeted warmly and, as you would expect in a small community, everybody seems to know everybody.

Visit Islay around the time of a Loganair / British Airways Express flight and you will find the neat terminal open with a small counter serving drinks and snacks. This will probably close just before the flight departs because the person serving is likely to be one of the airport firemen. Once the flight has departed, expect the firemen to return to clean the terminal and lock up.

The island itself is best known for its distilleries (seven at last count) and in the summer, whisky tasting and golf playing tours are the order of the day. But there's much more to see and do besides. Unfortunately our visit was too short to explore the island properly, but like many visitors we'll be back.

Landing Fee

Private light aircraft up to 3 tonnes £10.50 inc. if paid cash/cheque on arrival. Parking £1.56 per tonne per 24 hours.

To operate outside notified hours you must complete and have accepted an indemnity form obtained from Highland and Islands Airports Ltd (tel: 01667 462445, fax: 01667 462579), and send them a copy of your insurance certificate. Even if you do not *intend* to fly outside the published hours you are strongly recommended to consider doing this in advance, as the weather is more than capable of wrecking the best laid plans!

Fuel

Flying Organisations

Other Organisations

Car Hire

Bowmore Car Hire 01496 810206

Taxis

Richard Grey 01496 302382/302247
Angus McMilla 01496 302312

Public Transport

Bus services to Port Ellen & Bowmore, bus stop outside terminal

Nearby Places of Interest

Bowmore Distillery, Bowmore - 4 miles 01496 810441
Lagavulin Distillery, Port Ellen - 5 miles 01496 302250
Caol Ila Distillery, Port Askaig - 12 miles 01496 840207
Laphroaig Distillery, Port Ellen - 5 miles 01496 302418
Islay Natural History Trust Field Centre,
Port Charlotte - 14 miles 01496 850239
Dunyvaig Castle (ruin) - 2 miles
TIC 01496 810254

Food & Accommodation

Drinks and snacks in the terminal
Mrs Gallery Tea Rooms (opposite terminal)
Cottage Restaurant, Bowmore - 5 miles 01496 810422
The Old Granary (see Kintra Farm below)
Mrs Gallery Guest House & Tea Rooms (opposite terminal) 01496 302147
The Machrie Hotel & Golf Links - 2 miles from £35.00 01496 302310
The Trout Fly Guest House & Restaurant, Port Ellen - 5 miles 01496 302204

Kintra Farm, Kintra Beach (6 miles by road)
Located at the southern end the 7 mile Laggan Bay beach, Kintra Farm offers comfortable guest house accommodation in the main farmhouse (from £30), budget accommodation in the hostel, or even camping in the adjoining field. Either way you'll be assured of a warm welcome and true insight into the past and present Islay. We ate in the Old Granary Restaurant, with a good choice of food from bar snacks to suppers (very good) with a wide selection of wines. The restaurant is open to non-residents and is well worth seeking out, but phone first as the guest house and restaurant are mostly open only in the summer season. After we'd had our fill we walked along the fine sand beach in the soft light that these islands have at 10 o'clock on a summer's evening. The airport is only 1·5 miles along this beach if you don't mind climbing the odd fence to get in, the more conventional road route is nearer 6 miles.
When next morning our taxi failed to arrive due to a mix-up, the owners insisted on driving us to the airport themselves - refusing to take any money when we got there. Yes, we'll be back all right. 01496 302051

Isle of Skye (Broadford)

2 miles east of Broadford, off the A850
Roads and Transport, Regional Buildings, Glenurquhart Road, Inverness, IV3 5NX
Tel: 01478 612727 (Divisional Engineer)
Tel: 01463 702000 (Regional Buildings)
Fax: 01478 612255 (Divisional Engineer)
Fax: 01463 702606 (Regional Buildings)

The tarmac runway of this council-run airstrip was re-surfaced a few years ago, but the Portacabin next to the runway, and the frequency with which the windsock is blown away, remain the same!

Unlike many airfields in this region, Broadford does not have it's origins with airlines or the military - it is here as a community service. As well as providing a landing strip for business and pleasure visitors it also provides another link in the Scottish Air Ambulance service - although on this large and well-provided for island such visits are much more rare than elsewhere.

Skye itself is the best known and most visited of the Scottish islands. The opening in 1995 of the controversial (and expensive) bridge to the mainland is likely to increase the number of visitors - particularly day-trippers. As for the islanders, the bridge toll - and indeed its very presence - have not been universally accepted and the controversy looks set to drag on for some time. Broadford is at the south-eastern end of the island - an area renowned for the fertility of the land. Central Skye is for mountaineers and walkers and to the north, beyond the island capital of Portree, is the best place for peace and tranquillity.

Broadford, 1·5 miles from the airstrip, is the island's second largest town with plenty of food and accommodation on offer. If you are looking for something less commercialised, follow the B8083 west from Broadford to Elgol, from where you can take boat trips along the coast.

Landing Fee

£5.90 + per half tonne up to 3 tonnes. £11.80 + per tonne thereafter. First parking 2 hours free, then £1.47 + per tonne or part thereof per 24 hours or part thereof.

Fuel

Flying Organisations

Other Organisations

Car Hire

Sutherlands Garage	01471 822225

Taxis

Clarkin Private Hire	01471 534452

Public Transport

Regular buses connect Broadford with Portree and Kyleakin, (Skyeway 01599 534328)

Nearby Places of Interest

Balmacara Estate and Lochalsh Woodland Garden - 4 miles	01599 586325
Castle Moil Seal Cruises, Kyleakin - 2 miles	01599 584235
Talisker Distillery - 20 miles, the only distillery on Island	01478 640203
Clan Donald Visitor Centre - 8 miles	01471 534305/534227
TIC	01478 612137

Food & Accommodation

Seagreen, Kyle of Lochash - 3 miles, specialising in seafood, booking advisable (Egon Ronay)	01599 4388
Broadford Hotel - 2 miles from £30	01471 822204
Strathgorm, Breakish - 1 mile from £15	01471 822508
Corry Lodge, Broadford - 2 miles from £25	01471 822235
Cullin Hills Hotel ***, Portree - 20 miles from £40	01478 612003
Duisdale Hotel Sleat - 5 miles B&B from £37	01471 83363
Strathaird House - 8 miles B&B from £25	01471 866269
Ptarmigan - 1 mile B&B from £23	01471 822744

Kirkwall

3 miles south-east of Kirkwall
Kirkwall Airport, Kirkwall, Orkney Islands KW15 1TH
Tel: 01856 872421 Fax: 01856 875051

A small but surprisingly busy airport, the airport still retains that 'small-time' appeal, a refreshment counter offers sandwiches and snacks, accompanied by good tea and coffee.

Loganair / British Airways Express have direct several flights from mainland Scotland, which connect with short hops by Islander to many of the Orkney islands.

Kirkwall airport is on Mainland Orkney, which is surrounded by the 70 or so islands that make up Orkney. To the south of the airport is Scapa Flow. Here, on midsummer's day 1919, the sailors of the defeated German Fleet scuttled 50 warships rather than hand them over to the British navy, taking to the boats as the ships went down. Today the remaining sunken battleships make Scapa Flow one of the world's premier diving sites. More sombrely, HMS Royal Oak was torpedoed in Scapa Flow in 1939. She went down with the loss of 833 lives and is today a official War Grave, at low tide she is still clearly visible from the air.

The airport, and the town of Kirkwall are on 'East Mainland' which, like the rest of the Orkney Islands, is littered with historic and pre-historic sites dating back to at least 5000 BC and more wildlife and natural beauty than can be described here. Try the friendly folk at the TIC and you'll be captivated for sure.

Landing Fee
Private light aircraft up to 3 tonnes £10.50 inc. if paid cash/cheque on arrival. Parking £1.56 per tonne per 24 hours. Visa/Amex/Diners.
To operate outside notified hours you must complete an indemnity form obtained from Highland and Islands Airports Ltd, tel: 01667 462445, fax: 01667 462579. Even if you do not *intend* to fly outside the published hours you are strongly recommended to consider signing this form in advance, as the weather is more than capable of wrecking the best laid plans!

Fuel
AVGAS 100LL 68.46p + AVTUR JET A1 29.75+ S and J D Robertson Group Ltd 01856 872415/872961.
Visa/Amex/Diners

Flying Organisations

Other Organisations
Maintenance available via Loganair

Car Hire

W R Tullock	01856 875500/876262
Peace Car Hire	01856 872866
J W Tait	01856 872490/873003

Taxis

Brass's Taxis	01856 850750
Craigie's Garage	01856 872817

Public Transport

Bus services - J D Pearce & Co	01856 872866
Other details from TIC	

Nearby Places of Interest

Skara Brae - 7 miles. 4500 year old Neolithic village	
Maes Howe - 3 miles, chambered Kairn dating from around 2500 BC	
Scapa Flow Visitor Centre, Lyness, Hoy	01856 873191
Kirkwall historic town - 2 miles	
Highland Park Distillery and Visitor Centre, Kirkwall	01856 874619
TIC	01856 872856

Food & Accommodation

Light refreshments at airfield	
Quoyburray Inn (Orkney pub of the year 1994), Tankerness - 3 miles	01856 861255
Merkister Hotel & Skerries Restaurant (Egon Ronay), Harray - 10 miles	01856 771366
Hamnavoe Restaurant, Stromness - 10 miles	01856 850606
Ayre Hotel ***, Kirkwall from £50	01856 873001
Albert Hotel, Kirkwall, from £40.00	01856 876000
Whiteclett, Kirkwall, B&B from £14	01856 874193
Mrs M Bain, Kirkwall B&B from £14	01856 872862

Lerwick (Tingwall)

4 miles north-west of Lerwick, signposted from A971
Grantfield, Lerwick, Shetland, ZE1 0NT
Tel: 01595 744850 or 840306 Fax: 01595 694544

Although a much smaller and quieter airfield than Sumburgh to the south, Lerwick airfield is much closer to the administrative centre of Lerwick and, some would say, closer to the heart of Shetland. Islanders of Loganair / British Airways Express pass through en route to and from Fair Isle and Unst, otherwise traffic is mostly visiting light aircraft.

Although to many Shetland is a Scottish domain, its history and culture are far closer to the Vikings, Norsemen and Danes. Shetland was under Scandinavian rule for over 600 years, and only came to Scotland as a wedding dowry! These Nordic roots are clearly visible, from the place names to the mid-winter Up Helly Aa festival, where a replica Viking longship is paraded and then burnt by revellers dressed in full Viking regalia. All are welcome to watch this extraordinary celebration, but to participate you must be a Shetlander (a minimum residence of 5 years will suffice apparently).

Lerwick is undoubtedly the centre of Shetland for services and facilities. There are plenty of hotels, restaurants and shops; and most ferry services and visiting cruise ships dock at Lerwick harbour. The locals will delight in reminding the visitor that Lerwick is Britain's northernmost town, it is further from London than Milan, and closer to Norway and the Faroe Islands than it is to Glasgow and Edinburgh! You can cruise the harbour in a 40 foot replica longship, or venture east from the town to the island of Bressay and the bird sanctuary of Noss beyond, with its 600ft cliffs rearing vertically out of the North Sea. In fact, no point on Shetland is more than 3 miles from the sea - a point not to be forgotten if you are flying yourself.

Landing Fee
£3.38 per half tonne up to 3 tonnes. 3-20 tonnes £6.75 per tonne +. Parking fees £1.26 + per tonne per 24 hours or part thereof.
Cash or cheque only

Fuel
AVGAS 100LL 84.07p + AVTUR JET A1 31.62p +
Cash or cheque only

Flying Organisations

Tingwall Aero Club	01595 744850

Other Organisations

Car Hire

J Leask and Son	01595 693162
Bolts Car Hire	01595 693636

Taxis

Solidan	01595 694445
Willy Hunter	01595 692601

Public Transport
Details from TIC

Nearby Places of Interest

Lerwick Harbour Trust (for cruises on replica longship)	01595 692991
Island of Noss - 8 miles	
Lerwick historic town - 4 miles	
TIC	01595 693434

Food & Accommodation

Snacks at airfield	
The Noost (cafe), Lerwick	01595 693377
Westings Hotel - 1 mile from £30	01595 840242
The Old Manse, B&B from £18	01595 696301
Glen Orchy House, Lerwick from £25	01595 692031
Queens Hotel, Lerwick (overlooking harbour) from £60	01595 692826
The Shetland Hotel, Lerwick from £75	01595 695515

Perth (Scone)

3 miles north-east of Perth. From A85 follow signs for 'New Scone'
Perth Aerodrome, Perth Scotland PH2 6NP
Tel: 01738 552311 ext. 206/207 Fax: 01738 553006
Telex: 76265 ASTPTH G

Perth was conceived as a training site, and that has always been its primary purpose. Opened in 1936 and run by Airwork, who operating a civil flying training school; military training soon commenced on Tiger Moths. Perth (or Scone as it was better known then) officially became a military aerodrome in 1940, and indeed military training continued until 1954, when Airwork purchased the site for themselves.

Nowadays the airfield continues to train commercial pilots and engineers, and an atmosphere of quiet academia pervades the place, even when the circuit is full. The airfield is situated alongside the main A94 north of Perth, just outside New Scone (follow the A94 signs, not the signs to Scone Palace, which is on the old road), in the middle of some of Scotland's most beautiful countryside and is worth a visit just for that. The Grampian Highlands begin just 10 miles to the north.

The airfield has a pleasant pilots' rest area, excellent flight briefing facilities - as you would expect - and a restaurant, but the menu (which has a definite Middle/Far East flavour) can be a bit limited if you catch them at the wrong time. Most of the aircraft here belong to the training school, but the occasional unusual visitor can be seen passing through.

Landing Fee
Single £5.00 inc. multi £15 + .First 4 hours parking free, then single £2.75 +; multi £5.50 +
All major credit cards

Fuel
AVGAS 100LL 62.5p +
All major credit cards

Flying Organisations
Air Service Training Ltd 01738 552311

Other Organisations
Air Service Training Ltd (Maintenance) 01738 552311

Car Hire
Avis 01738 442646
Hertz 01738 624108
Europcar 01738 636888

Taxis
David Rhinde 01738 36098

Public Transport
Hourly buses from main gate to Perth. Perth railway station 3 miles.

Nearby Places of Interest
Scone Palace, Scone - 1 mile 01738 52300
Historic city of Perth (once Scotland's capital) - 4 miles. A visit strongly recommended
Art Gallery and City Museum, Perth - 4 miles
Balhousie Castle, Black Watch Museum, Perth - 4 miles 01738 621281
Caithness Glass Factory and Visitor Centre - 7 miles 01738 37373
Huntingtower Castle- 10 miles
Elcho Castle - 8 miles
TIC 01738 627958

Food & Accommodation
Restaurant and club facilities
Betty's Coffee Parlour, Perth - 4 miles (Egon Ronay) 01738 632693
Almond Villa Guest House - 4 miles B&B from £16 01738 629356
Pitcullen Guest House - 4 miles B& B from £17.50 01738 626506
Stakis Perth Hotel - Perth 4 miles from £25 01738 628281
Saluation Inn, Perth - 4 miles from £60 01738 630066

Prestwick

1 mile north-east of Prestwick, signposted from A77
Prestwick International Airport Ltd, Prestwick, Ayrshire, Scotland KA9 2PL
Tel: 01292 479822 Fax: 01292 671762
Telex: 778048 PIKLTD

For many years Prestwick was, for reasons that were (allegedly) more to do with politics than economics, the designated 'gateway' airport for transatlantic flights. Thus all flights across the Atlantic originating or ending in Scotland had to pass through here. Predictably, when this arrangement ended most airlines re-located to Glasgow or Edinburgh - which is what they wanted all along - and Prestwick became a very under-used airport.

The airport came under private ownership in 1992, and has since seen a number of changes. Catering and terminal facilities have been re-vamped, visitors are made more welcome and a new rail station serving the airport opened in September 1994. The result has been a doubling in passenger numbers (to about 350 000 in 1995) and the return of cargo and charter traffic, together with new scheduled services to Dublin, Belfast City and Stansted.

Prestwick is also home to the BAe Flying College, training pilots for the airlines, and is where the BAe Jetstream is built. On the northern side of the airfield is HMS Gannet, from where Royal Navy Sea King helicopters operate. Interesting aircraft ferrying across the Atlantic pass through, and Concorde comes here for circuit training.

Landing Fee
Singles £15 +; multi £20 + (private flights). First 24 hours parking free, then £10.85 + per 24 hours. Major credit cards (except amex)

Fuel
Via Air BP. AVGAS 100LL 66.26p + AVTUR JET A1 28.45p +
Major credit cards (except amex)

Flying Organisations

British Aerospace Flying College Ltd	01292 671022
(To find BAe Flying College follow the 'RNAS Prestwick' signs)	
Prestwick Flight Centre	01292 476523
Prestwick Flying Club / Scottish Airways Flyers	01292 475583

Other Organisations

British Aerospace Flying College Ltd (Maintenance)	01292 671022
Jetstream Aircraft Ltd (Maintenance)	01292 479888

Car Hire

Avis	01292 77218
Eurodollar	01292 77517
Hertz	01292 70666
Europcar	01292 678198

Taxis
Available at terminal

Public Transport
Local buses outside terminal 0141 332 9191. Citylink hourly coach service to Glasgow and Edinburgh. Courtesy coach connects to Prestwick railway station (1 mile), trains every 30 mins to Glasgow Central (Mon-Sat), hourly Sun.

Nearby Places of Interest
Golf at Troon, 2 miles
Racing at Ayr, 2 miles
Bachelors Club, (Robert Burns museum) 3 miles 01292 541940
TIC 01292 262555

Food & Accommodation
Restaurant, buffet and bar at airport. Viewing terrace on the 2nd floor
Local information from the helpful Information desk in the terminal

Travel Inn, Ayr £35 per room (next to airport at A77/A78 roundabout)	01292 678262
St Nicholas Hotel, Prestwick - 1 mile from £26	01292 76726
Marine Highland Hotel, Troon - 2 _ miles from £57	01292 314444
The Burns Monument Hotel, Ayr - 3 miles from £30	01292 442466
Glenmore Guest House, Ayr - 3 miles B&B from £16	01292 269830

Scatsta

20 miles north of Lerwick, next to the B9076
Scatsta Aerodrome, Brae, Shetland Scotland ZE2 9QP
Tel: 01806 242791

Scatsta owes its existence largely to Europe's largest oil terminal, Sullom Voe, just to the north of the airfield hidden in a remote inlet. Operated on behalf of BP the vast majority of visitors to the airfield are on oil company-related business rather than on leisure trips.

However, that is not to say that this corner of Shetland is any more industrialised than the rest, natural beauty, wildlife and historic sites are still the order of the day. Of the 100 or so islands that make up Shetland, only 15 are inhabited - the phrase 'unspoilt' really has meaning here. The 900 miles of coastline is strewn with inlets (voes) and bays where Viking longboats once sheltered, and with a population of just 24 000 over all the islands its easy to find a place of your own. It might be less easy to get away from all of Shetland's 300 000 sheep!

At the southern end of Sullom Voe is Mavis Grind, a strip of land barely 100 metres across which separates the North Sea from the Atlantic ocean. Carry on west across Mavis Grind and you enter the most mountainous and rugged part of Shetland Mainland. At the sea's edge cliffs, stacks and arches abound. Visit the lighthouse at Esha Ness in the far west and watch the puffins, or travel to Voe - a settlement with a distinctly Scandinavian flavour. Either way, the land is there for the exploring. Nature has also gifted another spectacle to Shetland. This far north the daylight hours in summer are almost never-ending - 19 hours of sunshine are possible in mid-summer. In winter the long nights are more than compensated for by the possibility of seeing greatest light show in the world - the Northern Lights (Aurora Borealis).

Landing Fee
Up to 1·5 tonnes £20 +, 1·5 to 2 tonnes £25 +

Fuel
AVTUR JET A1 - 2 hours PNR 33.54p +

Flying Organisations

Other Organisations

Car Hire
Bolts Car Hire 01595 693636

Taxis
Willie Hurson 01806 522550
Gary Johnson 01806 522443

Public Transport
Details from the TIC

Nearby Places of Interest
See main text
TIC 01595 693434

Food & Accommodation
Mid-Brae Inn and Restaurant, Brae - 3 miles 01806 522634
Westayre, Brae - 3 miles B&B from £14 01806 522368
Greystones Guest House, Brae - 3 miles from £26 01806 522322
Brae Hotel, Brae - 3 miles from £40 01806 522456
Busta House Hotel & Restaurant ***, Brae - 3 miles from £38. Attractions at the country house hotel include highly recommended food and accommodation, and around 120 malt whiskies! 01806 522506

Stornoway

2 miles east of Stornoway, signposted from A866
Stornoway Aerodrome, Isle of Lewis PA86 0BN
Tel: 01851 702256 Fax: 01851 703115
Telex: 75495

Like many airfields in the Highlands and Islands, Stornoway came into being in the 1930s as a landing strip for scheduled flights. The proposed runway ran through a golf course, and it took four years of protracted negotiations to agree a strip that left all 18 holes in place. By the time the grass runway was laid, war was threatening and it was never used. With the outbreak of war the Air Ministry arrived and promptly levelled everything in sight to build a major Coastal Command airfield!

The legacy of these beginnings is an airfield with good length runways, navaids and fuel and direct flights to Benbecula, Glasgow and Inverness. Stornoway is on the Isle of Lewis which is the largest and most populated of the Outer Hebrides; 20 000 of the Hebrides' 29 000 inhabitants live on Lewis. Like the neighbouring island of Harris, Lewis has a strong religious tradition. You will find virtually all shops, petrol stations, bars, cafes and restaurants etc. closed on a Sunday. There is no public transport on Sundays, the airport is closed all day and some B&B landladies will prefer you not to arrive or depart on a Sunday. Many shops also close on Wednesday afternoons.

The town of Stornoway is the administrative capital of the Outer Hebrides. On the bright side, this means it has very good facilities, however many visitors find it less enchanting than other settlements in the Highlands and Islands. The countryside is mostly moorland and many visitors head to the west coast which is littered with ruined castles and historical sites.

Landing Fee
Private light aircraft up to 3 tonnes £10.50 inc. if paid cash/cheque on arrival. Parking £1.56 per tonne per 24 hours. Visa/Amex/Diners.
To operate outside notified hours you must sign and have accepted a Highland and Islands Airports Ltd indemnity form, tel: 01667 462445, fax: 01667 462579. Even if you do not *intend* to fly outside the published hours you are strongly recommended to consider signing this form in advance, as the weather is more than capable of wrecking the best laid plans!

Fuel
AVGAS 100LL 90.66p + AVTUR JET A1 46.5p +
Visa/Amex/Diners

Flying Organisations

Other Organisations
Bristow Helicopters Ltd 01851 705577

Car Hire
Lewis Car Rentals 01851 703760
MacKinnon Self Drive 01851 702984

Taxis
Central cabs 01851 706900

Public Transport
Details from the TIC

Nearby Places of Interest
Port of Ness 27 miles
Tolsta Beach, 14 miles
Callanish Stones and visitor centre (second only to Stonehenge), 14 miles
Western Isles Museum, Stornoway 2 miles 01851 703773 ext. 266
TIC 01851 703088

Food & Accommodation
Cabarfeidh Hotel, Stornoway - 2 miles from £70 01851 702604
Caledonian Hotel, Stornoway - 2 miles from £40 01851 702411
Park Guest House, Stornoway
- 2 miles from £25 (food especially recommended) 01851 702485
Hebron, Stornoway - 2 miles B&B from £16 01851 702890
Ravenswood, Stornoway - 2 miles B&B from £18 01851 702673

Sumburgh

17 miles south of Lerwick, signposted from A970
Highlands & Islands Airports Ltd, Sumburgh Airport, Virkie, Shetland ZE3 9JP
Tel: 01950 460654 Fax: 01950 460218

Situated at the southern-most tip of the Shetland Islands, Sumburgh is the island's major airport.

As on many islands in this region the airfield came into being in the 1930's as a landing strip for Highland Airways, and was subsequently developed in the Second World War. Sumburgh might have slipped into obscurity but for the discovery of oil in the North Sea, which transformed this backwater into a thriving international airport and heliport. In part the pendulum has swung back. Most long range helicopters now operate directly from Aberdeen to the oil fields, although Sumburgh's role has not disappeared completely. British Airways have daily flights connecting to several points in mainland Scotland, and Sumburgh is also the base for Loganair / British Airways Express services to the other parts of the Shetlands in Islander aircraft. Some of the services to the smaller islands do not appear in the main timetables being virtually 'request' stops, dependant on passenger demand! Additionally Business Air operate services to Aberdeen, and Flyveselskap have a summer schedule from Bergen.

As a result of the expansion of the airport in the 1970's, facilities are good and the airport is also close to the Shetland's prime archaeological site - Jarlshof, a uniquely preserved settlement dating back to at least 1000BC.

Landing Fee
Private light aircraft up to 3 tonnes £10.50 inc. if paid cash/cheque on arrival. Parking £1.56 per tonne per 24 hours. All major credit cards.
To operate outside notified hours you must sign an indemnity form obtained from Highland and Islands Airports Ltd, tel: 01667 462445, fax: 01667 462579. Even if you do not *intend* to fly outside the published hours you are strongly recommended to consider signing this form in advance, as the weather is more than capable of wrecking the best laid plans!

Fuel
AVGAS 100LL 87.22p +, AVTUR JET A1 36.04 +
All major credit cards

Flying Organisations

Other Organisations

British International Helicopters (Maintenance)	01950 60321
Bristow Helicopters Ltd (Maintenance)	01950 60601

Car Hire

Bolts Car Hire (Europcar & Avis agents)	01950 460777
Star Rent a Car	01950 460444

Taxis
Available at terminal

Public Transport
Buses available at terminal. Details from TIC

Nearby Places of Interest
This part of Shetland has its share of early sites - notably Brochs, curious Iron Age defensive Towers. The wealth of natural features and wildlife sites are remarkable.
Jarlshof 1 mile
The island of Mousa, 10 miles north, is home to an impressive Broch (the best preserved in the UK apparently) and seals, seabirds and otters. Boat trips with Tom Jamieson 01950 431367
TIC 01595 693434

Food & Accommodation
Buffet and self service restaurant at terminal

Sumburgh Hotel - 1/4 mile from £50	01950 460201
Columbine, North Voe B&B from £15	01950 460582
Da Twa Merk, Toab B&B from £14	01950 460710

Tiree

3 miles north of Balemartine, Isle of Tiree
Tiree Aerodrome, Isle of Tiree, Argyll PA77 6UW
Tel: 01879 220456 Fax: 01879 220714

Although officially one of the Inner Hebrides, and situated close to the Isle of Mull, Tiree has the feel of one of the more remote islands. The airfield was established in 1934 for Midland and Scottish Airways, and owes its continuing existence almost wholly to Loganair / British Airways Express who are the airfield's main user. Tiree's published opening hours are based around the once a day service from Glasgow, outside these hours you will probably find that you have the airfield all to yourself! Contrary to what you might expect in such a remote spot the runways, and indeed the airport itself, are in very good condition.

With less than 1000 inhabitants, Tiree is not a bustling, busy sort of a place - but of course that is its very attraction. It offers remoteness and unspoilt beauty rather than scores of touristy hotspots; apparently the wartime NAAFI at the airfield was the island's first licensed premises! This is not to say that Tiree is a weather-beaten, desolate sort of a place – the locals claim that Tiree has more hours of sunshine per year than any part of the UK. Summer visitors support this claim and in fact many visitors do come for the weather - the windswept nature of this island has made it a popular windsurfing destination!

Landing Fee
Private light aircraft up to 3 tonnes £10.50 inc. if paid cash/cheque on arrival. Parking £1.56 per tonne per 24 hours.
To operate outside notified hours you must sign and have accepted an indemnity form obtained from Highland and Islands Airports Ltd, tel: 01667 462445, fax: 01667 462579. Given the limited opening hours of Tiree this is just about mandatory.

Fuel

Flying Organisations

Other Organisations

Car Hire
Tiree Motor Co 01879 220469
A MacLennan Motors 01879 220555

Taxis
J Kennedy 01879 220311/220419

Public Transport
Post bus - details from TIC. Caledonian MacBrayne (Ferries) 01879 220337

Nearby Places of Interest
A number of fine secluded beaches
Scarinish - pretty harbour
The Ringing Stone
Hynish village (at the southern tip of the island) Follow the track (after the road peters out) all the way to the beach and you pass down 'Happy Valley' - a beautiful grassy valley kept in perfect condition by the sheep!
A golf course (at Vaul bay)
TIC (Oban) 01631 563122

Food & Accommodation
The Glassary Guest House & Restaurant (reputedly the best food on the island), Sandaig - 3 miles from £18 01879 220684
Scarinish Hotel, Scarinish - 3 miles B&B from £19 01879 220308
Tiree Lodge Hotel, Gott Bay - 4 miles from £25 01879 220368

Unst

On the Isle of Unst, 2 miles south of Baltasound
Unst Aerodrome, Baltasound, Shetland ZE2 9DT
Tel: 01957 711404/5/6 Fax: 01957 711210

Situated on the most northerly of the Shetland Islands, Unst airfield is every pilot's idea of a remote outpost. Although the published opening hours (essentially 8:00-18:00 Monday to Friday) are far more generous than many airfields in the region, visitors arriving by air are expected to give good warning of their impending arrival - the airfield may well close when things are quiet, although it's difficult to imagine this airfield being busy! That is not to say that this is an unfriendly place. With Prior Permission by telephone you can expect a welcome as warm and helpful as anywhere in Shetland. There are a couple of Loganair / British Airways Express services each day (from/to Lerwick and Sumburgh), otherwise the airfield's main role is to support the off-shore oil platforms. As far as 'casual' visitors in light aircraft are concerned, there an average of less than 10 a year. One suspects that most have come to get the UK's most northerly airfield in their logbook.

In actual fact, apart from the abundant wildlife - and in particular bird life on the 600ft Hermaness cliffs - much of the island's attraction seems to be based on its latitude. Off the northern shore of Britain's most northerly island are the Muckle Flugga rocks. These are Britain's most northerly point, with a lighthouse that is Britain's most northerly lighthouse. Nearby is the large Radar station at Saxa Vord which – well you've probably guessed.

Unst has another claim to fame that may be closer to a pilot's heart. A few years ago Britain's strongest wind speed - 199mph - was recorded here. On the subject of weather, Shetland is not the grey and drizzly outpost you might imagine. April to June are reckoned to be the driest months, and in general the Gulf stream keeps the climate temperate - if not tropical! However, as you'd expect it pays to always monitor the weather closely and have some planned alternates up your sleeve. Then you can really enjoy the unique experience of travelling around these friendly islands.

Landing Fee
£15 for light aircraft. Parking fee on application.

Fuel
AVTUR JET A1 on application Out of hours fuel via ATC 2 hours PNR

Flying Organisations

Other Organisations

Car Hire

Taxis
P Y Mills 01957 81666

Public Transport
Details from TIC

Nearby Places of Interest
Muness castle, Muness 3 miles (Britain's most northerly...)
Unst is known for it's nature reserves, walking, fishing and bird life. Twitchers (bird watchers) come from all over the world to see rare bird species.
TIC 01595 693434

Food & Accommodation
Coffee bar at aerodrome
The Baltasound Hotel, Baltasound - 2 miles, from £38. Guess what? It's Britain's most northerly hotel. Bar meals and take-aways. Restaurant bookings 24 hours in advance preferred for 4 course meal. 01957 711334
Clingera Guest House, 500 metres from £15 01957 711579
Buness House, Baltasound - 2 miles from £29 01957 711315

Wick

1 mile north of Wick, signposted from A9
Wick Aerodrome, Wick, Caithness KW1 4QP
Tel: 01955 602215 Fax: 01955 604447

Wick is another airfield that was established in the 1930's by Highland Airways. It was developed in the Second World War, but was so visible in its open, treeless surroundings that it was frequently attacked. Eventually a decoy airfield (including decoy aircraft) was built on a nearby peat bog!

Today, Wick is a surprisingly active airfield given its location - it is the most northerly licensed airfield on the UK mainland. British Airways has a number of daily services, with direct flights to Edinburgh, Inverness, Kirkwall and Shetland. Gill Air also have direct services to Aberdeen and Newcastle. There is a flying school / Fixed Base Operator (FBO) on the airfield - Far North Aviation - and Bond Helicopters also operate here.

By all accounts, Far North Aviation are encouraging a lot of visitors to use Wick with the effectiveness of their handling services. They have based their operation on a USA style 'FBO' with the emphasis on slick and speedy turnarounds. Visiting pilots get free coffee and use of the briefing facilities. If you refuel, there are no handling fees. What's more, Far North have negotiated special accommodation rates locally, and will lay on courtesy transport to your hotel or guest house. Phone ahead, or call on the company frequency 130.375, callsign "Farnor", and they'll be waiting for you when you land. Let's hope this catches on in the rest of the UK!

Landing Fee

Private light aircraft up to 3 tonnes £10.50 inc. if paid cash/cheque on arrival. Parking £1.56 per tonne per 24 hours. Discount for AOPA members. All major credit cards accepted.

To operate outside notified hours you must sign and have accepted an indemnity form obtained from Highland and Islands Airports Ltd, tel: 01667 462445, fax: 01667 462579. Even if you do not *intend* to fly outside the published hours you are strongly recommended to consider signing this form in advance, as the weather is more than capable of wrecking the best laid plans!

Fuel

AVGAS 100LL 65.5p + AVTUR JET A1 34p + available during aerodrome hours from Far North. Outside aerodrome hours by arrangement 01955 602201 (H24)
All major credit cards accepted

Flying Organisations

Far North Flight Training	01955 602201

Other Organisations

Far North Aviation (handling)	01955 602201

Car Hire

Practical Car Hire	01955 604125

Taxis

Millers Taxis	01955 603192

Public Transport

Wick railway station 1 mile

Nearby Places of Interest

John O'Groats - 17 miles	
Caithness Glass, Wick - 2 miles	01955 602286
Northlands Viking Centre - 10 miles	01955 603761
TIC	01955 602596

Food & Accommodation

Buffet facilities available in the terminal, with a good view across the airfield
Accommodation and transport bookable through Far North

The Mercury Hotel, Wick - 1 mile from £35	01955 603344
Queens Hotel, Wick - 1 mile from £25	01955 602992
Harbour Guest House, Wick - 1 mile from £15	01955 603276
Bilbster House, Wick - 1 mile B&B from £15	01955 621212

Wales

Cardiff

9 miles south-west of Cardiff signposted from A4226. M4 J33 12 miles
Cardiff Wales Airport, Rhoose, Barry, South Glamorgan CF62 3BD
Tel: 01446 711111 Fax: 01446 711675
Telex: 497720 (Airport Authority)

Cardiff-Wales Airport, to give it its official title, compares in size to other regional airports such as Bristol and Teesside, having about a dozen scheduled services and about 1 million passengers a year. In the summer, it is fairly busy with charter jets plying the holiday routes, but in the winter traffic is light. A large maintenance hangar, recently constructed by British Airways for their 747s, now dominates the airport skyline.

Originally known as Rhoose, the airfield is some way from Cardiff City centre, and a longish bus or taxi ride is necessary to reach the town centre. However, the pleasant, modern terminal has good facilities and the upstairs cafeteria affords a good view of the airfield. On the South side of the airfield, the General Aviation community consists of the local flying schools, maintenance and a small cafe and viewing area for visitors.

The airport is less than 3 miles from St Athan, a major RAF maintenance station, and on quiet days it is not unknown for military aircraft make a low pass over the airport on their way through (for training, no doubt!). It's also not unknown for aircraft inbound to Cardiff to approach St Athan instead - there have been at least two such incidents already this year!

Landing Fee
£13.60 singles. Multi by weight. First 12 hours parking free. Thereafter £11.90 per night.
All major credit cards, but not Switch or Delta

Fuel
AVGAS 60p +, available H24 from Total (GA) Aviation Fuels Ltd on southside of airfield.
AVTUR Jet A1 25p + 0600-2245 by arrangement with Air BP 01446 710281
All major credit cards, but not Switch or Delta

Flying Organisations

Cardiff Wales Flying Club	01446 710000
Cardiff Aero Services	01446 711987

Other Organisations

Light Aircraft Maintenance (Cardiff) Ltd	01446 710106

Car Hire

Hertz	01446 711722
Europcar	01446 711924

Taxis
Available at terminal

Cardiff Airport Taxis	01446 710693
Amber Taxis	01446 777777

Public Transport
Buses from terminal to Barry and Cardiff bus station every hour
Barry railway station 4 miles
Cardiff central railway station 12 miles

Nearby Places of Interest
Note: the Wales Aircraft Museum near the terminal has now closed

Welsh Industrial and Maritime Museum 10 miles	01222 481919
Cardiff 10 miles	
Museum of Welsh Life, Nr St Fagans	01222 569441
TIC	01222 227281

Food & Accommodation
Bar and restaurant facilities in terminal and good viewing terrace
Cafe in Cardiff Wales Flying Club

La Brasserie restaurant, Cardiff	01222 372164
Le Monde restaurant, Cardiff	01222 387376
Riverside Cantonese restaurant, Cardiff	01222 372163
Wales Airport Hotel (close to terminal). Recently refurbished with new management.	01446 710787
Porville Hotel	01222 230951

Caernarfon

4 miles south-west of Caernarfon, signposted off the A499
Air Caernarfon Ltd, Caernarfon Aerodrome, Llandwrog, Caernarfon, Gwyedd LL54 5TP
Tel: 01286 830800 Fax: 01286 830280

RAF Llandwrog opened in 1941, training navigators, radio operators, air gunners and bomb aimers was the base's main function. Being so close to Snowdonia, techniques for mountain rescue of crashed aircraft (and their occupants) were developed here and a mountain rescue unit was operational by 1943. The airfield closed in 1945 and, apart from a brief re-activation for the investiture of the Prince of Wales in 1969, it remained dormant until it was re-opened as a civilian airfield in the late 1970s.

Nowadays the airfield, renamed Caernarfon - the ancient Welsh capital is only 4 miles away - is operated by Air Atlantique, the Coventry based DC3 operators. Facilities have been expanded of late, and the airfield is working hard to promote itself to visitors. There is a flying school and air taxi operation, pleasure flights in a DH Rapide, an air museum, a children's playground and rejuvenated catering in the tower. The Dakota Restaurant, under the supervision of Roy Kehoe, is open daily offering everything from breakfasts, teas, coffees, snacks and lunches to an evening a la carte menu. The beach is literally at the end of the runway and there are magnificent views of Snowdonia on a clear day.

The airfield offers a booking service for accommodation, taxis and car hire and is getting favourable reports from recent visitors.

Landing Fee
Singles £10, Twins £10.
All major credit cards except Amex and Diners

Fuel
AVGAS 100LL 67p inc. AVTUR JET A-1.
All major credit cards except Amex and Diners

Flying Organisations

Air Caernarfon Ltd	01286 830475

Other Organisations

Caernarfon Aircraft Maintenance Co Ltd (Maintenance)	01286 830782
Caernarfon Air World (Museum and Pleasure Flying)	01286 830800
Dakota Restaurant	01286 831600

Car Hire
Arranged via the airfield

Taxis
Arranged via the airfield

Public Transport
No convenient buses. Bangor railway station 11 miles

Nearby Places of Interest

The beach, 2 minutes down the lane from airport	
Snowdonia 10 miles	
Llanberis Lake Railway 8 miles	01286 870549
Snowdon Mountain Railway 12 miles	
Menai Straits and Menai Bridge 11 miles	
The Power of Wales, Llanberis (includes visit to Dinorwig Pumped Power Station)	01286 871331
Caernarfon: Maritime Museum, market square and (of course) the castle - 4 miles	

Food and Accommodation

Coffee shop and Restaurant	
Camping on airfield	
The Harp (comfortable pub with B&B, recommended) - 30 mins walk	01286 831071
Menai Bank Hotel, Caernarfon 5 miles from £16	01286 673297
Prince of Wales Hotel, Caernarfon 5 miles from £20	01286 673367

Haverfordwest

2 miles north of Haverfordwest, signposted from A40
Department Area Office, County Offices, Fishguard Road,
Haverfordwest, Dyfed SA62 4BN
Tel: 01437 764591 ext. 5190 (Licensee)
Tel: 01437 765283 (Aerodrome)

One of the less accessible airfields on the UK mainland, Haverfordwest sits close to the extreme south-west tip of Wales, almost at the end of the A40. Normally a quiet spot, the main activity being from the light aircraft and microlights of resident flying school, Haverfordwest recently made the national news as the base for pollution control Dakotas of Air Atlantique which were dispersing oil from the Sea Empress accident. This incident served to highlight the outstanding beauty of the local area, and the word is that the clean-up operation has been very successful.

Built in 1942 the airfield, known locally as Withybush, was a training base with for light bombers and closed in 1945 after the end of hostilities. Some of the airfield has been redeveloped on a modest scale, and a public road crosses the northern part of the original site. The airfield reopened in the early 1950s for an unsuccessful commercial service, and has been in use ever since by the local flying club who maintain the airfield. It is one of the few airfields in the area suitable for General Aviation, and the best aviation access to Pembrokeshire which remains a truly beautiful part of the country to explore, by air and on the ground.

Landing Fee
£5.50 (50% discount for training flights)
Cash and cheque only

Fuel
AVGAS 100LL 61p + AVTUR Jet A1 24p +
Cash and cheque only

Flying Organisations
Haverfordwest School of Flying — 01437 760822

Other Organisations

Car Hire
Dragon Car Hire — 01437 765357

Taxis
Rocky's Taxis — 01437 764822

Public Transport
Haverfordwest railway station 3 miles

Nearby Places of Interest
The narrow streets of Haverfordwest are well worth exploring. It is also the best place for food and shopping out-of-season.
Pembrokeshire Coast National Park, Britain's only coastal based National Park.
St David's 18 miles
Ramsey Island, famous for its seal colony 25 miles
Pembroke Dock, 11 miles. Former RAF seaplane base
Fine beach at St Brides Bay (8 miles)
TIC — 01437 763113

Food & Accommodation
Hot snacks and drinks Monday to Friday at airport
Something's Cooking, Letterson - 10 miles
(a very good fish and chip restaurant) — 01348 840621
Hotel Mariners, Haverfordwest - 3 miles, from £32.50 — 01437 763353
Wolfscastle Country Hotel, Wolfscastle - 6 miles from £33 — 01437 741225
Austalise, Camrose - 2 miles B&B from £15 — 01437 710303

Mona

2 miles west of Llangefni, Anglesey. Signposted from A5
RAF Valley, Holyhead, Gwynedd LL65 3NY
Tel: 01407 720581 (weekends Mona Flying Club) 01407 762241 (weekday OC Ops RAF Valley) 01407 720583 (RAF Mona)

The Mona airfield site was an airship base during the First World War, named Llangefni after the local town. When the airfield was constructed in 1942 it was first known as Henegwlys, the name of the nearest village, but soon became Mona, (maybe because of the difficulties in pronouncing the Welsh name!). An Air Gunnery School, operating Bothas and Ansons, operated from here, together with a number of other, temporary attachments.

Today the airfield is primarily a satellite for RAF Valley, whose training Hawks can be seen operating in the Welsh valleys most weekdays. It is also home to the Mona Flying Club, which operates a fleet of training aircraft, plus a number of privately owned aircraft which keep the airfield busy at weekends.

Landing Fee
On application

Fuel
AVGAS 100LL

Flying Organisations

Mona Flying Club	01407 720581

Other Organisations

Car Hire

Hertz	01407 763818

Taxis
Arranged via the Flying Club

Public Transport
Holyhead railway station 10 miles

Nearby Places of Interest
Menai Bridge and straits, 6 miles
Holyhead 10 miles
Llanfairpwllgwyngyllgogerychwyrndroewllllantysiliogogogoch, 5 miles. The longest place name in the UK. We've spelt it according to the platform ticket which is approximately six inches long. It also gave the spellchecker a fit. Unfortunately the railway station is no longer open

Penrhyn Castle, Bangor, 10 miles	01248 371337
Beaumaris Castle, 8 miles	
TIC	01407 762622

Food & Accommodation

Tea and coffee at Flying club at weekends	
Old Boathouse Cafe, Red Wharf Bay (Egon Ronay)	01248 852731
Jodies Bar and Bistro, Menai Bridge.	01248 714864
Presaddfed Hall, Bodedern 6 miles B&B from £27.50	01407 740484
Hendre, Holyhead - 10 miles B&B from £15	01407 762929
Tan-Y-Cytiau Country Guest House, Holyhead - 10 miles	01407 762763
Bulkeley Hotel, Beaumaris - 8 miles from £33.50	01248 810146

Swansea

5 miles west of Swansea, signposted from A4118
Swansea Aerodrome, Fairwood Common, Swansea SA2 7JU
Tel: 01792 204064 Fax: 01792 297923

Swansea was a busy fighter airfield under its original name of RAF Fairwood Common. It was used spasmodically after the war by civilian aircraft, but was properly re-opened as Swansea Airport in 1957, managed by Cambrian Airways. Various scheduled services have been tried at Swansea over the years, but it remains primarily a light and business aviation airfield with good access to Swansea and to the Gower peninsular.

Swansea is easier to find by air than by road - the mostly excellent airport signposting is absent at certain junctions and roundabouts. If you are visiting by road, the following might help:

From the M4 follow the Swansea signs that will take you along the A4067 road, parallel to the coast. At a set of lights the airport is signposted to the right. Go straight through the next set of lights (next to the hospital). At the mini-roundabout at the top of the hill TURN RIGHT (this is not signposted). At the next T junction turn left and after 1·5 miles turn left at the roundabout (this IS signposted). This road will now take you to the airport - but watch-out for the sheep on the Common!

Landing Fee
£10 per tonne +. Half price at weekends.
Visa/Access/Diners

Fuel
AVGAS 100LL 62p + AVTUR JET A1 30.75p+
Visa/Access/Diners

Flying Organisations

Cambrian Flying Club	01792 297275
Swansea Aero Club and Flying School	01792 204063

Other Organisations
636 Air Cadet Gliding Squadron

Car Hire

Avis	01792 460939
Eurodollar	01792 643336
Hertz	01792 586117
Europcar	01792 650526

Taxis
By arrangement

Public Transport
Regular bus services 18 and 18a links airport to The Quadrant bus station in Swansea.
Swansea railway station 6 miles.

Nearby Places of Interest

The Gower peninsula, lots of pretty walks etc.	
The Mumbles, for those who like walking by the sea - 4 miles	
Swansea - 5 miles	
Maritime Museum, Swansea	01792 650351
The Swansea Museum	01792 653763
Oystermouth Castle - 6 miles	01792 650821
Welsh Motor Sports Centre, Llanelli - 7 miles	
TIC	01792 468321

Food & Accommodation

Nice restaurant in terminal, especially good bacon butties and real coffee	
La Braseria Spanish restaurant, Swansea (Egon Ronay)	01792 469683
Langrove Lodge, Fairwood, close to airfield from £19	01792 232410
Hilton National, Swansea - 6 miles from £26.50	01792 797535
The Dolphin Hotel, Swansea - 6 miles from £22.50	01792 650011
Parkway Hotel, Swansea - 5 miles from £24.50	01792 201632
Norton House Hotel, The Mumbles - 4 miles from £35	01792 404891

Welshpool

2 miles south of Welshpool, next to the A490
Montgomeryshire/Welshpool Aerodrome, Welshpool, Powys
SY21 8SG
Tel: 01938 555062 Fax: 01938 555487

A beautiful greenfield site, originally just a grass strip, has been turned into an excellent little airfield with a tarmac runway, hangers, club house and cafe. All this has been done with the active support of the regional council - it's nice to find a local authority who actually recognise the importance of general aviation to the community. The airfield is modern, neat and clean and the cafe has a growing reputation for its food of the burger and bacon-roll variety, with picnic tables outside for warm summer days. The location is idyllic, with wonderful Welsh scenery and the river Severn passing just by the airfield boundary – it's no surprise that Welshpool is popular holiday break destination. Most of the resident aircraft are club tourers and trainers, but the airfield gets a lot of visitors so you will see a variety of types on a busy weekend.

The airfield is 3 miles south of Welshpool town, on the A490, just off the A483. The nearest motorway link is with the M54 at Shrewsbury, but the drive through the Welsh borders - whichever way you approach - is a pleasant one.

Landing Fee
£5.00 (single), £10.00 (multi)

Fuel
AVGAS 100LL 72p inc. AVTUR JET A-1 32.8p inc

Flying Organisations
Welshpool Flying School 01938 555062

Other Organisations
Pool Aviation Ltd (Maintenance) 01938 555062

Car Hire
Hertz Newtown 01686 625417

Taxis
Jeff's Taxis 01938 554473

Public Transport
Buses stop on main road 1 mile, both directions every 40 minutes. Welshpool railway station 4 miles

Nearby Places of Interest
Montgomeryshire - countryside of mountains, lakes, waterfalls and fascinating market towns and villages
Montgomeryshire Canal - 1 mile
Welshpool market town - 3 miles
Powis Castle - 4 miles
Welshpool and Llanfair Narrow gauge Light Railway - 4 miles
Montgomery - 5 miles. A hilltop market town with distinctive Georgian architecture. Offa's Dyke is nearby
TIC 01938 552043

Food & Accommodation
Cafe and restaurant on airfield - recommended
Powis Castle Tea Room, Welshpool - 3 miles. National Trust restaurant
Severn Farm B&B - 1 mile 01938 553098
Heath Cottage, Forden - 2 miles B&B from £17 01938 580453
Golf Hall Hotel, Welshpool
- 3 miles from £40 (food esp. recommended) 01938 553399
Royal Oak Hotel, Welshpool
- 3 miles from £40 (town center) 01938 552217
Gungrog House, Rhallt - 3 miles B&B from £21 01938 553381
Moat Farm, Welshpool - 3 miles from £36 01938 553179

Flying Clubs

A & G Aviation Ltd
Bournemouth
Tel: 01202 578558 Fax: 01202 570203
PPL(A), NR, IMC, Multi, PPL/IR, BCPL, FIC, AFIC, CPL, CPL/IR, NVQs, Aerobatics, Second pilot, Radionav
Membership: £15 joining and £60 subscription

Aircraft Type	Fleet	Training	Hire
PA-34	2	poa	
PA-28	1	poa	
C172	3	poa	
C152	4	poa	
C150	1	poa	

Trial lessons: 30 mins £42
Access Mastercard Visa
PPL Ground Tuition: available

A1 Aircraft
Biggin Hill
Tel: 01959 575088; 0860 872838
self-fly hire only

Aircraft Type	Fleet	Training	Hire
PA28-181		83.00	

No credit cards
Rate + VAT

Aardvark Aviation Ltd
Cranfield
Tel: 0181 810 9344 Fax: 0181 810 9344
PPL(A), NR, IMC
Membership fee:

Aircraft Type	Fleet	Training	Hire
C172	1	78	68

PPL Ground Training - cost generally included

Abbas Air
Compton Abbas
Tel: 01747 811767 Fax: 01747 811161
PPL(A), IMC, BCPL, FIC, AFIC, NVQs, Aerobatics, Foundation courses
Membership: Full £47; social £17.63

Aircraft Type	Fleet	Training	Hire
PA-28 Warrior	2	97.80	82.20
C150/152	5	82.20	69.60
Boeing Stearman	1	150	
Firefly T.67M		1	130

Trial Lesson: 30 mins £40
PPL Ground Tuition: available

Aberdeen Flying Club/Tayside Aviation Ltd
Aberdeen
Tel: 01224 725333
PPL(A), NR, IMC, Second pilot
Membership: £45

Aircraft Type	Fleet	Training	Hire
C152	5	79.80	69
Piper Archer	1	89.40	79.80

Trial lesson: £30 mins £38
PPL Ground Tuition: No charge

Aceair Flight Training
Halfpenny Green
Tel: 01384 221470
PPL(A), IMC, NR
Membership: £23

Aircraft Type	Fleet	Training	Hire
C150	1	75	65
PA28-161	1	85	75

Trial lesson: 30 mins £30
Membership: £23
PPL Ground Tuition: available

Aero Associates
Swanton Morley
Tel: 01953 850219; 0589 153586
Tailwheel, Aeros, Corporate days
Membership - on application

Aircraft Type	Fleet	Training	Hire
Tiger Moth	1	120	120
Zlin Z526	1	150	150

Aeros Flying Club
Gloucester
Tel: 01452 857419 Fax: 01452 856444
PPL(A), NR, IMC, Multi, Aeros, RNav, BCPL, CPL, IR, FIC, 2nd Pilot
Membership on application

Aircraft Type	Fleet	Training	Hire
PA30 (TwinCom)	1	155	140
Arrow Turbo	1	117.50	n/a
PA28.161	4	89.50	76.50
PA28.140	1	82.00	68.00
Seneca	1	205.00	190.00

Trial Lesson 30mins £40.00; 1hr £89.50
All major credit cards
PPL Ground Tuition: £10 per hour

The Gliding Centre
Little Rissington
Tel: 01295 678004

Aeroshow Flying Club
Gloucestershire
Tel:01452 857419

Air Alba
Inverness
Tel: 01667 462664 Fax: 01667 462696
PPL(A), NR, IMC, FIC, AFIC, Tailwheel, Second pilots, Radionav
Membership: £20

Aircraft Type	Fleet	Training	Hire
C152	2	72	67
PA28-161	1	92	92

Trial lesson: 30 mins £36
Visa Diners
PPL Ground Tuition: no extra cost

Air Caernarfon Ltd
Caernarfon
Tel: 01286 830475 Fax: 0286 830280
PPL(A), IMC, Second pilot

Aircraft Type	Fleet	Training	Hire
C152	1	68	58
Cessna FR172K	1	88	80
PA-28-140	1	78	68
PA-28-161	1	82	72

Air Service Training Ltd
Perth
Tel: 01738 552311 Fax: 01738 553006
PPL(A), NR, IMC, Multi, PPL/IR, BCPL, FIC, AFIC, CPL, CPL/IR, ATPL, NVQs, Aerobatics, Radionav, Simulator, ab-initio to CPL/IR (CAP509 approved), Engineering courses

Aircraft Type	Fleet	Training	Hire
C150	12	69.33	62.28
PA-28	14	84.60	72.85
C310	8	230	175
Simulators	5	75	

Trial lesson: 30 mins £30
All cards
PPL Ground Tuition: cost included in course fees
Other Ground tuition: ATPL; CPL Nav and tech

Air South Ltd
Shoreham
Tel: 01273 462874 Fax: 01273 440185
PPL(A), NR, IMC, Multi, PPL/IR, BCPL, FIC, AFIC, CPL, Tailwheel, Second pilot, Radionav

Aircraft Type	Fleet	Training	Hire
PA-28 Warrior/Archer	3	127.49	99.29
C152	3	107.51	79.31
Cub J3C-90	1	105.16	76.96
DH82A Tiger Moth	1	127.49	

Trial lesson: 25 mins £49 C152
Mastercard Access Visa
PPL Ground Tuition: cost: nil

Air Touring Flying Club
Biggin Hill
Tel: 01959 573133/573652 Fax: 01959 576478
PPL(A), NR, IMC, Multi, Second pilot, Radionav
Membership: £80 inc VAT annual; £11.75 monthly

Aircraft Type	Fleet	Training	Hire
Rallye 110ST	1	104.58	84.93
Rallye 150ST	1	109.86	89.70
Socata Tampico	4	125.14	101.61
Socata Tobago	1	149.87	120.86

Access Mastercard Visa Switch Amex
PPL Ground Tuition: available

Air Training Services
Wycombe Air Park
Tel: 01494 445412 Fax: 01494 445412
PPL/IR, IMC, Multi, Second pilot

Aircraft Type	Fleet	Training	Hire
PA-23E Aztec	1	200	150
Simulator	1	25	

Airbase
Shoreham
Tel: 01273 455532
Membership: £50
PPL(A), IMC, NR, multi, Second Pilot

Aircraft Type	Fleet	Training	Hire
C150	2	90	66
DR400	1	125	90
PA28-161	1	125	90
C310	1	288	229

Trial lesson: 30 mins £55
Mastercard Visa Switch
PPL Ground Tuition: £20/hr
BCPL and FIC courses planned for 1996

Airbourne School of Flying
Bournemouth
Tel: 01202 582181 Fax: 01202590442
PPL(A), NR, IMC, Multi, NVQs, PPL/IR, Aerobatics, Second pilot, PPL completions
Membership: £45 p/a

Aircraft Type	Fleet	Training	Hire
PA-28	2	from 85	80
C150	3	from 85	68
Cherokee 6	1	poa	69 dry

Trial lesson: 20 mins £29; 40 mins £59; 70 mins £99 with land away
Access Mastercard Visa Switch
PPL Ground Tuition: £350 including a free flight
All aircraft go onto discount rates for block hire. PPL assessment flight £45.

Airbourne School of Flying
Sandown (also at Bournemouth)
Tel: 01202 582181 Fax: 01202590442
PPL(A), NR, IMC, Multi, NVQs, PPL/IR, Aerobatics, Second pilot, PPL completions
Membership: £45 p/a

Aircraft Type	Fleet	Training	Hire
PA-28	2	from 85	80
C150	3	from 85	68
Cherokee 6	1	poa	69 dry

Trial lesson: 20 mins £29; 40 mins £59; 70 mins £99-land away
Access Mastercard Visa Switch
PPL Ground Tuition: £350 including a free flight
Aircraft available at discount rates for block hire - details on request

Airnova Flight Centre
Liverpool
Tel 0151 4277907/7908 Fax: 0151 4277908
PPL(A), NR, IMC, Multi, FIC, AFIC, BCPL, Second pilot
Membership: £75 p/a

Aircraft Type	Fleet	Training	Hire
PA-38-112	3	78	70
PA-28-151	1	88	80
PA-28-161	2	88	80
Beech 76	1	175	160
PA-28R	1	97	90

Trial lesson: 30 mins £49; 60 mins £76
Access Visa Mastercard Amex
PPL Ground Tuition: free to members
Block rates available on application

Airtime
Bournemouth
Tel: 01202 580676

Airways Flight Training (Exeter)
Exeter Airport
Tel: 01392 364216 Fax: 01392 368255
PPL/IR, NVQs, CPL/IR, ATPL, Simulator, GFT, Multi

Aircraft Type	Fleet	Training	Hire
PA34 200T Seneca	1	210	245
PA-28-161 Warrior	1	90	125
Beech 76	2	210	245

Simulator 142 Frasca
Visa Access Eurocard

Alan Mann Helicopters
Fairoaks
Tel: 01276 857471 Fax: 01276 857539
PPL(H), NR, Multi, Conversion training

Aircraft Type	Fleet	Training	Hire
Bell 47	2	317.25	317.25
Bell 206	4	528.75	470
Squirrel	1		646.25
Twin Squirrel	2		834.25

Visa Access Mastercard
PPL Ground Tuition: £15/hour

Aldergrove Flight Training Centre
Belfast International
Tel: 01849 423747 Fax: 01849 423777
PPL(A), NR, IMC, Multi, Second pilot, BCPL, CPL, ATPL, NVQs

Aircraft Type	Fleet	Training	Hire
C150	1	87.54	78.14
PA-28-140	1	92.83	83.43
PA-28-181	1	99.88	90.48
C152	1	87.54	78.14

Access Visa Diners
PPL Ground Tuition: no cost
Prices do not include VAT. PA-23 prices available on request

ALH Skytrain
Gamston
Tel 01777 838202 Fax: 0802 221373
PPL(A), NR, IMC, Multi, PPL/IR, Aerobatics, Tailwheel Second pilot, Radionav FAA Biannual IR renewal

Aircraft Type	Fleet	Training	Hire
PA-38	1	74	60
C175	1	75	75
PA-23	1	179	179
AT6	1	poa	
C152	2	74	60
PA28-235	1	95	95

Trial lesson: 30 mins £35 50
PPL Ground Tuition: 3 day course £85 or £10/hour

Alouette Flying Club
Biggin Hill
Tel: 01959 573243
PPL(A), NR, IMC, Second pilot
Continuation training and revision visiting lectures/ videos
QFIs: 2 F/time, 2 P/time

Aircraft Type	Fleet	Training	Hire
PA-38	1	59	44
C172	2	71	56

PPL Ground Tuition: Free

Andreas Flying Club
Andreas
Tel: 01624 880810 Fax: 01624 880278
PPL(A) Microlight, Gliding
Membership: £50

Aircraft Type	Fleet	Training	Hire
Motorglider	1	45	40
Blanik Glider	1	15	15
Hornet ZA	1	55	50
Pegasus Quantur	1	55	50
Blanik Single seater	1	poa	

PPL Ground Tuition: £5/hour for microlight PPL

Andrewsfield Aviation Ltd
Andrewsfield
Tel: 01371 856744 Fax: 01371 856500
PPL(A), PPL(Microlights), NR, IMC, Multi, Tailwheel, Radionav, BCPL, FIC, NVQ available

Aircraft Type	Fleet	Training	Hire
C150	2	86.50	71.50
C152	3	86.50	71.50
C172	1	95	87
PA-28	2	95	87
PA-23	1	156	141

Trial lessons: 20 mins £35; 30 mins £45
Visa Access Switch
PPL Ground Tuition: £15 per subject

ANT Flying Club
Blackpool
Tel: 01253 343102 Fax: 01253 345396
PPL(A), NR, IMC, Multi, FIC, AFIC, Aerobatics, Tailwheel, Second pilot, R/T
Membership: £58.75

Aircraft Type	Fleet	Training	Hire
Cherokee	3	82.25	76.38
Warrior	1	94	88
Aztec	1	270	246
Chieftain	1	470	420

Trial lesson: 30 mins £45; 60 mins £80
Card: Visa Mastercard Access Switch Amex
PPL Ground Tuition: Nil cost

Archer Flight Training
Gloucestershire
Tel: 01452 713830 Fax: 01452 857021
PPL(A), NR, IMC, Second pilots, Radionav

Aircraft Type	Fleet	Training	Hire
PA-38	1	65	65
DR400-100	1	65	
PA-28-180	1	75	70

Trial lesson: 30 mins £35
Visa Mastercard Access
PPL Ground Tuition: inc in course fee

Arrow Air Centre
Shipdham
Tel 01362 820162 Fax: 01362 821063
PPL(A), IMC, NR, multi, aerobatics, R/T, Radionav, second pilot
Membership: £75

Aircraft Type	Fleet	Training	Hire
PA28-140	2	85.31	62.43
PA28-161	1	109.86	89.83
C150	1	85.31	62.43

Trial Lesson: 30 mins £40
Access Visa
PPL Ground Tuition: £8/session
Multi engine by arrangement

Ashley Gardner School of Flying
Ronaldsway
Tel: 01624 823454 Fax: 01624 825744
PPL(A), IMC, NR
Membership on application

Aircraft Type	Fleet	Training	Hire
PA28-140	2	105.00	105.00
PA28-180	2	105.00	105.00

Trial Lesson 20mins (airborne) £40; 25 mins £50; 30 mins £60
Visa/Mastercard. NO Amex/Diners/Switch.
PPL Ground Tuition: 15.00/hr +VAT

Atlantic Flight Training
Coventry
Tel: 01203 303010
Approved abridged BCPL, Approved abridged IR Multi, FIC, IR renewals, tailwheel, 170A, 1179

Aircraft Type	Fleet	Training
C152	1	120
Maule	1	tba
C310	2	300
C402		tba
C404		tba

Access Mastercard Visa
Specialises in training its own internal cadets on a sponsorship scheme, but happy to assist with 3rd party training by arrangement

Avia Special Ltd

White Waltham and others by request
Tel: 01707 262774   Fax: 01707 251405
Aerobatics, Tailwheel aerobatic, pleasure flights, corporate hospitality

Aircraft Type	Fleet	Training
Mudry CAP10B	1	160
Zlin Z562	2	160
Tiger Moth	1	POA
Antonov AN2	1	POA

Aviators Flight Centre

Southend
Tel: 01702 542497
PPL(A), NR, IMC, NVQs, Second pilot, Tailwheel

Aircraft Type	Fleet	Training	Hire
C150	3	66.50	77.78
PA-28-151	1	73.32	84.60
C172	1	73.32	84.60

PPL Ground Tuition: variable costs

Avon Flying School

Wellesbourne
Tel: 01789 470727   Fax: 01789 470727
PPL(A), NR, IMC, Multi, Aerobatics, Tailwheel, Second pilot
Membership: £40 pa

Aircraft Type	Fleet	Training	Hire
PA-38	2	89.50	75
PA-28	2	96	85
C152 Tailwheel 1	89.50	75	
Beech 76	1	195	180

Trial lesson: 30 mins £45
Visa Mastercard Access
PPL Ground Tuition: £80/day

Barmoor Aviation

Top Farm
Tel: 01767 631377   Fax: 01767 631377
Self-fly hire, training by arrangement with local freelances

Aircraft Type	Fleet	Training	Hire
C152	1		55.00
C172 (IFR equip)	1		68.00
C182 (IFR)	1		75.00
TB20 (IFR++)	1		105.00 +VAT

No credit cards.
All prices plus VAT, all rates are airborne times

Barry Aviation Flying Club

Shoreham
Tel: 01444 451177 (course info); 01403 786767 (Flight Bookings); 01273 441767 (Club Room)   Fax: 01273 441768 (Club room fax)
PPL(A), NR, IMC, Second pilot, Airways training Group D to Group A, conversion courses (own a/c) career advice for airlines, Radionav

Aircraft Type	Fleet	Training	Hire
C150	2	79	47
TB9	1	99	79

PPL Ground tuition: 3 day intensive courses (inc exams) £299

Bateleur Aviation

Headcorn
Tel: 01233 613549   Fax: 01233 613549
PPL(A), IMC, NR, Multi, Tailwheel, Aerobatics, Second pilot, Radionav, CPL

Aircraft Type	Fleet	Training
C150	4	85 inc
C172	2	85 inc
PA-28 161	1	85
DR400 108	1	85
R3000	1	85
PA-34	1	85
PA-18	1	85
Jodel D150	1	85

Beccles Aviation Ltd

Beccles Heliport
Tel: 01502 475124

Bedfordshire School Of Flying
Cranfield
Tel: 01234 751403 Fax: 01234 750395
PPL(A), PPL(H), NR, IMC, Multi, Second pilot, Radionav, NVQ approved assessment centre

Aircraft Type	Fleet	Training	Hire
AA5A Cheetah	4	99	80
AA5B Tiger	1	90	90.00
GA7 Cougar	2	175	175
PA 28 Cadet		90	90
C150 Aerobat		90	80
R22	2	170	135

Trial lesson: fixed wing 60 mins £95; helicopter 30 mins £125; 60 mins £175
Visa Access Mastercard Switch accepted.
PPL Ground Training £600 including all equipment.
Other Ground Tuition: through Cabair College of Air Training short course, correspondence course or self study course.
All prices plus VAT. Special hire rates on 'Gold Rental' and 'Platinum Rental' available

Bembridge Flight Training
Bembridge
Tel: 01983 872050

Biggin Hill Ground School
Biggin Hill
Tel: 01656 57191
Tuition: PPL(A), IMC, PPL/IR fixed wing and Rotary, R/T groundschool

Biggin Hill School of Flying
Biggin Hill
Tel: 01959 573583 Fax: 01959 572163
PPL(A), NR, IMC, Multi, Tailwheel, Second pilot, Radionav, NVQs

Aircraft Type	Fleet	Training	Hire
AA5A Cheetah	6	99	80
AA5B Tiger	2	90	67.50
GA-7	1	135	127.50

Access Visa Switch
PPL Ground Tuition: £600+VAT including all equipment
Special Gold and Platinum rates, details on request.

Billins Air Services Ltd
Cranfield
Tel: 01234 751400 (eves 01895 232044)
PPL(A), NR, IMC, Multi, Safety Pilot
Membership fee £25/3 months, £60 pa

Aircraft Type	Fleet	Training	Hire
C150	4	75	56
C172	1	91.19	72
PA-32	1	134.19	115

Trial lesson: 30 mins £45; 60 mins £79
Visa Mastercard Access accepted with handling fee
PPL Ground Tuition £7.50 per 2 hour session
Training rate includes base landing fees. Call for details of PPL packages

Birmingham Aero Centre
Birmingham
Tel: 0121 782 7755 Fax: 0121 782 2094

Blackbushe School of Flying Ltd
Blackbushe
Tel: 01252 870999 Fax: 01252 871975
PPL(A), PPL(H) NR, IMC, Multi, Tailwheel, Second pilot, Aerobatics, Radionav, NVQs

Aircraft Type	Fleet	Training	Hire
AA5A Cheetah	6	99	80
AA5B Tiger	1		67.50
GA-7 Cougar	1		135
R22	2	170	135

Visa Mastercard Access Diners
PPL Ground Tuition: Yes; £600 + VAT including all equipment
All prices plus VAT. Gold and Platinum rental rates, details on request

Blackpool Air Centre
Blackpool
Tel: 01253 341871 Fax: 01253 341567
PPL(A), NR, IMC, Multi, Tailwheel, Banner towing, survival courses - emphasis on ditching procedures
Membership: £58.75

Aircraft Type	Fleet	Training	Hire
PA-28-140	4	85	75
C150	2	80	70
PA-23	1	190	
C185	1	12	
C205	1	120	
Auster J/1N	1	100	

Trial lesson: 30 mins £45; 60 mins £85
PPL Ground Tuition: £15 + VAT per hour

BM Aviation
Southampton
Tel: 01962 842555 Fax: 01962 842555
PPL(A), NR, IMC, Multi, PPL/IR, Aerobatics, Second pilot, FAA biennial flight reviews, FAA instrument competency checks

Aircraft Type	Fleet	Training	Hire
Cherokee 140	1	99.87	82.25
Grumman Tiger AA5B	1	111.62	94.00
C310Q	1	235	211.50

PPL Ground Tuition: £7.50 / hr

Bobbington Air Training School
Halfpenny Green
Tel: 01384 221292 Fax: 01384 221515
PPL(A), NR, IMC, Radionav
Membership: £23.50

Aircraft Type	Fleet	Training	Hire
C150	2	from 77	70
C152	3	80	73
PA-28 Warrior	2	93	86
PA-28 200R	1	110	102

Trial lesson: 30 mins £39.95
Access Visa Mastercard Switch Delta
PPL Ground Tuition: available

Bonus Aviation
Cranfield
Tel: 01234 751800 Fax: 01234 751096
PPL(A), NR, IMC, Multi, PPL/IR, BCPL, FIC, AFIC, CPL, CPL/IR, NVQ approved assessment centre, Second pilots, Radionav
Membership: £50

Aircraft Type	Fleet	Training	Hire
PA-38-112	7	87	72
PA-28-181	2	110	95
PA-28-201	1	135	120
PA-44-180	2	237	207

Trial lessons: 30 mins £49.50; 60 mins £94.50
Access Mastercard Visa Switch Diners and Amex
PPL Ground Tuition: £10/hr one to one
Other Ground tuition: Navigation, technical and performance subjects for CPL and BCPL

Border Air Training
Carlisle
Tel: 01228 573490 Fax: 01228 573490
PPL(A), NR, IMC, Multi, Second pilots, Radionav, Tailwheel conversions, Aerobatics
Membership: £40+ VAT pa

Aircraft Type	Fleet	Training	Hire
C152	1	76.38	64.63
PA-28 Warrior	1	88.13	76.38

Also Slingsby T.67 - prices on application
Trail Lessons: 40 mins £48 C152
Access Visa Mastercard
PPL Ground Tuition: included with membership

Bristol & Wessex Aero Club
Bristol
Tel: 01275 472514
PPL(A), IMC, Multi, NR
Membership on application

Aircraft Type	Fleet	Training	Hire
PA28-140	2	96.00	76.00
PA28-180	1	96.00	88.00
PA23 1	208.00	188.00	

Trial Lesson 30mins £50.00; 60mins £90.00
Visa/Mastercard/Switch. NO Amex/Diners.
PPL Ground Tuition: £70.00 per course.

Bristol Aero Club
Filton
Tel: 0117 936 8935 or 962 2678

Bristol Flying Centre
Bristol Lulsgate
Tel: 01275 474601 Fax: 01275 474851
PPL(A), PPL(H), NR, IMC, Multi, PPL/IR, BCPL, FIC, AFIC, CPL, ATPL, Aerobatics, NVQs
Membership fee: £90

Aircraft Type	Fleet	Training	Hire	Advanced Training
C152	5	93	75	120
C172	1	99	92	120
PA-28 Warrior	2	109	99	135
PA-28 Arrow	1	120	107	
PA-34 Seneca	5	210	180	240
PA-31 Chieftain	3	neg	390	
TB-20 Trinidad	1	160	140	
PA34-Seneca simulator	1	118		
R22	2	212	158	
Bell 206 JetRanger	1	470	410	

Trial Lesson 60 mins £96
Mastercard Access Visa Diners Amex accepted
PPL Ground Training, also nav and techs for CPL/ATPL, Perf A, Perf C, Perf E
QFIs: 5 F/Time,4 P/Time AFIs: 3 F/Time,1 P/Time

Bristows Helicopters Ltd
Redhill
Tel: 01737 822353 Fax: 01737 822694
CPL(H), QHI, Commercial helicopter training to all levels by arrangement

Aircraft Type	Fleet	Training	Hire
R22	6	poa	
Bell 206	2	poa	
Slingsby T67	1	poa	

Britannia Flying Club
Luton
Tel: 01582 428065

British Aerospace Flying College Ltd
Prestwick
Tel: 01292 671022 Fax: 01292 474016
BCPL, AFIC, CPL/IR, ATPL, NVQs

Aircraft Type	Fleet	Training	Hire
AS 202 Bravo	10		
PA-28 Warrior II	21		
PA-34 Seneca III	10		

30 mins Jet simulator £40
PPL Ground Tuition: by arr
Prices on request; Frasca and Seneca simulators available, poa. Other ground tuition: available only as part of full airline course (CPL/IR with frozen ATPL)

British Airways Flying Club
Wycombe Air Park
Tel: 01494 529262 Fax: 01494 461237
PPL(A), NR, IMC, FIC, AFIC, Second pilot, Radionav; Multi and tailwheel by arrangment
Membership: £20 joining, £50 pa Associates, BA staff £45 pa

Aircraft Type	Fleet	Training	Hire
PA-38	3	105.60	85.20
PA-28	7	110.64	90.24

Trial Lessons: 20 mins £39; 30 mins £53; 40 mins £69;
Visa Mastercard Access Diners Switch Delta accepted
PPL Ground tuition: structured courses by appointment
Special flying rates for BA staff

Burman Aviation Ltd
Cambridge
Tel: 01223 293396 Fax: 01223 293443
PPL(H), NR, FIC, conversions

Aircraft Type	Fleet	Training	Hire
R22	7	170	125
Bell 206 Jet Ranger	2	360	On application

Access Mastercard Visa Switch Amex
PPL Ground Tuition: Yes: £12.50 /hour
Course prices on application

Burman Aviation Ltd
Cranfield
Tel:01234 752220 Fax: 01234 752221
PPL(H), NR, AFIC, Turbine conversions
PPL Ground Tuition: Yes; Cost: £12.50/hour

Aircraft Type	Fleet	Training	Hire
R22	7	170	125
Bell 206 Jet Ranger	2	360	360

Visa Mastercard Access Switch Amex accepted

Burman Aviation Ltd
Gloucestershire
Tel: 01452 712388 Fax: 01452 713565
PPL(H), NR, AFIC, Turbine conversions

Aircraft Type	Fleet	Training	Hire
R22	7	170	125
Bell 206 Jet Ranger	2	360	360

Visa Mastercard Access Switch Amex
PPL Ground Tuition: £12.50 / hour

Bushpilots
Oaksey, Goodwood & Old Sarum
Tel: 01730 895034 Fax: 01730 895558
Glider tug training, tailwheel conversion, farm strips

Aircraft Type	Fleet	Training	Hire
Supercub 150	1	79	75
Citabria	1	79	75

Tailwheel conversion £350 inc call for details

C J Helicopters
Sywell
Tel 01604 760760 Fax: .01604 760760
PPL(H) NR, conversions, safety courses, mountain flying

Aircraft Type	Fleet	Training	Hire
Hughes 300c	1	229.12	176.25

PPL Ground tuition: available
Gazelle B206 and Hughes 500 by arrangement

Cabair College of Air Training
Cranfield
Tel: 01234 751243 Fax: 01234 751363
PPL/IR, BCPL, FIC, AFIC, CPL, CPL/IR, ATPL, NVQs
Ground tuition: Prices on application.
All courses to commercial licences - modular or integral - are carried out on AA5A/AA5B/PA-28/R22/B206

Cabair Flight Training (Redhill)
Redhill
Tel: 01737 822166 Fax: 01737 822147
PPL(A), PPL(H), NR, IMC, Multi, Tailwheel Second pilot, Radionav, NVQs
QFIs: 3 F/time

Aircraft Type	Fleet	Training	Hire
C172	3	124.90	80
R22	1	217	176
Bell 47	1		

Trial lesson: 30 mins £60 fixed wing; 30 mins £125 heli; 60 mins £175
Mastercard Visa Switch Access
PPL Ground Tuition: £600 + VAT including all equipment
All prices plus VAT. Gold and Platinum rental rates, details on request. Pre payment discount available. Bell prices on request

Caledonian Seaplanes
Cumbernauld
Tel: 01236 457777 Fax: 01236 738322
Seaplane/amphibian

Aircraft Type	Fleet	Training	Hire
Piper PA-18 Seaplane	1	120	120
CU206G Amphibian	1	199	199

PPL Ground Tuition: Cost - nil

Cambrian Flying Club
Swansea
Tel: 01792 297275
PPL(A), NR, IMC, FIC, AFIC, Second pilot

Aircraft Type	Fleet	Training	Hire
PA-38-112	2	72.26	62
PA-28-161	1	96.94	82.84

PPL Ground Tuition £4 for 1.5 hour course; £10 for 1 to 1

Cambridge Aero Club
Cambridge
Tel: 01123 373214 Fax: 01223 373833
PPL(A), NR, PPL/IR
Membership: £10 pa

Aircraft Type	Fleet	Training	Hire
C152	5	88.83	80.57

Trial Lesson: 30 mins £46.79; 40 mins £61.85
Visa Mastercard Amex Diners Switch

Cambridge Flying Group
Cambridge
Tel: 01223 293343 Fax: 01223 294147
PPL(A), IMC, NR, Aeros, Tailwheel
Membership £25 (short term)

Aircraft Type	Fleet	Training	Hire
Tiger Moth	2	92.40	84.60
Fuji	1	92.40	84.60

Trial lesson £46.20 (30mins)
No credit cards
PPL Ground Tuition - FOC

Capital Helicopters
Leicester
Tel: 01889 505 611

Cardiff Aero Services
Cardiff
Tel: 01446 711987
PPL(A), IMC, NR, Multi, FIC, IR (non-app), Second Pilot
Membership on application

Aircraft Type	Fleet	Training	Hire
PA38	3	82.66	76.05
C150	1	82.66	76.05
DR400-180	1	n/a	96.00
PA34	1	196.73	173.23
PN68	1	196.73	173.23

Trial Lesson 30mins £40.00, 1hr £80.00
Visa/Mastercard, no Diners/AMEX/Switch.
PPL Ground Tuition: on application

Cardiff-Wales Flying Club
Cardiff
Tel: 01446 710000 Fax:.01446 711135
PPL(A), PPL(H), NR, IMC, Second pilot, non approved IR
Membership: £60

Aircraft Type	Fleet	Training	Hire
PA38	4		
C150	1		
PA28-161	1	87	63.50
PA28-181	1	97	73.50
PA44	1	169	144
R22	1	190	140

Trial lesson: 30 mins £38 fixed/wing; 30 mins £90 helicopter
Access Visa Switch Visa
PPL Ground Tuition: no cost

Carill Aviation Flying School
Southampton
Tel: 01703 627225 Fax: 01703 643528
PPL(A), NR, IMC, Multi, PPL/IR, NVQs, BCPL, Second pilot, Radionav
Membership: £35

Aircraft Type	Fleet	Training	Hire
PA-28-161	4	104.86	99.88
PA-28-180	1	104.86	99.88

Trial lesson: 30 mins £59; 60 mins £99 for two people to land away
Visa Mastercard Amex
PPL Ground Tuition: £10/hr; ground briefings at no charge
Special rates for 'Warrior Group', (Warrior group pay £11.75 pcm)

Channel Aviation Ltd
Guernsey
Tel: 01481 37217 Fax: 01481 38886
PPL(A), NR, IMC, Multi, Second pilot, Radionav

Aircraft Type	Fleet	Training	Hire
PA-38	4	65	55
PA-28	1	85	70
PA-34	1	165	130

Trial lesson: 30 mins £35
Access Visa
PPL Ground Tuition: cost: inclusive with courses

Chase Aviation
Bournemouth
Tel: 01202 485172 Fax: 01202 480492
Self-fly hire mainly. All types of PPL tuition available by arrangement.
Membership - on application

Aircraft Type	Fleet	Training	Hire
B55 Baron	1		180.00
AA5	1		65.00

Trial Lesson £50, 30 mins
No credit cards

Cherokee Flying Group
Rochester
Tel: 01322 666345 Fax: 01322 667547
PPL(A), NR, Tailwheel, IMC

Aircraft Type	Fleet	Training	Hire
PA-28-160	1	82	72
Piper Super Cub 150	1	79	69

Trial Lesson: 30 mins £40
PPL Ground Tuition: Nil cost to group members

Cheshire Air Training School
Liverpool
Tel 0151 4868383 Fax: 0151 359464
PPL(A), NR, IMC, Multi, BCPL, FIC, AFIC, aerobatics, farm strip flying
Membership: £70 standard or £370 premium pa

Aircraft Type	Fleet	Training	Hire
C150	2	75	67.50
C172	1	86	78.50
T67B	1	90	82.50
T67C	1	125	117.50

Trial lessons: 30 mins £43.50 C150; 60 mins £81 C150
Access Mastercard Visa Switch Delta
PPL Ground Tuition: £120 all subjects inc exam
Premium rates available - details on request, all prices + landings

Chester Flying School
Hawarden
Tel: 01244 534353 Fax: 01244 534353
PPL(A), NR, IMC
Membership: £52 pa

Aircraft Type	Fleet	Training	Hire
PA-38	1	56	70
PA-28	1	56	70

Trial Lesson: 30 mins £40
PPL Ground Tuition: £15 for non-members, included for members

City Air Charter (London) Ltd
Cranfield
Tel: 01234 751417/750592 Fax: 01234 751246
PPL(A), NR, IMC, Multi, Aerobatics, Second pilot, Radionav
Membership: £58.75; Full social membership FOC

Aircraft Type	Fleet	Training	Hire
C150	1	70	
C172	1	75	
PA-28-181 Archer II	1	95	

Trial lesson: 30 mins £38; 40 mins £58; 60 mins £85;
Mastercard Access Visa Amex Diners accepted
PPL Ground Tuition: Free with lesson or £15 per hour1 to1
PA23 Aztec and Pa34 available block bookings - ring for prices Instructors add £15 PPL £20 IMC and £30 Multi

Civilair Flying Club
Biggin Hill
Tel: 01959 573853/573989
PPL(A), NR, IMC, Multi, Second pilot, Radionav, R/T
Membership: £50

Aircraft Type	Fleet	Training	Hire
C152	4	95.88	76.85
AA5	1	101.52	81.78
PA-28-150	1	108.10	88.13
PA-23-250	1	209.39	170.61
C172	1	101.52	81.78

Access Mastercard Visa Switch Amex
PPL Ground Tuition: £12/hr inc
Landing fees additional

Clacton Aero Club (1988) Ltd
Clacton Airfield
Tel: 01255 424671 Fax: 01255 475364
PPL(A), IMC, FIC, AFIC, Aerobatics, Tailwheel, Second pilot, Tailwheel, PPL, residential courses also available on Cessna 152

Aircraft Type	Fleet	Training	Hire
Piper Super Cub	3	74	68
C172	2	79	74
C152	3	69	62
C206	1	110	100 (not weekend)
DH82a Tiger Moth	2	95	79

PPL Ground Tuition: included in residential courses

Direct Helicopters
Southend
Tel: 01702 546420 Fax: 01702 542104
PPL(A), PPL(H), NR, Multi, Aerobatics

Aircraft Type	Fleet	Training	Hire
Jet Ranger	2	395	355
Hughes 300	1	225	195
R22	1	195	165

PPL Ground Tuition: all in hourly rate
All prices + VAT

Classair
Biggin Hill
Tel: 01959 540495
PPL(A), NR, IMC, Second pilot
Membership: £40

Aircraft Type	Fleet	Training	Hire
Robin 3000	1	105	88

Access Visa Mastercard
PPL Ground Tuition: nil charge with flying

Cleveland Flying School Ltd
Teesside International Airport
Tel: 01325 332855/332043 Fax: 01325 332855
PPL(A,) NR, IMC, Multi, Aerobatics, Radionav
Membership: £35 p/a

Aircraft Type	Fleet	Training	Hire
C150	2	83.50	68.50
C152	1	83.50	68.50
C172	1	94	80.50
PA-28 Warrior	1	97	76.50
Firefly T.67B	1	90.50	72.50
Piper Seneca	1	209.52	187.68

Trial Lessons: 30 mins £50 C172/PA28; 30 mins £35 C150/152; 45 mins £70 T67
Access Mastercard Visa
PPL Ground Tuition: Included in a/c training charge
Block rates available

Cloudbase Aviation
Redhill
Tel: 01737 822423
PPL(A) Microlights

Aircraft Type	Fleet	Training	Hire
CFM Shadow	5	69	22

PPL Ground Tuition: £10 per session
Solo charges on own aircraft

Cloudbase Aviation
Goodwood
Tel: 01293 522465 Fax: 01293 852610
PPL(A, Microlight

Aircraft Type	Fleet	Training	Hire
CFM Shadow	2	69	22
Flexwing	1	64	

PPL Ground Tuition: £10 per session
Solo charges on own aircraft

Comed Aviation Ltd
Blackpool
Tel: 01253 349072 Fax: 01253 349073
PPL(A), NR, IMC, Multi, PPL/IR, BCPL, FIC, AFIC, CPL, CPL/IR approved and non approved, ATPL, NVQs, Aerobatics, Second pilot, Radionav
Membership: £58.75

Aircraft Type	Fleet	Training	Hire
PA-28-140	5	85	75
PA-28-151	1	90	85
PA-23-250F	1	240	220
PA-31-350	2	440	411
T67A Slingsby	1	90	85
C172	1	85	75

Trial lessons: 30 mins £45; 60 mins £85
Access Mastercard Visa Switch Amex
PPL Ground Tuition: free

Cornwall Flying Club
Bodmin
Tel: 01208 821419/821463 Fax: 01208 821419
PPL(A), NR, IMC, Second pilots, Radionav
Membership: £90

Aircraft Type	Fleet	Training	Hire
C152	2	75	56
C150	1	75	56
C172	1	86	66

Trial Lesson: 30 mins £45; 60 mins 90
Visa Access Mastercard
PPL Ground Tuition: £12 per hour
All prices + VAT

Cotswold Aero Club
Gloucestershire
Tel: 01452 713924
PPL(A), NR, IMC, Aerobatics, Second pilot, Silver C conversions, Tailwheel conversions on own aircraft, Radionav
Membership: £40

Aircraft Type	Fleet	Training	Hire
Robin 2160	1	86.96	76.99
Robin DR400/120	2	82.94	74.66
Robin DR400/160	1	92.30	83.90

Trial lesson: 30 mins £50
PPL Ground Tuition: £30 per course

Coventry Flying School/Coventry Aeroplane Club
Coventry
Tel: 01203 301428 Fax: 01203 306417
PPL(A), NR, IMC, Multi, Second pilot, Radionav
Membership: £45

Aircraft Type	Fleet	Training	Hire
C152	3	79.20	69
C172	2	82.62	
PA-28-181 Archer	1	88.62	
PN68B (dry)	2	111.63	111.63
PN68B (wet)	2	165	165

Trial lesson: 30 mins £45
Access Visa Mastercard Delta Switch
PPL Ground Tuition: £25 per subject
Subs scheme on 152 only: £30 per month, £45 per hour

Coventry Helicopters
Coventry
Tel: 01203 639206

CPM Enterprises
Gloucestershire
Tel: 01452 855796
Tuition: PPL, IMC groundschool

Crowfield Flying School
Crowfield
Tel: 01449 711017 Fax: 01449 711054
PPL(A), NR, IMC
Membership: £58.75

Aircraft Type	Fleet	Training	Hire
C150	3	70.80	59.93
PA-28 Warrior	1	89.30	76.38

Trial lesson: 25 mins £40
PPL Ground Tuition: as an integral part of the package

Cubair Ltd
Redhill
Tel: 01737 822124 Fax: 01737 822115
PPL(A), NR, IMC, Aerobatics, Tailwheel Second pilot, Radionav, PPLs on tailwheels
Membership: £50 p/a insurance excess

Aircraft Type	Fleet	Training	Hire
PA-18	3	from 108	from 93
D140	1	by arr	by arr
C150	2	from 95	from 81
C172	1	from 115	from 99
T62A	1	114	93
Citabria	1	108	93
Tiger Moth	1	by arr	

Trial lesson: 30 mins £59.75; 60 mins £89.00
Mastercard Access Visa
PPL Ground Tuition: free as part of training or £15/hour one to one

Cumbria Aero Club
Carlisle
Tel: 01228 573633 Fax: 01228 573633
PPL(A) NR IMC Multi Aerobatics Tailwheel conversions Second pilots Radionav R/T
Membership: £45 pa, £25 if living more than 50 miles away

Aircraft Type	Fleet	Training	Hire
C152	7	79.61	67.62
C172	1	84.49	73.50
C337	1	164.50	146.88

Trial lessons: 30 mins £37.50 C152; 60 mins £75 C152
Access Mastercard Visa
PPL Ground Tuition: £35.75 per subject + exam fee

Delta Helicopters
Luton
Tel: 01582 405250 Fax: 01582 401084
PPL(H), NR, Multi, FIC, AFIC, CPL

Aircraft Type	Fleet	Training	Hire
R22	2	175	145
Bell 206	1	410	390
AS355	1	prices on application	

Trial lessons: 20 mins £75
Visa Mastercard Access accepted
PPL Ground Tuition: £25

Deltair Aviation Services Ltd
Liverpool
Tel 0151 4942040 Fax: 01782 513101
PPL(A), NR, IMC, Multi, PPL/IR, BCPL, FIC, AFIC, CP,L CPL/IR, Aerobatics, Tailwheel, Second pilot, Radionav

Aircraft Type	Fleet	Training	Hire
Bulldog	3	98	88
PA-38	3	70	60
C172	1	78	68
C152	1	70	60
PA-18	1	70	60

Trial lesson: 45 mins £55
Access Visa
PPL Ground Tuition: available

Denham School of Flying
Denham
Tel 01895 833327 Fax: 01895 835048
PPL(A), NR, IMC, Multi, NVQs, Tailwheel, Second pilot, Radionav
Membership: £120+VAT

Aircraft Type	Fleet	Training	Hire
PA-28 Cadet	6	99	80
PA-28 Warrior	1	99	80
AA5B Tiger	1	90	67.50
GA-7 Cougar	1	135	127.50
PA-32	1	135	127.50

Trial lesson: 1 hour land away double £99
Access Mastercard Visa Switch
PPL Ground Tuition: Yes; £600 + VAT including all equipment.
Special rates available

Derby Aero Club and Flying School
Derby Airfield
Tel: 01283 733803 Fax: 01283 734829
PPL(A), IMC, FIC, AFIC, Multi, Tailwheel, Second pilots, Radionav
Membership: £47 full; £15 social

Aircraft Type	Fleet	Training	Hire
C152	4	78	71
C152 tailwheel	1	78	71
C172	1	90	83
PN 68	1	poa	
PA23	1	poa	

Trial lessons: 30 mins £39
PPL Ground Tuition: £40 per course £8/hour private tuition
All prices inc VAT and homebased landing fees. Discounts given for pre-payment.

Devon School of Flying
Dunkeswell Aerodrome
Tel: 01404 891643 Fax: 01404 891456
PPL(A), NR, IMC, Multi, BCPL, FIC, AFIC, Aerobatics, Tailwheel, Second pilots, Radionav
Membership: Annual: £55; Temporary £7.05(1 month)

Aircraft Type	Fleet	Training	Hire
C152	1	88.30	74
PA-28-151 Warrior	1	95	89.50
PA-28-161 Warrior II	3	95	89.50
PA-28-180 Cherokee	1	103.00	92.50
Tiger Moth	1	137.50	

Trial lessons: 15 mins £25 (C152) or £30 (Warrior); 30 mins £43.50 (C152) £56.25 (Warrior); 15 mins £49.50 (Tiger Moth)
Access Visa Mastercard Switch Delta
PPL Ground Tuition: £15 per hour one to one tuition

Donair Flying Club
East Midlands
Tel: 01332 810444 Fax: 01332 853852
PPL(A) NR IMC Multi Aerobatics
Membership: £50 p/a

Aircraft Type	Fleet	Training	Hire
C150	1	75	65
C150 Aerobat	1	75	65
C152	2	75	65
PA-28	1	85	75
C182	1	95	85
PA-34	1	188	188

Trial Lesson: 30 mins £38; 60 mins £70
Access Mastercard Visa Switch Delta Amex Diners
PPL Ground Tuition: available

Dragon Aviation
Chirk
Tel: 01691 774137/01691 772659 Fax: 01691 772659
PPL(A) Microlight 3 axis and flex wing

Aircraft Type	Fleet	Training	Hire
BMW Thruster (3 axis)	1	55	50
Pegasus XL (Flex wing)	1	55	

PPL Ground Tuition: £15/hr

EAA Aviation Ltd (Safelight)
Fairoaks
Tel: 01276 856969 Fax: 01276 855349
IMC, Multi, PPL/IR, BCPL, CPL, CPL/IR, Second pilot

Aircraft Type	Fleet	Training	Hire
Partenavia P.68	1	240	
PA-28	1	160	
PA-23	1	240	200
Frasca 142	1	70.	

Non-PPL Ground tuition: Tutor/correspondence courses

Eagle Flight Training
Luton
Tel: 01582 20007 Fax: 01582 435130
PPL(A), NR, IMC, Second pilot, Radionav, FAA PPL - ATPL ground/flight training, FAA biennial flight reviews,- FAA instrument competency checks, Multi.

Aircraft Type	Fleet	Training	Hire
PA-28-161	2	85	70
PA-34	1	215	200

Trial lessons: 30 mins £45; 60 mins £85, 90 minutes land away £130
Visa Access Mastercard accepted - 4% surcharge
Ground Tuition: cost depends upon the licence/cert/rating.
Also: FAA CPL/IR/ATPL ground tuition

Eaglescott School of Flying
Eaglescott Airfield
Tel: 01769 520404
PPL(A), IMC, Tailwheel, Second pilots

Aircraft Type	Fleet	Training	Hire
PA-12 Super Cruiser	1	80	68
PA-38 Tomahawk	2	80	68
PA-28-161 Warrior II	1	90	86
Hatz Biplane	1	80	80
C150	1	80	68

Group details available for PA-12 and PA-28
PPL Ground Tuition: £12/hour

East Coast Flight Training Ltd
Norwich Airport
Tel 01603 787187
PPL(A), NR, IMC, Multi, aerobatics
Membership: £49 pa

Aircraft Type	Fleet	Training	Hire
C150M	1	89	79
C152	1	89	79
C150M Aerobat	1	89	79
C172	1	97	85

Trial lesson: 30 mins £35; 45 mins £69
PPL Ground Tuition: £10 per hour (individual tuition)

East Herts Flying School
Panshanger
Tel: 01707 391791 Fax: 01707 392792
PPL, IMC, NR, Multi, Aeros, Tailwheel, RadioNav, Second Pilot
Membership £60

Aircraft Type	Fleet	Training	Hire
PA-38	4	94	70
C150	2	94	70
PA28	1	111.60	90
C182	1		94
Pitts S-2A	1	165	

Trial Lesson - on application
Major credit cards
PPL Ground Tuition: FOC

East Midlands Flying School Ltd
East Midlands
Tel: 01332 850383 Fax: 01332 853088
PPL(A) NR IMC
Membership: £55 inc personal accident insurance

Aircraft Type	Fleet	Training	Hire
C152	5	76	64
PA-28-161 Warrior	2	80	68
PA-28-181 Archer	1	83	71

Trial lessons: 30 mins £40; 60 mins £70
Access Visa
PPL Ground Tuition: £35 per subject inc. exam
All prices include VAT landing fees & Nav charges at EMA Pre-payment discounts available

East Midlands Helicopters
Costock
Tel: 01509 856444
PPL(H), AFI(H) course, Night/Instrument training

Aircraft Type	Fleet	Training	Hire
Robinson R22 Beta	3	229.15	164.50
Bell 47	1	287.88	217.88
Bell Jetranger	2	499.38	499.38

PPL Ground Tuition: Normally in with the price of the course

East Staffordshire Flying Club
Tatenhill
Tel: 01283 575283 Fax: 01283 575283
PPL(A), NR, IMC, Multi, Tailwheel, Radionav, Tailwheel on own aircraft
Membership: £20 p/a

Aircraft Type	Fleet	Training	Hire
C152	1	70	55
Robin	1	85	70
BE76	1	155	140
Arrow 4	1	100	85
Piper Seminole	1	poa	

Visa Access Mastercard
PPL Ground Tuition: cost on application

Eastern Air Centre Ltd
Gamston
Tel: 01777 838222 Fax: 01777 838035
PPL(A), NR, IMC, Multi, Radionav
Membership: £72 pa

Aircraft Type	Fleet	Training	Hire
C152	2	75	59.50
C172	1	85	75
PA-34 Seneca I	1	180	150

PPL Ground Tuition: £680 inc VAT
(ex Doncaster Aero Club for all our friends in the area).

Eastwest Flying Training
East Midlands
Tel: 01332 811418

Edinburgh Air Centre
Edinburgh
Tel: 031 3398888 Fax: 031 3394059
PPL(A), NR, IMC, Multi, PPL/IR, BCPL, CPL, CPL/IR Aerobatics, Second pilot
Membership: £42

Aircraft Type	Fleet	Training	Hire
C152	7	77	66.50
C172	4	89	74.50
C182	1	130	101.60
C210	1	179	151
CT210	1	179	151
C310	3	245	245
Frasca sim	1	85	

Trial lesson: 30 mins 4£9.50
Access Visa Mastercard Eurocard
PPL Ground Tuition: free

Edinburgh Flying Club
Edinburgh
Tel: 0131 3394990
PPL(A), NR, IMC, Radionav
Membership: £80

Aircraft Type	Fleet	Training	Hire
PA-38	3	77.85	69.63
PA-28-Archer	1	96.95	82.20
PA-28-Warrior	1	92.25	77.50

Trial lesson: 30 mins £49.50
Access Mastercard Visa
PPL Ground Tuition: free with PPL

EFG Flying School
Biggin Hill
Tel: 01959 540400/540054
PPL(A), NR, IMC, Multi
Membership: £58.75 p/a

Aircraft Type	Fleet	Training	Hire
C152	3	103.40	82.95
PA-28-161	2	123.96	104.93
PA-23 Aztec E	1	227.95	204.45
PA-23 Aztec F	1	233.82	210.33

Access Visa Mastercard Amex Switch
PPL Ground Tuition: no charge
Pre payment discount £1000 7%; £1500+10%

Eglinton Flying Club
Eglinton
Tel: 0504 810962
PPL(A), NR, IMC

Aircraft Type	Fleet	Training	Hire
C152	1	54	52
PA-28-161 Warrior	1	64	60

PPL Ground Tuition: available,

Enstone Eagles Gliding Club
Enstone
Tel: 01608 677461
Gliding - from ab initio upwards
Membership: £120 pa
Aircraft Type Fleet Training Hire
T.21, Twin Astir, K7(M) KA 8 gliders: all £4 per launch and 25p per minute airtime.
Instruction is free. 5 day course £255
Trial lesson: £20 per launch
PPL Ground Tuition: free

Enstone Flying Club
Enstone
Tel: 01608 678204 Fax: 01608 643424
PPL(A) NR, IMC, Second pilot, Radionav

Aircraft Type	Fleet	Training	Hire
PA-28 Warrior II	1	99	83.50
PA-38 Tomahawk	1	89	73.50
Robin DR400	1		83.50
TB-10 Tobago	1		85 00
PA-28-235	1		112

Trial lesson: 60 mins £80
Amex
PPL Ground Tuition: inclusive

Essex Flying School Ltd
Earls Colne
Tel: 01787 223676 Fax: 01787 224246
PPL(A), NR, IMC, Multi, PPL/IR, Aerobatics Second pilots

Aircraft Type	Fleet	Training	Hire
C152	2	74.50	64
C150	2	74.50	64
C172	1	85.50	77
PA-28-140	2	82.50	74
C150 Aerobat	1	78.50	68

PPL Ground Tuition: £14 per hour

Euroair
Cranfield
Tel: 01234 752262 Fax: 01234 752262
PPL(A), NR, IMC, Aerobatics, Second pilots, Radionav
Membership: £10 temp, £35/year inc insurance waiver

Aircraft Type	Fleet	Training	Hire
C150 aerobat	1	86	69
C152	1	86	69
C172	1	94	78

Trial lessons: 30 mins £40 (C152); 25 mins £40 (Aerobat); 30 mins £45 (C172)
PPL Ground Tuition: £10 per hour

European Flyers
Blackbushe
Tel: 01252 873747 Fax: 01252 876177
PPL(A), IMC, Multi, FIC, Night, Aerobatics, AFIC, Radionav, Simulator, NVQ assessment centre
Membership: Full PPL £76.38; family £94; Social 29.38; Veteran £41.13; Daily £5.88

Aircraft Type	Fleet	Training	Hire
C152	7	99.88	95 88.13
C172	3	111.63	99.88
AA5A	2	106.75	99.88
Archer II	2	111.63	99.88
Seneca	1	182.13	123
Arrow	1	123.38	111.63
Simulator	1	29.38	

PPL Ground Tuition: £17.62
Prices are represenative of the numerous flying rate options offered.

Exeter Air Training School
Exeter
Tel: 01392 445197 Fax: 01392 445197
PPL(A), NR, BCPL, Radionav, Multi, IMC, NVQ
Membership: £45 pa; £7 per month

Aircraft Type	Fleet	Training	Hire
C152	1	83	70
C172	1	93	80
PA23	1	220	n/a

Trial lessons: 30 mins £42; 45 mins £65
PPL Ground Tuition: £140 (inc all exams)
Landing fee C152 and C172 £3 - PA23 £17

Exeter Flying Club Ltd
Exeter
Tel: 01392 367653 Fax: 01392 367653
PPL(A), NR, IMC, Multi BCPL, FIC, AFIC, Aerobatics, Tailwheel conversions, Second pilot, Radionav, NVQs pending
Membership: £38 Flying; £10 Associate

Aircraft Type	Fleet	Training	Hire
C152	3	84	69
C172	2	94	79
Robin DR400/120	1	89	69
PA-28-181 Archer	1	95	85

Trial lessons: 40 mins £50; 60 mins £75
Access Visa Mastercard - 2.5% surcharge
PPL Ground Tuition: £140 including exams or £7.50 per hour

Fairoaks Flight Centre
Fairoaks
Tel: 01276 858075 Fax: 01276 857677
PPL(A), NR, IMC, Multi, Second pilot, Radionav
Membership: £47

Aircraft Type	Fleet	Training	Hire
Warrior II	4	116.63	122.50
PA-28-180	1	111.69	117.80
PA-30	1	175.37	175.37

Trial lesson: 30 mins £60
Access Visa Amex Diners Mastercard
PPL Ground Tuition:, normally free by flying instructors; if individual special requirements £16/hr

Falcon Flying Services
Biggin Hill
Tel: 01959 575923/572339 Fax: 01959/576857

Aircraft Type	Fleet	Hire
C152	1	33

Block 50hrs
Access Visa Mastercard Switch Amex
Also available PA-23, PA-28, Warrior, PA-38, PA-34

Far North Aviation
Wick
Tel: 01955 602201 Fax: 01955 602201
PPL(A), NR, IMC, Multi
Membership: Free

Aircraft Type	Fleet	Training	Hire
Cessna F172P	1	85	70

Trial lesson: 20 mins £40
PPL Ground Tuition: free

Fast Helicopters Ltd
Thruxton
Tel: 01264 772508 Fax: 01264 773824
PPL(A), NR, IMC, PPL/IR, AFIC, PPL(H), AFIC helicopter only

Aircraft Type	Fleet	Training	Hire
C150	1	77.50	64.63
R22	3	211.50	152.75
Bell 206 Jet Ranger	2	407	399.50
Enstrom	1	246.75	205.63

Trial lessons: 20 mins £75 R22; £156 Bell 206
30 mins £110 R22; £235 Bell 206; £41.13 C150, 60 mins £82.26 C150
Visa Mastercard
PPL Ground Tuition: no cost

Fast Helicopters Ltd
Shoreham
Tel: 01273 465389 Fax: 0836 702388
PPL(H), NR

Aircraft Type	Fleet	Training	Hire
R22	2	211.50	146.88
Bell 206 Jetranger	1	470	411.25

Trial lesson: 30 mins £110
Visa Mastercard Access
PPL Ground Tuition: available

Felthorpe Flying Group
Felthorpe
Tel 01603 867691

Aircraft Type	Fleet	Training	Hire
DHC-1 Chipmunk	1	Price on application	

Fenland Flying School
Fenland
Tel: 01406 540461 Fax: 01406 540461
PPL(A), PPL(H), NR, IMC, Aerobatics (by arrangement), second pilot, Radionav
Membership: £95 pa

Aircraft Type	Fleet	Training	Hire
C150	2	69.50	79.50
C172	1	87.50	

Trial Lesson: 20 mins £30; 40 mins £55; 60 mins £80
PPL Ground Tuition: by arrangement

Fenland Helicopter Centre
Fenland
Tel: 01406 540115
PPL(H), Second pilot, Turbine conversions
Membership: £97

Aircraft Type	Fleet	Training	Hire
Schweizer	2	235	190
Bell 206 Jetranger	1	470	376
R22	1	200	152.75

Trial lesson: 30 mins £100 R22; 30 mins £107.50 Schweizer
Discount for full time courses

Fife Flying Club/Tayside Aviation Ltd
Fife
Tel: 01592 753792
PPL(A), NR, IMC, Second pilots, AFIC, FIC, BCPL aerobatics, R/T, NVQs
Membership: 35

Aircraft Type	Fleet	Training	Hire
C152	3	79.80	69
DV20 Katana	3	84.60	74.40
Piper Warrior	1	89.40	79.80

Trial lesson: 30 mins £35
PPL Ground Tuition: no charge
Special rates available to club members at certain times of year

Firecrest Aviation Ltd
Elstree
Tel: 0181 207 6201 Fax: 0181 207 4204
PPL(A), NR, IMC, Multi, Tailwheel, Second pilot, Radionav

Aircraft Type	Fleet	Training	Hire
C150	3	99.85	52.87
C172	2	114.00	68.00

Trial lesson: 30 mins £59.50
Access Mastercard Visa Switch Delta
PPL Ground Tuition: £12.50/evening class

Fleetlands Flying Association
Lee-on-Solent
Tel: 01329 318037
Membership only available to current or ex-service/ex-civil service staff.

Flylight Airsports Ltd
Sywell
Tel 01604 494459
PPL(A) Microlight, FIC Microlight, AFIC Microlight
Membership: £90 pa or £50 pa training

Aircraft Type	Fleet	Training
Mainair Blade 582	1	60
Solar Wings Quantum 582	1	60
Mainair Scorcher	1	60
Cyclone AX3	1	60

Trial lesson: 30 mins £35; 60 mins £60
PPL Ground Tuition: £12 per hour
Prices include landing fees

Frank Morgan School of Flying
Humberside
Tel: 01652 688859 Fax: 01652 688859
PPL(A), NR, IMC, Multi, FIC, AFIC, Aerobatics, Tailwheel, Second pilot, Radionav 1179/170A test, NVQs
Membership: £55 p/a

Aircraft Type	Fleet	Training	Hire
C172	1	79	67
PA-28-140	1	79	67
C150 Aerobat	1	70	58
C150	1	70	58

Trial lesson: 30 mins £42.50 C150; 30 mins £55 aerobatics or C172/PA28
Access Mastercard Visa Switch Delta
PPL Ground Tuition: £120 per subject, £500 pack
The only full time flying school approved to teach disabled people for the PPL(A) who do not have the use of their lower body. The approved aircraft is a C172 and the special equipment is made by Union Aviation Inc.The individual is able to obtain an unrestricted licence to fly solo and carry passengers

Freestyle Aviation
White Waltham
Tel: 01628 37732 Fax: 01628 777083
Aerobatics, Tailwheel, Spinning
Membership: 95 pa

Aircraft Type	Fleet	Training	Hire
Pitts S-2A	1	162	144

Visa Access Mastercard - 4% surcharge
Non-PPL Ground tuition: Aerobatic ground school, no charge for flying students.
Freestyle graduates have achieved over 30 podium finishes at BAeA contests since 1992.

Full Sutton Flying Centre
Full Sutton
Tel: 01759 372717; 373277 Fax: 01759 372991
PPL, IMC, NR, Multi
Membership £65

Aircraft Type	Fleet	Training	Hire
C150	2	On Application	
C172	1	On Application	
PA28	1	On Application	

Trial lesson - on application
Credit cards- on application
PPL Ground Tuition - on application

Furness Aviation Ltd
Barrow/Walney Island
Tel: 01229 472404 (Office); 01229 829708 (Secretary)
PPL(A), NR
Membership: £24
Hire: £80 per hour Mon-Fri; Please book at least 10 days in advance. Short notice bookings subject to availability
Trial lesson: 30 mins £42
PPL Ground Tuition: R/T

Glasgow Flying Club
Glasgow
Tel: 0141 889 4565
PPL(A), NR, IMC
Membership: £95

Aircraft Type	Fleet	Training	Hire
PA-38	2	88.50	67
PA-28-140	2	91.50	70
C172	1	99.50	78

Trial lesson: 30 mins £55

Gloucester and Cheltenham School of Flying
Gloucestershire
Tel: 01452 857153 Fax: 01452 857153
PPL(A), NR, IMC, Multi, Second pilot, Radionav
Membership: £36 pa

Aircraft Type	Fleet	Training	Hire
PA-28 Archer	1	93	85
PA-28 Warrior	1	85	85
PA-38	3	75	75
BE76 Duchess	1	135	125

Trial Lesson: 30 mins £40
PPL Ground Tuition: no charge
Hour building on PA-38 £55 per hour. Call for details. AOPA Ground instructors course and FAA ground school

Goodwood Flying School
Goodwood
Tel: 01243 774656 Fax: 01243 536497
PPL(A), NR, IMC, Multi, BCPL, FIC, AFIC, Aerobatics, Tailwheel, Second pilot, Radionav
NVQ approved

Aircraft Type	Fleet	Training	Hire
PA-38 Tomahawk	6	112	74
PA-28 Warrior	2	121	86
PA-28 Archer	1	125	91

Trial lesson: 30 mins £49.50
Access Visa Switch Delta
PPL Ground Tuition: from £15/hr

Guernsey Flight Training Ltd
Guernsey
Tel: 01481 65254 Fax: 01481 63830
PPL(A), NR, IMC, Multi, Aerobatics by arrangement
Membership: £15 (overseas)

Aircraft Type	Fleet	Training	Hire
C152	2	78	66
C172	1	72	
Beechcraft Musketeer	1	72	

Trial Lesson: 35 mins £35; 60 mins £65
Visa, Switch, M/card, Delta Eurocard
PPL Ground Tuition: included in course.

Halfpenny Green Flying Centre
Halfpenny Green
Tel: 01384 221456 Fax: 01384 221006
PPL(A), NR, IMC, Aerobatics, Second pilot, Radionav, R/T

Aircraft Type	Fleet	Training	Hire
PA-28-161	3	89	83
C150	2	75	70.71
TB10	1	98	88
Robin 2160	1	98	88
TB20	1	130	108

Trial lesson: 30 mins £39
Access Visa - 2.1% surcharge
PPL Ground Tuition: £6 per evening

Hall Aviation
Biggin Hill
Tel: 01689 855359
PPL(A), NR, IMC, Second pilot, Radionav, Cross channel and European touring training

Aircraft Type	Fleet	Training	Hire
Robin DR400	2	85	60
Robin 3000	1	85	60
Grumman AA5	1	105	80
Piper PA28 Cadet	1	110	85

PPL Ground Tuition: £15 per hour

Haverfordwest School of Flying
Haverfordwest
Tel: 01437 760822 Fax: 01437 760822
PPL(A), PPL(A), Microlight NR, IMC, Multi, Aerobatics
Membership: £10

Aircraft Type	Fleet	Training	Hire
C150	4	70	60
C172	2	85	85
PA-34	1	poa	
Snowbird	1	50	
Weightshift	1	50	

Trial lesson: 35 mins £40
PPL Ground Tuition: available

Heli Air Ltd
Denham
Tel 01895 835899
PPL(H), NR, mountain flying, low flying, instrument appreciation, turbine conversions

Aircraft Type	Fleet	Training	Hire
Bell 206 Jetranger	2	poa	
R22	4	poa	
Schweizer	a/r	poa	
R44	3	poa	
Hughes 500	a/r	poa	

Trial lesson: 30 mins £95

Heli Air Ltd
Wellesbourne
Tel: 01789 470476 Fax: 01789 470466
PPL(H), NR, mountain flying, FIC, 1179

Aircraft Type	Fleet	Training	Hire
R22	7		
R44	3		
Bell 206	2		
Hughes 300	1		
Hughes 500	1		
AS355	1		

Prices on application. Discounts for block booking

Helicentre Ltd
Blackpool
Tel: 01253 343082 Fax: 01253 407351
PPL(H), NR, Type conversions, safety courses

Aircraft Type	Fleet	Training	Hire
R22	3	135	175
Bell Jet Ranger	2	345	390
R44	1	370	315
AS355 Twin Squirrel		590	

Trial Lesson: 30 mins £95
Visa, Switch, M/card
PPL Ground Tuition: included in PPL training; extra tuition £15/h
All prices plus VAT

Helicopter Services
Luton
Tel: 0181 9686630 Fax: 0181 9686630
PPL(H), NR, IMC, Multi, FIC, AFIC, NVQs, Second pilot, 170A approval for commercial GFT, Mountain courses turbine conversions

Aircraft Type	Fleet	Training	Hire
R22	4	211.50	158.60
Hiller 12E	1	258.50	258.50
Hughes 269	1	246.75	211.50
Hughes 369	1	470	470
Bell 206 Jetranger	2	470	470
Twin Squirrel	1	793	793

PPL Ground Tuition: tailored to student or full ground course £199

Helicopter Training and Hire Ltd
Belfast International
Tel: 01849 453663 Fax: 01849 423233
PPL(H), NR, Helicopter turbine conversion mountain flying, R22 safety courses, RT

Aircraft Type	Fleet	Training	Hire
R22 Beta	2	170	120 (wet)
JetRanger	2	340	340 (Safety pilot only)

Trial lesson: 30 mins £95
PPL Ground Tuition: Yes; call for price details
Prices + VAT

Helicopter Training and Hire Ltd
Newtownards
Tel: 01247 820028 Fax: 01247 820357
PPL(H), NR, Helicopter turbine conversion, mountain flying, R22 safety courses, RT

Aircraft Type	Fleet	Training	Hire
R22 Beta	2	170	120(wet)
JetRanger	2	340+VAT	340(Safety pilot only)

Trial lesson: 30 mins £95
PPL Ground Tuition: Yes, call for details
Prices + VAT

Heliscott Flight Training
Walton Wood Airfield
Tel: 01977 621378 Fax: 01977 620868
PPL(H), NR, FIC, AFIC, CPL, NVQs, Seaplane ratings in Florida

Aircraft Type	Fleet	Training	Hire
R22	2	199.75	152.75
Schweizer	1	258.50	211.50
Bell Jet Ranger	2	470	470

PPL Ground Tuition: free with PPL course

Heliwest
Bodmin
Tel: 01326 312371
PPL(H) only.
Membership - on application

Aircraft Type	Fleet	Training	Hire
R22	1 185	130	

Trial Lesson £95 30 mins
No credit cards.
PPL Ground Tuition: FOC
Prices plus VAT

Henlow Flying Club
RAF Henlow
Tel: 01462 851936 Fax: 01462 851936
PPL(A), NR, IMC, Aerobatics, Second pilot, Radionav, Silver conversions

Aircraft Type	Fleet	Training	Hire
C150	1	95	from 42
C152	1	95	from 42
PA-28-161	1	105	from 60
PA-28-181	1	105	from 60

Trial lessons: 30 mins £45
PPL Ground Tuition: no charge

Herefordshire Aero Club Ltd
Shobdon
Tel: 01568 708369 Fax: 01568 708935
PPL(A), NR, IMC, Aerobatics, Radionav
Membership: £58 p/a; £30 senior; £15 affiliated

Aircraft Type	Fleet	Training	Hire
C152	3	72	57
C172	1	81.60	70.80
Grumman AA5B Tiger	1	85	75
C150	1	72	57

Trial lessons: 30 mins £40; 60 mins £72
Mastercard Access Visa Delta Switch
PPL Ground Tuition: £10 per hour
Syndicate system available to licensed pilots, details on request.

Horizon Flying Club Ltd
Ipswich
Tel: 01473 714840 Fax: 01473 718365
PPL(A), NR, IMC, Multi, FIC, AFIC, Aerobatics, Tailwheel, Second pilot, Radionav, Formation, Ground instructor
Membership: £52 p/a

Aircraft Type	Fleet	Training	Hire
C152	1	73.92	70.92
C150	2	73.92	70.92
A150L Texas			
Taildragger Aerobat	1	73.92	70.92
PA-28-140	1	84.72	81.72

Trial lesson: 30 mins £37
Visa Access Mastercard
PPL Ground Tuition: POA

Hull Aero Club
Linley Hill
Tel: 01964 544994 Fax: 01964 544994
PPL(A), NR (by arrangement), IMC, Aerobatics, Second pilot
Membership: £100 pa; £60pa

Aircraft Type	Fleet	Training	Hire
C150	3	77	65
AA5A Cheetah	1	75	65

Trial Lesson: 20 mins £25, 30 mins £35, 60 mins £60
PPL Ground Tuition: inc in PPL

Humber Flying Club
Humberside
Tel: 01652 680746 Fax: 01652 688492
PPL(A), NR, IMC, Multi, CPL/IR, PPL/IR, CPL and ATPL, GFTs NVQs
QFIs: 1 F/time 3 P/time

Aircraft Type	Fleet	Training	Hire
C150	2	70	65
C172	1	80	75
Beech 76	1	175	165

Trial lesson: 30 mins £30; 60 mins £60
PPL Ground Tuition: £25 per subject incl exam
C150 for hour building (min 10 hrs) £37.50 / hr. Ground tuition for CPL and ATPL, GFT support

Humberside Flight Training Ltd
Humberside
Tel: 01652 688056 Fax: 01652 688056
PPL(A), NR, IMC, Multi, approved BCPL PPL
Membership: £24

Aircraft Type	Fleet	Training	Hire
C150	2	74	68
C152	1	74	68
C172	1	85	85
PA-28-140	1	80	70

Trial lesson: 30 mins £39
Visa Access Mastercard
Ground Tuition: £15 per subject

India Mike Charlie
Turweston
Tel 01280 705749 Fax: 01280 705749
PPL (A), NR, IMC, Multi, Second pilot, FIC aerobatics,
PPL Ground Tuition: Yes; one to one instruction free
Membership: £60 pa

Aircraft Type	Fleet	Training	Hire
PA-28	2	95	85
PA-38	3	75	70
T67B	1	95	85
PA-34 Seneca 1	1	175	

Trial lesson: 30 mins £40 PA-38
Access Mastercard Visa
Specialise in full time residential courses

Invicta Air Sports
Coldharbour Farm, Kent
Tel: 01227 700441 Fax: 01227 700441
PPL(A) Microlight, Microlight flexwings

Aircraft Type	Fleet	Training	Hire
Pegasus XL 447	2	60	40
Pegasus Q 462	1	60	40
Quantum 48L	1	60	40

PPL Ground Tuition: FOC to students

Ipswich School of Flying
Ipswich
Tel: 01473 729510 Fax: 01473 721000
PPL(A), NR, IMC, Multi, Aerobatics, Tailwheel, Second pilot
Membership: £35

Aircraft Type	Fleet	Training	Hire
C182G	1	94	84
PA-28-161	2	84	74
PA-38	1	74	66
C150	1	74	66
Citabria	1	80	70

Trial lesson: 30 mins £40
Visa Access Mastercard
PPL Ground Tuition: available

Jersey Aero Club
Jersey
Tel: 01534 43990 Fax: 01534 41290
PPL(A), NR, IMC, Multi, PPL/IR FIC, AFIC, Aerobatics, Tailwheel, Radionav

Aircraft Type	Fleet	Training	Hire
PA-28	6	94	75
Chipmunk	1	94	
PA-23	1	155	135
Cessna 150	1		39

Trial lesson: 30 mins £44
Access Visa Switch Delta
PPL Ground Tuition: no charge, included in course costs
Special 'standby' flying rates - details on request.

Jones Aviation
Birmingham
Tel: 0121 7061845

Kingair Flight Centre
Biggin Hill
Tel: 01959 575088 Fax: 01959 572163
PPL(A), NR, IMC, Multi, Tailwheel, Second pilot, Radionav, NVQs

Aircraft Type	Fleet	Training	Hire
C152	5	from 50	
C172	4	from 50	
GA-7	1	from 50	
PA-28	1	from 50	
DV20 Katana	1	from 50	

Access Switch Visa Mastercard Diners
PPL Ground Tuition: Yes; £600+VAT including all equipment Mastergold and Platinum Gold Frequent flyer schemes - call for details

Klingair Flying Club
Peterborough Conington
Tel: 01487 832022 Fax: 01487 832614
PPL(A), NR, IMC, Aerobatics, Second pilots, Radionav
Membership: £117.50 p/a , joining fee £58.75

Aircraft Type	Fleet	Training	Hire	Aerobatic training
C152	3	83.43	65.80	
C152 Aerobat	1	85.78	65.80	89.30
PA-28-161 Warrior	1	106.92	83.42	

Trial Lesson: 30 mins £40
Visa Mastercard Diners
PPL Ground Tuition: Yes: various courses available from £35.25.
Reduced rate on block bookings

Knight Air Flying School
Leeds Bradford
Tel: 0113 2391339 Fax: 0113 2391326
PPL(A), NR, IMC, Multi, PPL/IR, BCPL, CPL, CPL/IR, ATPL, NVQs, Radionav, R/T , 1179 type ratings, approved and unapproved IR and BCPL GFT courses
Membership: £44.26 flying membership; £63.53 family

Aircraft Type	Fleet	Training	Hire
C150/152	3	75.74	59.57
C172	1	86.07	76.59
PA-28-140	1	80.85	
Beech Duchess	1	100	

Trial lesson: 30 mins £42.55; 60 mins £76.59; 30 mins £53.61; 60 mins £85.10
All major cards taken
PPL Ground Tuition: Yes; £15.32/hour
Prices exclude VAT

Lancashire Aero Club
Barton
Tel: 0161 787 7326 Fax: 0161 787 8782
PPL(A), NR, IMC, Multi, FIC, AFIC, Aerobatics, Second pilot, Radionav
Membership: £145 pa; £50 joining fee

Aircraft Type	Fleet	Training	Hire
C150	1	85.78	74.03
C150 Aerobat	1	85.78	74.03
C152	4	85.78	74.03
G115	2	85.78	74.03
C172	1	90.48	78.73
PA-28-161	2	90.48	78.73
PA-28-181	1	90.48	81.08

Trial lessons: 30 mins £45; 60 mins £80
Access Mastercard Visa - 4% surcharge
PPL Ground Tuition: £17.63/hour

Lands End Flying Club
Lands End
Tel: 01736 788771/788719 Fax: 01736 787274
PPL(A) NR IMC Tailwheel
Membership: £45 + £10 enrolment

Aircraft Type	Fleet	Training	Hire
C152	2	65	62.50
PA-28-140	2	70	67.50
C172	1	140	140

Trial Lessons: 30 mins £40
Access Mastercard Visa
PPL Ground Tuition: £12 per hour

Leicestershire Aero Club
Leicester
Tel: 0116 259 2360 Fax: 0116 259 2712
PPL(A), PPL(H), NR, IMC, Multi, FIC, AFIC, Aerobatics, second pilot, Radionav
Membership: £50 joining fee, £135 annual sub

Aircraft Type	Fleet	Training	Hire
C152	5	64	79.50
C172	1	67	83
PA-28	1	69	88

Trial Lesson: 20 mins £35
Visa Access
PPL Ground Tuition: £200 inc

Lincoln Aero Club
Sturgate
Tel: 01427 838305 (weekends); 01777 702417 and 01522 721411 (midweek)
Fax: 0427 838423
PPL(A), NR, IMC, Second pilot
Membership: £56

Aircraft Type	Fleet	Training	Hire
C152	2	59	50
PA-28-180	1	76	50

Trial lesson: 30 mins £32 C152
PPL Ground Tuition: cost included in flying training costs

Liverpool Flying School
Liverpool
Tel 0151 4277449 Fax: 0151 4278816
PPL(A), NR, IMC, Multi, BCPL, Aerobatics, Tailwheel, Second pilot, Radionav, Bi-plane flying in a Boeing Stearman
Membership: £60 p/a

Aircraft Type	Fleet	Training	Hire
PA-38	2	74.50	69.50
PA-28 Cherokee	2	79.50	74.50
PA-28 Warrior	1	87	82
Piper Aztec	2	197	192
DHC-1 Chipmunk	1	89.50	84.50
Boeing Stearman	1	130	
PA28-180	1	96	82

Trial lesson: 30 mins £45
PPL Ground Tuition: £11.75 per hour

London Aerial Tours
Rochester
Tel: 0181 946 6950
Multi

Aircraft Type	Fleet	Training	Hire
GA7 Cougar	1	135	

Complete multi engine package £1,095 inc VAT

London Flight Centre
Lydd
Tel: 01797 321549 Fax: 01797 321947
PPL(A), NR, IMC, PPL/IR, FIC, CPL
Membership: £58.75

Aircraft Type	Fleet	Training	Hire
C152	7	86	65.80
C172	1	101	83.43
PA-28-161	2	101	83.43
PA-28-181	1	111	92.83
PA-34	1	POA	

Call for package deals
Trial lessons: 30 mins £39; 45 mins £69 inc land away
Access Mastercard Visa Switch Delta
PPL Ground tuition: £15 per hour + VAT

London Flights (Biggin Hill) Ltd
Biggin Hill
Tel: 01959 540079

London Guildhall University Department of Civil Aviation Studies
Tel: 0171 320 1757
Tuition: PPL, IMC, CPL & ATPL Nav subjects

London School of Flying
Elstree
Tel: 0181 9534343 Fax: 0181 2071509
PPL(A), PPL(H), NR, IMC, Multi, Second pilot, Radionav, NVQs
Membership: £120

Aircraft Type	Fleet	Training	Hire
AA5A Cheetah	12	99	80
AA5B Tiger	4	90	67.50
R22 Beta	3	170	135
GA-7 Cougar	4	135	127.50
DV20 Katana	2	50	

Trial lessons: 60 mins £99 fixed wing; 30 mins £125 helicopter
Access Mastercard Visa Switch Delta
PPL Ground Tuition: £600+VAT including all the equipment.
All prices plus VAT. PA-32 Saratoga, prices on application Special pre-paid prices available - details on request

Manchester Helicopter Centre
Barton
Tel: 0161 787 7125 Fax: 0161 787 7892
PPL(H), Turbine conversions, 1179/H on all types
Membership: £145 pa; £50 joining fee

Aircraft Type	Fleet	Training	Hire
Enstrom F280C	1	195+VAT	165+VAT
Enstrom F280	1	195+VAT	165+VAT
Enstrom F28C	1	195+VAT	165+VAT

Trial lesson: 30 mins £100
PPL Ground Tuition: cost included in flying rate

Manx Flyers Aero Club
Ronaldsway
Tel: 01624 822926
PPL(A), NR, IMC, Multi, Second pilots
Membership: £94

Aircraft Type	Fleet	Training	Hire
PA-28-140	2	101.23	90.48
PA-28-181	1	112.80	101.05

Trial lesson: 30 mins £49.99
PPL Ground Tuition: free

Marchington Gliding Club
Tatenhill
Tel: 01543 878479 Fax: 01283 820108
Gliding Certificate - basic through to diamond

Aircraft Type	Fleet	Training	Hire

Super Blanik, ASK 21, ASK 23, D G 500: prices for training or hire - 26 pence per minute

Martin Evans
Biggin/Rochester
Tel: 0181 9466950
PPL(A), NR, IMC, Multi, BCPL, FIC, AFIC, CPL, NVQs

Aircraft Type	Fleet	Training
C172	1	80
GA7	1	135

PPL Ground Tuition: included
Freelance instructor examiner London/South East. A/c selected as required.

McCarthy Helicopter Services Ltd
Wycombe Air Park
Tel: 01494 451111 Fax: 01494 450627
PPL(H), NR, AFIC, Mountain flying, low flying, instrument appreciation
Membership: £250

Aircraft Type	Fleet	Training	Hire
R22	6	185	159
Bell Jet Ranger	3	464	425
Bell 47	1	305	
Enstrom 280	1	270	230
AS355	1	POA	

Trial lessons: 20 mins £85
Visa Mastercard Amex Dines
Non PPL Ground tuition: NRs, mountain flying

Medway Flight Training
Rochester/Farthing Corner
Tel: 01634 389757 Fax: 01634 264011
PPL(A), NR, IMC, Tailwheel, Second pilot, Radionav, Farm strip and glider towing, Silver C conversions, R/T
Other Ground tuition:
Membership: £30

Aircraft Type	Fleet	Training	Hire
PA-18	2	89.30	77.55
PA-22	1	80	63.30

Trial Lesson: 30 mins £40
Visa Access Mastercard Switch
PPL Ground Tuition: Free with flying training. Specialist one to one £13 per hour
Ground R/T operator licence courses £94 inc exam fees

Merseyside Aviation
Liverpool
Tel 0151 4943924/mobile: 0402 201341 Fax: 0151 4943924
PPL(A), NR, IMC, multi, Aerobatics, Second pilot, Radionav
Membership: £50 p/a

Aircraft Type	Fleet	Training	Hire
PA-38	2	79.50	74.50
T67B	1	90	

Trial lesson: 60 mins £75
PPL Ground Tuition: £50 per subject
Special rates for hours building

Metropolitan Police Flying Club (Biggin Hill Section)
Biggin Hill
Tel: 01959 572350
PPL(A), NR, IMC, Multi, Aerobatics, Radionav

Aircraft Type	Fleet	Training	Hire
C152 Aerobat	1	63	48
C152	1	63	48

PPL Ground Tuition: Yes; No charge to students
£15 per 2 hour instruction slot for instructor; local (discounted) landing fees additional

Microflight Ireland Ltd
Mullaghmore/Aghadowey
Tel: 01265 868002 Fax: 01265 824625
PPL(A) Microlight

Aircraft Type	Fleet	Training	Hire
Cyclone AX-3	1	55	
Pegasus XL	1	55	

PPL Ground Tuition: free

Midland Air Training School
Coventry
Tel: 01203 304914
PPL(A), NR, IMC, Multi

Aircraft Type	Fleet	Training	Hire
PA-28-140	3	86	76

Trial lesson: 30 mins £48
PPL Ground Tuition: no charges for PPL training
Multi available on application

Midland Flight Centre
Halfpenny Green
Tel: 01384 221011
PPL(A), IMC, NR, Multi, Aerobatics
Membership: £23

Aircraft Type	Fleet	Training	Hire
C152	3	75	70
PA-28-161	1	85	80
PA-28-181	1	95	90
PA-44	1	165	155

Trial lesson: 30 mins £30
Access Visa
PPL Ground Tuition: cost - only exam fees

Modern Air
Fowlmere
Tel: 01763 208281 Fax: 01763 208861
PPL(A), NR, IMC, Multi
Membership: £70.50 p/a

Aircraft Type	Fleet	Hire
PA-38-112	1	96
PA-28-181	5	111.62
PA-32R-301	1	164.50
PA-34-200	1	176.25
PA-34-200T	2	223.25
PA-34-220T	1	235.00

PPL Ground Tuition: Free
All rates are for airborne times only to the nearest 5 mins. Experience restrictions apply - ring for details

Mona Flying Club
RAF Mona
Tel: 01407 720581 (weekends) 01248 722782 (weekdays) Fax: 01407 720581
PPL(A), IMC, NR
Membership on application

Aircraft Type	Fleet	Training	Hire
C150	1	65.00	60.00
C152	1	65.00	60.00
PA28-180	1	76.00	71.00

Trial Lesson 30mins £35.00
Mastercard /Visa. No Amex/Diners/Switch
PPL Ground Tuition: £50.00 per course

Moorland Flying Club
Davidstow Moor
Tel: 01840 261517 Fax: 01840 213844
Tailwheel, FIC, AFIC, Microlight weightshift and 3 axis

Aircraft Type	Fleet	Training
Thruster TST	2	59
Mainair Blade	1	59
Pegasus Flash	1	59

PPL Ground Tuition: £315 inc exams

MSF Aviation (UK) Ltd
Manchester International
Tel: 0161 4991444 Fax: 0161 4980569
PPL(A), NR, IMC, Multi, Second pilots, Radionav
Membership: £99.88

Aircraft Type	Fleet	Training	Hire
PA-38	4	93.41	85.19
PA-28-140	1	110.63	99.88
C172	1	115.15	104.58

Trial Lessons: 45mins £79.90; 60 mins £92.82
Access Visa Mastercard Switch
PPL Ground Tuition: £85 per subject or £23.50 + VAT per hour
PA-38 and PA-28 landing fee £13.50; C 172 landing fee £19.38

Newcastle Upon Tyne Aero Club Ltd
Newcastle
Tel: 0191 2861321 Fax 0191 2861321
PPL(A), NR, IMC, Multi, Second pilot
Membership: £50

Aircraft Type	Fleet	Training	Hire
PA-28	5	85	65
TB-9	1	85	65
Beech 76	1	150	130

Trial lesson: 30 mins £42.50
PPL Ground Tuition: £12 per course

Norfolk County Flying Club
Norwich
Tel 01603 404600 Fax: 01603 404200
PPL(A), NR, IMC, Multi, non approved IR, Second pilot
Membership: £95 full flying; £25 social - £15 airport pass holder - £190 super membership

Aircraft Type	Fleet	Training	Hire
PA-38 Tomahawk	2	89	79
PA-28 Warrior II	1	105.75	95.75
C172	1	95	85
PA-23 Aztec E	2	225	195

Trial lesson: 30 mins £45
Access Mastercard Visa Switch
PPL Ground Tuition: Individuals free - £10 per evening session
Special discounts for 'super' membership

Northamptonshire School of Flying Ltd and Air Charter
Sywell
Tel 01604 644678 Fax: 01604 495324
PPL(A), NR, IMC, Multi, Aerobatics, Tailwheel, Second pilot, Radionav, Non-approved I/R courses
Membership: £500 - then hire from as little as £40/hour wet

Aircraft Type	Fleet	Training	Hire
PA-23	1	200	175.02 wet
Pitts S2A	1	158.50	132.50
C172	2	91.85	75
C152	1	83.50	68.50
B.121 Beagle Pup	3	83.50	68.50

Trial lesson: 20 mins £35; 30 mins £45; 20 mins £62.66 Pitts; 30 mins £84 Pitts
Visa Access Mastercard
PPL Ground Tuition: Day courses £70 + VAT inc exam
Block rates available on Pitts

Northern Helicopters (Leeds) Ltd
Private Heliport known as Coney Park, 0.5 miles north of Leeds/Bradford Airport
Tel: 0113 2500588 Fax: 0113 2508161
PPL(H), NR, CPL, F170A check rides

Aircraft Type	Fleet	Training	Hire
R22 Beta	3	185	145
Schweizer 300	1	210	170
JetRanger	2	380	350
Longranger	1		
Twin Squirrel IFR	1	595	
Hughes 500E	1	380	350

Trial lesson: 30 mins £100
All major cards taken
PPL Ground Tuition: £20/hour

Old Sarum Flying Club
Old Sarum
Tel: 01722 322525 Fax: 01722 323702
PPL(A), PPL(H) PPL(A) Microlights, NR, IMC, Multi, PPL/IR, BCPL, FIC, AFIC, NVQs, Aerobatics, Tailwheel, Second pilot, Radionav, Unapproved IR training
Membership: £65

Aircraft Type	Fleet	Training	Hire
C150	4	92	77
C152 Taildragger	1	92	77
Robin HR200/100	1	92	77
Slingsby T67A	1	92	77
Super Cub 150	1	94	79
Citabria 150	1	94	79
PA-28-161 Warrior	2	99	84
Beagle Pup	1	100	87
PA-28-R200	1	112	97
Seneca I	1	165	150
C172	1	99	84
Pegasus M/light	1	60	45
Thruster M/light	1	64	
Chevvron M/light	1	68	
R22	1	205.63	152.75

Trial lesson: 30 mins £46; 20 mins £65 helicopter
Access Visa Mastercard
PPL Ground Tuition: £100 for full course or £10 per session
Discounts for pre-paid blocks

Old Sarum Microlight School
Old Sarum
Tel: 0850 516404

Aircraft Type	Fleet	Training	Hire
Pegasus Flexwing	2	60	45
Thruster	1	64	

Trial lesson: 30 mins £37.50
PPL Ground Tuition: £12/hr

Osprey Flying Club
Cranfield
Tel: 01234 750197 Fax: 01234 751157
PPL(A), NR, Aerobatics, Radionav, IMC, Multi, PPL/IR, AFIC
Membership: £35 p/a

Aircraft Type	Fleet	Training	Hire
C152A	2	68	83
C172	2	78	88

PPL Ground Tuition: £12/hr

Oxford Air Training School
Oxford/Kidlington
Tel: 01865 841234 Fax: 01865 841234
PPL(A), PPL(H), NR, IMC, Multi, PPL/IR, BCPL, FIC, AFIC, CPL, CPL/IR, ATPL NVQs, Aerobatics, Radionav, Second pilot

Aircraft Type	Fleet	Training	Hire
PA-28-161			
Cadets and Warriors	19	100	80
T67C Firefly	2	100	80
PA-34-200T	11	275	275

Trial lesson: 30 mins £65
Access Mastercard Visa Switch
PPL Ground Tuition: free if training there
These rates are for PPL, + VAT - commercial rates on application. Also ground tuition: for all Nav-group courses for CPL & ATPL; tech courses also

Oxfordshire Sportflying Ltd
Enstone
Tel: 01608 677208 Fax: 01608 677015
PPL(A), SLMG PPLs

Aircraft Type	Fleet	Training	Hire
C152	1	69	60
Super Cub	1	69	60
G109	3	69	60
Vivat	1	69	60

PPL Ground Tuition: in flight price

Pegasus Flight Training
Kemble Airfield
Tel: 01285 770077
PPL(A) Microlights, FIC (Microlights), PPL(A) Powerchutes, FIC (Powerchutes) Powered Paraglider

Aircraft Type	Fleet	Training
Quantum 582		74
AX3		74

Trial lesson: 30 mins, £38
PPL Ground Tuition: poa

Pegasus Flight Training
Enstone
Tel: 01608 678741/0860 864445
PPL(A) Microlight, AFIC, Instructor test, all flight and ground training and exams

Aircraft Type	Fleet	Training	Hire
Pegasus Quantum 15	2	59	59
Pegasus XL	1	59	

Visa Amex
PPL Ground Tuition: £12/hour

Perranporth Flying Club (Truro Aviation Ltd)
Perranporth
Tel: 01872 553310 Fax: On request
PPL(A,) NR, IMC, Second pilots, Tailwheel conversions on own aircraft, Holiday courses specialist
Membership: £40 p/a

Aircraft Type	Fleet	Training	Hire
C150	2	74	58

Trial Lessons: 30 mins £35
PPL Ground Tuition: Free with flying course; evening lectures £5 per head

Phoenix Flying School
Netherthorpe
Tel: 01909 481802 Fax: 01909 481802
PPL(A), IMC

Aircraft Type	Fleet	Training	Hire
C150	3	65	55
C172	1	poa	

Trial lesson: 30 mins £32
PPL Ground Tuition: no charge

Pilot Flight Training
Hinton-in-the-Hedges
Tel 01295 812775
PPL(A), NR, IMC, Second pilot, PPL (SLMG), FAA ratings, NVQ available
Membership: £50 pa - free for students

Aircraft Type	Fleet	Training	Hire
Warriors	2	95	85
C152	2	80	70
Cherokee	1	85	75
Venture	2	50	40
C150	1	80	70
Condor	1	65	55
Frasca	1	from 25	

Trial Lesson: 30 mins £45
PPL Ground Tuition: £25 per subject
Also PPL training at Kidlington Airport

Pilot Flight Training
Oxford
Tel: 01865 370814 01865 370814 Fax: 01865 370814
PPL(A), NR, IMC, Silver C conversions, FAA ratings, NVQ available
Membership: £50 pa - free for students

Aircraft Type	Fleet	Training	Hire
Warriors	2	95	85
C152	3	80	70
Cherokee	1	85	75
Condor	1	65	55
Frasca	1	45	35

Trial lesson: 30 mins £45
PPL Ground Tuition: £25 per subject

PLH Associates Ltd
Tel: 0151 648 2947 / 0831 091959
Training advisory and consultancy services

Plymouth School of Flying Ltd
Plymouth City Airport
Tel: 01752 773335 Fax: 01752 770252
PPL(A), NR, IMC, PPL/IR, BCPL, FIC, AFIC, CPL, Aerobatics, NVQs
Membership: £85 p/a; 10 p/m

Aircraft Type	Fleet	Training	Hire
PA-28 Warrior	2	98	84
C152	3	91	74.50
Slingsby T.67	1	120	105

Trial lessons: 20 mins £35
Visa Mastercard Access Switch
PPL Ground Tuition: £17.63 per hour

Polo Aviation
Bristol
Tel: 01275 474100 Fax: 01275 472526
PPL (H), NR, AFIC (H)
Membership £75

Aircraft Type	Fleet	Training	Hire
R22	3	180	135
Bell 206	1	400	350
AS350	1	550	
AS355	1	700	

Trial Lesson £105 (30 mins in R22)
Access, Visa, Amex
PPL Ground Tuition: included
All prices plus VAT

Premier Flying and Social
Shoreham
Tel: 01273 462277
PPL(A), NR, IMC, Multi, Radionav

Aircraft Type	Fleet	Training	Hire
C150/152	2	80	55
PA-28-161	1	97	72

Trial lesson: 30 mins £40 C150; 30 mins £60 PA-28
PPL Ground Tuition: Yes; £15/hr

Prestwick Flight Centre
Prestwick
Tel: 01292 476523 Fax: 01292 475991
PPL(A), NR, IMC, Multi
Membership: £53.00 pa

Aircraft Type	Fleet	Training	Hire
Grumman GA7	1	210.09	181.89
Grumman AA5B	2	98.00	86.95
Grumman AA5A	3	92.12	80.37
PA-28-181	1	98.00	86.95
PA-38-112	4	84.60	71.91

Trial lesson: 30 mins £49; 45 mins £70; 60 mins £92.50
PPL Ground Tuition: Yes
Reduced monthly rate available through monthly standing order

Prestwick Flight Centre
Carlisle
Tel: 01292 476523 Fax: 01292 475991
PPL(A), NR, IMC, Multi
Membership: £53pa

Aircraft Type	Fleet	Training	Hire
Grumman GA7	1	210.09	181.89
Grumman AA5B	2	98.00	86.95
Grumman AA5A	3	92.12	80.37
PA-28-181	1	98.00	86.95
PA-38-112	4	84.60	71.91

Trial Lessons: 30 mins £49; 45 mins £73; 60 mins £92.50
PPL Ground tuition: available
Reduced monthly rate available through monthly standing order
Carlisle Flight Centre ??

Prestwick Flying Club
Prestwick
Tel: 01292 475583 Fax: 01292 671974
PPL(A), NR, IMC, Aerobatics

Aircraft Type	Fleet	Hire
C150	1	55.20
C152	1	55.20
PA-28	1	72
Victa Airtourer	1	67

PPL Ground Tuition: £5 per hour
Instruction rate is additional £12/hr

Professional Air Training
Bournemouth
Tel: 01202 593366 Fax: 01202 581151
NR, PPL/IR, FIC, AFIC, BCPL, IMC, Multi, CPL, CPL/IR NVQs approved assessment centre Simulator 1179s

Aircraft Type	Fleet	Training	Hire
Cessna 172	1	150	
Seneca II	2	295	
Frasca 142 Simulator 1	94		

Non-PPL Ground tuition: Only in connection with courses
Rates charged take-off to landing only; hire rates on application; charges fully inclusive of VAT and landing fees etc.

R S Pilot Training
Wellesbourne
Tel: 01789 470434 Fax: 01789 470465
PPL(A), NR, IMC, Second pilot, Radionav

Aircraft Type	Fleet	Training	Hire
C152	3	89	73
PA-28	1	98	89

Trial lesson: 25 mins £39 35
PPL Ground Tuition: one to one free of charge
10 hour block £80/hr dual

Ravenair
Manchester International
Tel: 0161 4368848 Fax: 0161 4991632
PPL(A), NR, IMC, Multi, PPL/IR, BCPL, FIC, AFIC, CPL, Simulator, RT , 1179
Membership: £70

Aircraft Type	Fleet	Training	Hire
PA-38 Tomahawk	8	74	60
PA-28-180	1	90	72
PA-23-250E Aztec	2	235	205
PN 68B	1	195	165

Trial Lessons: 45 mins £80
Access Mastercard Visa Switch
PPL Ground Tuition: £16
All prices + VAT and landing fees . Aerosoft 200 Flight Sim includes PA-28 (VFR); PA-28 (IFR); PA23 and Boeing 747-200. Prices on application

Real Aeroplane Club
Breighton
Tel: 01757 289065 Fax: 01757 289065
Aerobatics
Membership: £25

Aircraft Type	Fleet	Training	Aerobatics
C152 Aerobat	1	55	60

Visa

Redhill Aviation
Redhill
Tel: 01737 822959 Fax: 01737 822163
PPL(A), NR, IMC, Multi, PPL/IR, BCPL, FIC, AFIC, CPL, CPL/IR, NVQs, Aerobatics, Second pilot, Radionav
Membership: £80 p/a

Aircraft Type	Fleet	Training	Hire
C152	8	91	79.25
C152 Aerobat	2	91	79.25
PA-28-181 Archer	2	112.15	94
PA-34-220T Seneca III	2	240.88	211.50

Trial lesson: 30 mins £50
All cards accepted
PPL Ground Tuition: £15/hour 1 to 1 or Evening lectures £10

Redhill Helicopter Centre
Redhill
Tel: 01737 823287 Fax: 01737 823118
PPL(H)

Aircraft Type	Fleet	Training	Hire
R22	1	190	190
Hughes 300	1	205	205
Hughes 500	1	395	365
Bell 206	2	430	365

Ground Tuition: Free in fees
Discounts for off-peak flying.

Ribble Valley Microlight Club
Tarn Farm (Cockerham)
Tel: 01772 313437
PPL(A) Microlight, Tailwheel

Aircraft Type	Fleet	Training
Cyclone AX-3	1	55
Pegasus Quasar	1	55

PPL Ground Tuition: £15 per evening

Rochester Aviation Ltd
Rochester
Tel: 01634 816340
PPL(A), NR, IMC, Radionav

Aircraft Type	Fleet	Training	Hire
Robin DR400/2+2	6	108	81
Robin DR400/140B	1	123.93	96.93
C172A	1	n/a	82

Trial lesson: 25 mins £50; 60 mins £120
Access Visa Amex Switch
PPL Ground Tuition: £50 per course subject.

Rod Humphries School of Flying
Seige Cross Farm Strip
Tel: 01703 600786/0850 264080
PPL (microlight)

Aircraft Type	Fleet	Training	
Shadow BD	1	69	£40 per hour dual
Thruster TST	1	59	£40 per hour dual

PPL Ground Tuition: £10 per session

Roger Savage (Gyroplanes) Ltd
Great Orton
Tel: 017684 83859 Fax: 017684 83693

Romney Marsh Aviation
Lydd
Tel: 01797 320734
PPL(A), NR, IMC, Multi, FIC, AFIC, Tailwheel, Second pilot, Radionav
Membership: £42.30

Aircraft Type	Fleet	Training	Hire
C152	2	82.25	58.75
PA-28 Warrior	1	92.83	70.50
PA-28 Archer	1	92.83	70.50
PA-23 Aztec	1	200	180

Trial lesson: 25 mins £35 C152
PPL Ground Tuition: £11.75 inc per hour

Rotorvation Helicopter Training School
Rochester
Tel: 01322 865992/862289 0468 368620 Fax: 01322 865992
PPL(H), NR

Aircraft Type	Fleet	Training
R22	3	148+VAT

Trial lessons: 30 mins airborne, £85
PPL Ground Tuition: included in hourly rate

Rotorvation Helicopter Training School
Redhill
Tel: 01322 865992/862289 0468 368620 Fax: 01322 865992
PPL(H,) NR

Aircraft Type	Fleet	Training
R22	3	178+VAT

Trial lesson: 30 mins airborne £85
PPL Ground Tuition: cost included in hourly rate

Roylair Services Ltd
Gamston
Tel: 01777 839049
FIC courses ground tuition only
No aircraft

RS Pilot Training
Wellesbourne
Tel: 01789 470434 Fax: 01789 470465
PPL(A), NR, IMC, Second Pilot
Membership on application

Aircraft Type	Fleet	Training	Hire
C152	3	89.00	73.00
PA28-161 (airways)	1	98.00	89.00

Trial Lesson 25mins £41.00
No credit cards.
PPL Ground Tuition: FOC

Rural Flying Corps
Bourn
Tel: 01954 719602 Fax: 01767 640632
PPL(A), NR, IMC, Multi, FIC, AFIC, Aerobatics, Tailwheel conversion, Second pilots
Membership: £50 pa; Gold card £50 extra

Aircraft Type	Fleet	Training/Hire	Stand-by
C150 Aerobat	1	72.50	62.50
C152	2	72.50	
C310	1	175	

Trial lessons: 30 mins £50
Visa
PPL Ground Tuition: Ground subjects and long briefings: £20 per individual session; group sessions by arrangement

Sabre Airsports
Shobdon
Tel: 01568 708168 Fax: 01568 708553
PPL(A) Microlight; Flexwing and 3-axis
Membership £10 p/a

Aircraft Type	Fleet	Training	Hire
Mainair Blade	1	55	15
Mainair Mercury	1	55	15
Mainair Alpha	1	55	15
Mainair Spectrum	1	68	15

Trial lesson: 30 mins £30; 60 mins £60
PPL Ground Tuition: yes; £12/hour
Own machine if purchased through Sabre - £38 p/hour

Sandra's Flying Group
Deenethorpe
Tel 01933 53870/0831 455134 Fax: 01933 53870
Monthly membership: £50

Aircraft Type	Fleet	Hire
AA5 Traveler	1	46.40
C150	1	36.50

Sandtoft Aero Club
Sandtoft
Tel: 01427 873676 Fax: 01427 874656
PPL(A), NR, IMC, Multi, Aerobatics, Tailwheel, Second pilot, Helicopters, flexwing & 3 axis microlights
Membership: £70

Aircraft Type	Fleet	Training	Hire
C172	1	88.50	75
PA-28	1	88.50	75
C152	1	74.50	65
Chipmunk	1	120	100

Trial lesson: 25 mins £35
Access Visa
PPL Ground Tuition: £17.63/hr

Sandwell Valley Aero Club
Derby
Tel: 1922 648556 Fax: 01922 616383
PPL(A) IMC Second pilots Tailwheel

Aircraft Type	Fleet	Training	Hire
C152	1	78	

Trial Lesson: 30 mins £39
PPL Ground Tuition: Air law, Human perf £30; Nav, met and aeroplanes general £40

Scottish Airways Flyers
Prestwick
Tel: 01292 477583 Fax: 01292 671974
PPL(A), NR, IMC

Aircraft Type	Fleet	Training	Hire
C150	1	72	60
PA-28 Warrior	1	84	72
PA-38 Tomahawk	1	75	63

PPL Ground Tuition: £5/hour

Seawing Flying Club Ltd
Southend
Tel: 01702 545420
PPL(A), NR, IMC, Aerobatics, Second pilot
Membership: £30 pa

Aircraft Type	Fleet	Training	Hire
C150/152	6	72	60
C150 Aerobat	1	83.80	71.80
C172	2	83.80	71.80
PA-28-180	2	83.80	71.80

Trial Lessons: 30 mins £39.50
Visa Access Mastercard Switch
PPL Ground Tuition: available

Seawings Instruction Services
Medway Marine
Tel: 01797 223400 Fax: 01797 224834

Secoat's Flying Club
Manston
Tel: 01843 822022 Fax: 01843 821228
PPL(A), NR, IMC, Multi, PPL/IR, FIC, AFIC, CPL, CPL/IR, ATPL, NVQs, Aerobatics, Second pilot, Radionav
Membership: £55+VAT

Aircraft Type	Fleet	Training	Hire
PA-38	2	79.90	68.15
PA-28 Warrior	6	90.48	81.08
Aztec	2	235	
PA34	1	336	235
PA28 Archer	1	99.88	88.13

Trial lesson: 20 mins £35
PPL Ground Tuition: £192/wk; £100 weekend + VAT
Also ground tuition for PPL/IR, CPL, ATPL

Senair
Coventry
Tel: 01203 307003

SFT Aviation Ltd
Bournemouth/Florida
Tel: 01202 599888 Fax: 01202 599119
NR, IMC, Multi, PPL/IR, BCPL, FIC, AFIC, CPL, CPL/IR, ATPL, NVQs approved assessment centre, Aerobatics BCPL upgrade, CAA approved integrated CPL/ATPL

Aircraft Type	Fleet	Training	Hire
PA-23-250F Aztec	5	311	187
PA-28-161 Warrior	4	183	103
Fuji 200-160	1	183	103
Pitts S2B	1	259	
Frasca 142 simulator	1	94	12
PA23 motion simulatior	2	130	
HS125 Jet simulator	1	194	

Mastercard Access Visa - 2% surcharge
Non-PPL tuition: through The European College of Aviation

Shadow Flight Centre Ltd
Old Sarum
Tel: 01722 410567 Fax: 01722 410678
PPL(A) Microlights, FIC, Second pilot, Group (A) conversions Aircraft adapted for disabled pilots
Membership: £80 inc

Aircraft Type	Fleet	Training
CFM Shadow	2	68
CFM Shadow(Adapted)	2	by arr
Streak Shadow	1	by arr

Trial lesson: 30 mins £38.50
PPL Ground Tuition: £15/hr

Shakespeare Flying Group
Birmingham
Tel: 0121 7111717

Sheffield Aero Club
Netherthorpe
Tel: 01909 475233 Fax: 01909 475233
PPL(A), IMC, Radionav
Membership: £90

Aircraft Type	Fleet	Training	Hire
C152	5	75.50	59
PA-28-181 Archer	1	75.50	73

Trial lesson: 30 mins £39.50
PPL Ground Tuition: from £40 per course

Sherburn Aero Club Ltd
Sherburn-in-Elmet
Tel: 01977 682674 Fax: 01977 683699
PPL(A), PPL(H), IMC, NR, Multi, Aerobatics, Radionav, Safety pilot courses
Membership: £72

Aircraft Type	Fleet	Training	Hire
PA-28-161 Cadet	4	82	60
C150	3	74	52
C152	1	76	54
PA28-181	2	91	70
Slingsby T67M	1	101	79
PA-23	1	183	

Trial lesson: 30 mins £36
Visa Mastercard Switch
PPL Ground Tuition: £5 per 2 hour night class or 1 to 1 by arr.

Shropshire Aero Club Ltd
Sleap
Tel: 01939 232882 Fax: 01939 235058
PPL(A), NR, IMC, Aerobatics,
Membership: £65 pilots; £18 associate

Aircraft Type	Fleet	Training	Hire
C150/152	5	71	65
PA-28 Archer	1	88.50	80
TB-20	1	90	90

Trial lesson: 30 mins £46, 60 mins £90
Visa Mastercard Access
PPL Ground Tuition: available

Sir Armstrong Whitworth Flying Group
Coventry
Tel: 01203 301498 Fax: 01203 312639
PPL(A), IMC, NR, Tailwheel
Membership £50, £25 joining fee

Aircraft Type	Fleet	Training	Hire
C140	1	75.00	75.00
C152	1	55.00	55.00
PA28-140	1	55.00	55.00

Trial Lesson 30mins, £35.00 (C152/Pa28)
No Credit Cards.
PPL Ground Tuition: around £30.00 per course

Sky Leisure Aviation Ltd
Shoreham
Tel: 1273 464422 Fax: 01273 464422
PPL(A), NR, IMC, Multi, PPL/IR, Tailwheel, Aerobatics, Second pilot
Membership: £24

Aircraft Type	Fleet	Training	Hire
C152	3	77.50	66
PA-38 Tomahawk	1	81.50	69
Grumman AA5	1	92.50	79
C172	1	92.50	79
PA-28-180 Cherokee	1	97.50	poa
PA-23 Aztec F	1	212.50	poa
PA28-161	1	97.50	87

Trial lesson: 30 mins £37
Visa Mastercard Eurocard
PPL Ground Tuition: £20 per hour

Sky Systems Ltd
Edburton
Tel: 1273 857700
Paragliding, Paramotoring, Hangliding, Microlighting
Call for details and prices
Access Visa Switch delta Amex

Skyline School of Flying
Little Gransden
Tel: 01767 651950 Fax: 01767 651950
PPL(A), NR, IMC, Aerobatics, Tailwheel, Second pilot, Radionav

Aircraft Type	Fleet	Training	Hire
Cessna Aerobat	1	55.60	32
PA-28 Cherokee	3	60.60	32
PA-18 Cub	1	65.00	56
DR253 Regent	1	price on application	

Trial lesson: 30 mins £39.95
PPL Ground Tuition: £15.00 per hour
All rates + VAT

Skysport
Elstree
Tel: 0181 866 0562 Fax: 0181 866 0562
PPL(A) training limited, at Andrewsfield. Training for British Air Racing Championship organised by the Royal Aero Club RRR Assn. The only school in the country for this purpose

Aircraft Type	Fleet	Training	Hire
Beagle Pup 150	1	98	79.80
Beagle Pup 100	1	92	72
SA Bulldog	1	124	113

All rates reduced by 7% if block booked. All times tacho; no VAT

Sloane Helicopters Ltd
Northampton/Sywell (also at White Waltham)
Tel: 01628 829369 Fax: 01628 829368
PPL(H), NR, Second pilots, Career courses, Conversion courses, R22 safety course, NVQs
Membership: £125 pa

Aircraft Type	Fleet	Training	
R22	8	190	140
R44	4	330	265
Bell 206 Jetranger	1	430	380

Trial Lesson: 30 mins £99.99
Visa Access Mastercard Amex
PPL Ground Tuition: No fee
Prices do not include VAT. Block rates on application. R22 factory approved ground courses

Solent Flight Ltd
Southampton
Tel: 01703 650300/01703 650005 Fax: 01703 650005
PPL(A) NR, IMC, Tailwheel, Second pilot, Radionav, Aerobatics, NVQs
Membership: £50 p/a

Aircraft Type	Fleet	Training	Hire
Grumman Cheetah	4	94	84
Grumman Tiger	1	100	89
C150 Aerobat	1	74	74
AT6 Harvard	1	250	250

Trial lessons: 30 mins £55; 45 mins £75; 60 mins £100
Switch Visa Mastercard Amex Diners Access
PPL Ground Tuition: no charge for Solent Flight PPL students
Special frequent flyers rates. All prices exclude VAT

Solihull Flying Club
Coventry
Tel: 01564 826235
NR, IMC, Multi, PPL/IR, Second pilot, Radionav

Aircraft Type	Fleet	Training	Hire
PA-32 Seneca I	1	180	112 dry
Partenavia P.68B	1	180	112 dry
Tobago TB-10	1	99	89 wet

Ground Tuition: £10/hr (one to one)
Landing fees additional

Soloflight Captains Club
Humberside
Tel: 01652 688833 Fax: 01652 688833
PPL(A), NR, IMC, Multi, PPL/IR, Aerobatics, Tailwheel, Second pilot, Radionav, Specialist in FAA IRs, FAA, BFR
Membership: £35 + £15 joining

Aircraft Type	Fleet	Training	Hire
PA-28 Warrior	2	79	69
C172	1	79	69
PA-34 Seneca	1	225	195
C310	1	255	

Trial lessons: 30 mins £45
Access Visa
PPL Ground Tuition: Course £60

South Warwickshire Flying School
Wellesbourne
Tel: 01789 840094 Fax: 01789 842593
PPL(A), NR, IMC, Multi, Second pilot, Radionav
Membership: £40 pa

Aircraft Type	Fleet	Training	Hire
C152	5	83	73
C172	1	95	85
Piper Cadet	1	95	85
DV20 Katana	2	83	73

Trial lesson: 30 mins £41.50
All cards accepted
PPL Ground Tuition: FOC

Southend Flying Club
Southend
Tel: 01702 545198 Fax: 01702 543756
PPL(A), NR, IMC, Multi, PPL/IR, BCPL, FIC, AFIC, CPL CPL/IR, Second pilot, Radionav, NVQs

Aircraft Type	Fleet	Training	Hire
PA-28-140	4	96.50	88
PA-28-180	1	99.50	91
PA-28-151	1	104	95
PA-34-200	1	188	175
C152 Aerobat	1	93	84.50

Trial lessons: 30 mins - 2 seaters £39.50; 60 mins £79; 30 mins - 4 seaters £47.50; 60 mins £95 65
Visa Mastercard Access
PPL Ground Tuition: free of charge
Special 'hour builder' rates available.

Southern Air Ltd
Shoreham
Tel: 1273 461661 Fax: 1273 454020
PPL(A), PPL(H), NR, IMC, Multi, Tailwheel, Second pilot, Radionav, Turbine conversions
Membership: £30

Aircraft Type	Fleet	Training	Hire
PA-28-161	3	102	77
C152	1	88	63
Chipmunk	1	128	113
C310	2	266	206
Robin DR200	1	102	77
TB9	1	poa	
PA34	1	poa	
Enstrom F28A	2	203	163
Enstrom F28F	1	228	183
Bell Jet Ranger	2	410	410
Enstrom 480T	2	poa	

Trial lesson: 30 mins £45 C152;
All cards taken except Diners
PPL Ground Tuition: £25/hr + VAT

Southern Flight Training Ltd
Bournemouth
Tel: 01202 590940 Fax: 01202 590920
PPL(A), NR, IMC, Multi, BCPL, Second pilots, Radionav, NVQs

Aircraft Type	Fleet	Training	Hire
C152	2	55	70 90
PA28	2	65	80 105

All major credit cards
PPL Ground Tuition: Yes: £10/hr for exam subject
All prices + VAT; discount block booking - call for details

Southport and Merseyside Aero Club
Liverpool
Tel 0151 7097494 Fax: 0151 7093774

Aircraft Type	Fleet	Training	Hire
C172	1	Prices on application	

Spitfire Aviation
Bournemouth
Tel: 01202 582282 Fax: 01202 590784
PPL(A), NR, IMC, BCPL, AFIC, Second pilots, Multi
Membership: Nil

Aircraft Type	Fleet	Training	Hire
Cherokee 140	1	£70	£60
Partenavia	1	£150	£130

Trial lesson: 30 mins £35; 60 mins £70
PPL Ground Tuition: available
Can supply safety pilots. All prices + VAT.

St Angelo Aviation
Enniskillen
Tel: 01365 322771 Fax: 01365 322771
PPL(A), IMC, NR
Membership on application

Aircraft Type	Fleet	Training	Hire
PA28-151	1	70	65

Trial Lesson 30mins £35.00
No credit cards.
PPL Ground Tuition: FOC

St George Flying Club
Teesside
Tel: 01325 333431. 332195 after hours
PPL(A), NR, IMC, BCPL, NVQ, Radionav
Membership: £35 p/a

Aircraft Type	Fleet	Training	Hire
PA-28-161	1	86.50	76.50
C172	1	89.50	79.50
PA28-151	1	82.50	72.50

Trial Lessons: 20 mins £30
Access Mastercard Visa Switch
PPL Ground Tuition: included in PPL course
Also BCPL ground tuition.

Stapleford Flight Centre
Stapleford
Tel: 01708 688380 Fax: 01708 688421
PPL(A), NR, IMC, Multi, PPL/IR, BCPL, CPL/IR, NVQs, Second pilot, Radionav
Membership: £55 pa

Aircraft Type	Fleet	Training	Hire
C172	3	105	93
C152	13	95	85
Piper Warrior	3	107	95
PA-31 Seneca	4	195	235

PPL Ground Tuition: £5 evening class; £40 per day; 5 days £190 including exams

Staverton Flying School
Gloucestershire
Tel: 01452 712388 Fax: 01452 713565
PPL(A), PPL(H), NR, IMC, Multi, Aerobatics, Second pilot, Radionav

Aircraft Type	Fleet	Training	Hire
C152	5	82.48	71.91
C172	4	95.17	84.60
Robinson R22	2	170.37	135.12

Trial lesson: 30 mins £43.50 - C152
PPL Ground Tuition: Normally free

Stephenson Aviation
Goodwood
Tel: 01243 530165 Fax: 01243 539921
PPL(H), NR, Mountain Flying Courses, Helicopters Training, type conversion to turbine

Aircraft Type	Fleet	Training	Hire
Enstrom F280 Shark	3	235	199.75
Bell 206 Jetranger	1	470	470

Trial lesson: 30 mins £125
Visa Access Mastercard
PPL Ground Tuition: Individual tuition: £20 per hour
Discount rates for advance payments

Sterling Helicopters Ltd
Norwich
Tel 01603 417156 Fax: 01603 410791
PPL(H), NR, 1179 conversions for rotary wing

Aircraft Type	Fleet	Training	Hire
Schweizer 300c	1	255	230
Bell 206 Jetranger	1	POA	
AS350		POA	
AS355		POA	
BO105		POA	

Trial lesson: 30 mins £135
Visa only
PPL Ground Tuition: cost by negotiation: free to PPL(H) customers

Suffolk Aero Club
Ipswich
Tel: 01473 713312
PPL(A), NR, IMC, Multi, Aerobatics, Second pilot, Radionav

Aircraft Type	Fleet	Training	Hire
C150/152	3	72	65
C172	1	83	76
Piper Aztec	POA		

PPL Ground Tuition: nil cost

Surrey and Kent Flying Club Ltd
Biggin Hill
Tel: 01959 572225/540579 Fax: 01959 571357
PPL(A), NR, IMC, Multi, BCPL, FIC, AFIC, CPL, NVQs, Aerobatics, Second pilot, Radionav
Membership: £85

Aircraft Type	Fleet	Training	Hire
PA-38 Tomahawk	3	84.60	64.43
C152	2	84.60	64.43
TB9	3	95.98	77.17
TB10	1	113.19	90.94
PA34 Seneca I	1	114.49	127.39

Access Visa Switch
PPL Ground tuition: Yes, cost by negotiation
Prices do not include landing fees

Sussex Flying Club Ltd
Shoreham
Tel: 01273 440852 Fax: 01273 440852
PPL(A), NR, IMC, R/T, Aerobatics, Second pilot, Radionav, AOPA basic aerobatics course
Membership: £58.75

Aircraft Type	Fleet	Training	Hire
C150/C152	2	92	75
C150 Aerobat	1	117	86
PA-28 Warrior	2	103	86
PA-28R Arrow	1	poa	

Trial lesson: 30 mins £37
Visa Mastercard Access
PPL Ground Tuition: £10/hr by arr
Discounts available for 10 hour blocks on all but the Arrow.

Swansea Aero Club and Flying School
Swansea
Tel: 01792 204063 Fax: 01792 297923
PPL(A), NR, IMC, Multi, Second pilot
Membership: £25 pa

Aircraft Type	Fleet	Training	Hire
C150/152	3	74	67
C172	1	94	86
Beech F33 Bonanza	1	140	130
PA-23 Aztec	Price on application		

Trial lesson: 30 mins £39
Mastercard Visa Switch
PPL Ground Tuition: £4 per evening class. Private instruction by arr.

Take Flight
Wellesbourne
Tel: 01789 470424
PPL(A), NR, IMC, Multi, BCPL
Membership: Free

Aircraft Type	Fleet	Training	Hire
C152	2	83	70
C172	1	poa	84
PA-28 161	1	poa	84
PA-28 Cherokee	1	poa	84

Trial lesson: 30 mins £38
Visa Mastercard Access
PPL Ground Tuition: Yes

Tayside Aviation
Fife
Tel: 01592 753792 Fax: 01592 612812
PPL(A), NR, IMC, BCPL, AFIC, FIC, CPL, Aerobatics, Second pilot, Radionav
Membership: £35pa

Aircraft Type	Fleet	Training	Hire
Katana	1	60	69
C152	3	60	69
PA-28 Warrior	1	79.80	89.40

Trial Lesson: 30 mins £35; 45 mins £52; 60 mins £69
Visa, Switch, Mastercard, Delta, Euro
PPL Ground Tuition: inc in PPL course

Tayside Flying Club/Tayside Aviation Ltd
Dundee
Tel: 01382 644372 Fax: 01382 644531
PPL(A), NR, IMC, Multi, NVQs, BCPL, FIC, AFIC, Aerobatics, Second pilot

Aircraft Type	Fleet	Training	Hire
C152	5	79.80	69
DV20 Katana	6	84.60	74.40
Piper Warrior	1	89.40	79.80
Grumman AA5	1	85.80	75.60
Piper Aztec	1	235	235

PPL Ground Tuition: no charge
Special offers available for members at certain times of the year

Teesside Aero Club/Teesside Flight Centre
Teesside
Tel: 01325 332752/333142 Fax: 01325 333916
PPL(A) NR, IMC, Royal Air Force Scholarship course (7 year's approval), PPL(H) by arrangement
Membership: £40 p/a; Student and Senior citizen £25

Aircraft Type	Fleet	Training	Hire
PA-38	6	82.50	69
PA-28-161	1	89.50	77.50
C172N	1	90.50	80.50

Trial Lessons: 30 mins £35 Helicopter trial lesson by arrangement
Access Visa Mastercard Switch
PPL Ground Tuition: normally free with PPL flight training

TG Aviation Ltd/Thanet Flying Club
Manston
Tel: 01843 823656/823520 Fax: 01843 822024
PPL(A), NR, IMC, Multi, BCPL, FIC, AFIC, CPL/IR, Aerobatics, Second pilot, Radionav, NVQs
Membership: £24

Aircraft Type	Fleet	Training	Hire
C152	6	79	79
PA-28 Warrior	2	89	89
PA-34 Seneca II	1	204.73	185

Trial lesson: 20 mins £35; 60 mins £79
PPL Ground Tuition: POA

The European College of Aviation
Bournemouth
Tel: 01202 599509 Fax: 01202 591509

The Field Club
Long Marston
Tel: 01789 720607 Fax: 01789 721531
PPL(A), PPL(A) microlights, IMC, Tailwheel, Second pilot
Membership: £65 pa

Aircraft Type	Fleet	Training	Hire
C152 tailwheel	1	70	79
C152	1	70	79

Trial Lesson: 30 mins £40
PPL Ground Tuition: £15 per hour

The Flight Centre
Gamston
Tel: 01777 838222
PPL(A), IMC, Radionav, type conversions Multi
Membership: £66 p/a; £25 joining fee

Aircraft Type	Fleet	Training	Hire
C152	2	75	59.50
C172	1	85	75
PA34	1	170	140/80 dry

Trial lesson: 30 mins £36; 60 mins £72
PPL Ground Tuition: all ground subjects, courses from £80

The Microlight School
Fenland
Tel: 01406 540542 Fax: 0973 677703
PPL(A) Microlights

Aircraft Type	Fleet	Training
Flexwing	2	55

PPL Ground Tuition: free with course or £10/hour
Training on own microlight £35/hour

The Norwich School of Flying
Norwich
Tel 01603 403107
PPL(A), NR, IMC, Multi, Tailwheel, Second pilot, Radionav
Membership: £39 pa

Aircraft Type	Fleet	Training	Hire
PA-38	2	90	78
PA-28-180	1	102	90

Trial lesson: 30 mins £39
Amex only
PPL Ground Tuition: £10 per evening class; £9 per hour individual tuition
Block rates available on PA-38

The Pilot Academy
Gloucestershire
Tel: 01452 713555 Fax: 01452 855744
PPL(A), NR, IMC, Tailwheel, NVQs
Membership: £50 p/a

Aircraft Type	Fleet	Training	Hire
C152	2	84	69
PA-28-161	1	106	91
PA-38	2	84	69

Trial lesson: 30 mins £49.50
PPL Ground Tuition: £10/hour

The Pilot Centre Ltd
Denham
Tel 01895 833838 Fax: 01895 832267
PPL(A), NR, IMC, Multi, Aerobatics, Tailwheel, Second pilot, Radionav

Aircraft Type	Fleet	Training	Hire
C150/152	4	from 80.00	from 64.00
C172	3	from 90.00	from 72.00
PA-28-161	2	from 90.00	from 72.00

PPL Ground Tuition: normally free, but a nominal charge may be made for evening lectures
Airborne times only charged.

The Sherwood Flying Club Ltd
Nottingham
Tel: 01159 332334 Fax: 01159 332442
PPL(A), NR, IMC, Aerobatics, Tailwheel, Second pilot, Radionav
Membership: Joining fee £20; £75 p/a; Country membership joining £20 £30 p/a

Aircraft Type	Fleet	Training	Hire
PA-38	2	69.48	62.28
PA-28 Warrior II	1	78.24	71.04
Bellanca 8K CAB	1	72.96	72.96

Trial lesson: 20 mins £25; 30 mins £35
PPL Ground Tuition: nominal cost

The Tiger Club
Headcorn
Tel: 01622 891017 Fax: 01622 891017
Aerobatics, Tailwheel, Formation; farmstrips

Aircraft Type	Fleet	Training	Hire
Tiger Moth	2	97.52	97.52
Stampe	1	114.56	114.56
Slingsby T.67 M200	1	135	135
Piper Cub	1	70.50	70.50
Jodel D150	1	60	60

Three Point Flying
Rochester
Tel: 01634 861265 Fax: 01634 816620

Aircraft Type	Fleet	Training	Hire
Stampe	1	From £90	

Trial lessons: 30 mins £85 inc aeros if required
Prices + VAT per hour, may vary according to usage

Thurston Helicopters Ltd
Headcorn
Tel: 01622 891158 Fax: 01622 890876

Aircraft Type	Fleet	Training	Hire
R22	1	185+VAT	POA

Trial lessons: 20 mins £117.50; 40 mins £170
Access Mastercard Visa
PPL Ground Tuition: available

Tiger Helicopters
Shobdon
Tel: 01568 708028 Fax: 01568 708005
PPL(H), NR, CPL(H), Turbine transition courses for jet engined helicopters, mountain training courses, NVQs

Aircraft Type	Fleet	Training	Hire
R22	2	193.87	141
Bell 206	1	440	440

Trial lesson: 30 mins £94
Visa Switch Mastercard Access
PPL Ground Tuition: available

Tingwall Aero Club
Lerwick

TripleA Flying Ltd
Humberside
Tel: 01652 680564 Fax: 01652 680579
PPL(A), NR, IMC, Multi, PPL/IR, CPL, CPL/IR, ATPL, NVQs

Aircraft Type	Fleet	Training	Hire
C150	2	poa	poa
Grumman Cougar GA7	2	185 I/R and multi	
C172	2	poa	poa
Frasca 142 Simulator	1	87.25	29

Card: Access Visa Amex, with surcharge
PPL Ground Tuition: £10/hr

Tropair Air Services
Biggin Hill
Tel: 01959 576767 Fax: 01959 540033
NR, IMC, Multi

Aircraft Type	Fleet	Training	Hire
Robin DR46	1	80	
C172	1	80	
Grumman Cheetah	2	79.90	73.44
PA-28 Cadet	1	85.78	
Rockwell 114	1	114.56	
Grumman Cougar	1	146.87 T	

Non-PPL Ground tuition: available

Truman Aviation Ltd
Nottingham
Tel: 0115 9815050 Fax: 0115 9811444
PPL(A), NR, IMC, Multi, BCPL, FIC, AFIC, Tailwheel, Second pilot, Radionav, 1179s Panel examiner, NVQs
Membership: Joining £60 + VAT; £40 +VAT early renewal £30 +VAT

Aircraft Type	Fleet	Training	Hire
PA-38	8	77.55	64.63
PA-28-181	1	84.50	72.60
C172	1	86.77	74.70
Duchess	1	by arrangement	
Tiger Moth	1	98	
PA28-161	1	84.50	72.60

Trial lesson: 20 mins £35; 40 mins £65; 60 mins £95
Access Mastercard Visa Diners Switch Delta
PPL Ground Tuition: available

Turnhouse Flying Club
Edinburgh
Tel: 0131 3394706 Fax: 0131 3171429
PPL(A), NR, IMC, Multi, FIC, Aerobatics
Membership: £45

Aircraft Type	Fleet	Training	Hire
C152	3	72	61.80
C172	2	79	68.80
C182RG	1	120	109.80
PA-28-181	1	88	78
Beech 76	1	199	160

Trial lesson: 30 mins £48
Access Mastercard Visa
PPL Ground Tuition: free

Ulster Flying Club
Newtownards
Tel: 01247 813327 Fax: 01247 814575
PPL(A), PPL(H), PPL(A) Microlights, NR, IMC, Multi, Second pilot, Aerobatics, R/T
Membership: £150+VAT

Aircraft Type	Fleet	Training	Hire
C152	2	75	65
PA-28-140	1	88	78
PA-23	1	poa	
PA28-151	1	poa	

Trial lesson: 40 mins £50
Access Visa Mastercard
PPL Ground Tuition: foc

Vectair 95 Ltd
Goodwood
Tel: 01243 781652
PPL(A), NR, IMC, multi, silver C conversions, Aerobatics

Aircraft Type	Fleet	Training	Hire
C150 aerobat	2	95.76	74.61
C152	1	99.29	78.14
C172	1	105.75	84.60
PA28-161	1	109.86	88.71

Trial lesson: 30 mins £49.50
PPL Ground Tuition: available

Walkbury Flying Club
Peterborough Sibson
Tel: 01832 280289 Fax: 01832 280289
PPL(A), NR, IMC, Multi, Aerobatics, Second pilot, Radionav, RT

Aircraft Type	Fleet	Training	Hire
C152	2	84.95	71.68
C152 Aerobat	1	84.95	71.68
C172	1	88.95	82.84
PN68	1	210	

Trial Lesson: 20mins £30; 30mins £40; 45mins £60
Visa Mastercard
PPL Ground Tuition: £12/hr one to one

Warwickshire Aerocentre
Birmingham
Tel: 0121 7821011 Fax: 0121 7824256
PPL(A), NR, IMC, Multi, BCPL FIC AFIC Aerobatics, Second pilot
Membership: £65

Aircraft Type	Fleet	Training	Hire
PA-38	2	80	65
C152	1	80	65
C172	1	95	80
Piper Warrior	1	95	80
Piper Lance	1	170	155
Piper Commanche	1	122.50	107.50
Piper Seneca	1	200	185
PA28-181	1	105	90

Trial Lesson: 30 mins £46.50
Visa Access Mastercard Delta Eurocard
PPL Ground Tuition: £45 per subject

Weald Air Services
Headcorn
Tel: 01622 891539
PPL(A), NR, IMC, Multi
Membership: £40

Aircraft Type	Fleet	Training	Hire
C150	3	75	54 tacho
DR400/108	1	80	66.20 tacho
PA-28-161	1	80	66.20 tacho
R3000	1	80	66.20 tacho
PA-34 Seneca I	1	170	140 tacho
C172	2	90.00	66.20

Trial lesson: 30 mins £40; 60 mins £80
PPL Ground Tuition: Yes; £12.50 per hour

Wellesbourne Aviation Ltd
Wellesbourne
Tel: 01789 841066 Fax: 01789 841067
PPL(A), NR, IMC, Multi, Second pilot, Radionav
Membership: £35 pa

Aircraft Type	Fleet	Training	Hire
PA-38	2	89	70
PA-28 161	2	95	89
PA-34 Seneca 3 1	220	205	

Trial lesson: 25 mins £39
Visa Mastercard Access
PPL Ground Tuition: from £70 per subject evening courses

Welshpool Flying School
Welshpool
Tel: 01938 555062 Fax: 01938 555487
PPL(A), NR, IMC, Multi, BCPL, FIC, AFI,C Second pilot
Membership: £35 p/a

Aircraft Type	Fleet	Training	Hire
PA-38	3	72	58
C152	1	72	58
PA-28	2	82	70
Baron 55	1	230	200

Trial lesson: 30 mins £40
Visa Amex Diners
PPL Ground Tuition: £30/hr
Fixed price courses available on request

Wensum Vintage Flying Group
Swanton Morely
Tel: 01362 638193 Fax: 01362 638113

West Lancs Aero Club Ltd
RAF Woodvale
Tel: 01704 72610
PPL(A), NR, IMC, Radionav
Membership: £40 p/a

Aircraft Type	Fleet	Training	Hire
C150	3	71.79	71.79
PA-28-161	2	78.26	71.03
C172	1	78.26	71.03

Trial Lesson: 30 mins £38
PPL Ground Tuition: Evening lectures £19.98 per subject

West London Aero Club
White Waltham
Tel: 01628 823272 Fax: 01628 826070
PPL(A), PPL(H), NR, IMC, Aerobatics, Tailwheel, Second pilots, NVQs, Radionav
Membership: £95 pa

Aircraft Fleet	Hire	Training	WeekdayTouring
PA-28-161 Warrior	8	78.75	99.87
PA-28-140 Cherokee	4	86.67	95
PA-28-200R Arrow	1	108.60	130
PA-28-180 Cherokee	1	86.67	95
PA-22 Colt	1	80	100
Slingsby T67B	2	78.75	99.87
Pitts Special	1	162	

Trial lessons: 30 minutes £59; 60 mins £99
Visa Mastercard Access Diners Amex
PPL Ground Tuition: £35 per day/subject per exam

West Midlands Police Flying Club
Coventry
Tel: 0121 5502644
PPL(A), NR, IMC, Second pilot, Radionav
Membership: £240

Aircraft Type	Fleet	Training	Hire
C150	1	40 Tacho	40 tacho
C172	1	72	62

Trial lesson: 30 mins £30
PPL Ground Tuition: £10-20 per subject inc exams

West of Scotland Flying Club
Cumbernauld
Tel: 01236 451000 Fax: 02123 722100
PPL(A), NR, IMC
Membership: £64

Aircraft Type	Fleet	Training	Hire
PA-28-140	1	89	76
PA-28-161	2	96	83
PA-28-181	1	96	83
TB10	1	96	83
VT4	1	92	79

Trial lesson: 30 mins £39.75; 60 mins £103.75
Access Visa
PPL Ground Tuition: no charge to members

Westair Flying School
Blackpool
Tel: 01253 404925 Fax: 01253 401121
PPL(A), NR, IMC, Multi, FIC. AFIC. Second pilot
Membership: £40 + VAT

Aircraft Type	Fleet	Training	Hire
C401	2	300	300
Beech 76	1	170.50	160
TB10 Tobago	1	88.50	78
Warrior II	1	80.50	70
C172	1	80.50	70
C152	1	77.00	64.20
C150	1	72.34	60.00
PA-28R 200T	1	100	100

Trial lesson: 20 mins £25; 30 mins £40;
Visa Access Mastercard
PPL Ground Tuition: no charge
All rates + VAT; C150 Monday to Friday £50 + VAT hire only

Western Air Training
Thruxton
Tel: 01264 773900 Fax: 01264 773913
PPL(A), NR, IMC, Multi, Aerobatics, Tailwheel, Second pilot, Radionav, Formation Flying
Membership: £52.88 p/a

Aircraft Type	Fleet	Training	Hire
PA-38	3	76.96	68.15
PA-28-181 Archer	1	88.73	82.95
C172 N	1	82.95	76.96
Slingsby T67B	1	76.96	68.15
Aztec E	1	180	160
C150 tailwheel	1	76.96	68.15

Trial lesson: 20 mins £30
Visa Access Mastercard
PPL Ground Tuition: £14.10/hr
10% off all flying charges between Monday and Friday

Wickenby Aviation Ltd
Wickenby
Tel 01673 885345 Fax: 01673 885346
PPL(A), NR, IMC, Multi, Tailwheel, Aerobatics
Membership: £80 + VAT

Aircraft Type	Fleet	Training	Hire
C150	2	67	67
C152	2	67	67
Auster J1N	1	72	72
Pitts S2A	1	150	135

Trial lesson: 30 mins £33.50 + VAT
PPL Ground Tuition: No charge

Willowair Flying Club
Southend
Tel: 01702 531555 Fax: 01702 542070
PPL(A,) PPL(H), NR, IMC, Aerobatics
Membership: £50 p/a, £10 p/m

Aircraft Type	Fleet	Training	Hire
C150	2	65.60	56
C152	1	65.60	56
C172	1	77.60	68
C337	1	175	150
PA-28-180	1	77.60	68
PA-28 Warrior	1	77.60	68
Jetranger	1	499	POA
R22	1	225	195

Trial lesons: 30 mins 2 seaters, £39.95; 60 mins £74.95; 30 mins 4 seater £49.95; 60 mins £86.95; Helicopter 30 mins £99; 60 mins £198
Visa Mastercard Switch
PPL Ground Tuition: free

Woodgate Air Services
Belfast International
Tel: 0849 422789 Fax: 0849 423307
PPL(A), NR, IMC, FIC, AFIC, Aerobatics, Tailwheel, Second pilot, Radionav

Aircraft Type	Fleet	Training	Hire
PA-28-161	2	79	72
PA-28-181		84	70

PPL Ground Tuition: cost: £100

Woodvale Aviation Co Ltd
RAF Woodvale
Tel 01704 874456/874497 Fax: 01704 832327
PPL(A), NR, IMC, Multi,, Aerobatics, Tailwheel, Second pilot

Aircraft Type	Fleet	Training	Hire
DHC1 Chipmunk	1	94.00	94.00
PA-28-140	2	76.38	75.00
PA-28-180	1	price on application	

Trial lesson: 30 mins £38
PPL Ground Tuition: Free

Wycombe Air Centre Ltd
Wycombe Air Park/Booker
Tel: 01494 443737 Fax: 01494 465456
PPL(A), NR, IMC, Multi, PPL/IR, BCPL, FIC, AFIC, CPL, CPL/IR, NVQ approved assessment centre, Aerobatics Second pilots, Radionav, Simulator
Membership: £10 per month, £80 per year, £260 per year premium

Aircraft Type	Fleet	Training	Hire
C152	6	89	69
C172	4	93	73
C182RG	1	113	98
Piper Archer	2	98	77
Beech Duchess	2	139	124
Frasca	1	45	30

Trial lessons: 30 mins £55
Access Mastercard Visa Diners Amex Switch
PPL Ground Tuition: £260 including exams
All prices are NVQ rates net of 25% tax relief including VAT

York Gliding Centre
York (Rufforth)
Tel: 01904 738694 Fax: 01904 738694
SLMG PPL, Gliding training
Membership: £123 full member

Aircraft Type	Fleet	Training	Hire
Falke 2000 Motor glider	1	49	44
T61 Motor Glider	2	43	38

PPL Ground Tuition: Yes; £15/hr
Also 4 x 2-seat gliders; 3 x 1-seat gliders and 12 syndicated gliders

Yorkshire Aeroplane Club
Leeds Bradford
Tel: 0113 2503840 Fax: 0113 2500464
PPL(A), NR, IMC, Multi, FIC, BCPL, CPL/IR, Aerobatics, NVQs
Membership: £70.75

Aircraft Type	Fleet	Training	Hire
C150/152	8	90	65
PA-28-180	1	105	75

Trial lesson: 30 mins £48
Visa Access Mastercard Switch
PPL Ground Tuition: free to club members

Yorkshire Helicopter Centre Ltd
Swinton Meadows
Tel: 01709 571720 Fax: 01708 571721
PPL(H), NR, FIC, AFIC, CPL, ATPL, Second pilot, NVQs, Turbine conversions

Aircraft Type	Fleet	Training	Hire
R22	1	poa	
Bell 206	3	poa	

Visa Mastercard Access
PPL Ground Tuition: £85+VAT per day

Gliding Clubs

BRITISH GLIDING ASSOCIATION MEMBER CLUBS

Reproduced by kind permission of the British Gliding Association.

ANGUS GLIDING CLUB Tel: 01241 8714100
Drumslade Farm, Roundyhill, Glamis, By Forfar.
Secretary: Miss. P. Elrick, 64 Kinnaird Street, Arbroath, DD11 4EE.
Tel: 01241 8714100

AQUILA GLIDING CLUB Tel: 01295 811056
Hinton in the Hedges Airfield, Steane, Brackley, Northants, NNI3 5NS
Secretary: M. Eastburn, Home Farm, Beachampton, Milton Keynes, MK19 6DX.
Tel: 01908 562592

BATH WILTS & NORTH DORSET GLIDING CLUB Tel: 01985 844095
The Park, Kingston Deverill, Warminster, Wilts, BA12 7HF.
Secretary: K. Stephens, 2 Ethendun, Brattonn, Wiltshire, BA13 4RX.
Tel: 01380 830986

BIDFORD GLIDING CENTRE LTD Tel: 01789 490298
Bidford Airfield, Bidford on Avon, Warks. B50 4PD
Secretary: Mrs. Doreen Bailey - Site Address.

BLACK MOUNTAINS GLIDING CLUB Tel: 01874 711463
Troed Yr Harn, Talgarth, Powys, LD3 0EF
Secretary: M. Brockington, Cysgody Deri, Cefntiresgob, Landeilo, Dyfed SA19 7HS.
Tel: 01558 823250

BOOKER GLIDING CLUB Tel: 01494 442501
Wycombe Air Park, Marlow, Bucks, SL7 3DR.
Secretary: N. Gibson, 51 Haw Lane, Bedlow Ridge, Bucks, HP14 4JH

BORDERS GLIDING CLUB Tel: 0166 86284
Galewood Airfield, Milfield, Northumberland.
Secretary: C. Brown, Bilsdale, Ulgham, Morpeth, Northumberland, NE61 3AR
Tel: 01670 790465

BOWLAND FOREST GLIDING CLUB Tel: 01995 61267
Lower Cock Hill Farm, Fiddlers Lane, Chipping, Preston, PR3 2WN
Secretary: C. Wright, 12 Duke Street, Settle, North Yorkshire, BD24 9DW
Tel: 01729 824165

BRISTOL & GLOUCESTERSHIRE GLIDING CLUB Tel: 01453 860342
Nympsfield, Nr Stonehouse, Gloucestershire, GL10 3TX.
Secretary: G. Lloyd, Court Cottage, 27 Hampton Street, Tetbury, Gloucestershire, GL8 8JN
Tel: 01666 503196

BUCKMINSTER GLIDING CLUB Tel: 01476 860385
Saltby Airfield, Sproxton Road, Skillington, Grantham, Lincs, NG33 5HL.
Secretary: Mrs. C. Lawrence, Holmwood, 3 Towns Lane, Goadby Marwood,
Melton Mowbray, Leicestershire.
Tel. 01664 78244

BURN GLIDING CLUB Tel: 01757 270296
Park Lane, Burn, Selby, YO8 8LW
Secretary: M. Wakefield, 61 The Mount, Selby, North Yorkshire, YO8 9BD.
Tel: 01757 703601

CAIRNGORM GLIDING CLUB Tel: 01540 651317
Blackmill Airstrip, Feshiebridge, Kincraig, Inverness-Shire
Secretary: R. Lambert, 48 McIntosh Drive, Elgin, Moray, IV30 3AW.
Tel: 01343 547701

CAMBRIDGE UNIVERSITY GLIDING CLUB Tel: 01767 677077
Gransden Lodge Airfield, Lodge Farm, Longstowe Road, Little Gransden, Sandy, Beds, SG19 3EB.
Secretary: Penny Minnitt, 5 Ratfords Yard, Great Wilbraham, Cambridge.
Tel: 01223 880544 or John Birch 01279 777328

CARLTON MOOR GLIDING CLUB Tel: 01642 778234
(Weekends only).
Carlton Moor, Nr. Stokesley, N. Yorks.
Secretary: R. Evans, 17 Clepstone Avenue, Linthorpe, Middlesborough, Cleveland, TS5 5LL.
Tel: 01642 815160

CHANNEL GLIDING CLUB Tel: 01304 824888
Waldershare Park, Nr Whitfield, Dover, Kent, CT15 5NH.
Secretary: R. Armitage, Blenheim Villa, 150 Gladstone Road, Walmer, Deal,
Kent, CT14 7EN.
Tel: 01304 363111

CONNEL GLIDING CLUB Tel: 01631 71428
North Connel Airfield, Nr Oban, Argyll.
Secretary: R. Worters, Glenfinart Park, Ardentinny, Nr. Dunoon, Argyll.
Tel: 0136981 256

CORNISH GLIDING & FLYING CLUB Tel: 01872 572124
Trevellas Airfield, St. Georges Hill, Perranporth, Cornwall.
Secretary: R Gillow, "Homeleigh", 60 East End, Redruth, Cornwall, TR15 2EL.
Tel: 01209 216583

COTSWOLD GLIDING CLUB Tel: 01285 760415
The Control Tower, Aston Down Airfield, Nr. Minchinhampton, Stroud, Glos. GL6 8HT
Secretary: M. Smith, 2 Lodgemoor Close, Stroud, Glos, GL5 3HU.
Tel: 01453 757732

DARTMOOR GLIDING SOCIETY Tel: 01822 810712
Challacott Lane, Mary Tavy.
Secretary: K. Basterfield, Old Rectory, Gulworthy, Tavistock, PL19 8JA.
Tel: 01822 832281

DEESIDE GLIDING CLUB Tel: 013398 85339
Aboyne Airfield, Dinnet, Aboyne, Aberdeen, AB34 5LB.
Secretary: G. Douglas, 23 Eider Road, Newburgh, Ellon, Aberdeen, AB41 0FD.
Tel: 01358 789761

DERBY & LANCASHIRE GLIDING CLUB Tel: 01298 871270
Great Hucklow, Tideswell, Derbyshire, SK17 8RQ.
Secretary: John Hogarth - Club address.

DEVON & SOMERSET GLIDING CLUB Tel: 01404 841386
North Hill Airfield, Broadhembury, Honiton, Devon.
Secretary: J. Phillips, 31 Cop Hill Lane, Budleigh Salterton, Devon, EX9 6DX.

DRA FARNBOROUGH GLIDING CLUB Tel: 01256 703157
Clubhouse or 01256 702134 RAF Ops.
RAF Odiham, Odiham, Hants.
Secretary: R. Weeks, 4 Pedlars Grove, Yateley, Surrey, GU17 7AS
Tel: 01252 890313

DORSET GLIDING CLUB Tel: 01929 405599
Eyres Field, Puddletown Road, Hyde, Wareham, Dorset, BH20 7NG
Secretary: D. Piercy, 6 Boswells Close, Bere Regis, Dorset, BH20 7JE.
Tel: 01929 471447

DUKERIES GLIDING CLUB 01909 501032
Gamston Airfield, Gamston, East Retford, Nottingham.
Secretary: J. Pellatt, 32 Colsterdale, Worksop, Notts, S81 0XH.
Tel: 01909 501032

DUMFRIES & DISTRICT GLIDING CLUB Tel: 01387 76601
Falgunzeon, By Dalbeattie, Dumfries & Galloway.
Secretary: R. Slack, 25 Hardthorn Road, Dumfries, DG2 9HY.
Tel: 01387 64612

EAST SUSSEX GLIDING CLUB Tel: 01825 840347
Kitson Field, The Broyle, Ringmer, West Sussex. BN8 5AP
Secretary: S. Forster, 17 Ironstone Way, Hempstead Fields, Uckfield,
West Sussex, TN22 0XX
Tel: 01825 768796

ENSTONE EAGLES GLIDING CLUB Tel: 01608 677535
Control Tower, Enstone Airfield, Nr Chipping Norton, Oxon, OX7 4NP.
Secretary: G. Burton, 3 Manor Cresent, Standlake, Oxon, OX8 7RX.
Tel: 01865 300518

ESSEX GLIDING CLUB 0181 8026663
North Weald Airfield, North Weald, Essex.
Secretary: I. Whitaker, 11 Savana Court, Yoakley Road, London, N16 0BG.
Tel: 0181 8026663

ESSEX & SUFFOLK GLIDING CLUB Tel: 01206 242596
Wormingford Airfield, Colchester, Essex. CO6 3AQ
Secretary: Kevin Bye, 199 Sheldrake Drive, Ipswich, Suffolk, IP2 9LE
Tel: 01473 682279

GLYNDWR SOARING CLUB Tel: 01745 813774
Lleweni Parc, Mold Road, Denbigh.
Secretary: Rod Witter, 5 Skips Lane, Christleton, Chester, CH3 7BE.

HEREFORDSHIRE GLIDING CLUB Tel: 01568 708908
Shobdon Airfield, Herefordshire, HR6 9NR.
Secretary: M. Dodd, 20 Hollymount, Worcester, WR4 9SE.
Tel: 01905 28318

HIGHLAND GLIDING CLUB Tel: 01343 86272
Easterton, Birnie, Elgin, Morayshire.
Secretary: J. Thomson, Rosela, Drum Road, Keith, Banffshire, AB55 3ER.
Tel: 01542 887585

IMPERIAL COLLEGE GLIDING CLUB
Lasham Airfield, Lasham, Alton, Hants.
Secretary: G. Kenny, 11 Holroyd Road, Putney, London, SW15 6LN.
Tel: 0181 7885489

ISLANDERS GLIDING CLUB
Jurby Airfield, Jurby, Isle of Man.
Secretary: J. Melling, 7 Mannix Court, Mooragh Promenade, Ramsey, Isle of Man.
Tel: 01624 816550

KENT GLIDING CLUB Tel: 01233 740274 & 01233 740307
Squids Gate, Challock, Kent.
Secretary: Simon Noad, 54 Middletune Avenue, Sittingbourne, Kent, ME10 2JE.
Tel: 01795 471865

LAKES GLIDING CLUB Tel: 01229 471458
Walney Airfield, Barrow In Furness, Cumbria.
Secretary: A. Dennis, 1 Crosslands Park, Barrow In Furness, Cumbria LA13 9LA.
Tel: 01229 828120

LASHAM GLIDING SOCIETY Tel: 01256 381322
Lasham Airfield, Alton, Hants, GU34 5SS.
Secretary: Phil Phillips - Site address

LINCOLNSHIRE GLIDING CLUB Tel: 01507 450698
Strubby Airfield, Alford, Lincolnshire, LN13 1AA.
Secretary: J. Kitchen, 17 May Street, Cleethorpes, S. Hums, DN35 7HH.
Tel: 01472 600770

LONDON GLIDING CLUB Tel: 01582 663419
Tring Road, Dunstable, Beds. LU6 2JP.
Secretary: K. Downham, 7 Creenways, Abbots Langley, Herts, WD5 0EU.
Tel: 01923 267058

MARCHINGTON GLIDING CLUB Tel: 01282 575578
Tatenhill Airfield, Newborough Road, Burton On Trent, Staffs.
Secretary: Val Roberts, 10 Windmill Drive, Marchington, Nr. Uttoxeter, Staffs.
Tel: 01283 820108

MENDIP GLIDING CLUB Tel: 01749 870312
Halesland Airfield, New Road, Draycott, Cheddar, Somerset, BS27 3SJ.
Secretary: G. Taylor, 48 Silverberry Road, Weston-Super-Mare, Avon.
Tel: 01934 512620

MIDLAND GLIDING CLUB Tel: 01588 650206
The Long Mynd, Church Stretton, Shropshire, SY6 6TA.
Secretary: W. Duckett, "Fairfield", 57 New Church Road, Wellingford, Telford, Shropshire.
Tel: 01952 255355

NENE VALLEY GLIDING CLUB Tel: 01860 693479
RAF Upwood, Ramsay, Huntingdon, Cambs.
Secretary: Fay Keddie, Shelley Morane, Huntingdon Road, Warboys, Cambridgeshire, PE17 2SG

NEWARK & NOTTS GLIDING CLUB Tel: 01636 707151
The Club House, Drove Lane, Winthorpe, Newark, Notts, NG24 2NY.
Secretary: M. Evans, 1 Randall Close, Newark, Notts, NG24 2LF.
Tel: 01636 704293

NORFOLK GLIDING CLUB Tel: 01379 677207
Tibenham Airfield, Long Stratton, Norfolk, NR16 1NT.
Secretary: Dr Josie Briggs, "Avondale", Norwich Road, Besthorpe, Attleborough, NR17 2LB
Tel: 01953 456310

NORTH DEVON GLIDING CLUB Tel: 01769 520404
Eaglescott Airfield, Burrington, Umberleigh, North Devon.
Secretary: B. Pearson, Burrington, Umberleigh, North Devon.

NORTH WALES GLIDING CLUB Tel: 01745 582286
Bryn Cwyn Bach Farm, Rhuallt, St. Asaph, Clwyd.
Secretary: P. Cassidy, 51 Limekiln Row, Castlefields, Runcorn, Cheshire, WA7 2LT.
Tel: 01928 575366

NORTHUMBRIA GLIDING CLUB Tel: 01207 561286
Currock Hill, Chopwell, Newcastle Upon Tyne, NL17 7AX.
Secretary: J. Richardson, 3 Laburnum Avenue, Durham City, DH1 4HA.
Tel: 0191 3862884

OXFORDSHIRE GLIDING CLUB Tel: 01869 343265
RAF Weston On The Green, Nr. Bicester, Oxon. OX6 8TQ.
Secretary: B. Taylor, 30 Desalis Road, Hillingdon, Middlesex.
Tel: 0181 7561284

OXFORDSHIRE SPORTFLYING LTD Tel: 01608 677208
Enstone Aerodrome, Church Enstone, Oxon, OX7 4NP.
Secretary: John Blackmore - Site address

PETERBOROUGH & SPALDING GLIDING CLUB Tel: 01234 261079
Postland Airfield, Crowland, Lincs.
Secretary: G. Willows, 6 Malvern Walk, Oakhain, Leics. LE15 6NJ.
Tel: 01572 723885

RAE BEDFORD FLYING CLUB Tel: 01234 261079
Building 109, Defence Research Agency, Farnborough, MK41 6AE.
Secretary: M. Riley, 11 Poplar Avenue, Bedford, MK41 6AE.
Tel: 01234 347567

RATTLESDEN GLIDING CLUB Tel: 01449 737789
Rattlesden Airfield, Hightown Green, Rattlesden, Bury St. Edmunds, Suffolk, I30 0SX
Secretary: Humphrey Chamberlain, Hill House, Gt. Yeldham, Halstead, Essex.
Tel: 01787 237241

R.S.R.E. FLYING CLUB Tel: 01386 552123
DRA Pershore, Long Lane, Throckmorton, Pershore, Worcs, WR10 2LW
Secretary: Dr. D. Rodway, 2 Bellars Lane, Malvern, Worcs. WR14 2DN.
Tel: 01684 567588

SACKVILLE GLIDING CLUB Tel: 01234 708877
Sackville Lodge Farm, Riseley, Beds, MK44 1BS.
Secretary: D. Wales, Bolinder House, 70 Ome Gardens, Bolbeck Park, Milton Keynes.
Tel: 01908 234141

SCOTTISH GLIDING UNION Tel: 01592 840355
Portmoak Airfield, Scotlandwell By Kinross, KY13 7JJ.

SHALBOURNE SOARING SOCIETY Tel: 01264 731204
Rivar Hill Airfield, Henley, Nr. Marlborough, Wilts, SN8 3RJ
Secretary: Julia Reid, 77 Bryans Close Road, Calne, Wilts, SN11 9AD.
Tel: 01249 815598

SHENINGTON GLIDING CLUB Tel: 01295 688121
Edgehill Airfield, Shenington, Oxon.
Secretary: Sue Edmunds, 3 Homestead Road, Bodicote Chase, Banbury, Oxon, OX16 9TW.
Tel: 01295 251716

SHROPSHIRE SOARING GROUP Tel: 01939 32045
Sleap Airfield, Nr Wem, Shropshire, SY4 3HE
Secretary: D. Triplett, The Thatches, Aston, Wem, Shropshire SY4 5JQ

SOUTHDOWN GLIDING CLUB Tel: 01903 746706
Parham Airfield, Pulborough Road, Cootham, Pulborough, W. Sussex, RH20 4HP.
Secretary: E. Nicholson, 11 Faithful Cresent, Storrington, Pulborough, West Sussex.

SOUTH WALES GLIDING CLUB Tel: 01291 690536
The Airfield, Cwernesney, Usk, Gwent.
Secretary: N. Spencer Jones, 53 Momon Park Road, Rhoose, South Glamorgan.
Tel: 01446 711749

STAFFORDSHIRE GLIDING CLUB Tel: 01785 282575
Seighford Airfield, Seighford, Stafford.
Secretary: Peter Gill, 9 Malory Close, Stone, Staffs, ST15 0JQ.
Tel: 01785 817972

STRATHCLYDE GLIDING CLUB Tel: 01357 520235
Strathaven Airfield, Coudlaw Farm, Strathaven, Lanarkshire.
Secretary: Martin Robertson, 10/2 West Winnelstrae, Edinburgh, EH5 2ES

STRATFORD ON AVON GLIDING CLUB Tel: 01789 731095
Snitterfield Airfield, Bearley Road, Snitterfield, Stratford on Avon, Warks., CV37 0EG
Secretary: M. Davies, 26 Falstaff Avenue, Hollywood, Birmingham, B47 5EP.
Tel: 01564 822309

SURREY & HANTS GLIDING CLUB Tel: 01256 381270
Lasham Airfield, Lasham, Alton, Hants.
Secretary: C. Ross, Shaftesbury, Fuersley Road, Yateley, Camberley, Surrey.
Tel: 01252 874081

SURREY HILLS GLIDING CLUB Tel: 0181 7630091
Kenley Airfield, Caterham On The Hill, Surrey, CR8 5YG.
Secretary: Peter Wann. - Site address

THE GLIDING CENTRE Tel: 01295 688151
Shenington Airfield, Banbury, Oxon, OX15 6NY
Secretary: Mike Cuming - Site address

THE MOTOR GLIDER CENTRE Tel: 01295 812775 or 0836 787421
Hinton-in-the-Hedges Airfield, Steane, Brackley, Northants, NN13 5NS.
Secretary: Mrs Susan Eagles, 101 Martial Daire Boulevard, Brackley, Northants, NN13 6LX

THE SOARING CENTRE Tel: 01858 880521 or 01858 880429
Husbands Bosworth Airfield, Lutterworth, Leicestershire, LE17 6JJ
Secretary: J. Langrick, 8 Tower Court, Luhenham, Market Harborough, Leicestershire. Tel: 01858 424927

THRUXTON GLIDING CLUB Tel: 01264 773274
Thruxton Airfield, Andover, Hants.
Secretary: T. Walker, 3 Northlands Drive, Winchester, Hants, SO23 7AR.
Tel: 01962 865503

TRENT VALLEY GLIDING CLUB Tel: 01652 648777
The Airfield, Kirton In Lindsey, Gainsborough, Lincs.
Secretary: J. Williams, Ridgewood Mount Pleasant, Northcliff Road, Kirton In Lindsey, Gainsborough, Lincs.
Tel: 01652 648519

ULSTER GLIDING CLUB Tel: 015047 50301
c/o, F.J. McGuigan & Co., 16 Main Street, Limivady, Co. Down, N. Ireland, BT49 0EU
Secretary: J. Lamb, 137 Temnamore Road, Duneannon, Co. Tyrone, BT71.
Tel: 018687 23736

UPWARD BOUND TRUST GLIDING CLUB
Aylesbury/Thame Airfield, Haddenham, Bucks. (NOT A POSTAL ADDRESS).
Secretary: P. Chamberlain, 89 Leverstock Green Rd, Hemel Hempstead, Herts.
Tel: 01442 61747

VALE OF NEATH GLIDING CLUB Tel: 01685 811023
Rhigos Airfield, Mount Road, Cefn Rhigos, Nr Glynneath, Mid- Glamorgan.
Secretary: R. Nalder, 3 Court Walk, Cwrt Herbert, Neath, West Glamorgan.
Tel: 01636 637241

VALE OF WHITE HORSE GLIDING CLUB Tel: 01793 783685
Sandhill Farm, Shrivenham, Swindon, Wilts.
Secretary: Mrs. P. Leach, 15 Beech Lea, Blunsdon, Swindon, Wilts.
Tel: 01793 725265

VECTIS GLIDING CLUB
Bembridge Airfield, Bembridge, Isle of Wight.
Secretary: C. Waghorn, 33 Stenbury View, Wroxall, Isle of Wight.
Tel: 01983 853611

WELLAND GLIDING CLUB Tel: 01832 5237
Lyvdon Airfield, Harley Way, Lyvdon Road, Brigstock, Kettering, Northants.
Secretary: K. Wells, 95 Hyholmes, Bretton, Peterborough, Cambs, PE3 8LL
Tel: 01733 266355

WEST WALES GLIDING CLUB
Templeton Airfield, Templeton, Narberth, SA67 8RZ
Secretary: P. Harris, 11 Pentle Close, Pentlepoir, Saundersfoot, Dyfed, SA69 9BW

WOLDS GLIDING CLUB Tel: 01759 303579
The Airfield, Pocklington, York, YO4 2NR
Secretary: Derek Roddie, 9 Elm Street, Selby, YO8 7AR
Tel: 01757 708955

YORK GLIDING CENTRE Tel: 01904 738694
Rufforth Aerodrome, Rufforth, York, YO2 3QA
Secretary: S. Lee, 22 West Lane, Baildon, Shipley, W. Yorks, BD17 5HD.
Tel: 01274 583053

YORKSHIRE GLIDING CLUB Tel: 01845 597237
Sutton Bank, Thirsk, North Yorkshire, Y07 2EY.
Secretary: John Goodall, Market House, 3 Devonshire Place, Long Preston, Skipton N. Yorks, BD23 4NE

Microlight Schools

KEY

I	Flying Instruction Available
IS	Flying Instruction Available via affiliated school
F	Flying Instructor Training
G	Ground School
C	Courses to suit the individual
NS	No solo flying on school aircraft after first solo flight
L-R	Solo training to restricted PPL (M) on club / school aircraft
L-U	Solo training to unrestricted PPL (M) on club / school aircraft

ENGLAND

Aerolite Limited
Long Marston Airfield
Stratford upon Avon, Warks. CV37 8RT
Contact: Tony Blackwell — 01789-299229
Key I.NS.G.C.

Aerosport U.K
Full Sutton Airfield
Pocklington Nr York YO4 1HS
Contact: Steve Grzybowski — 01924-493990 (H)
01759 373063 (Airfield)
Key I.G.C.

Airbourne Aviation
Popham Airfield, Nr.Basingstoke, Hants S021 3HB
Contact: Mac or Paula Smith (Booking Office) — 01202-822486
01256-398254 (Airfield))
Key I.F.G.C.L-R.L-U

Air School Instruction
Lower Mount Pleasant, Stonea,
March, Cambs. PE15 0EA
Contact: Chip Smith — 01354-740953 (W)
01354-741209 (Fax)
Key I.S.

Avon Microlight Club
Long Marston Airfield
Stratford upon Avon
Wawickshire CV37 8RT
Contact: S Comben — 01789 261811

Baxby Airsports Club
Baxby Manor
Husthwaite, York YO6 3SW
Contact: David or Elaine Smith — 01347-868572 (H)
01347-860443 (Airfield)
Key I.G.C. L-U

Bedford Microlight Centre
Long Acres Farm, Sandy, Bedford. SG19 1ND
Contact: Snowy Barton — 01767-691616 (Airfield)
Key I.G.C.

Berkshire Microlight Club
2 Larkswood Road, Tilehurst,
Reading RG3 6NP
Contact: P Anderson — 01734 423137
No Instruction Club Only

Bristol Microlight Aircraft Club
1 Magnon Road, Bradford-on-Avon, Wilts
Contact: Ron Huntley
No Instruction Club Only

Bristol Microlight School
The Swallows, Cameley Road,
Temple Cloud, Bristol BS18 5AF
Contact: Phil Reed — 01761 452436
Key I.C.G.L-R. L-U.

Buckingham Microlight Club
5 Pelham Road, Thame, Oxon. 0X9 3WN
Contact: P Woodliffe-Thomas — 01844 213881 (H)
01442 229291 (W)
No Instruction Club Only

C10 Airsports
Deenethorpe Aerodrome
Weldon, Nr Corby
Northants
Contact: Simon James — 0832 205273 (Airfield)
Key I.C.G.L-U.

Cambridgeshire Microlight Club
114 High Street, Sutton, Cambs CB6 2NW
Contact: Peter Robinson — 01353-778446
Key IS.

Central Airsports Flying Club
2 Tudor Cottage
North Kilworth, Leics. LE17 4HQ
Contact: Samantha Hunt — 01858-880627

Charmey Down Microlight Club
186 Henleaze Road, Henleaze,
Bristol BS9 4NE
Contact: David Murray — 01179 620833
No Instruction Club Only

Cheshire Flyers
Cranbar
Birch Heath Lane
Chrisleton. Cheshire. CH3 7AP
Contact: Will Edwards — 01244 336162
Key IS.

Cheshire Microlight Centre
4 Adlington Drive, Sandbach
Cheshire CW11 0DX
Contact: John or Bernadette Bradbury — 01270-764713
Key I.NS.G.

Chevron Foxtrot Golf Syndicate
Saling Airfield
Stebbing
Gt. Dunmow
Essex CM6 3TH
Contact: Miss N J Ingelson — 01371-856744
Key I.C.S

Chilbolton Flying Club
50 Headley Road
Liphook, Hants
Contact: M.Treveil — 01428-723966
No instruction Club Only

Chiltern Park Microlight Club
Chiltern Park Airfield
Ilpsden
Wallingford
Oxon 0X10 6AS
Contact: Dennis Pearson — 01491-875080 (Airfield)
(Evenings) — 01491-874242
Key I.NS.

Cloudbase Aviation
Redhill and Goodwood
28 Saunders Close, Poundhill, Crawley, Sussex RH10 7AE
Contact: Phil James — 01293-522465
01737-822423
0850-852610
Key I.G.C.

Cumbria Microlights
Lorton Aero Club
Kirkbride Airfield.Nr Wigton
Cumbria. CA4 6AL
Contact: John Houldershaw — 01768 772762 (H)
01697 351006 (Airfield)
Key I.G.S. L-U

David Clarke Microlight Aircraft
Norfolk and Norwich Flying Club
Unit 1, The Black Hangar
Dereham, Norfolk NR20 5HR
Contact: David Clarke — 01362-637405 (W)
0831 222172 (M)
Key I.NS.IS.F.C.G.

Derby & Nottingham
Microlight Aircraft Club
38 Wallett Avenue, Beeston,
Nottingham, NG9 2QR
Contact: Dr Andy Buchan — 01159-222807 (H)
0850-942096 (Mobile)
01159-259900 (Fax)
Key I.IS.G.C.L-R. L-U.

Devon Microlight Centre
Sweetfield House
Bow, Crediton, Devon EX17 6JS
Contact: Ron Andrews — 01363-82480 (H)
01363-8258l (W)
Key I.G.C.

Dragon Aviation
Chirk Airfield
Shropshire LL14 5BG
Contact: R.Everitt — 01691 774137 (H)
J.Pearce — 01691 772659 (Airfield)
Key IS.C.G.L-U.

East Midlands Microlights
2a Townsend Lane
Donnington Le-Heath, Coalville
Leicester LE67 2GF
Contact: Simon Barnard 0860 788753
John Hollings 01332 865336
Key I.G.C. L-U

Eshott Airfield Limited (Felton)
30 Humford Way, Bayards Wood,
Bedlington, Northumberland NE22 5ET.
Contact: Roger Rhodes 01670-825427 (H)
Bill Emerson 01912-644022 (H)
01670 787881(Airfield)
Key IS.G.L-R.L-U.

Fenland Aero Club
Fenland Airfield
Holbeach, Nr Spalding, Lincs PE12 8RQ
Contact: Paul Feasey 01406-540542 (Airfield)
Key I.IS.C.NS.G.

Flylight Airsports
Sywell Aerodrome
Sywel1, Northants.
Contact: Paul Dewhurst 01604 494459 (A/F)
0378 792862 (M)
Kevin Jones 0850 367275 (M)
Key I.F.C.G.L-R. L-U.

Gordon Faulkner Flight Training
3 Goosemoor Green
Gentleshaw
Staffs WS15 4NL
Contact: Gordon Faulkner 01543-673075 (Office)
01831-811783
(Airfield)
Key I.G.C.L-R. L-U.

G.S. Aviation Ltd
Clench Common Airfield,
Nr Marlborough, Wilts SNB 4NZ
Contact: Graham Slater 01672-515535 (Airfield)
01672-512578 (H)
Key I.IS.NS.G.C.

Hampshire Microlight Flying Club
16 Fairfield Square, Cosham
Portsmouth, Hants PO6 3JS
Contact: Mark Henson: 01705-640122 (Home)
0850-868354 (Mobile)
Key I.NS.G.C.

Hanningfield Leisure
Crowsheath Farm,
Hawkswood Road, Downham,
Billericay, Essex, CM11 1JT
Contact: Tony Gunn/Angie Nicol or Debbie Leathlean 01268 710468
Key I.G.C.L-R.L-U.

Hertfordshire Flying Club
Hilary, Old House Lame, Roydon
Nr. Harlow, Essex CM19 5DJ
Contact: Brian Curtis 01279 792151 (H)
0860-756281 (W)
Key I.IS.G.C.

H V A Partnership
9 Tysea Close, Harlow, Essex, CM18 7EU
Contact: Phil Lee 01279 421121 (H)
01279 842255 (Airfield)
Key C.NS.I.G.

Invicta Air Sports
Rose Cottage
Watery Lane
Petham
Canterbury, Kent CT4 5QR
Contact: David Hadley 01227-700441 (H)
0850-216629 (Mobile)
Key IS.C.G.L-U.

Kent Microlight Aircraft Club
Valleyside, The Street
Petham, Canterbury, Kent CT4 SQY
Contact: Geoff Hall 01227-700463
David Brooker 01233-770231
David Hadley 01227-700441
Key IS.

Leading Edge
16 Edward Street, Rusthall,
Tunbridge Wells
Contact: Reg Whittall — 01892-545535 (H)
01836-583359 (W)
Key I.G.C.L-R.L-U.
(Bristol Area at Weekends)

Leicestershire Microlight Aircraft Club
8 Pope Crescent, Enderby,
Leicestershire LE9 5QT
Contact: Barry Underwood — 0116 2864699 (Instructor)
01455 558791 (Airfield)
David Thorpe (Inst&Safety Officer) — 01476-72632
Key I.G.C.

M4 Microlight Club
Redlands Airport, Lower Wanborough,
Swindon, Wilts, SN4 0LH
Contact: Don Law — 01793-740854 (H)
01793-790052 (W)
Key I.S.

Medway Airsports Club
268 Hoo Marina Park
Hoo, Rochester
Kent ME3 9TL
Contact: John F Nicholls — 01634-255063
Key IS.

Medway Microlights
Burrows Lane, Middle Stoke
Rochester, Kent ME3 9RN
Contact: Keith Reynolds — 01634-270236
0860-346349
Key I.NS.C.S.G.

Mercury Flying School
7 Bury Lane, Brinscall
Withnell, Lancs PR6 8RX
Contact: Tony Wells — 01254-831345 (H)
0831 841271 (W)
Key I.G.S.

Meridian Ultralights
51 Wold Road, Pocklingtom
E.Yorks YO4 2QG
Contact: Brian Godden — 01759 304337
Key IS.G.

Metheringham Microlight Club
The Old Airfield
Martin Moor, Metheringham,
Lincolnshire
Contact: Richard Roberts — 01526 378783
Key I.G.

Microlight Aircraft Flight Training
13 Collinson's, Ipswich, Suffolk, IP2 0DS
Contact: Mike Farr — 01473 232733 (H)
Key I.G.S.

Microlight Sport Aviation
3 Silver Lane, West Wickham
Kent BR4 0SG
Contact: Deepak Mahajan — 0181 7761178
0585 485122 (M)
Key I.G.C.

Midland Microlight Flying Club
The Laurels, Derby Road
Melbourne, Derbyshire DE73 1DE
Contact: Chris Brookes — 01332-863605 (H)
Key I.IS.C.G.L-R. L-U.

Moorland Flying Club
Davidstow Aerodrome
Davidstow, Camelford, Cornwall PL32 9YE
Contact: Ian Stokes — 01840 261517 (Daytime)
(24 hr fax & Answerphone) — 01840-213844
Key I.IS.F.G.C. L-R. L-U.

Morris Airsports Ltd
North Lakes Flying Club
Gt. Orton Airfield, Nr. Wiggonby
Carlisle, Cumbria
Contact: Mike Morris — 01228-42109 (H)
Key I.G.C L-U

Newton Peverell Flying Group
Newton Peverell Farm
Sturminster Marshall
Dorset
Contact: Tim Trenchard — 01258-857439
No instruction club only

Northampton Microlight Club
10 St Crispin Road, Earls Barton
Northampton NN6 0PG
Contact: Mrs Jenny Gardner — 01604-812290
No Instruction Club only

North Beds Microlight Flying Club
31 Keswick Drive, Rushden
Northants. NN10 0JJ
Contact: Paul Risdale — 01933-311413
No Instruction Club Only

North Derbyshire Microlight Club
2 Duke Street, Whittington Moor
Chesterfield, Derbyshire S41 9AD
Contact: Graham Clayton — 01246 451546
Ian Dawson — 01246-202683
Key IS

Northern Lites
20 Priestley Close, Pudsey,
Leeds LS28 9NJ
Contact: Graham Wilkins — 01132-563049 (H)
0860-496060 (W)
Key I.G.C.L-R.

Northern Microlight School
2 Ashlea Cottage
St Michaels Road, Bilsborrow
Preston, Lancs PR3 0RT
Contact: Graham Hobson — 01995-604694 (Bookings)
01995-640713 (Airfield)
Key I.F.C.G.L-R L-U

Northumbrian Microlights
1 Bockenfield Cottage, Nr.Felton,
Northumberland, NE6S 9QS
Contact: Steve Clarehugh — 0831-382375 (Mobile)
01670-787067 (Airfield)
Key IS.G.C.L-U.

Northwest Microlight Aircraft Club
5 Glenmore Close, Prestwich,
Manchester M25 7BH
Contact: Karl or Dorothy Wedl — 0161-7980690 (Evenings)
01204-24845 (W)
01204-365531 (Fax)
No instruction Club only

North Yorkshire Flying Club
68 Sandhill Drive, Harrogate
North Yorks, HG1 4JS
Contact: Stephen Bell — 01423-509302
No instruction Club only

Old Sarum Microlight Club
Hanger 3, The Portway
Salisbury, Wilts 5P4 6BJ
Contact: Lesley Maynard — 01722 322525 (H)
01722 414770 (W)
Key I.IS.F.G.C.L-R. L-U.

Pegasus Flight Training
Sutton Meadows Airfield, The Gault,
Sutton,Ely,Cambs. CB6 2BJ
Contact: Dave or Shaun Garrison — 01487 842360
0585 173877
Key F.G.C.I.NS. L-R.L-U.

Pegasus Flight Training
The Control Tower
Kemble Airfield, Kemble
Cirencester, Gloucs, GL7 6BA
Contact: David Young — 01285 770077 (W)
0836 591596
Key I.NS.G.C.

Pegasus Flight Training (Oxford)
The Microlight School
Enstone Airfield, Church Enstone,
Oxford 0X7 4NP
Contact: Geoff Weighell
01608 678741 (Airfield)
0860-864445 (Mobile)

Key I.C.G.F.NS.

Robin Hood Microlight Aircraft Club
715 Hucknall Road, Heathfield
Nottingham NG5 1NX
Contact: Cohn Bodill
01159-626279
0850-634624

Key I.G.NS.IS.C.

Rod Humphries School of Flying
6 Ridge Way Walk
Chandlers Ford, Eastleigh, Hants
Contact: Rod Humphries
01703-255534
0850-264080 (M)

Key I.G.C

Ribble Valley Microlight Club
Tarn Farm, Gulf Lane, Cockerham Lancs.
Contact: Tony Wells
01254-831345 (H)
0831 841271 (W)

Key IS

Sabre Air Sports
Shobdon Airfield, Nr. Leominster
Hereford HR6 9HR
Contact: S Hillyer-Jones
01568-708168
Key I.G.C.L-R.

Severn Valley Microlight Club
c/o Catsbury Cottage, Hartpury,
Glos. GL19 3BP
Contact: John Hamer
01452-700314 (H)
01242-661820 (W)

Key G.

Slipsteam Aviation
1 Oaklands Avenue
Romford
Essex RM1 4DB
Contact: Pete McEvoy
01708-728448 (H)
Key I.C.G.L-R.

Somerset Microlights
4 Gravelands Lane, Henlade
Taunton, Somerset. TA3 5DL
Contact: Jim Greenshields
01823 442391
0836 613544

Key I.NS.G.C. L-R. L-U

Staffordshire Aero Club
17 Belmont Close,
Churchbridge, Cannock WS11 3SS
Contact: Simon Ganecki
01922 416381
Key IS.

Surrey Microlight Club
25 Harrow Road
Carshalton, Surrey. SM5 3QH
Contact: John W.O'Connor
0181 643 2314
No instruction Club only

The Microlight Aviation Club
3 Woodlinken Close
Verwood, Dorset BH21 6BP
Contact: Paula Smith
01202 822486
Key I.F.G.C.L-R.L-U

The Microlight Flying School
Rufforth Airfield
York Road, Rufforth, York YO2 3QA
Contact: Steve Heward
01904 628105 (H)
0831-417499

Key I.G.C.L-R.L-U.

The Shadow Flight Centre Ltd
Hanger 3, Old Sarum Airfield
Salisbury, Wilts, SP4 6BJ
Contact: Fiona Luckhurst
01722 410567 (W)
Key I.

The Wealden Microlight Club
2 Coles Hall Cottage, Five Ashes,
Mayfield, East Sussex, TN20 6JH.
Contact: Mark Phillips — 01825-830573 (H) ??
Key I.IS.NS.C.G.

The Wealden Microlight Club
15 Treetops, Tonbridge, Kent TN9 2UT
Contact: Mark Phillips — 01836-214393 (Airfield) ??
Key I.IS.NS.G.C.

Three Counties Microlight School
397 Bretch Hill
Banbury, Oxon. OX16 0JA
Contact: David Marshall — 01295 259551
Key I.G.C.L-R.L-U.

Trent Valley Microlight Club (Ghost Squadron)
Hangar No.7, Haywood Heights, Little Haywood,
Staffs ST18 0UR
Contact: Terry Travis — 01889-882364 (H)
0836-363370
0543 462551 (W)

Ultraflight Aviation
Roddige Lane, Fradley
Lichfield, Staffs, WS13 8QS
Contact: Mark Amu — 01283 791917
Key I.NS.F.G.C.

West Essex Microlight Group
Hilary, Old House Lane, Roydon
Nr. Harlow, Essex CM19 5DJ
Contact: Brian Curtis — 0127979-2151 (H)
0860 756281 (W)
Key I.IS.G.C.

West Lancashire Microlight School
Ince Blundell, Nr Formby, Lancs
Contact: John North — 01772-311288 (H)
0850-882309 (M)
Key I.G.C.NS. L-U.L-R.

West Midlands Microlight Club
36 Hyde Lane, Kinver, South Staffordshire. DY7 6AF
Contact: Albert Tristram — 01384 873365 (H)
Key G.

West Riding Microlight Aircraft Club
93 Lea Farm Road, Hawksworth Estate
Leeds LS5 3PU
Contact: Peter Gilfoyle — 01132-333402 (W)
01132-588401 (H)
Key IS.C.

Wiltshire Microlight Centre
"The Old Barn", Rhyls Lane, Lockeridge
Nr. Marlborough, Wilts
Contact: Tony Hughes — 01672-86554/5
0860-246555
Key I.IS.C.G.

Windsports Training
The Control Tower, Wombleton Aerodrome
Kirbymoorside, N. Yorks YO6 5RY
Contact: John Teesdale — 01751-433358
Key I.G.C.L-R.L-U.

Wright Flight
Stoodleigh Barton
Stoodleigh, Tiverton,
N. Devon EX36 4RB
Contact: Will Knowles — 01398 355235
0850 384000
Key.I.G.C.L-R. L-U.

York Flying Club
Rufforth Airfield
York Road, Rufforth, York YO2 30A
Contact: Andrew Walmsley — 01482 865518
Key I.G.C.L-R.L-U

Yorkshire Dragons Microlight Club
8 Heys Gardens, Miry Lane, Thongsbridge
Huddersfield HD7 2FS
Contact: T. Jenkins — 01484 687479
Key IS.C.

Yorkshire Eagles Microlight Club
284 Selby Road, Leeds LS15 0PS
Contact: Martin O'Hearne
Key IS.C.

Yorkshire Microlight Aircraft Club
20 Priestley Close, Pudsey, Leeds LS28 9NJ
Contact: Lynda Wilkins 01132-563049
Key IS.G.C.

Yorkshire Microlight Centre
The Airfield, Sandtoft, Nr Belton, Doncaster, DN19 1PN
Contact: Graham Wilkins 01132 563049
0860 496060
Key I.IS.C.G.

SCOTLAND

Connel Flying Club
Tulach Ard, Balvicar,
Oban, Argyll PA34 4TF
Contact: David Whitelaw 01852 300411
Key I.G.C.L-U.

East of Scotland Microlights
Catcune Cottage Gorebridge, Midlothian EH23 4QF
Contact: Gordon Douglas 01875-820102 (H)
01620-880332 (Airfield)
Key I.G.C. L-U.

Grampian Microlight Flying Club
Conifers 3 Corseduick Park, Newmachar
Aberdeen AB2 0PF
Contact: Fiona Whyte 01651-862567 (H)
01651-862211 (W)
Key IS.

North Scottish Microlight Flying Club
21 Gordon Terrace, Dyce, Aberdeen AB2 0BB
Contact: Alex Lowe 01224-722517
No instruction club only

Scottish Flying Club
17 Crawurds View
Lochwinnoch
Remfrewshire, PA12 4EJ
Contact: Graeme Park 01505-842721 (H)
01505-704142 (W)
Key IS.G.

WALES

Ceredigion Flying Club
Cottage No 4, Drefach
Aberaeron Dyfed SA46 0JR
Contact: Nigel Hemmings 01545 571329
No Instruction Club Only

Haverfordwest School of Flying
Withybush, Aerodrome, Haverfordwest,
Dyfed.
Contact: John Rees 01437 766226 (H)
01437 760822 (W)
Key IS

North Wales Micro1ight Flying Club
15 Rhodfa Gofer
Dyserth, Clwyd. LL1B 6LP
Contact: Peter Tabberer 01745 571093
No Instruction Club Only

ISLE OF MAN

Manx Eagle Club,
Solway, Windsor Mount,
Ramsey, Isle of Man.
Contact: Carol Carine 01624-814738 (H)
01624 816526 (W)
No instruction club only

NORTHERN IRELAND

Microflight Ireland

2 Princes St, Portrush
County Antrim BT56 8AX
Contact: Mark Holmes

01265-824625 (Also Fax)
01265-868002 (Airfield)

Address of Airfield:
Mullagh More Airfield, Agivey Road, Aghadowey.
Key I

Maintenance Organisations

Approvals:

British Civil Airworthiness Requirements - BCAR

M3 Organisations approved for maintenance of aeroplanes and rotorcraft not exceeding 2730kg.

M5 Organisations approved for maintenance of aeroplanes and rotorcraft of military origin above 2730kg.

JAR Joint Aviation Requirement Part 145 approved maintenance organisations

– Aeroplanes / Airships / Helicopters

A1 Aeroplanes/airships above 5700 kg
A2 Aeroplanes/airships 5700 kg and below
A3 Helicopters

– Engines

B1 Turbine Engines
B2 Piston Engines
B3 Auxilary Power Units

– Components

C1 Air Conditioning & Pressurisation
C2 Autopilots
C3 Comm & Nav radios
C4 Doors & Hatches
C5 Electrical Power
C6 Equipment
C7 Engine - auxilary power unit
C8 Flight Controls
C9 Fuel - Airframe
C10 Helicopter - rotors
C11 Helicopter - transmission
C12 Hydraulic
C13 Instruments
C14 Landing Gear
C15 Oxygen
C16 Propellers
C17 Pneumatic
C18 Protection ice/rain/fire
C19 Windows
C20 Structural

Acebell Aviation (Acebell) Ltd BCAR AMR/342 M3	01737 822212
Aeromedicare T/A Wessex Air Maintenance JAR CAA.00165 A1	01202 590251
Aeromega Helicopters (Engineering) Ltd JAR CAA.00058 A3.C10.C11	01708 688361
Air Fabrication Services	01452 859878
Air Hanson Engineering Ltd BCAR AI/8686/81 A2.E2.E3 JAR CAA.00063 A1-A3.C10.C14	01252 890089
Air Kilroe Ltd JAR CAA.00091 A1.A2.C5.C6.C14	0161 4362055
Air Navigation & Trading Company Ltd JAR CAA.00406 A2.C16	01253 405093
Air Nova BCAR AMR/350 M3 JAR CAA.00355 A2	0151 4278093
Air Service Training Ltd JAR CAA.00044 A2.B2.C1.C3.C5-C7.C9.C13.C16	01738 52311
Air South Engineering Ltd JAR CAA.00199 A2	01273 462874
Air Touring Services Ltd JAR CAA.00006 A2.	01959 573652
Air Training Services JAR CAA.00456 A2	01494 473664
Air UK Engineering Ltd BCAR DAI/6210/61 A2.B4.E1 JAR CAA.00127 A1.C1.C3.C5.C7-C9.C12-C18	01603 424244
Aircraft Engineers JAR CAA.00107 A2	0131 3334150
Aircraft Instruments Ltd JAR CAA.00478 C13	01405 860856
Aircraft Servicing (Guernsey) Ltd BCAR AMR/289 M3	01481 65750
Airline Instruments Ltd JAR CAA.00064 C13	0181 9534912
Airspeed Aviation Ltd BCAR AMR/179 M3	01283 575407
Airways Aero Associations Ltd BCAR AMR/228 M3	01494 532997
Alan Mann Helicopters Ltd BCAR AI/9408/93 A2 JAR CAA.00032 A3.C8.C10.C11.C14	01276 857441
Alan Mann Helicopters Ltd JAR CAA.00032 A3.C8.C10.C11.C14	01603 417156
Allied Signal Ltd JAR CAA.00259 B1.B3.C16	01582 402040
American Airlines Inc. JAR CAA.00455 A1	01293 502030
Anglo American Airmotive Ltd JAR CAA.00220 A1.A2.B1.C1.C14.C16	01202 570023
Anglo Normandy Aeroengineering Ltd JAR CAA.00264 A1.A2.C1.C5-C7.C13.C14.C16	01481 35675
Arrow Air Services (Engineering) Ltd BCAR AMR/61 M3	01362 820337
ATC-Lasham Ltd JAR CAA.00442 A1.C1.C2.C4-C9.C12.C14. C19.D1	01256 56123
Atlantic Aeroengineering Ltd JAR CAA.00216 A1.A2.C2.C3.C5.C6.C8.C9.C12-C14.C16.C18	01203 307566
Avtech Ltd JAR CAA.00314 A1.A2.B2.C5.C7.C18	01959 575767
B-17 Preservation Ltd (Engineering) BCAR AI/9468/94 M5	01293 883213
B Las	01208 821535
Battleward Ltd **T/A Executive Aircraft Maintenance** JAR CAA.00333 A2.A3 BCAR AMR/306 M3	01203 511414
Bigginair Ltd BCAR AMR/278 M3	01959 575923

Bodmin Light Aeroplane Services Ltd BCAR AMR/277 M3	0120882 535
Bond Helicopters Ltd BCAR DAI/8444/75 A2.E2 JAR CAA.00007 A2.A3.C1-C14.C18	01224 725505
Bond Helicopters Ltd JAR CAA.00007 A2.A3.C1-C14.C18	01253 405222
Bond Helicopters Ltd JAR CAA.0007 A2.A3.C1-C14.C18	01652 688417
Bonus Aviation Ltd BCAR AMR/309 M3	01234 751800
Booker Air Services BCAR AMR/227 M3	01494 529263
Bostonair (Engineering) Ltd JAR CAA.00248 A2	01652 680411
Brian Seedle Helicopters JAR CAA.00471 A3	01253 342754
Brintel Helicopters Ltd T/A British International Helicopters JAR CAA.00167 A3.C1-C14.C17.C19.D1	01224 771353
Brintel Helicopters Ltd T/A British International Helicopters JAR CAA.00167 A3.C1-C14.C17-C19.D1	01950 60321
Bristow Helicopters Ltd JAR CAA.00055 A1-A3.B1. C2-C14.C18.D1	01293 502131
Bristow Helicopters Ltd JAR CAA.00055 A1-A3.B1.C2-C14.C18.D1	01851 705577
Bristow Helicopters Ltd JAR CAA.00055 A1-A3.B1.C2-C14.C18.D1	01950 60601
Bristow Helicopters Ltd in association with Caledonian Helicopters Ltd JAR CAA.00055 A1-A3.B1.C2-C14.C18.D1	01224 723151/2
Britannia Airways Ltd BCAR AD/1789/94 E2.E3 JAR CAA.00112 A1.A2.B1.B3.C1-C9.C12-C15.C17-C19	01582 424155
Britannia Flying Club CAR AMR/397 M3	01582 428065
British Aerospace Flying College Ltd BCAR AMR/268 M3	01292 671022
British Airways Maintenance Cardiff JAR CAA.00048 A1.C6	01446 747100
British Airways plc BCAR DAI/8566/78 A2.B3.B4.E1 JAR CAA.00021 A1.B1.B3.C1-C9.C12-C19.D1	01293 567000
British Airways plc BCAR DAI/8566/78 A2.B3.B4.E1. JAR CAA.00021 A1.B1.B3.C1-C9.C12-C19.D1	0141 8871111
British Airways plc JAR CAA.00021 A1.B1.B3.C1-C9.C12-C19.D1	0181 5625531
British Midland Airways Ltd BCAR AI/2838/51 A2.B3. JAR CAA.00171 A1.B1.B3.C1-C9.C12-C19.D1	01332 854000
British Midland plc BCAR AI/2838/51 A2.B3 JAR CAA.00171 A1.B1.B3.C1-C9.C12-C19.D1	0181 9905033
Burman Aviation Ltd JAR CAA.00193 A2.A3.C11	01234 752220
Busy Bee Aero Engineering BCAR AMR/51 M3	01832 280579
CAA Flight Calibration Service JAR CAA.00420 A1.C3.C6	01325 333317
Cabair Maintenance Ltd JAR CAA000109 A2.C5	0181 9533586
Caernarfon Aircraft Maintenance Co Ltd JAR CAA.00368 A2	01286 830782
Caledonian Airborne Engineering Ltd JAR CAA.00183 A1.A2.C5	01224 72224
Carrill Aviation Ltd JAR CAA.00190 A2	01747 812128
CAS Engineering Ltd JAR CAA.00382 A2	01255 424671

CDS Aviation Services Ltd BCAR AMR/254 M3	01787 223006
Central Flying Services BCAR AMR/117 M3	01702 540380
Channel Island Aero Services Ltd (Engineering) BCAR AMR/9 M3	01534 42373
Cheshire Flying Services Ltd T/A/ Ravenair JAR CAA.00324 A2	0161 4368848
Cityflyer Express Ltd JAR CAA.00052 A1	01293 507482
Claddagh Air Maintenance (N.I.) Ltd BCAR AMR/355 M3	012665 58609
Cobaircraft Co Ltd BCAR AMR/109 M3	01959 571553
Cooper Aerial Surveys Engineering Ltd CAA.00104 A2	01427 874423
Cormack Aircraft Services Ltd JAR CAA.00150 A2	01236 457777
Cotswold Aero Engineering Ltd BCAR AMR/366 M3	01452 714525
Coventry Aircraft Maintenance Ltd JAR CAA.00033	01203 302553
Cranfield Aeronautical Research Ltd JAR CAA.00377 A2.C5.C6.C9	01234 750111
CSE Aviation Ltd BCAR DAI/2250/46 A1.B3.B4.E1 JAR CAA.00027 A1-A3.B1.B2.C2.C3.C5.C7-C14.C16.C17	01865 841234
Denham Aircraft Maintenance BCAR AMR/74 M3	01895 834187
Devon School of Flying BCAR AMR/281 M3	01404 891643
DF Ranger T/A Wiltshire Aircraft Maintenance BCAR AMR/322 M3	01256 398372
Donington Aviation Engineering Ltd JAR CAA.00358 A1.A2	01332 812694
Dukeries Aviation Ltd BCAR AMR/145 M3	01909 481802
Dunlop Ltd JAR CAA.00241 C1.C4-C14. C16-C18	0181 7591086
Eagles Aviation Services Ltd BCAR AMR/352 M3	01666 77988
Earthline Ltd - Aviation Services JAR CAA.00476 A2	01264 771327
East Midlands Flying School Ltd BCAR AMR/391 M3	01332 850383
Eastern Air Executive Ltd JAR CAA.00154 A2.D1	01427 838280
Eurojet Aviation Engineering Department JAR CAA.00092 A1.A2.C5.C9.C12.C17	01452 713456
European Helicopters Ltd JAR CAA.00003	01236 457567
European Helicopters Ltd JAR CAA.00003 A3.C8.C10.C11	01895 834777
Evans Aviation Ltd BCAR AMR/403 M3	01481 824081
Farnborough Aviation Services Ltd JAR CAA.00443 A1.A2	01252 372400
Fast Helicopters Ltd JAR CAA.00133 A3	01264 772508
Fenland Aeroservices Ltd BCAR AMR/162 M3	0140634 255
The Fighter Collection Ltd BCAR AI/9480/95 M5	01223 834973
FLS Aerospace (Light Aircraft) Ltd BCAR DAI/8586/79 B cond. G-70 A1.A2.B3. BCAR AMR/405 M3	01202 500200
FLS Aerospace (Lovaux) Ltd JAR CAA.00260 A2.C3-C6.C8.C12-C14.C17-C19	0161 4989388

FLS Aerospace (Lovaux) Ltd JAR CAA.00260 A2.C3-C6.C8.C12-C14.C17-C19	01722 321812
FLS Aerospace Ltd JAR CAA.00101 A1.A2.C1-C9.C12-C15.C17-C19.D1	01202 570380
FLS Aerospace Ltd BCAR DAI/2677/48 A2.B3.B4.E2.E3 JAR CAA.00101 A1.A2.C1-C9.C12-C15.C17-C19.D1	01279 680068
FLS Aerospace Ltd BCAR DAI/2677/48 A2.B3.B4.E2.E3 JAR CAA.00101 A1.A2.C1-C9.C12-C15.C17-C19.D1	0161 4993999
Ford Motor Company Ltd JAR CAA.00084 A1.C5	01279 680941
FPT Industries Ltd BCAR DAI/3067/50 A1	01705 662391
FR Aviation Ltd JAR CAA.00131 A1.A2.B1. C1-C9.C15.C17-C19	01202 474115
G-Air Aviation Services Ltd JAR AA.00280 A2	0181 9538363
Gatwick Avionics Ltd CAA.00487 A2.A3.C3.	01737 822215
GB Airways Ltd JAR CAA.00313 A1	01293 664226
GEC Avionics Ltd BCAR AMR/104 M3	01634 844400
Gill Aviation Ltd JAR CAA.00118 A1.C5-C7.C14	0191 2869665
Goldstar Engineering Ltd JAR CAA.00312 A2.C16	01253 404615
Goodwood Aerodrome & Motor Circuit Ltd **Aircraft Maintenance Division** JAR CAA.00017 A2	01243 781934
Graham Fox Aircraft Engineering BCAR AMR/376 M3	01845 597707
Hawker Restorations Ltd (Head Office) BCAR DAI/9454/94 E2.E4.M5	01449 740544
Heavylift Aircraft Engineering Ltd JAR CAA.00054 A1.C3-C8.C16.C19	01279 680611
Heavylift Aircraft Engineering Ltd JAR CAA.00054 A1.C3-C8.C16.C19	01702 541616
Helitech (Luton) Ltd JAR CAA.00086 A3.B2.C1.C6.C7.C10-C12.D1	01582 27828
Heliwork Services Ltd BCAR AI/8441/74 A2.B4 JAR CAA.00019 A3.B1.C5.C7.C8.C10-C12.C14.D1	01264 773422
HFI Helicopters JAR CAA.00403 A3	01767 651887
Historic Flying Ltd BCAR AMR/358 M3	01799 528084
Holdcroft Aviation Services Ltd BCAR AMR/54 M3	01295 810287
Hunting Aviation Ltd **Business Aviation Division** JAR CAA.00090 A1.A2.B1.B3.C5.C9.C14	01279 680167
Hunting Aviation Ltd **Contracts Services Division** BCAR AMR/375 M3	01748 875238
Hunting Business Aviation Ltd BCAR AI/8030/68 A2 JAR CAA.00090 A1.A2.B1.B3.C5.C9.C14	0181 7592141
Hunting Cargo Airlines Ltd JAR CAA.00149 A1	01332 810081
IAP Aircraft Maintenance Ltd JAR CAA.00136 A1	01293 502288
IDS Aircraft Ltd JAR CAA.00255 A1.A2.C5.C6.C8.C14.C15	01202 573243
Inflite Engineering Services Ltd BCAR DAI/9104/87 A2.B4.E1.E2.E3 JAR CAA.00028 A1.A2.C4-C6.C12.C14.D1	01279 680736
International Aerospace Engineering Ltd JAR CAA.00039 A1-A3.C2.C3.C5.C6.C13	01234 750198

Jade Air Engineering Ltd JAR CAA.00080 A1.A2.C5.C6.C7.C16	01273 464013
JEA Engineering (UK) Ltd BCAR DAI/8668/80 B4.E2.E3 JAR CAA.00008 A1.A2.B1.C1.C4-C9.C12-C14.C16-C19	01392 364520/362415
Jersey Aircraft Maintenance Ltd BCAR AI/9327/91 B1.M3 JAR CAA.00046 A1.A2.C5.C6	01534 45124
Jetstream Aircraft Ltd BCAR DAI/9386/92 B cond. G-4 A1.A2 JAR CAA.00269 A1.A2.C1-C9.C12-C19	01292 479888
John Durkin Technical Services BCAR AMR/359 M3	01670 736624
JRB Aviation Ltd JAR CAA.00325 A2.C5	01702 545430
Justgold Ltd T/A Blackpool Air Centre JAR CAA.00341 A2.C6.C16	01253 41871
KB Aviation BCAR AMR/349 M3	01273 453333
Keenair (North West) Ltd BCAR AMR/108 M3	0151 4273275/4274048
Kenboag Aviation Ltd JAR CAA.00384 A2.A3.C2.C3.C5	01247 811241
Kennet Aviation BCAR AI/9478/95 M5	01234 752153
Klingair Ltd BCAR AMR/134 M3	01487 832022
Lambson Aviation Ltd T/A Knight Air JAR CAA.00009 A1.A2.C2.C3.C6.C13.C16	0113 2391339
Lambson Aviation Ltd T/A Knight Air JAR CAA.00009 A1.A2.C2.C3.C6.C13.C16	01777 83521
Light Aircraft Engineering (Elstree) Ltd BCAR AMR/49 M3	0181 9539341
Light Aircraft Maintenance (Cardiff) Ltd BCAR AMR/404 M3	01446 710106
Light Planes Lancashire Ltd JAR CAA.00050 A2	0161 7877326
Lincoln Flight Centre Limited BCAR AMR/90 M3	01673 885345
Littlewings Engineering Ltd BCAR AMR/220 M3	0191 2716485
Loganair Ltd JAR CAA.00079 A1.A2.C1-C9.C12-C19.D1	0141 8891311
London Flight Centre (Engineering) Ltd JAR CAA.00357 A2	01679 21839
Maersk Air Engineering Ltd JAR CAA.00240 A1.A2.B1.C3.C5.C6.C14.C16	0121 7823232
Maersk Air Engineering Ltd JAR CAA.00240 A1.A2.B1.C3.C5.C6.C14.C16	01224 724825
Maersk Air Engineering Ltd JAR CAA.00240 A1.A2.B1.C3.C5.C6.C14.C16	01752 705151
Magec Aviation Ltd BCAR DAI/9172/88 A1.E2.E3 JAR CAA.00056 A1.A2.C3.C5.C6.C12.C14.C16	01582 24182
Mann Aviation Ltd JAR CAA.00059 A1-A3.C4.C6.C8.C14.C18.C19	01252 395179
Mann Aviation Ltd BCAR AI/8054/68 A2 JAR CAA.00059 A1-A3.C4.C6.C8.C14.C18.C19	01276 857441
Mann Avionics Ltd BCAR AI/9362/91 A2 JAR CAA.00043 A1-A3.C2.C3.C5.C6.C13	01276 857444/5
Manx Airlines Ltd JAR CAA.00051 A1.A2.C3.C5.C7.C14.D1	01624 82411
March Helicopters Ltd JAR CAA.00310 A3	01604 493137
Markspire Ltd T/A Airtime Aviation JAR CAA.00467 A2	01202 580676

Marshall of Cambridge Aerospace Ltd BCAR DAI/1853/45 B cond. G-52 A1.B3.B4.E1.E2.E3 JAR CAA.00031 A1.A2.C3.C5-C7.C13.C19.D1	01223 61133
Martin-Baker Aircraft Company Ltd BCAR DAI/2779/48 A2.B3.E2 JAR CAA.00315 A2	01895 832214
McAlpine Helicopters Ltd BCAR DAI/8677/80 A2.E2 JAR CAA.00124 A3.B1.C3.C5.C10.C11	01865 841188
McCarthy Helicopter Services Ltd JAR CAA.00499 A3.C10.C11	01494 451111
Merlin Maintenance BCAR AMR/188 M3	01667 462642
Midair Aviation Ltd JAR CAA.00254 A2	01202 581925
Midland Aircraft Maintenance BCAR AMR/185 M3	01384 221302
Mitchell Aircraft Co. Ltd BCAR AI/9451/94 M5	01223 833113
Modern Air BCAR AMR/378 M3	01763 208281
Modern Jet Support Centre Ltd JAR CAA.0004 A1.B1.C5.C7.C14	01843 823661
Monarch Aircraft Engineering Co. Ltd BCAR DAI/8021/68 A2.E2.E3 JAR CAA.00029 A1.B3.C1-C9.C12-C15.C17-C19	01582 424211
Nordic Aero Ltd JAR CAA.00350 A1	01293 502512
North Weald Flying Services Ltd	01992 524510
Northamptonshire School of Flying JAR CAA.00299 A2	01604 644678
Northbrook College of Further & Higher Education T/A Northbrook Aviation JAR CAA.00431 A2	01273 461198
Northern Executive Aviation (Maintenance) Ltd JAR CAA.00066 A1.A2.C3.C5.C6	0161 4364300
Ogden Aviation Engineering Ltd JAR CAA.00175 A1	01293 507331
Old Sarum Engineering BCAR AMR/390 M3	01722 322525/410711
Osprey Aviation Ltd JAR.CAA00267 A1.C4.C5.C8.C13	01703 620727
Personal Plane Services Ltd BCAR AI/4514/55 B1.M3	01494 529432
Pilatus Britten-Norman Ltd BCAR DAI/7384/64 B cond. G-51 A1.B1.B3.B4I JAR CAA.00337 A2.C2-C5.C8.C13.C14.D1	01983 872511
Plymouth Executive Aviation Ltd JAR CAA.00087 A1.A2.B1.C1.C3.C5.C12-C14	01752 786611
Police Aviation Services Ltd BCAR DAI/9420/93 A2.E2.E3 JAR CAA.00163 A2.A3	01452 857999
Pool Aviation Ltd JAR CAA.00347 A2.C5	01938 555062
Popular Flying Association BCAR DAI/1172/48 Unclassified	01273 461616
Premier Aircraft Maintenance Ltd BCAR AMR/399 M3	01384 221009
Prestwick Aircraft Maintenance Ltd BCAR AMR/125 M3	01292 678170
Quantel Ltd BACR AMR/186 M3	01959 574545
Ragwing BCAR AMR/192 M3	01799 527621
Raytheon Corporate Jets Incorporated BCAR DAI/9496/95. A1.A2.B1.B4.E2.E3 JAR CAA.00095 A1.B3	01244 520444
RD Aviation Ltd BCAR AI/9419/93 A2	01865 841441

Redhill Engineering
A division of Redhill Aviation 01737 822959
JAR CAA.00319 A2

RFS Aircraft Engineering Ltd 01702 543000
JAR CAA.00038 A2.B1.B2.C3.C7

RGV Aviation Ltd 01452 855501
JAR CAA.00215 A2

RN Aviation (Leicester Airport) 01533 593629
BCAR AMR/165 M3

Rollason Aircraft & Engines Ltd 01273 462680
BCAR AI/3902/53 A2.M3
JAR CAA.00233 B2.C7

Rotortech Ltd 01954 210765/210901
BCAR DAI/6883/63 A2.E2
JAR CAA.00067 A3.B1.C4-C6.C10-C12.C14.D1

Rotortech Ltd 01954 210901
JAR CAA.00067 A3.B1.C4-C6.C10-C12.C14.D1

Routair Aviation Services Ltd 01702 540380
BCAR AMR/117 M3

Royal Aircraft Establishment Aero Club Ltd 01252 392047/393649
BCAR AMR/93 M3

Samson Aviation Services Ltd 0191 2144111
JAR CAA.00407 A2

Scottish Aerotech Services Ltd 0141 8480040
BCAR AI/9356/91 B1
JAR CAA.00105 A1

Seething Aviation Ltd 01508 558013
JAR CAA.00025 A2

SFT Aviation Ltd 01202 499888
JAR CAA.00249 A2

Shendley Farms Engineering Ltd 01622 890226
JAR CAA.00421 A2

Shenley Farms (Engineering) Ltd 01622 890226
CAA.00421 A2

Sherburn Engineering Ltd 01977 685296
BCAR AMR/237 M3

Shipping & Airlines Ltd 01959 573404
JAR CAA.00343 A2

Shobdon Aircraft Maintenance Ltd 01568 708855
BCAR AMR/246 M3

Short Brothers plc 01752 707477
JAR CAA.00363 A2.C3.D1

Short Brothers plc Support Services Division 01202 572271
HDA/125
JAR CAA.00363 A2.C3.D1

Skycare Handling 01959 574679

Skyline Helicopters Ltd 01494 451111
JAR CAA.00108 A3.C10.C11

Sloane Helicopters Ltd 01604 790595
JAR CAA.00097 A3.C10.C11

Source Aviation Services Ltd 01202 578999
BCARAI/9490/95 M5

Southern Air Ltd 01273 461664
JAR CAA.00317 A2.A3.C1.C3.C5.C6.C11

Stapleford Flying Club Maintenance 01708 688449
JAR CAA.00012 A2

Stephenson Aviation Ltd 01243 530165
JAR CAA.00022 A2.A3.C3.C8.C10.C11.C14

Sterling Helicopters Ltd 01603 417156
JAR CAA.00440 A3.C8.C10.C11.C14

Tatenhill Aviation 01283 575283
BCAR AMR/370 M3

Taurus Air Services 0161 707 7064
JAR CAA.00370 A3

Taylor Aircraft Services Sales and Brokerage 01604 492160
BCAR AMR/284 M3

Tayside Aviation (Engineering) Ltd 01382 68838
JAR CAA.00045 A2

TG Aviation Ltd 01843 823656
JAR CAA.00311 A2